COMIC-CON

EPISODE IV: A FAN'S HOPE

LONDON, NEW YORK, MUNICH,
MELBOURNE, AND DELHI

Senior Editor Michele Wells
Designer Carol Stamile
Editor Tim Cox
Jacket Designer Jessica Park
Production Designer Tracy Wehmeyer

First American Edition, 2011

Published in the United States by DK Publishing
375 Hudson Street, New York, New York 10014

Published in Great Britain by Dorling Kindersley Limited
DK books are available at special discounts when purchased in bulk for sales promotions, premiums, fund-raising, or educational use.
For details, contact:
DK Publishing Special Markets
375 Hudson Street
New York, New York 10014
SpecialSales@dk.com

A catalog record for this book
is available from the Library of Congress

ISBN: 978-0-7566-8342-9

Color reproduction by Hung Hing
Printed and bound in China

Executive Producer
Alba Tull

Producers
Peter McCabe and David Newsom

Production Coordinator
Kevin Warnecke

An 8-Eyes Pictures Production

PHOTOGRAPHERS

Fine Art Formal Portraits
Celebrity/Interviewee Portraits - Alba Tull
Civilian/Costumed Portraits - Peter McCabe

Reportage
Paul Taggart
Josh "CuriousJosh" Reiss
David Newsom
Richard Coleman
Jesse Dhein
Doug Wylie
Stephanie Dana
Sean Cassidy

Special thanks to
Leica Camera
Marty Glickman, for Mamiya Camera and Profoto Lighting

COMIC-CON
EPISODE IV: A FAN'S HOPE

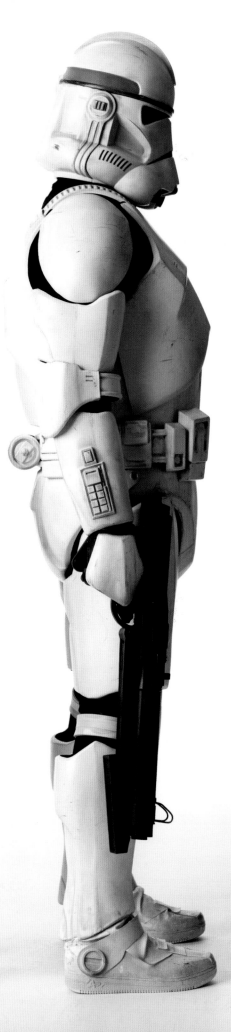

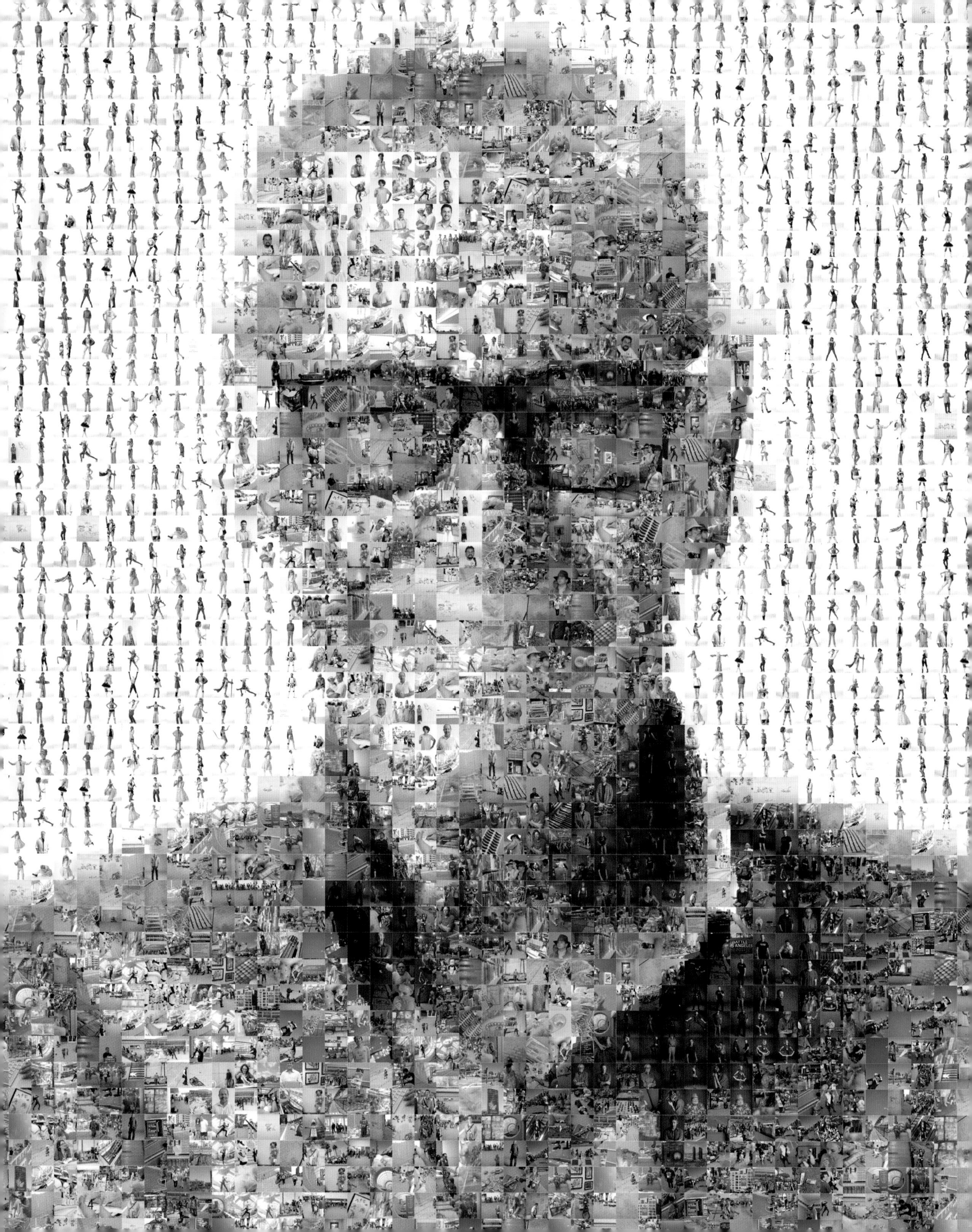

foreword

by Stan Lee

comic book writer, editor, and publisher; former president and chairman, Marvel Comics; producer; actor; television personality

One of my first memories of comic book conventions was as a fan. When I first attended them, there were perhaps a few dozen people wandering around. And the image that sticks in my mind is—most of the convention-goers were young children. Occasionally there'd be an adult or two holding a child's hand because the kid was too young to come by himself.

Now, everything's reversed. The thousands of convention-goers are mostly grown-ups, adults who are interested in movies, television, DVDs, and, of course, comic books. Now and then you'll see a few adults holding a child's hand, usually because they couldn't find a babysitter that day.

These fans are tremendously important to the comic book business, just as they are to any creative endeavor. Without fans, no comic book artist or writer can hope to achieve meaningful success. Indeed, while some foolish people mock or disregard them, those very fans can make you or break you.

On a personal level, it's both gratifying and flattering to know that another human being is enthusiastic about something you've done. That's why I'm grateful for any fans I might have. I love their enthusiasm, their loyalty, and—just between us—I admire their judgment.

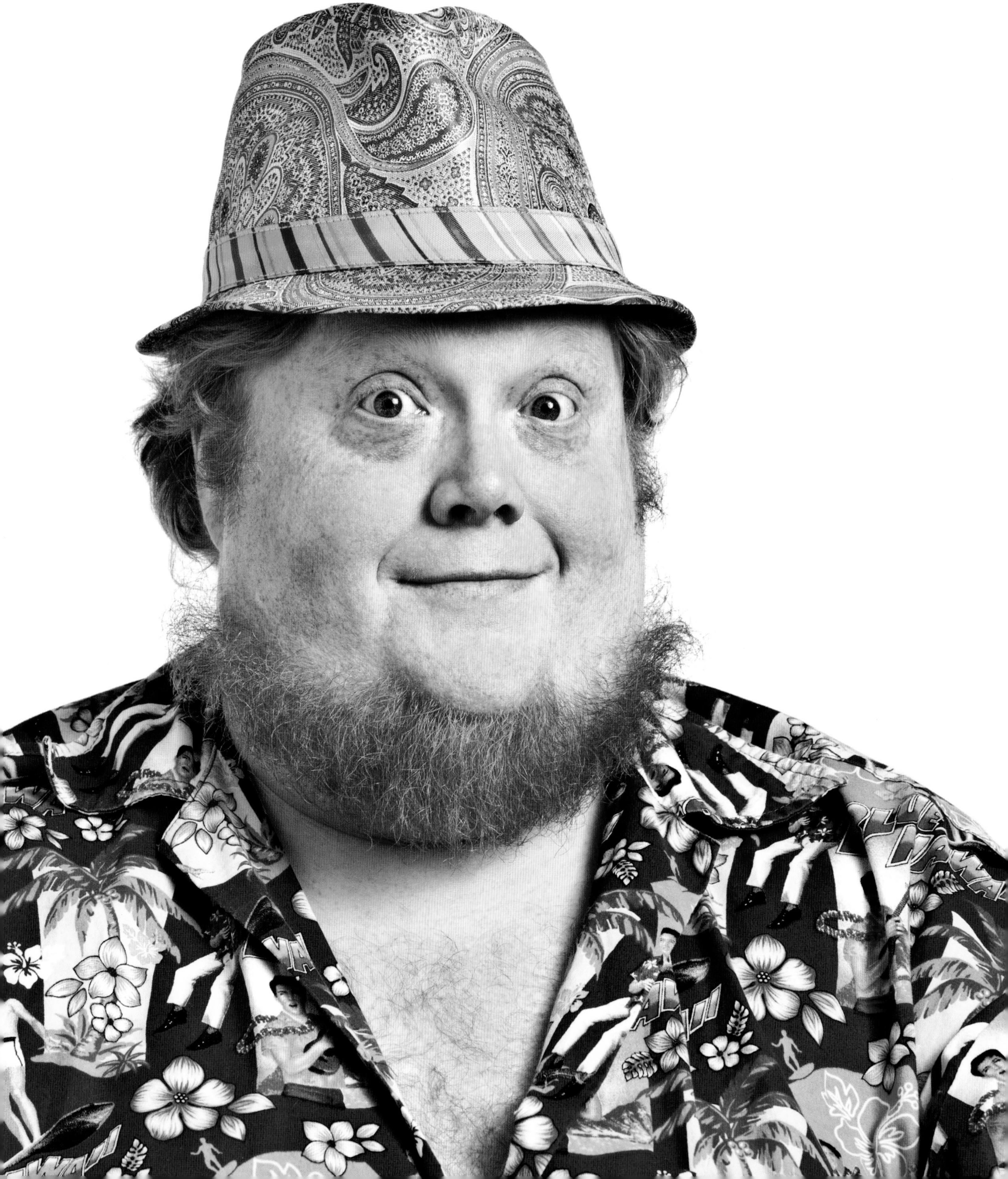

foreword

by Harry Knowles

founder | Ain't It Cool News

Welcome, dear reader...

The tome in your hands is a glimpse at the big carnival of geek culture.

Beginning in 1973, I began to go to San Diego yearly with the purpose of attending Comic-Con. I was attending the year when the Fire Marshal shut the convention down and all the dealers had to march out of the hotel, carrying their tables, so they would be set up in the same order at the new hotel that was booked at the last minute.

At this magical place, I've met many of the Nine Old Men who created the miracle of Disney animation. I was given the nickname "Fuzzy" by Jack Kirby. And I've bought Frazetta art here. I've met friends, had debates, and even sold collectibles. I've been a dealer, a fan, a guest, and a host at the San Diego Comic-Con—but most of all, I've been in awe of its growth.

Many bemoan the growth, but to me, it reveals a growing culture of which I'm a part. Geek culture—comics, animation, film, games, toys, collectibles...a way to live this life we are given. There's more to all of us than Comic-Con, but we're never really more ourselves than we are at this beautiful assembly.

For most, Comic-Con is the one point in the year where we don't care what people think of us, because we are amongst family—the more than 100,000 people who are "one of us." That's empowering. We could fill a major football stadium with that number (we wouldn't, but we could). Instead, we take over the city of San Diego and its fabled Convention Center. We come in costume, we come to buy...but most of all, we come to belong. To take our place in Hall H and have the gigantic entertainment companies of the world pitch us their wares.

Within these pages, you'll find many extended members of your family. Perhaps you saw them at Comic-Con last year. Or perhaps not, but this book conjures memories of Comic-Con, and that, dear reader, is a Linus blanket of comfort. To remind you, wherever you are, Comic-Con is coming. And nothing will stop it from taking over the world.

foreword

by Thomas Tull
founder | Legendary Pictures

I love Comic-Con. I love what it represents, what it feels like to immerse yourself in the place. I love to wander and rediscover the endless supply of the heroes and images that have thrilled me since I was a kid; to see dads experience it with their kids, a next generation of fans.

It's difficult to describe to someone who has never been to Comic-Con the level of energy and passion that is so real you can feel it as you roam the huge halls. The visitors who make the pilgrimage are all in and committed to celebrating the culture they have helped to create—all without a hint of self-awareness. I am in awe of how far the culture has come in the past few decades, with new comics, movies, toys, and collectibles going from fringe to leading the world of entertainment and grabbing it by the throat.

I feel unbelievably lucky because in my work with Legendary I have had a chance as an adult to work with many of the heroes I had as a kid. These are heroes who come alive in San Diego and torpedo through Hall H and onto pages and movie screens so fans around the world can be a part of the stories.

So when Morgan Spurlock asked if I would like to produce the movie with him, I thought it was a way to truly honor the culture and people who are the Con in a way that brings the experience to a wider audience. I hope you feel that this project celebrates one of the most powerful cultural zeitgeists of our time, and mostly is a tribute to the fans who keep coming back every year.

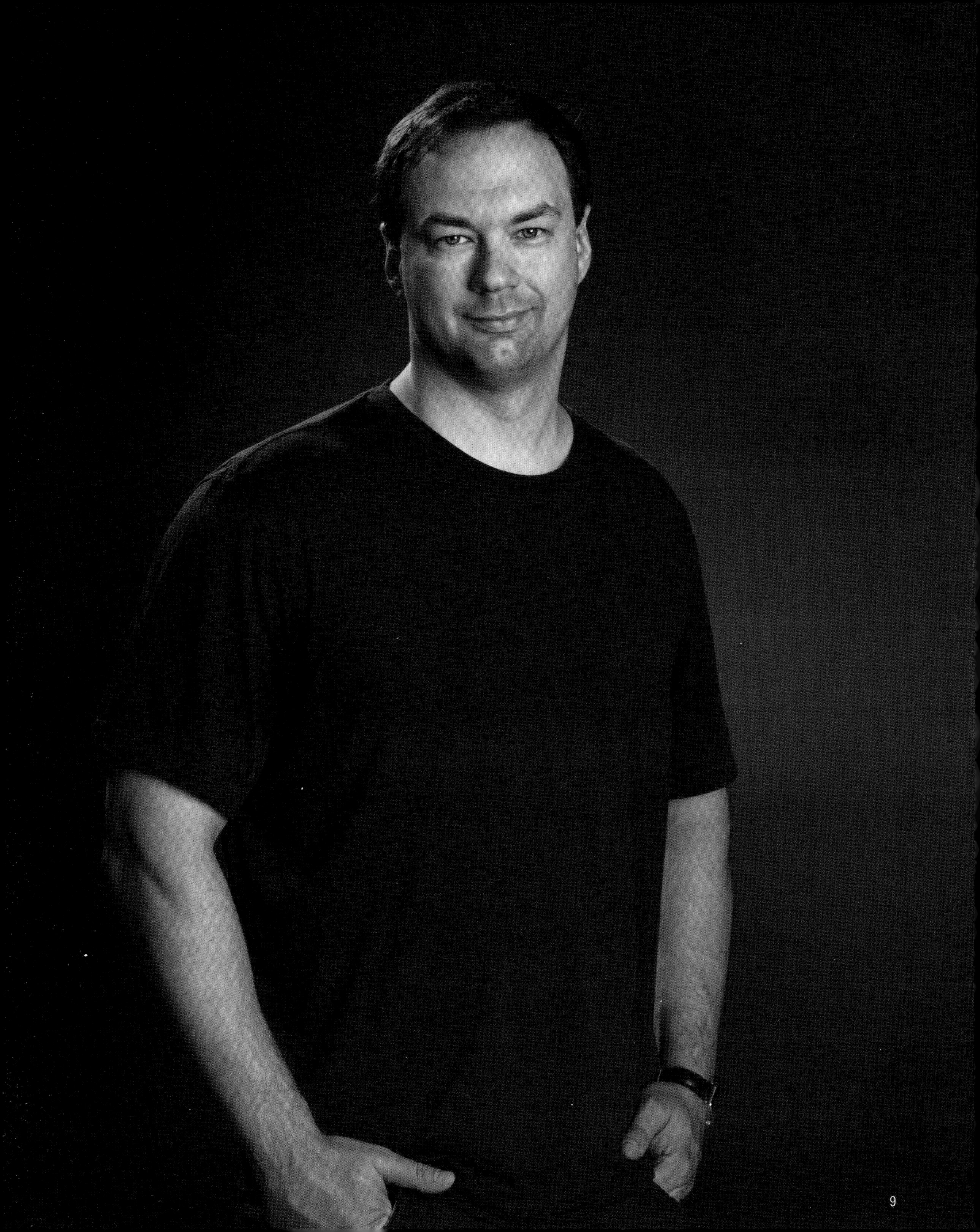

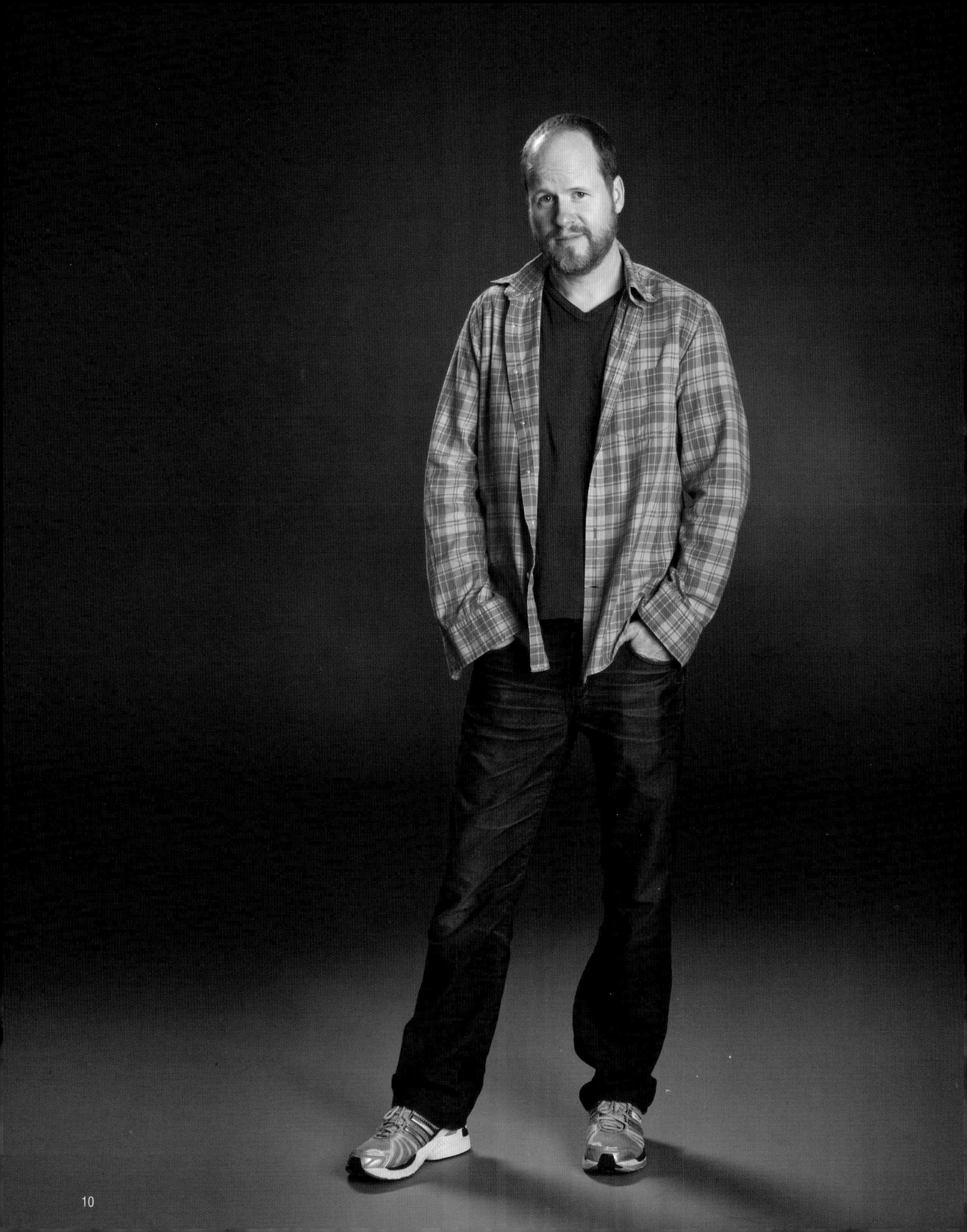

foreword

by Joss Whedon

producer, director, creator, screenwriter | Buffy the Vampire Slayer, Angel, Firefly, Dollhouse, The Avengers

The first comic convention I ever attended was in New York when I was ten years old. It was probably four rooms total, but it seemed like the most magnificent event ever held. My second Comic-Con was in San Diego as an adult. *Buffy the Vampire Slayer* had just come out, and I honestly came to find out if we had any fans. (We totally did.) I remember walking the halls and having that same sense of grandeur, of goofy excitement. The energy and enthusiasm was overwhelming. I realized I had finally found my home.

Comic-Con has definitely gotten bigger and more mainstream. The industry has figured out where the true fans are. This has created a dichotomy between the comic fans and the movies—in some cases, a bitter rift. But I believe there could be harmony between the comic book folk and movie makers. Ultimately, they just need to sit down or possibly make out. This is the kind of place Comic-Con is: It's a place where people with the same passion—whether their obsessions are similar or very, very different—come together. To make out.

Meeting the fans and being around the fans is what Comic-Con is all about. The fans here are responding to the work you do, and are sincerely trying to connect with you. This is the place where it all happens. Something as simple as an autograph is actually more significant; it's a connection. And you only really connect with a fan, not just by being around them, but by being one yourself. I've never been anything but. So enjoy this tour of my home.

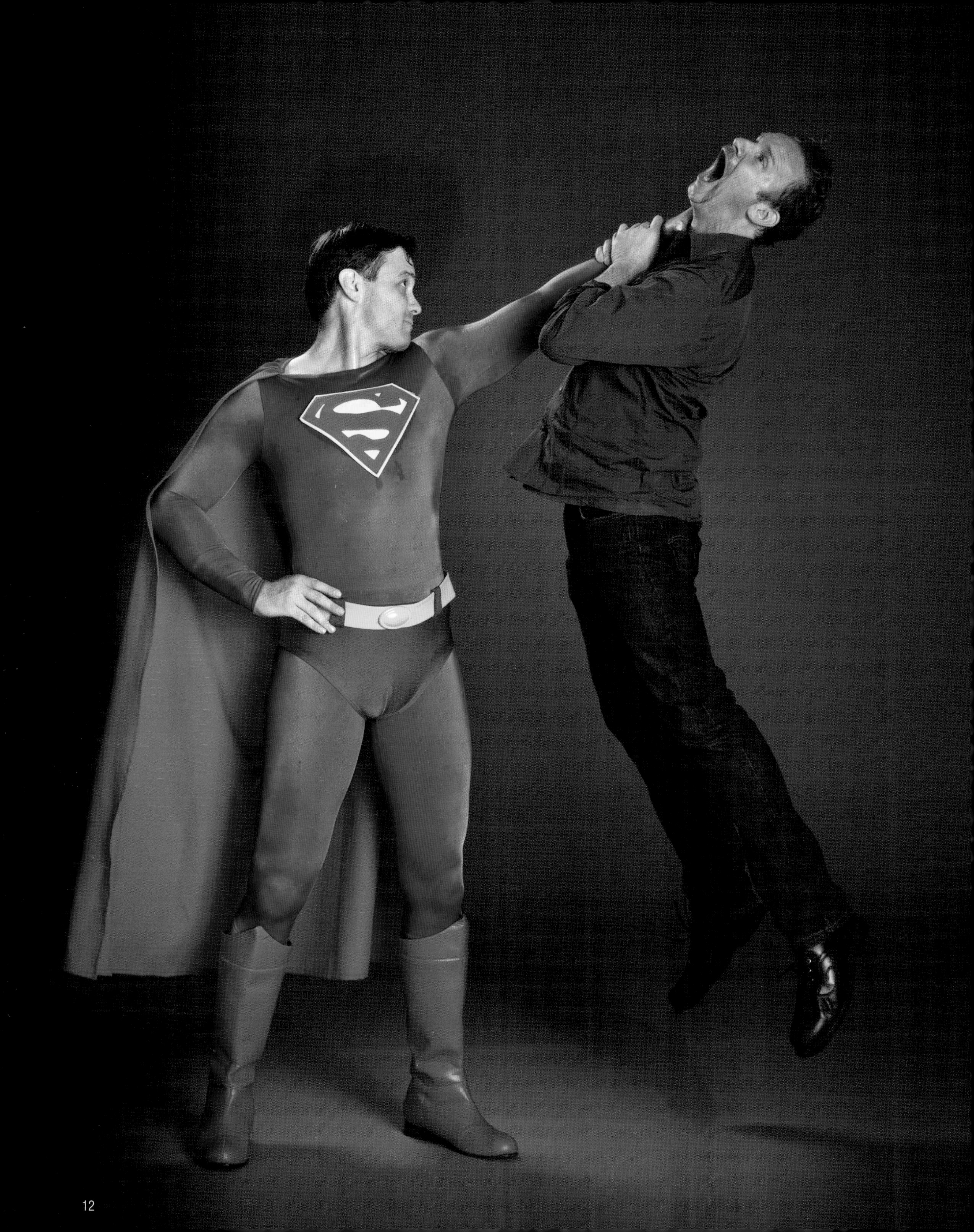

introduction

by Morgan Spurlock

As a geeky kid growing up in West Virginia, I consumed comics and horror films and *Mad* magazines like they were meals. It was as if they were the only things keeping me alive; and in a way they were. You see, I wasn't just a fan. I was addicted. And these books and stories gave my brain and my soul everything they were craving—a look at the world that I couldn't get anywhere else, and the knowledge that there were other people out there who were just as off and confused and as twisted as I was.

It was the summer of 2009 when I finally made it to my first-ever San Diego Comic-Con. For years I had wanted to take this trip, my own personal Haj to the Mecca of Geekdom, but it always seemed as though I was doing something that prohibited me from being there.

But now, finally, I was here! It was a dream come true for me. For my first hour on the Comic-Con floor, I was in awe. I was transported back into the body of that wide-eyed twelve-year-old boy, staring in disbelief at my idols and inspirations—Sergio Aragones, Frank Miller, and the man himself, Stan Lee.

When I shook Stan's hand, I thanked him for giving that young boy the confidence and the desire to want to tell stories, and I thanked him for helping me become who I am today. He looked at me, smiled that Stan Lee smile, and said, "You know what, Morgan? We should make a movie together. We should make a documentary! We should make a documentary about Comic-Con!"

So when people ask me to explain to them exactly what Comic-Con is, I smile and tell them, "That's easy. It's a place where heroes still save the day."

preview night

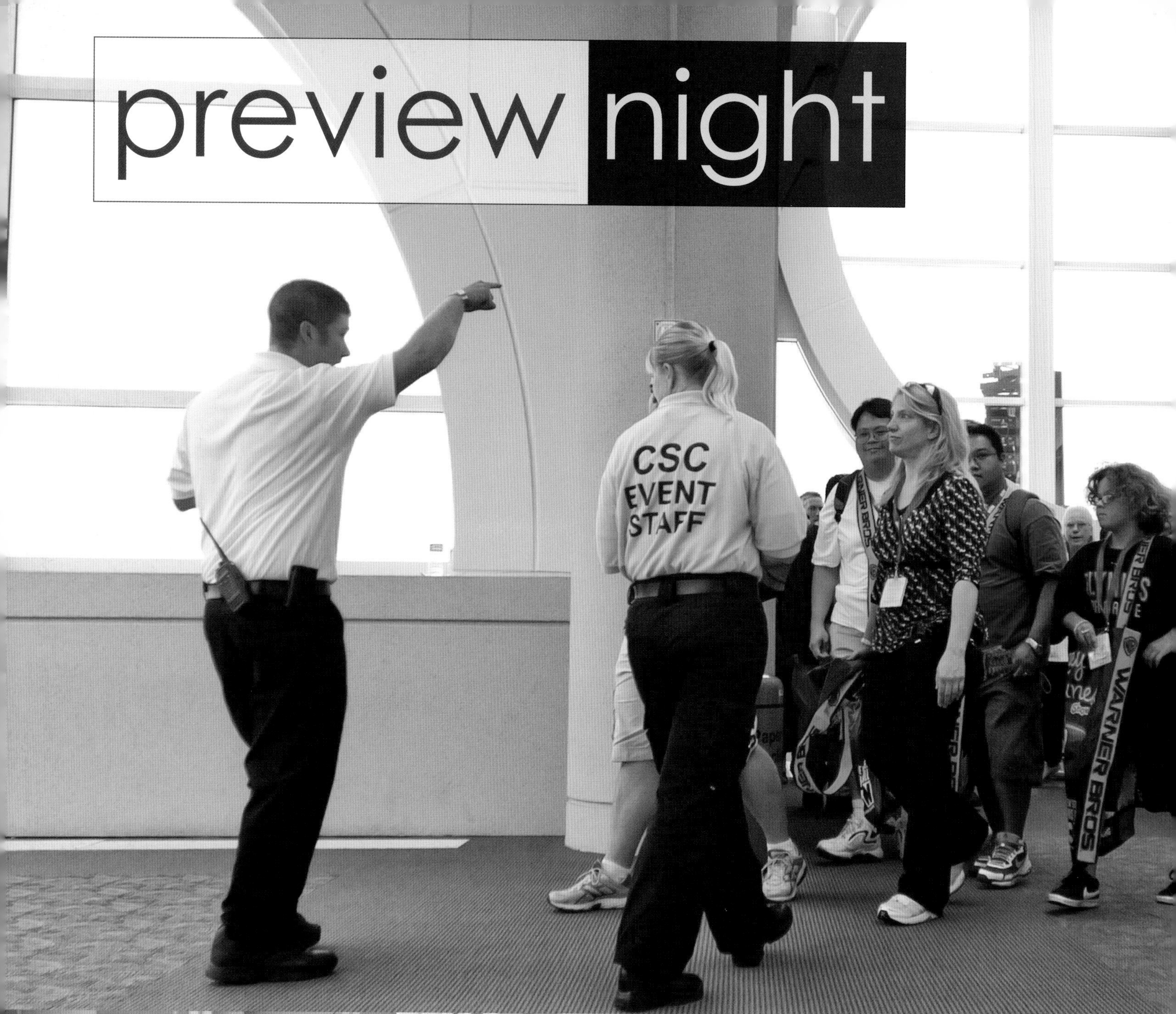
CSC
EVENT
STAFF

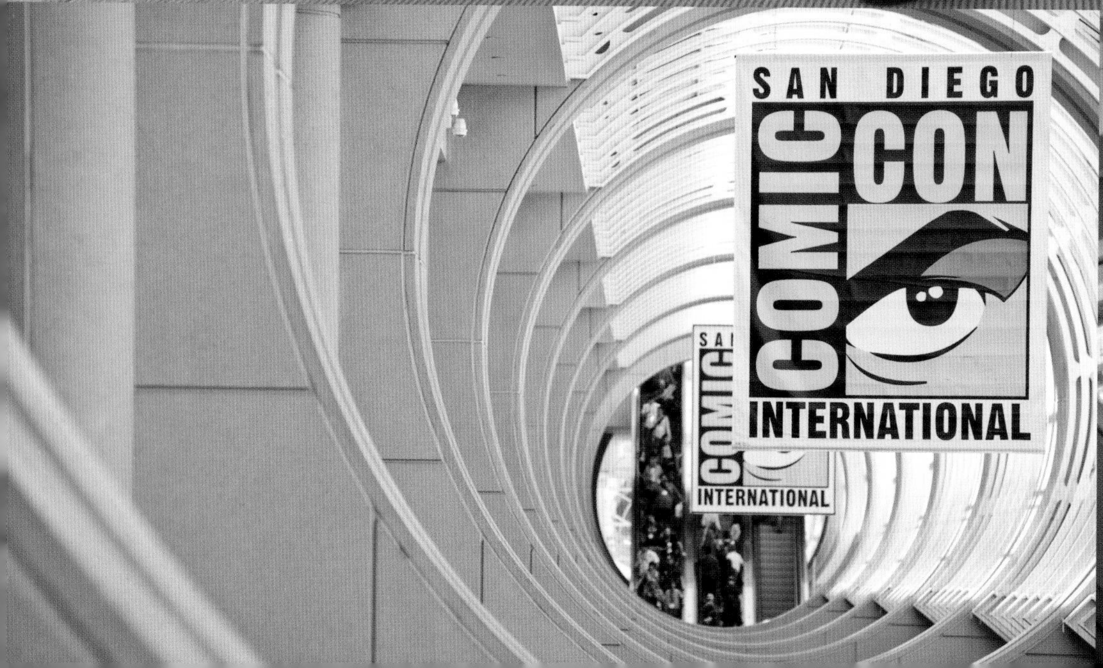
SAN DIEGO
COMIC CON
INTERNATIONAL

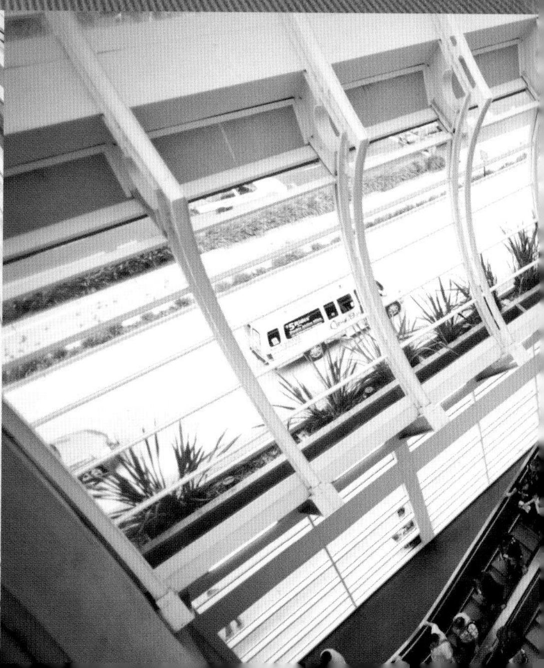

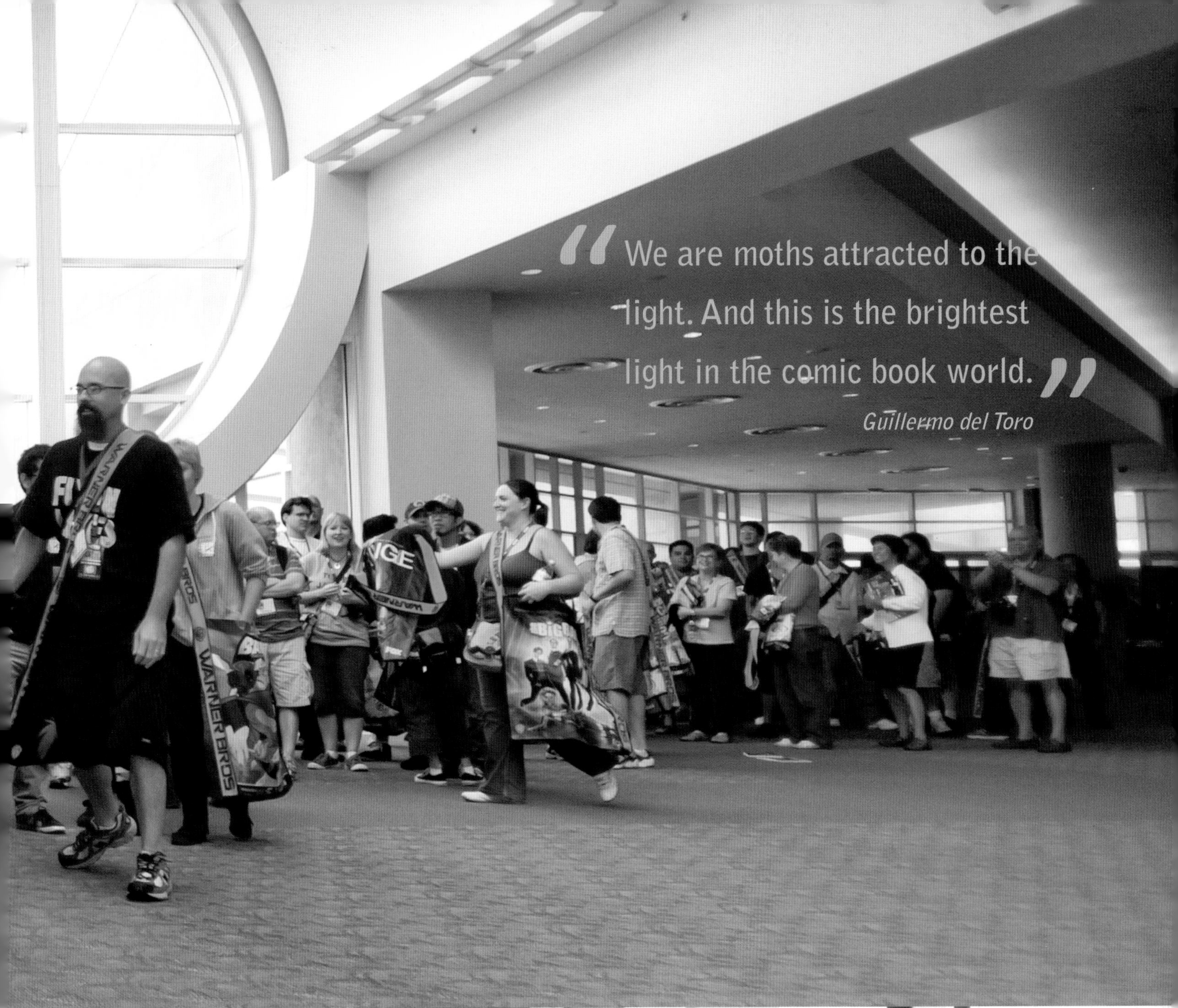
WARNER BROS

> We are moths attracted to the light. And this is the brightest light in the comic book world.
>
> *Guillermo del Toro*

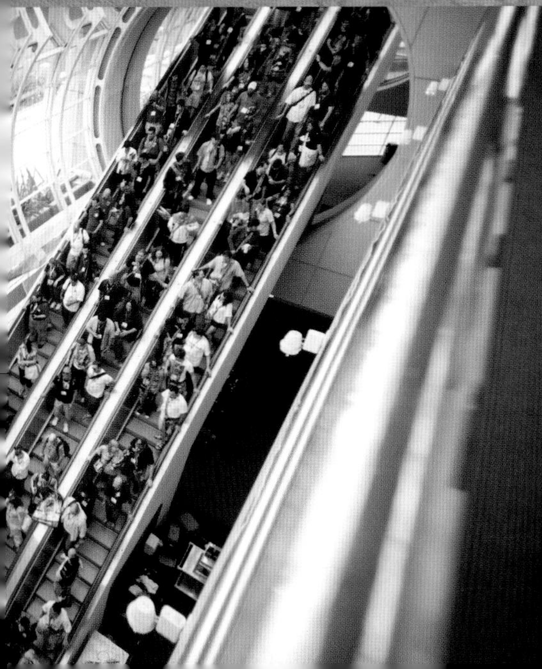

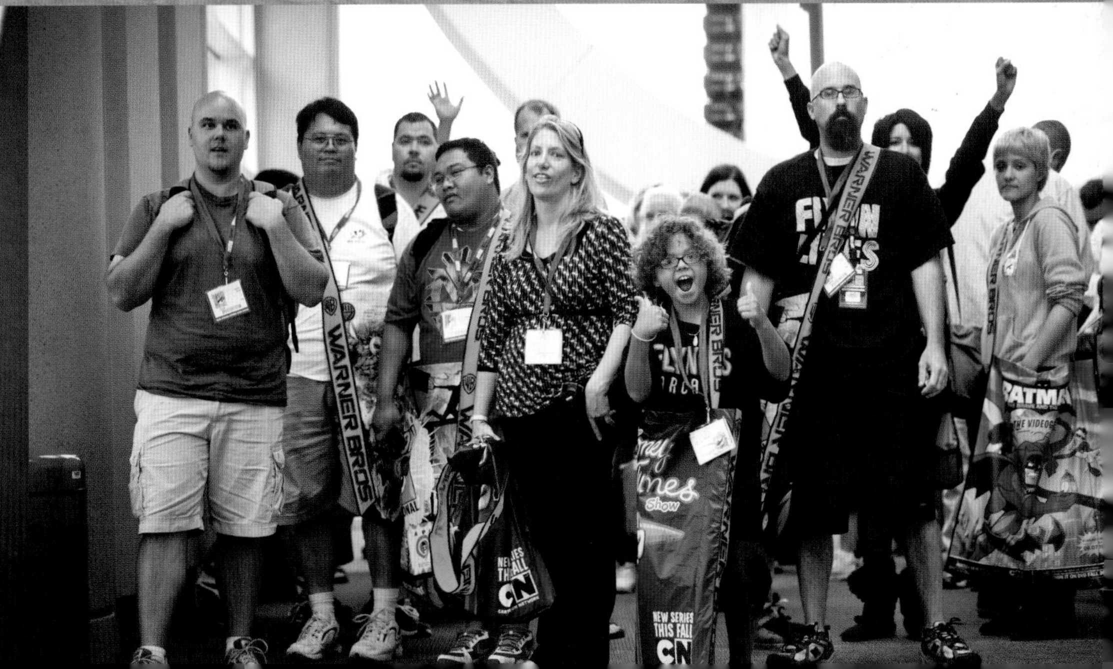
WARNER BROS
NEW SERIES THIS FALL

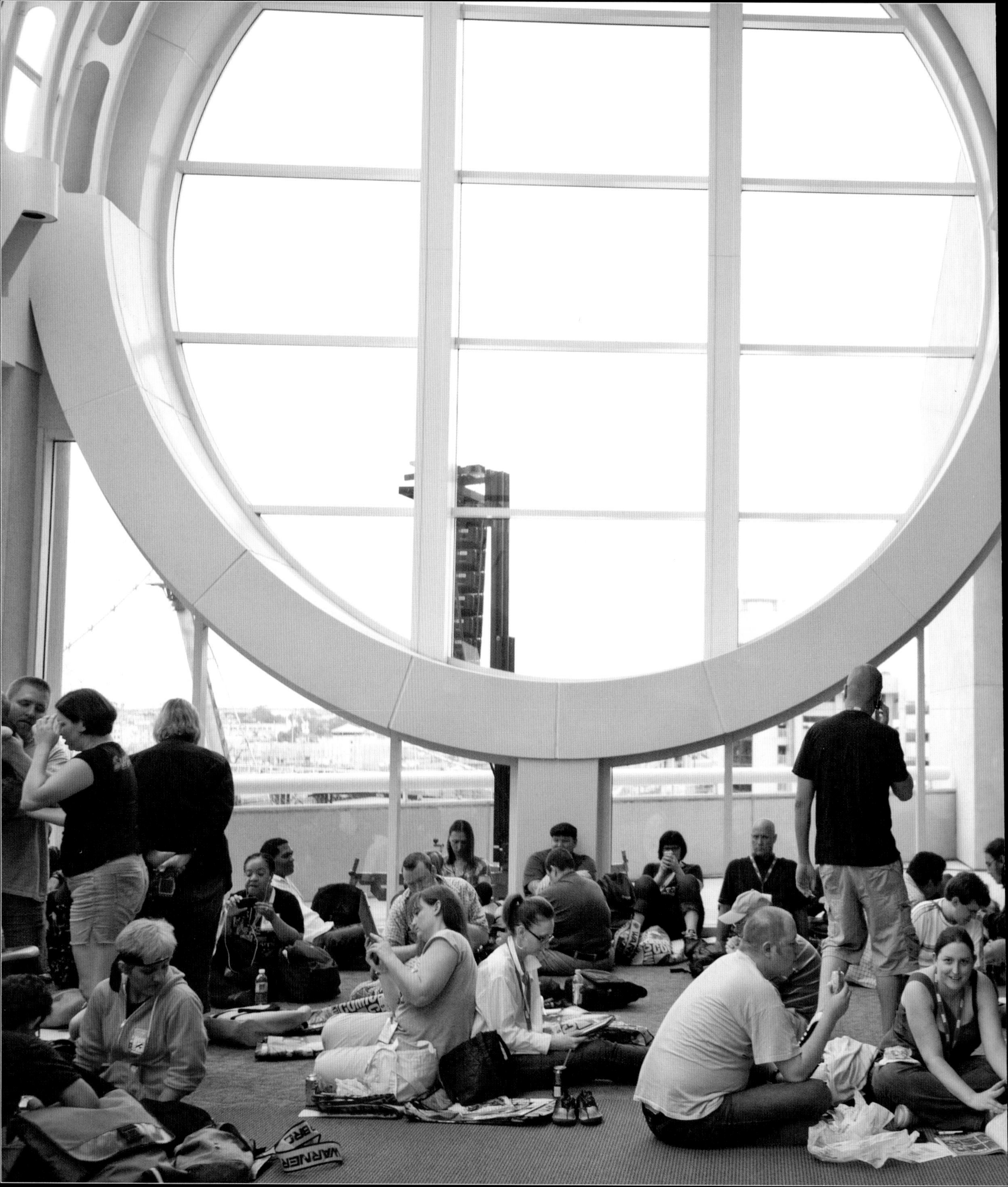
WARNER

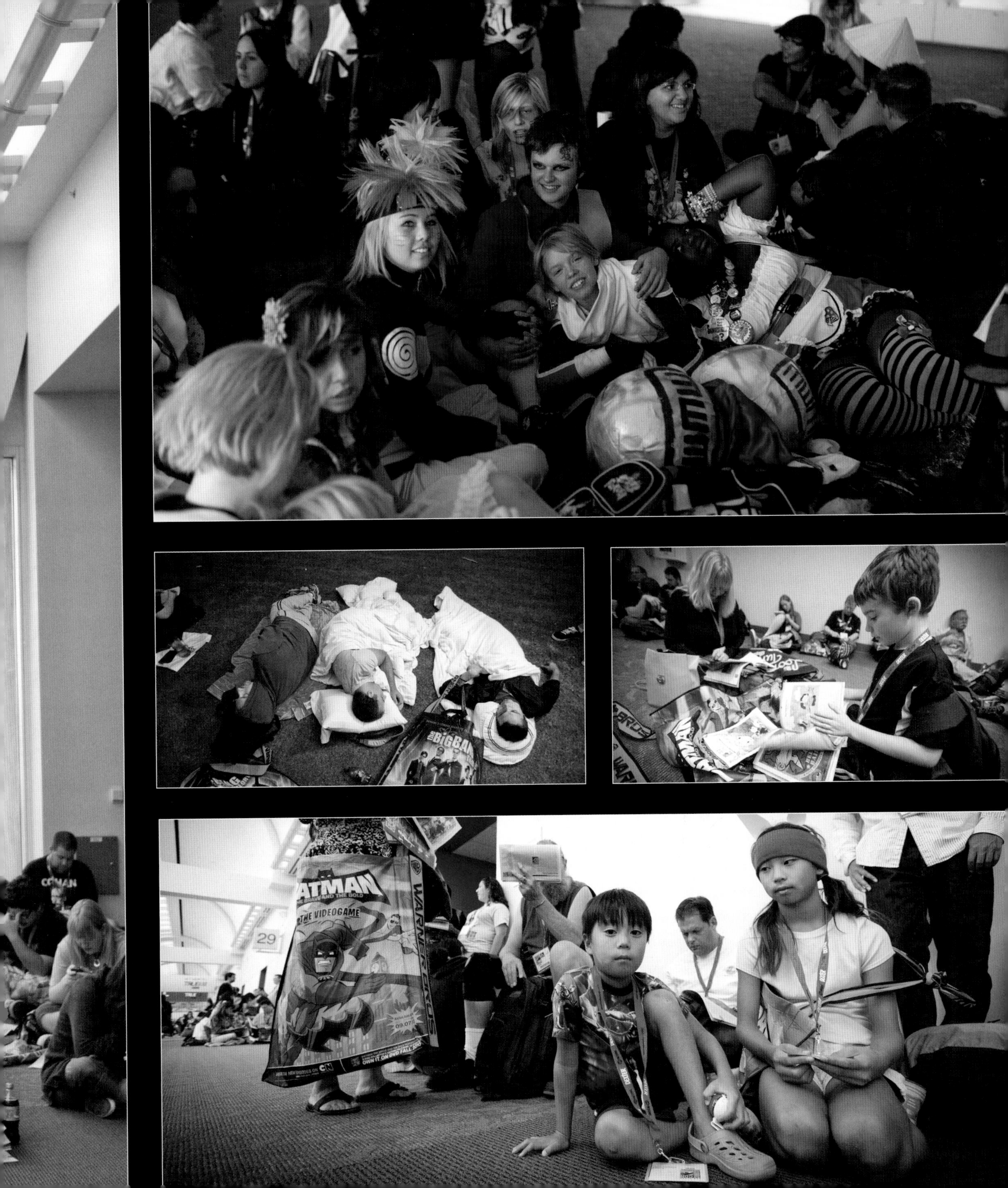
ATMAN
THE VIDEOGAME
29

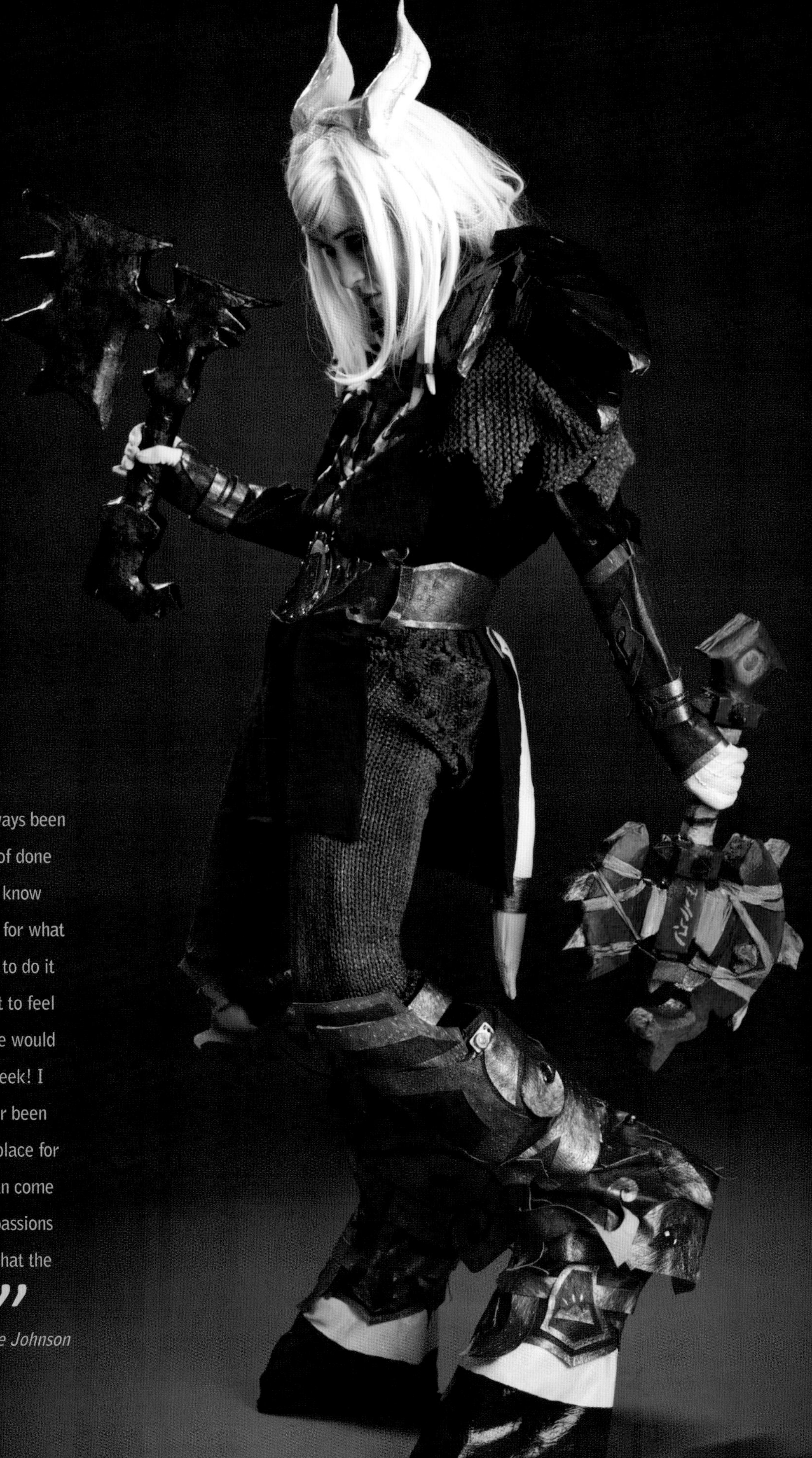

> "I've always been a geek. I've always been kind of an outcast, and just kind of done my own thing. Even now, when I know people probably make fun of me for what I do. But I love it. And I'm going to do it because I love it. So I don't want to feel shame for it anymore, like people would expect you to. It's good to be a geek! I would tell people who have never been to Comic-Con that this is a safe place for you. This is a place where you can come and be yourself, and enjoy your passions without having to worry about what the rest of the world thinks of you."

Erin Marie Johnson

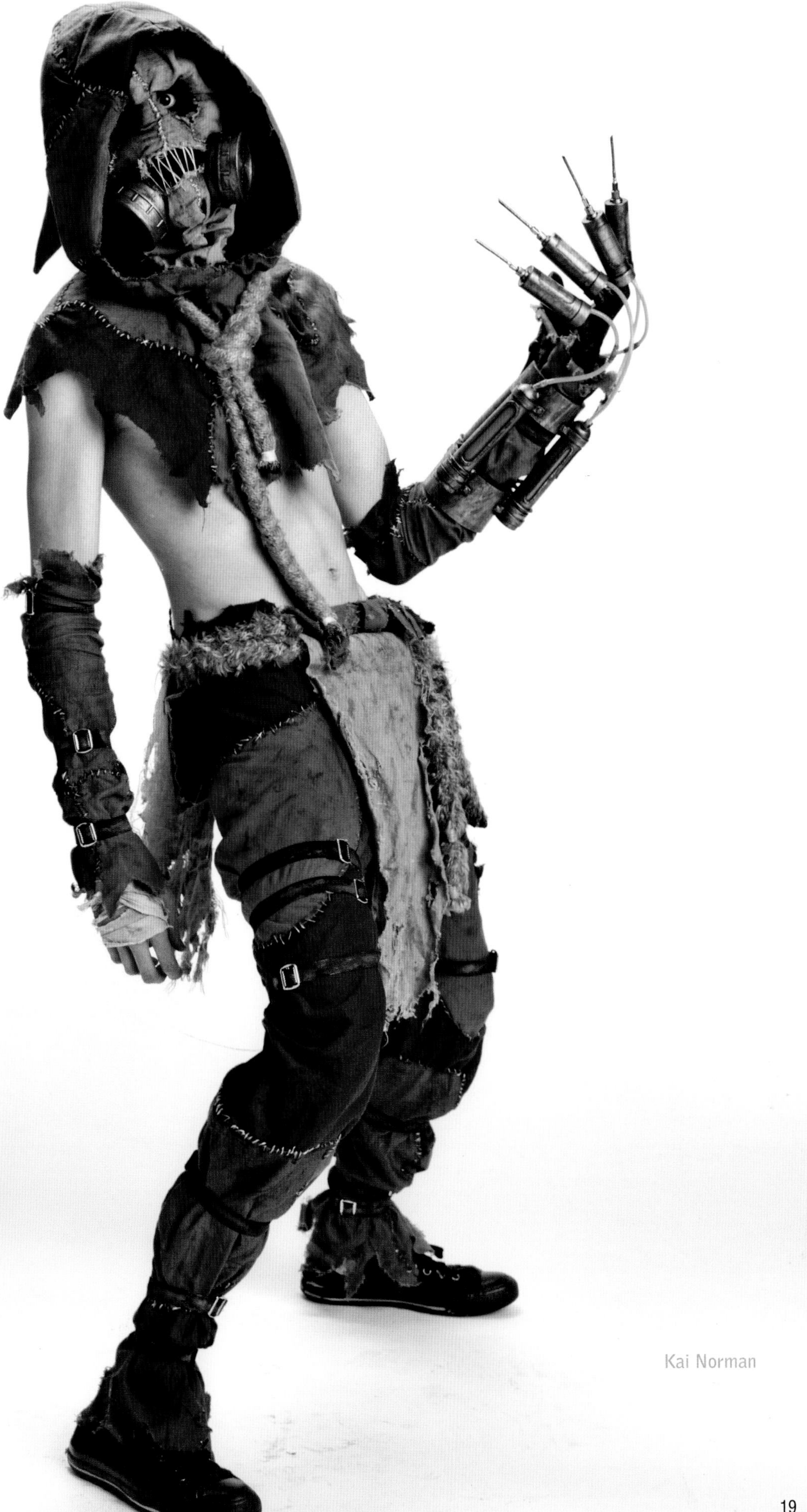

Kai Norman

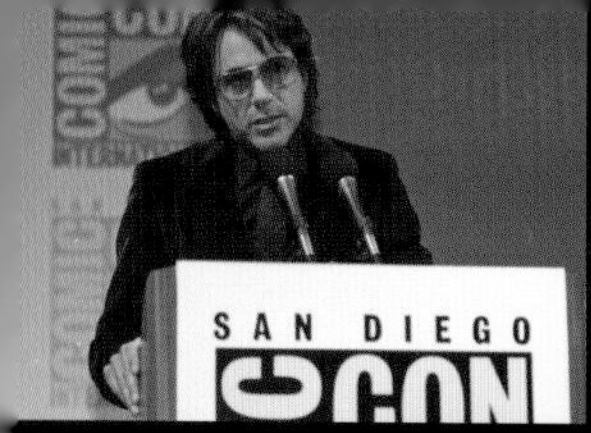
SAN DIEGO
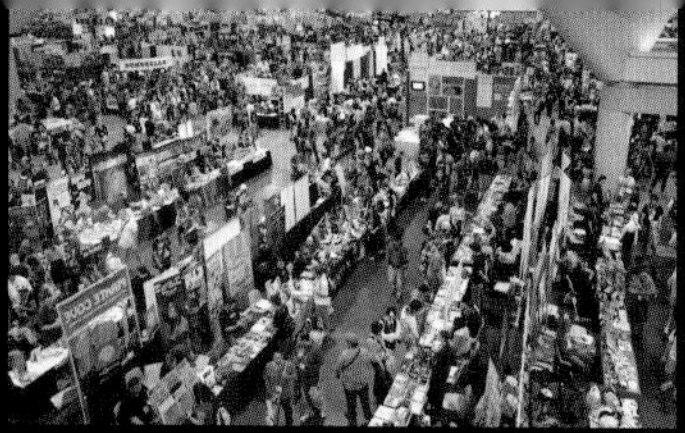
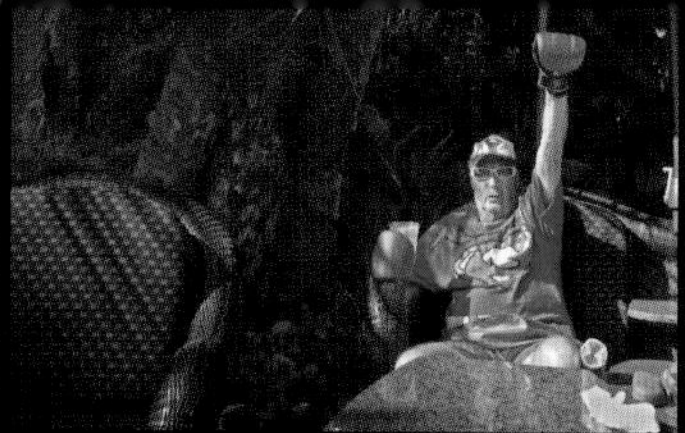
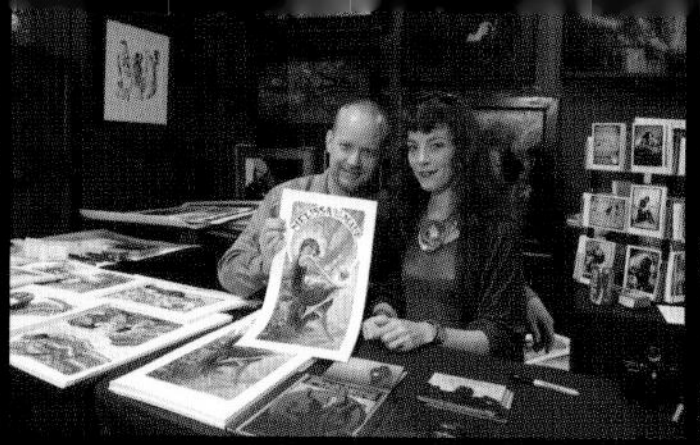
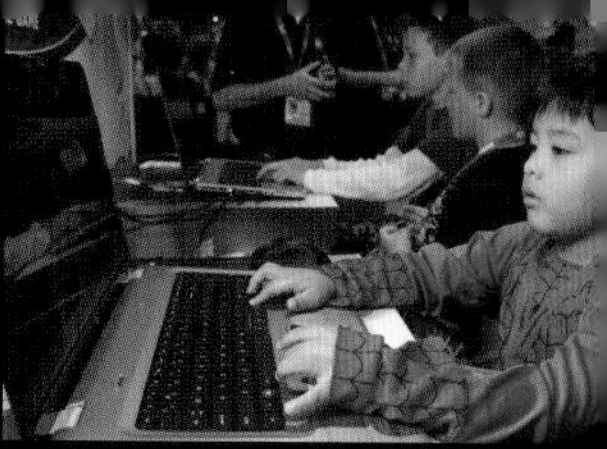
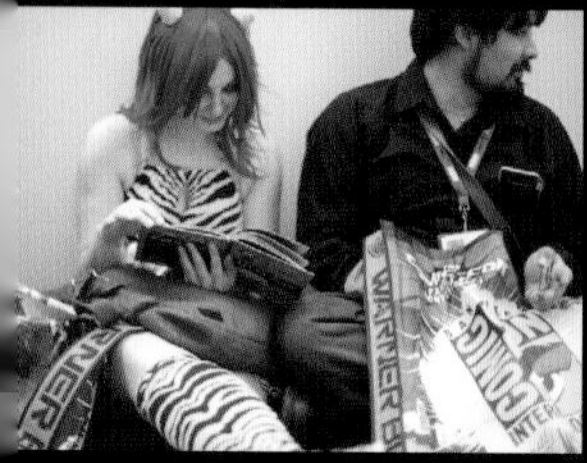
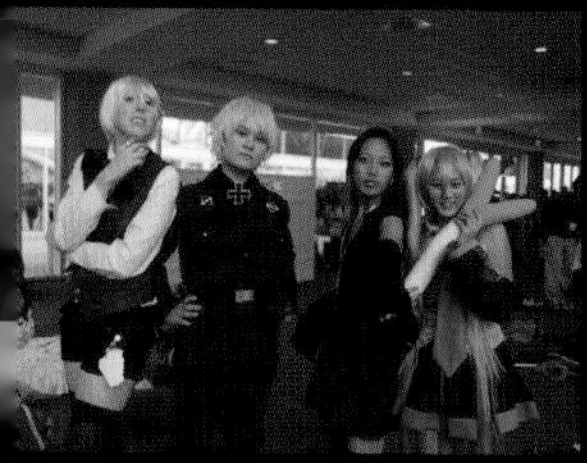
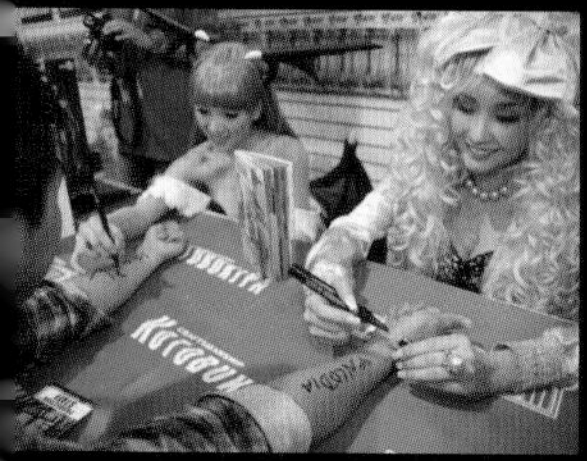
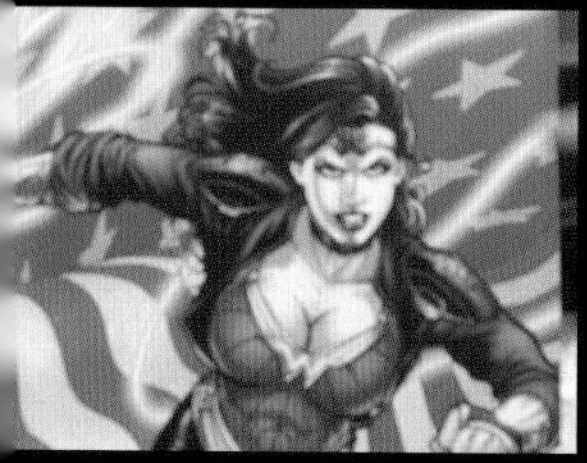
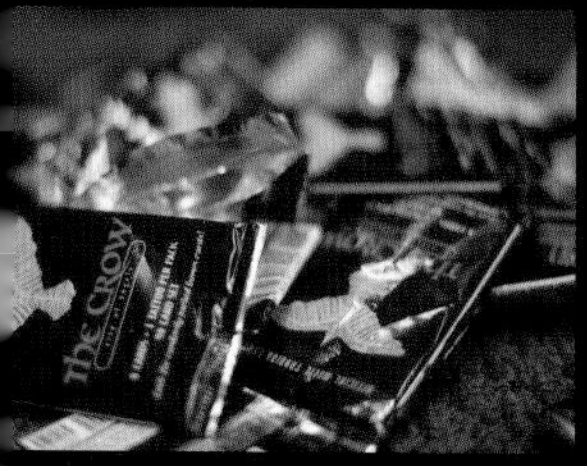
THE CROW
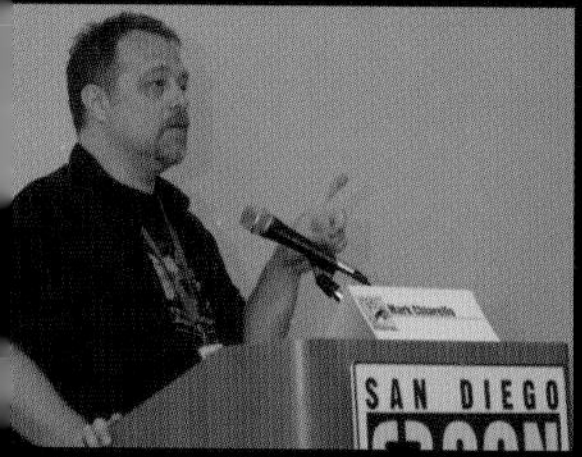
SAN DIEGO
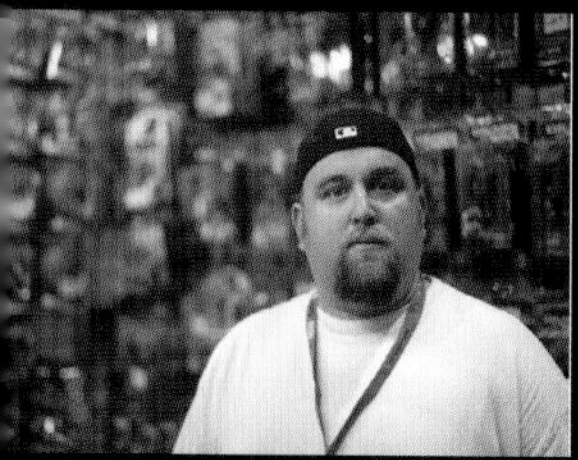
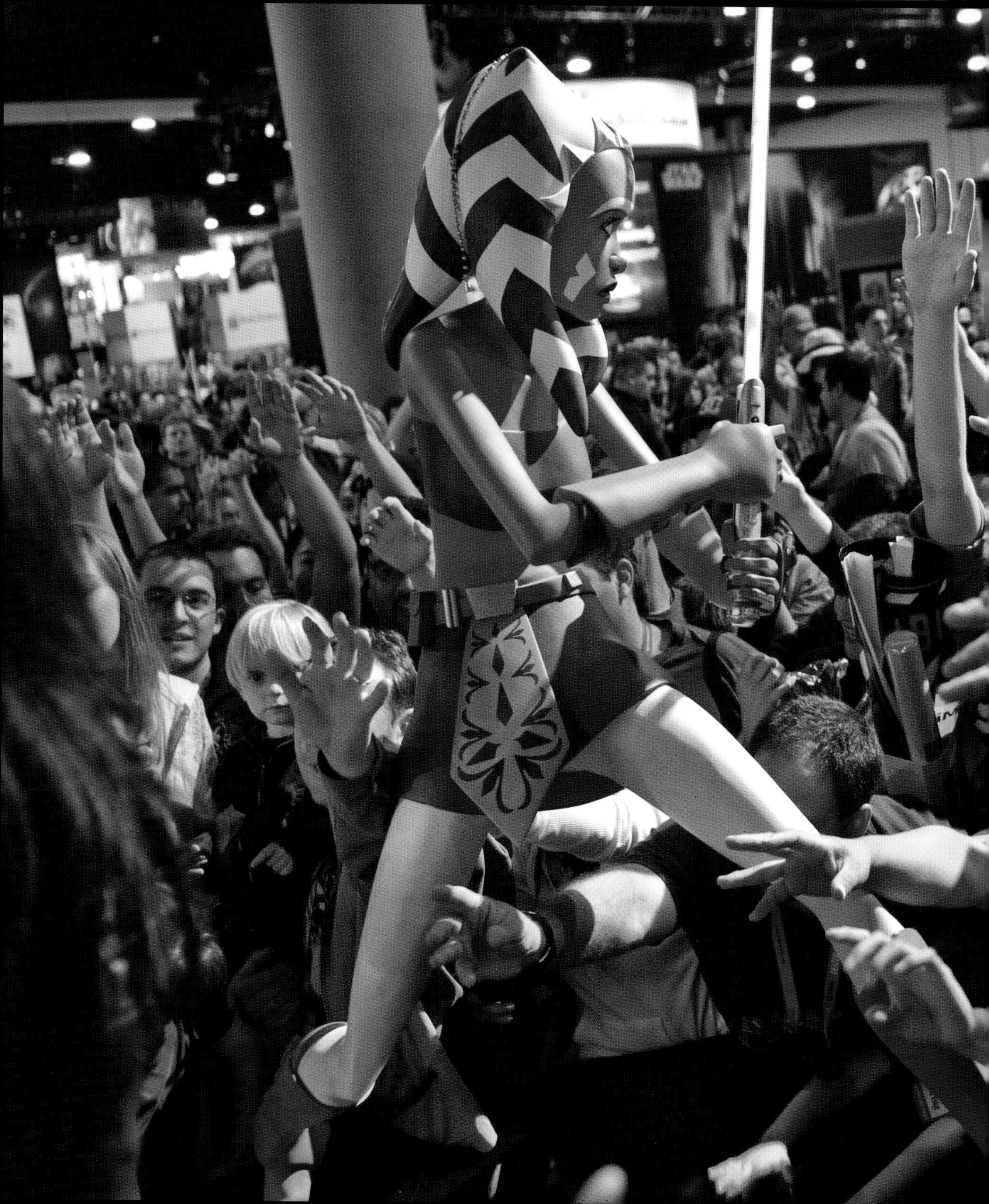
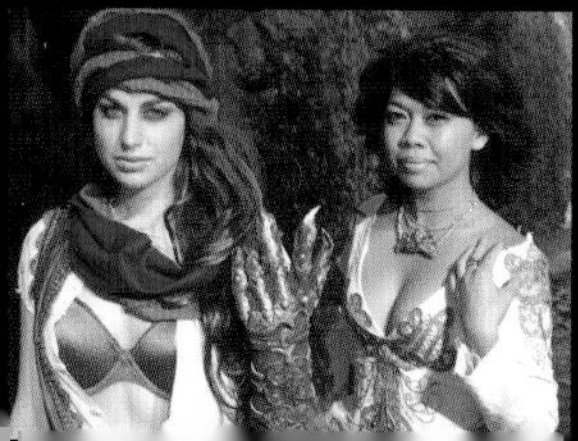
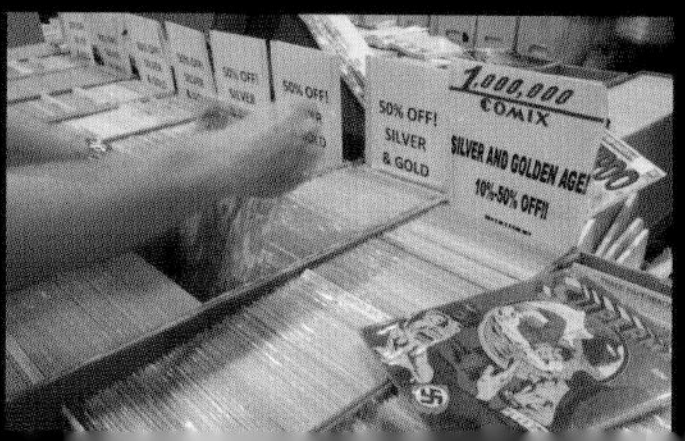
50% OFF!
SILVER
& GOLD
1,000,000
COMIX
SILVER AND GOLDEN AGE!
10%-50% OFF!
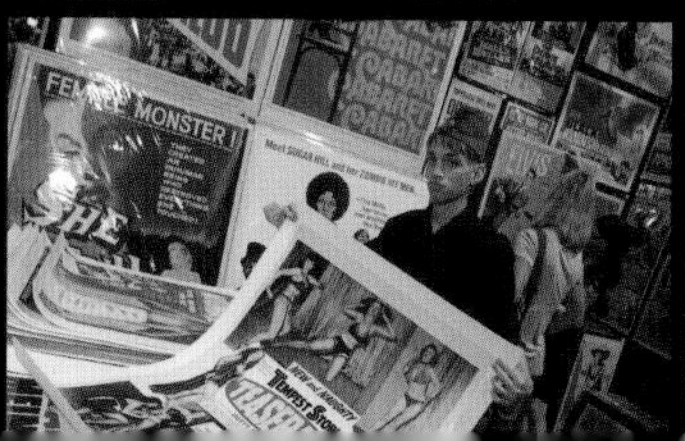
FEMALE MONSTER
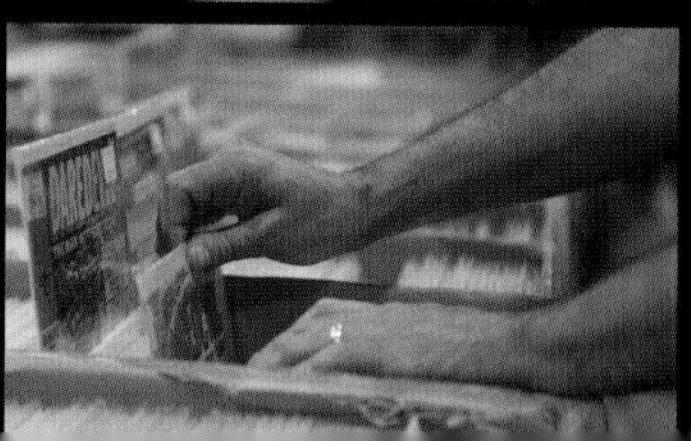
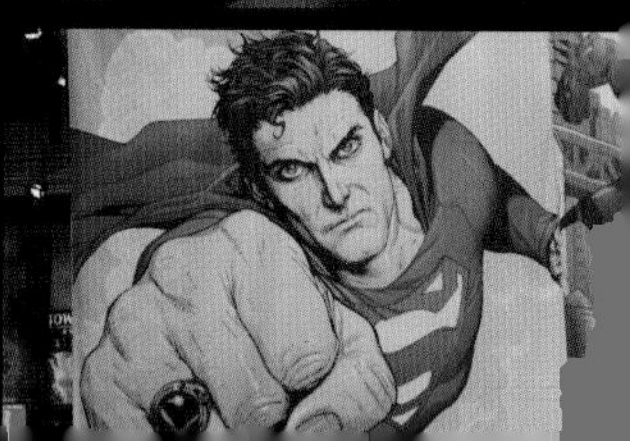

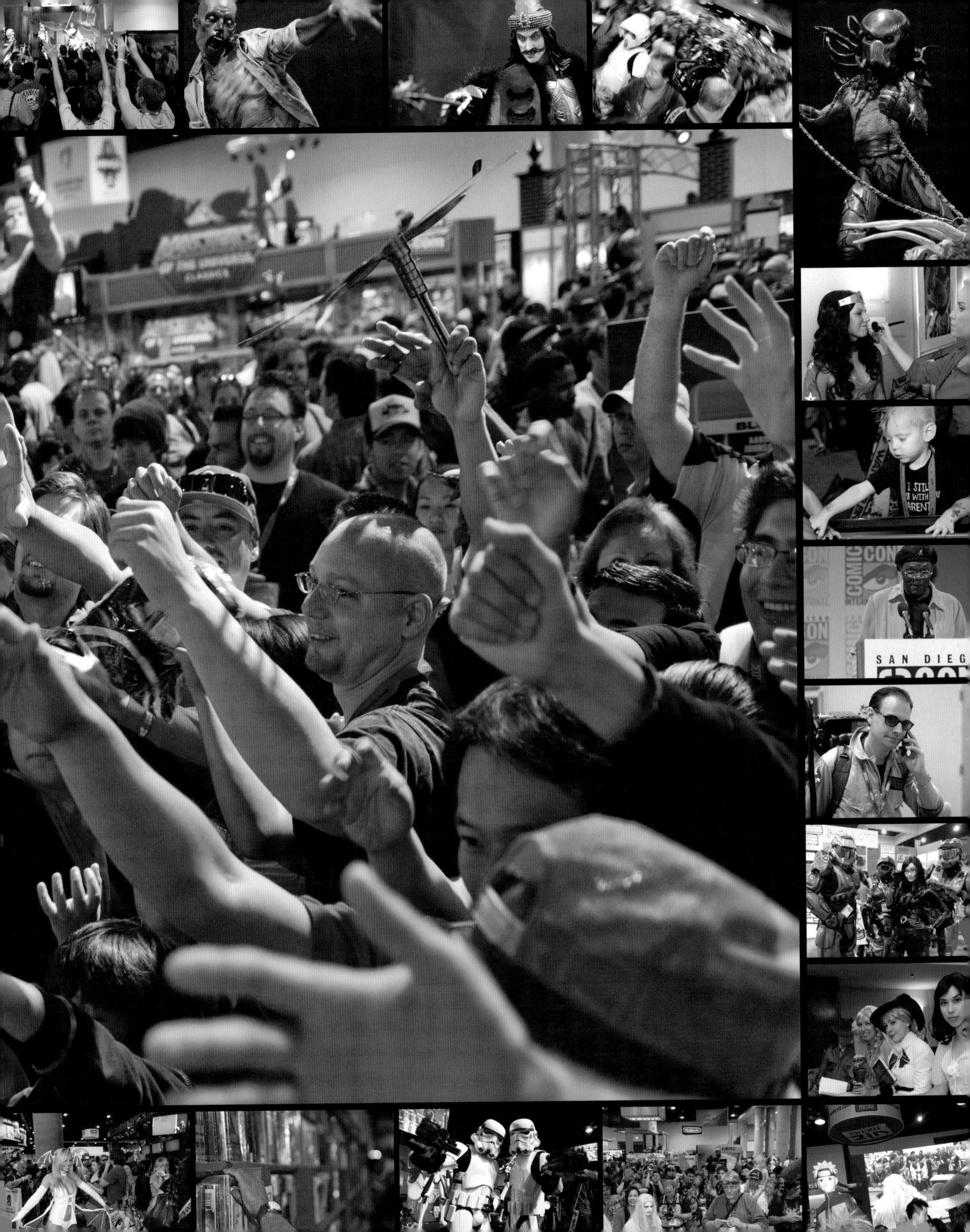
SAN DIEG

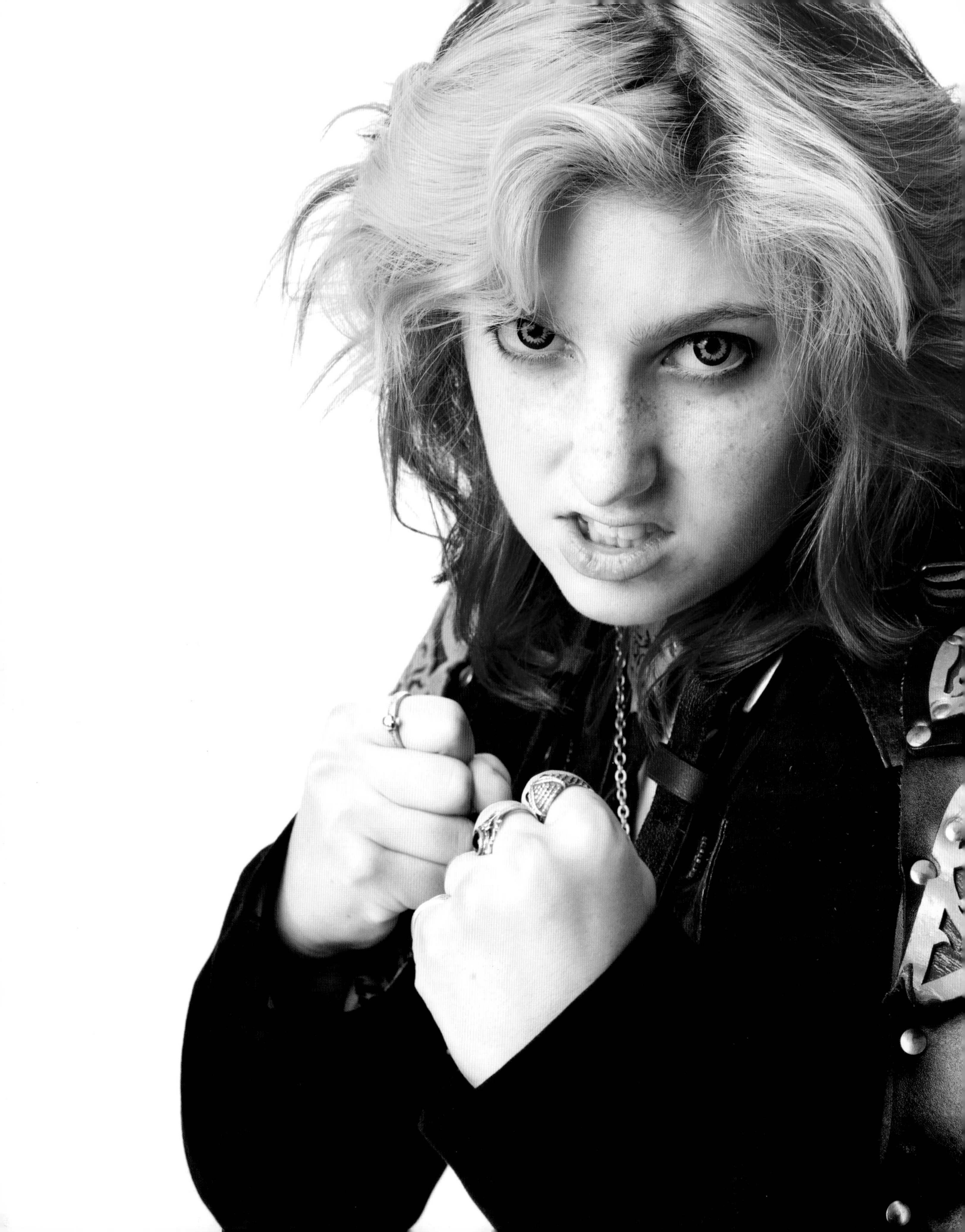

day one

> "The first day of Comic-Con is the closest thing to Christmas morning that you'll ever experience as an adult. The excitement, the wonder, the anticipation... you have no idea what's inside, but you can't wait to rip it open to find out."
>
> *Morgan Spurlock*

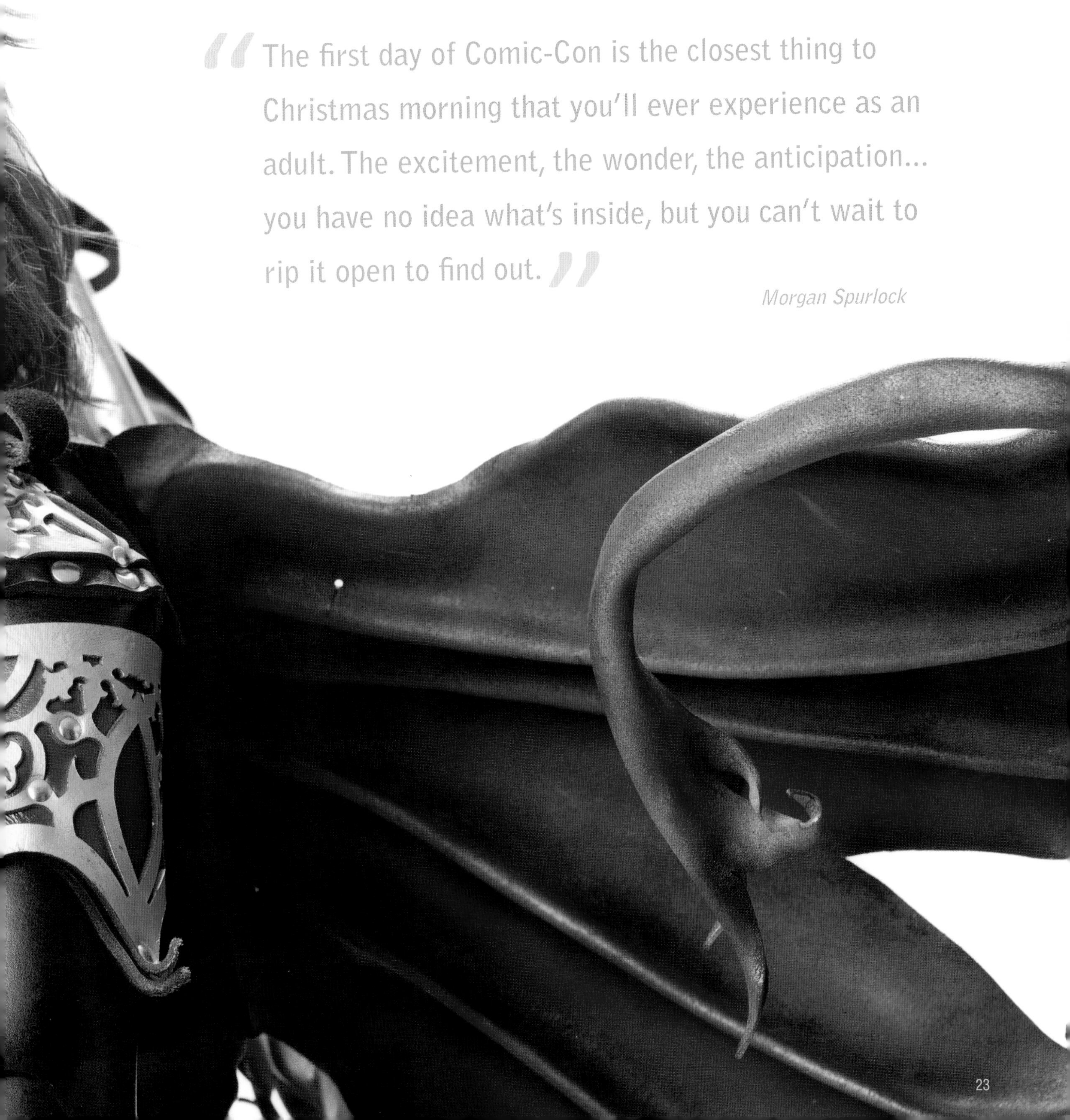

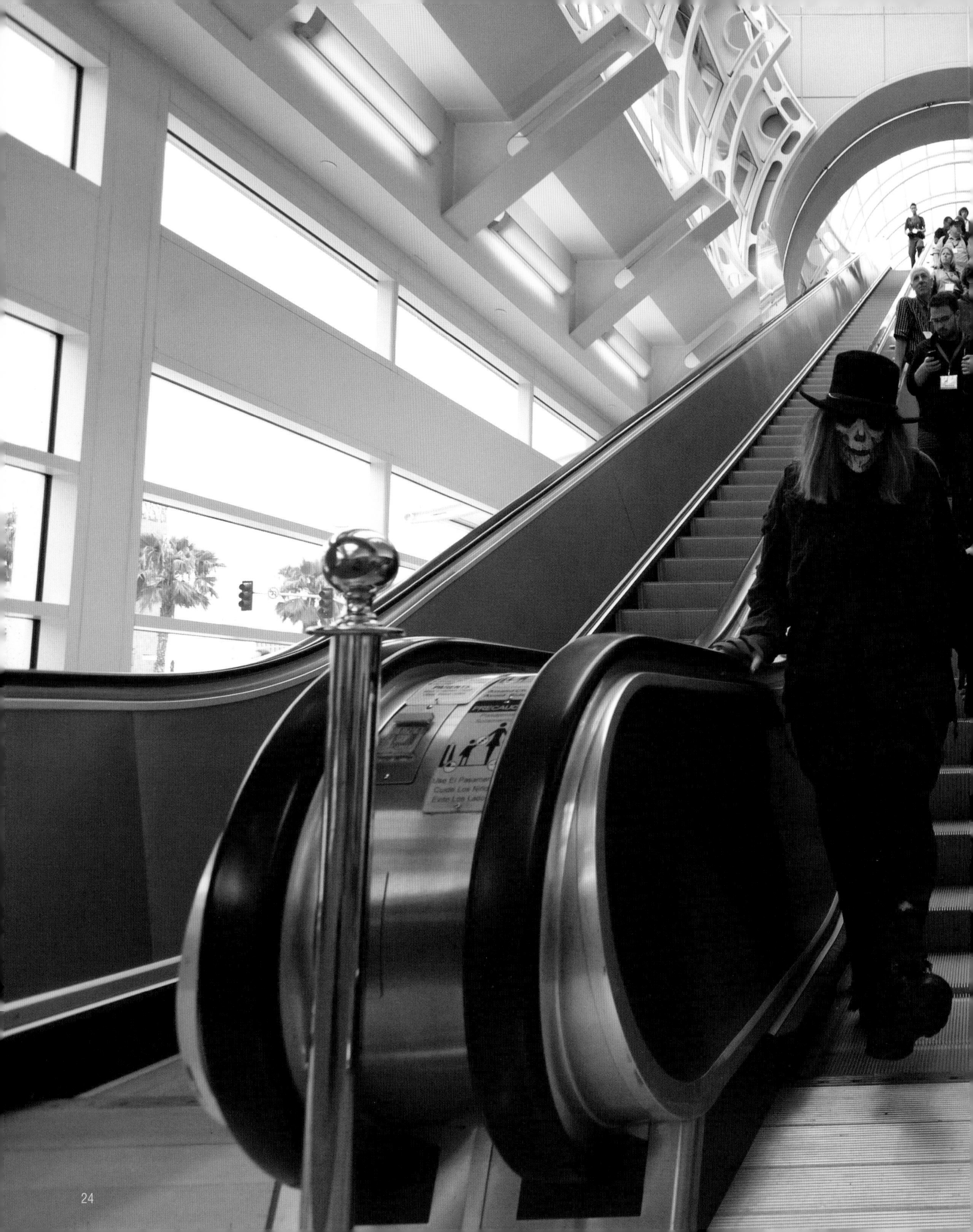

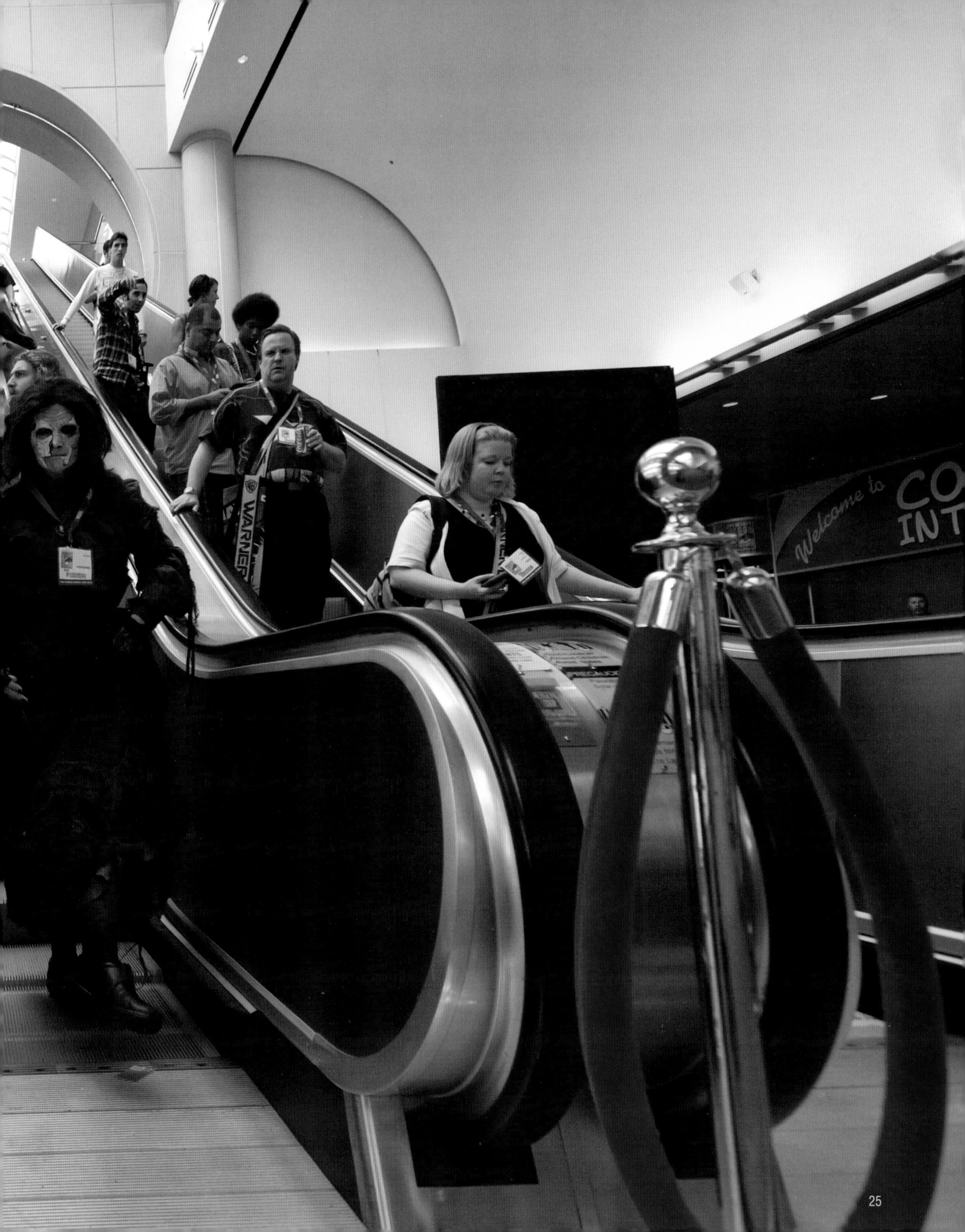
WARNER
Welcome to

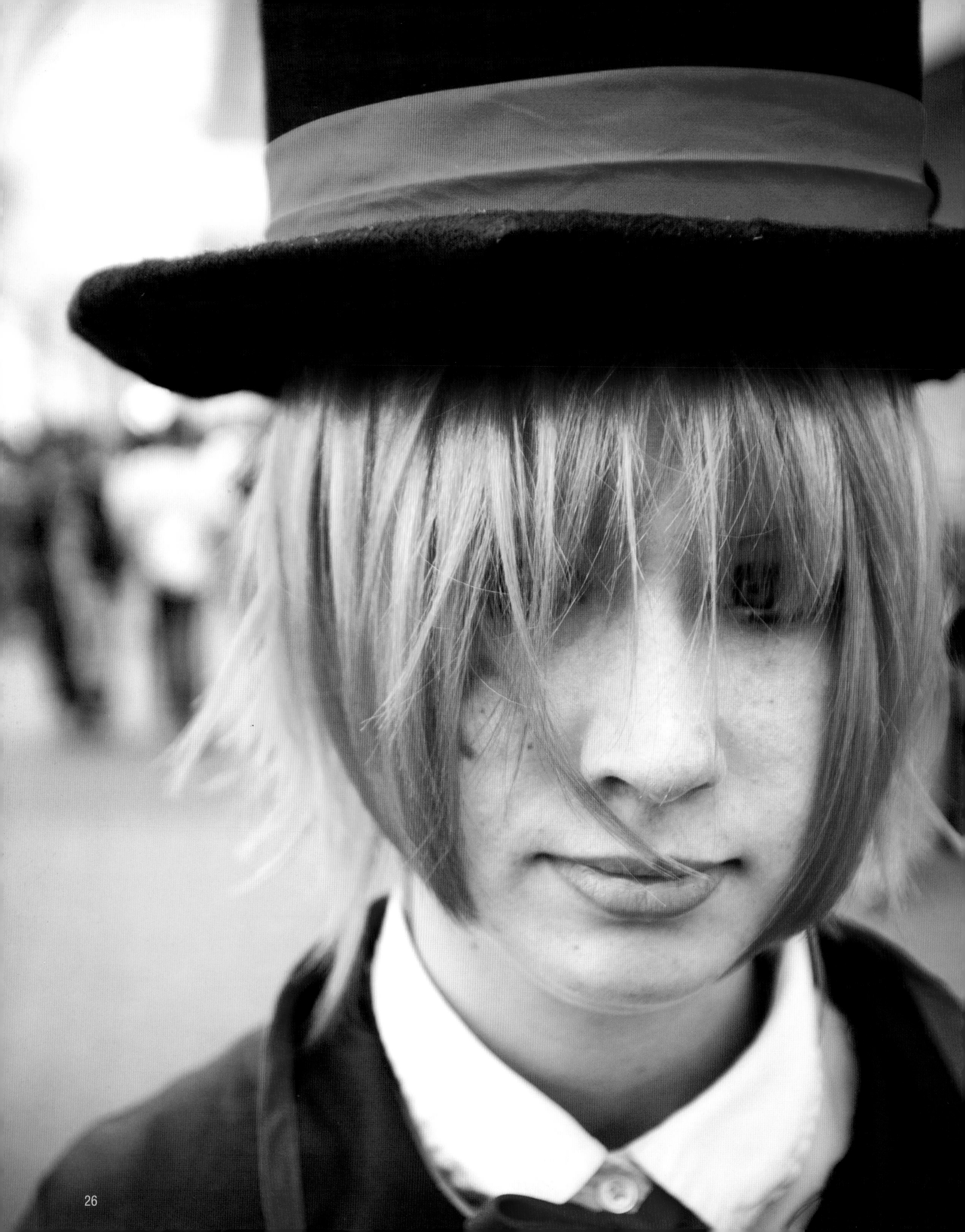

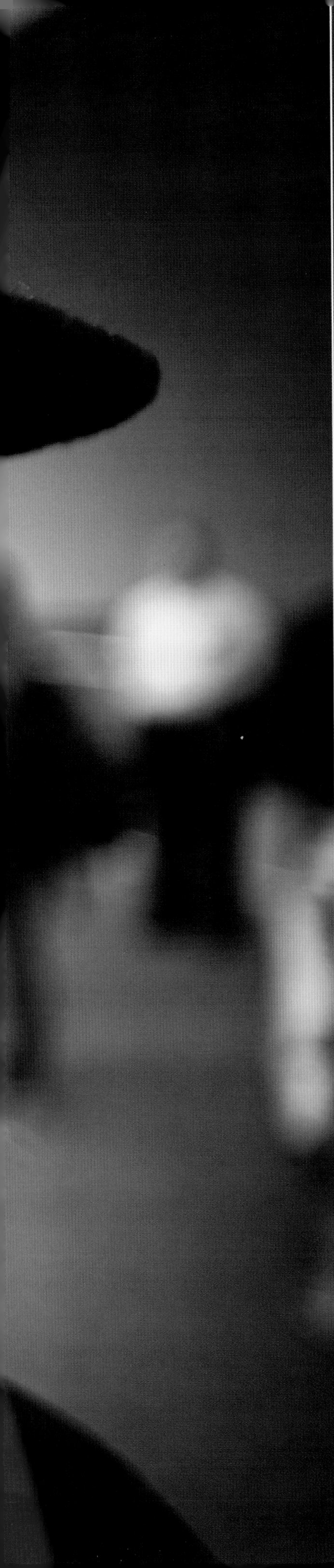

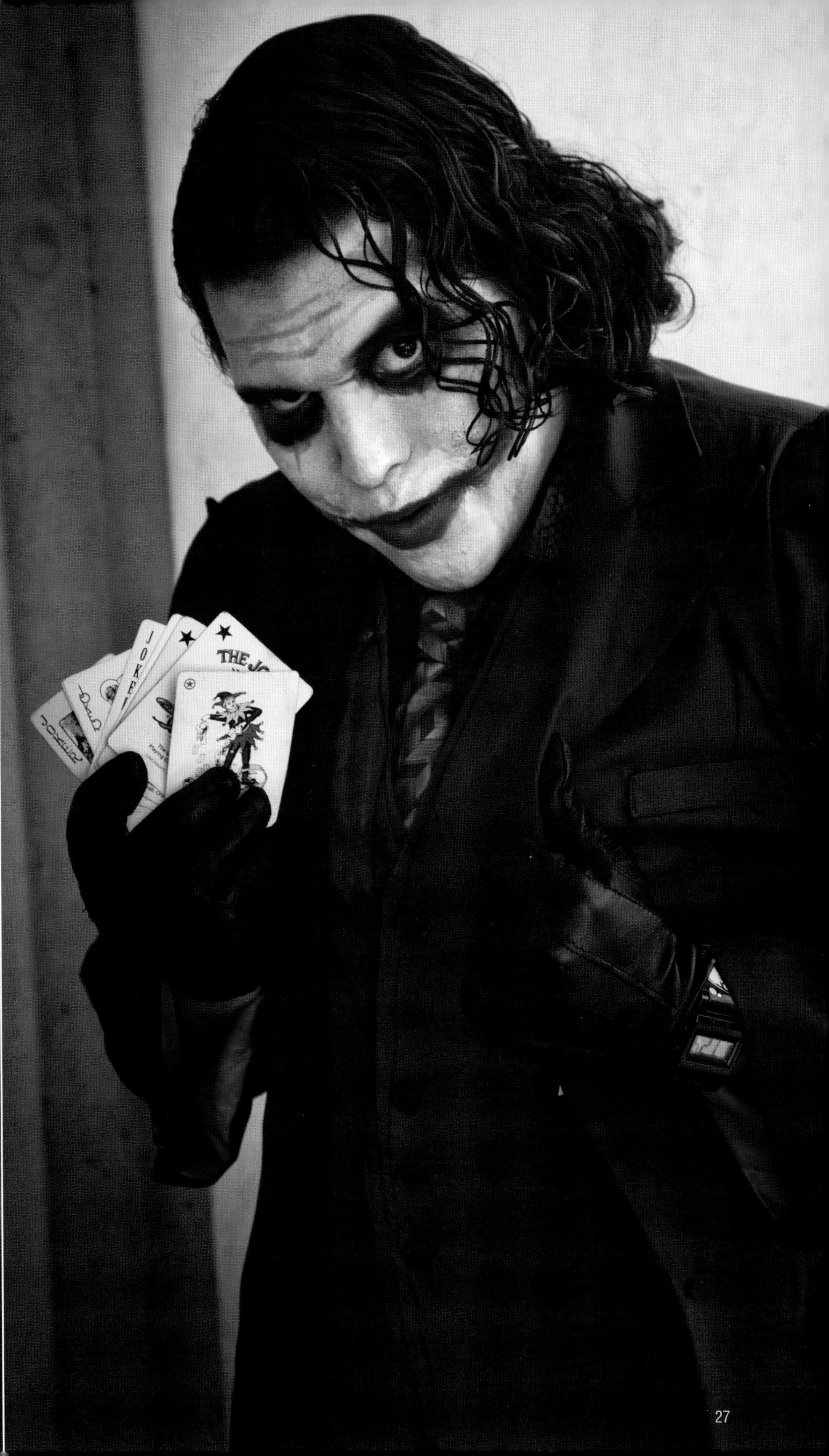

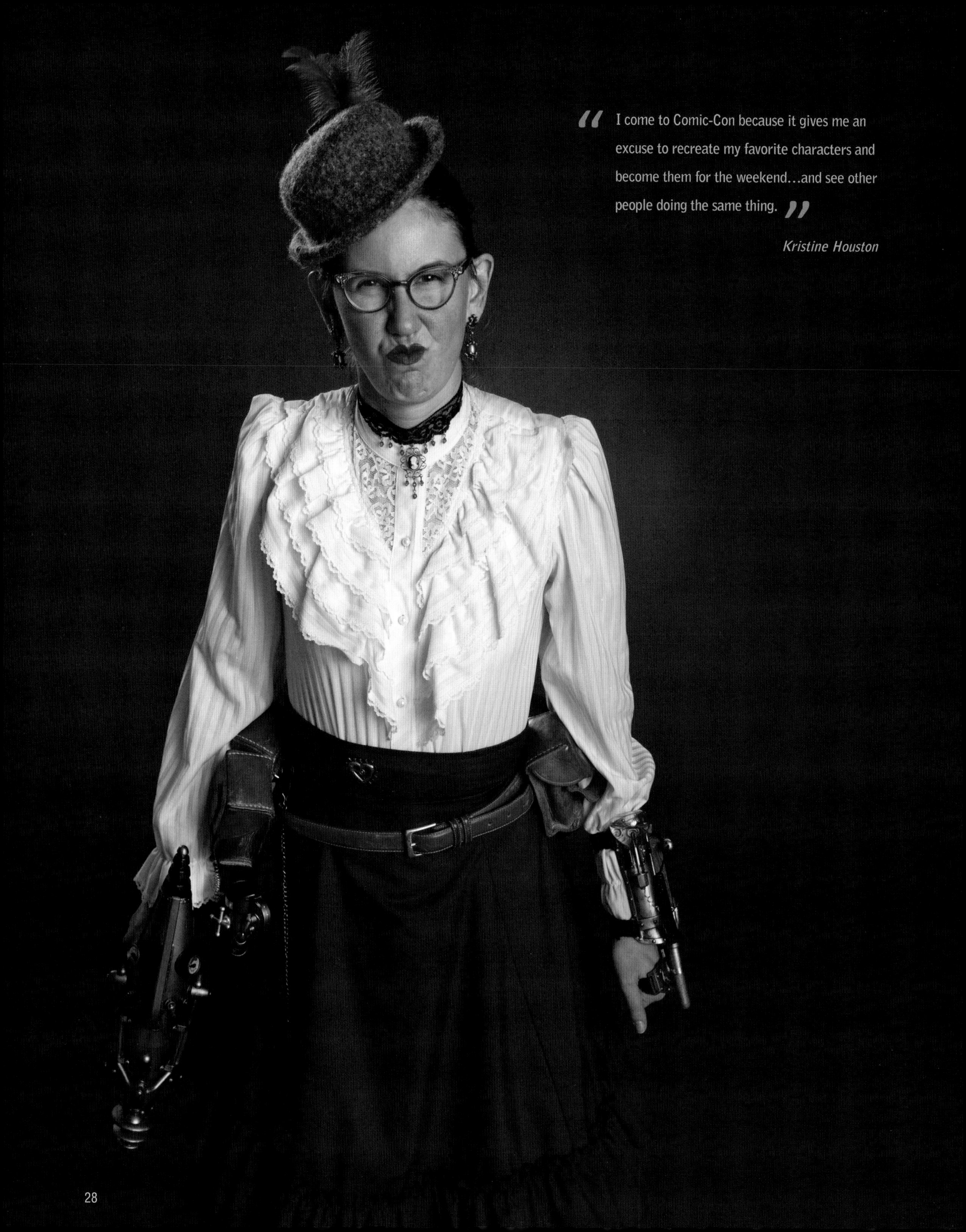

“I come to Comic-Con because it gives me an excuse to recreate my favorite characters and become them for the weekend...and see other people doing the same thing.”

Kristine Houston

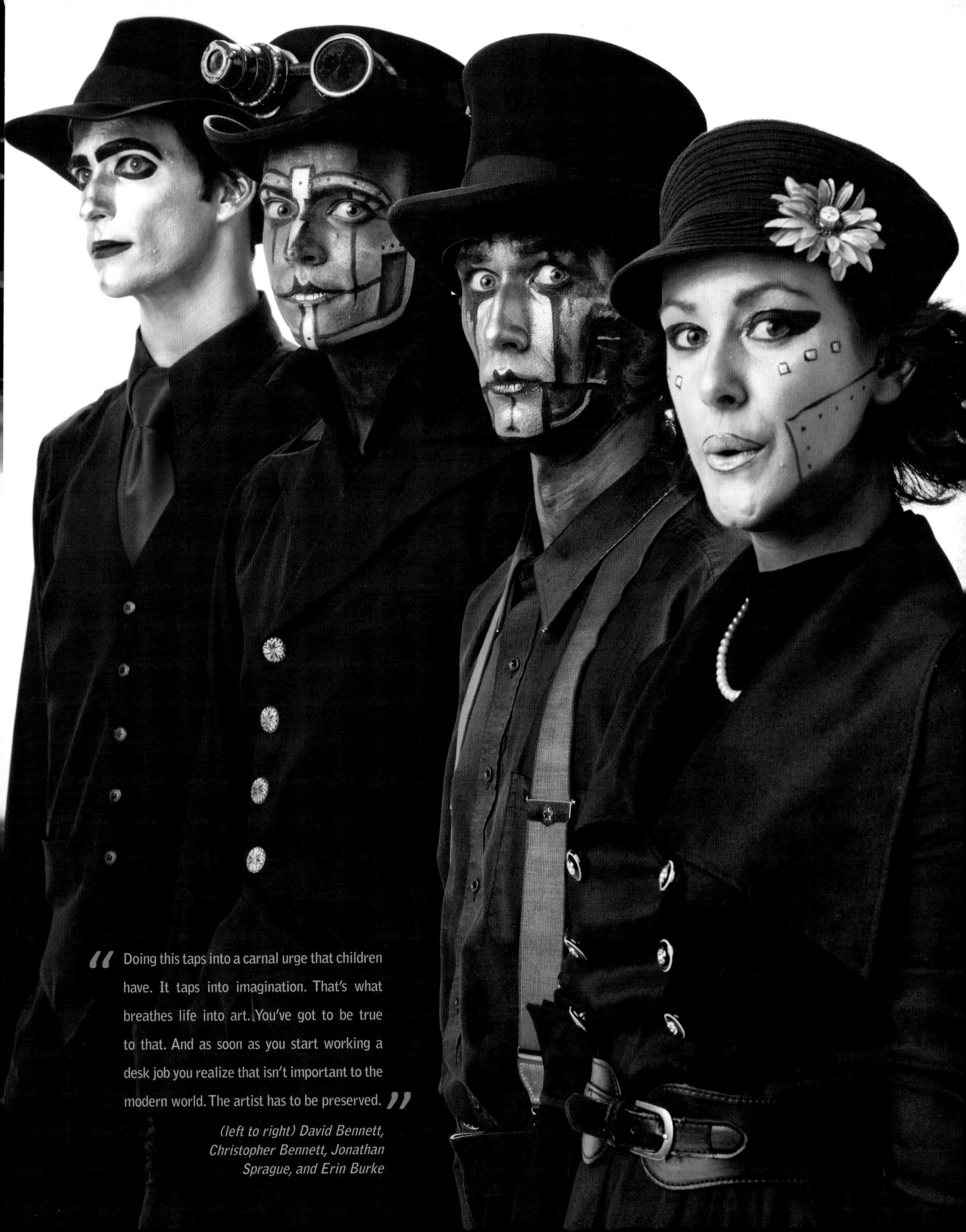

"Doing this taps into a carnal urge that children have. It taps into imagination. That's what breathes life into art. You've got to be true to that. And as soon as you start working a desk job you realize that isn't important to the modern world. The artist has to be preserved."

(left to right) David Bennett, Christopher Bennett, Jonathan Sprague, and Erin Burke

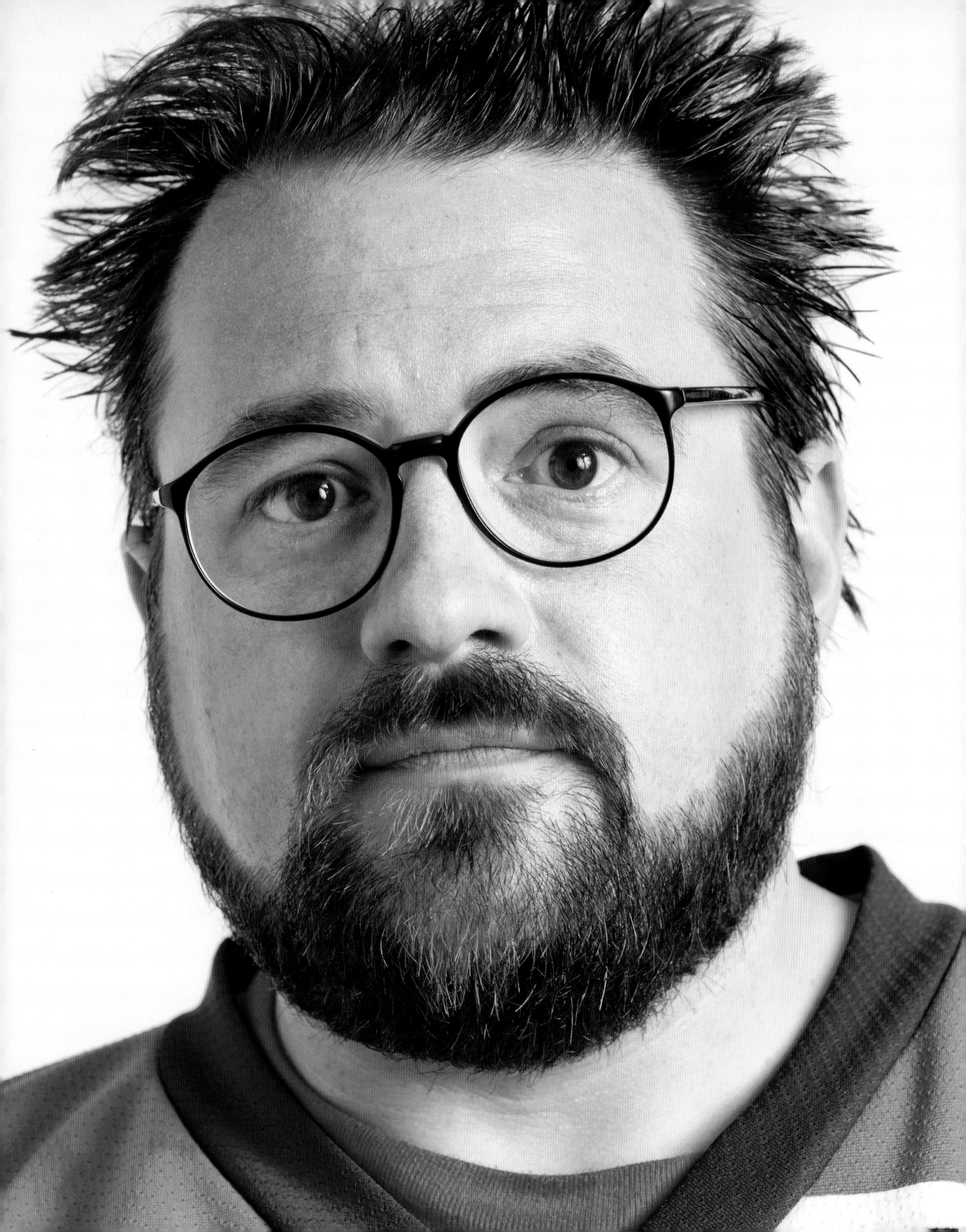

kevin smith

screenwriter, film producer, director, comic book writer, author, podcaster, actor

" In the mind of every collector, of every comic book fiend, San Diego Comic-Con is the answer to all your prayers. It's like heaven, inasmuch as they tell you that everything that you have ever lost is going to come back to you. Everything that you have ever wanted will come your way. "

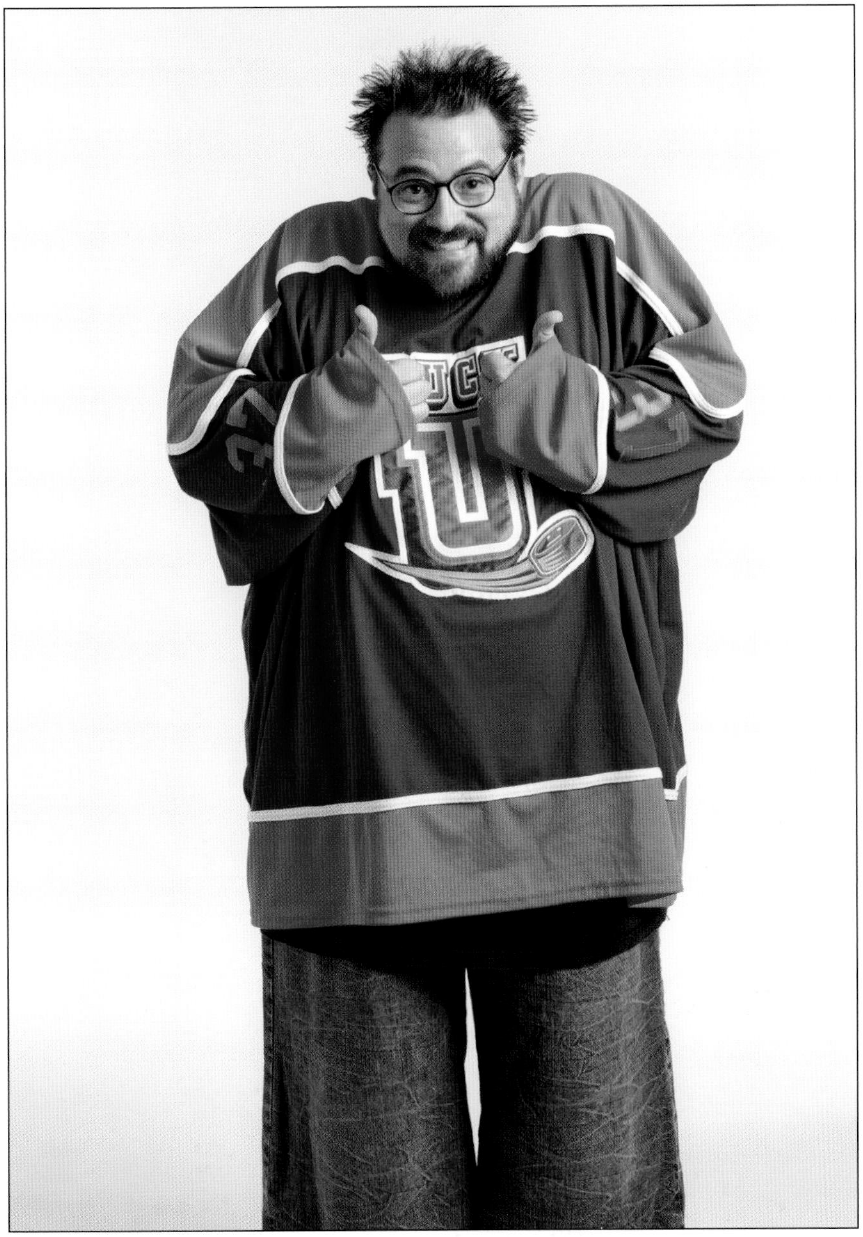

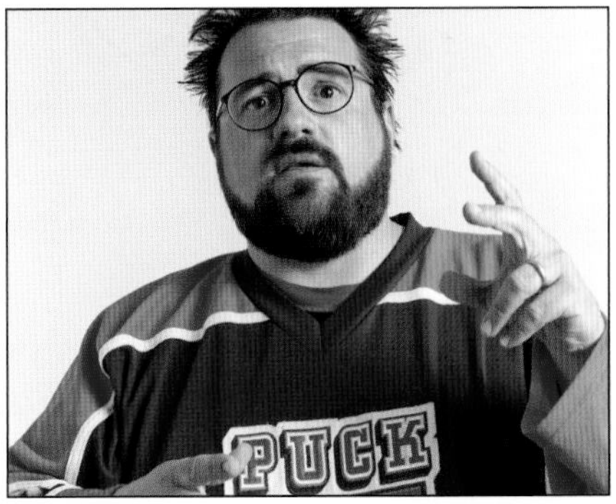
PUCK

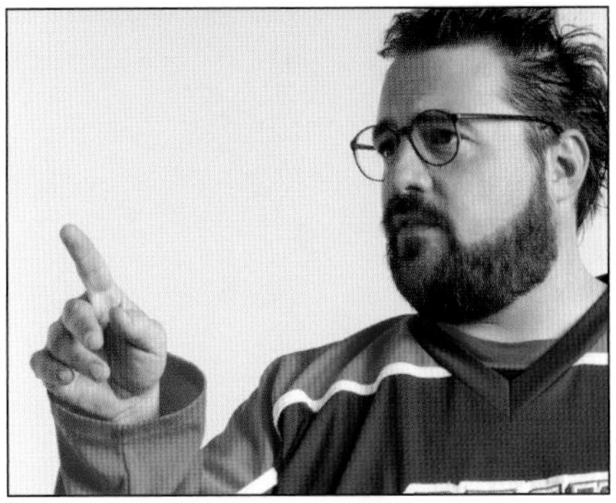

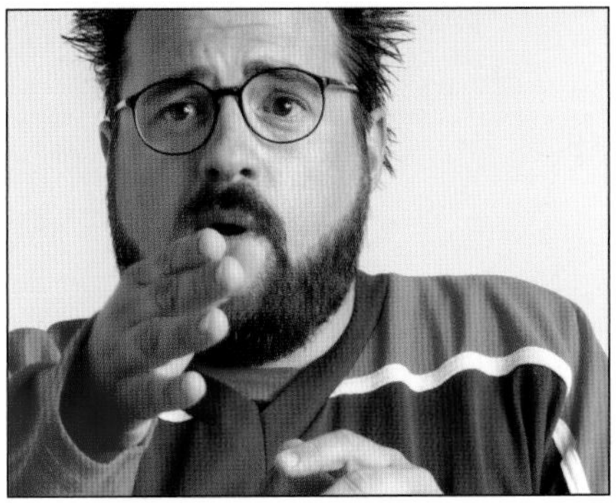

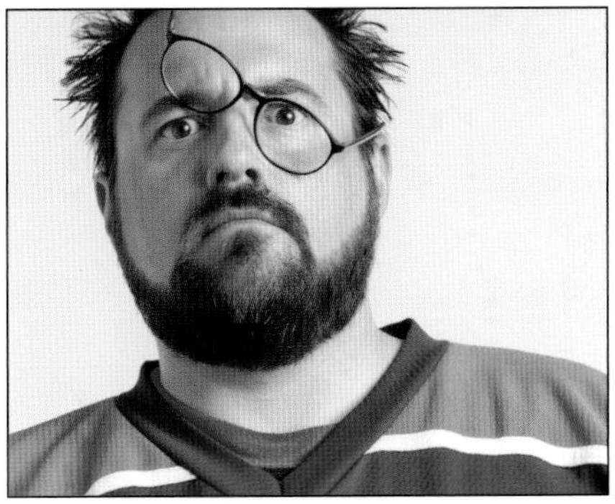

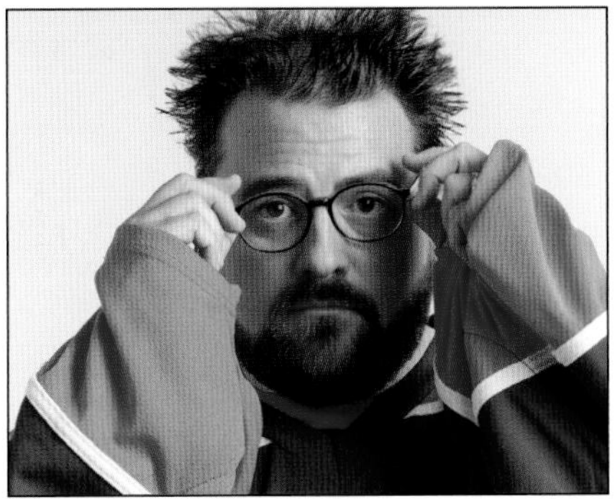

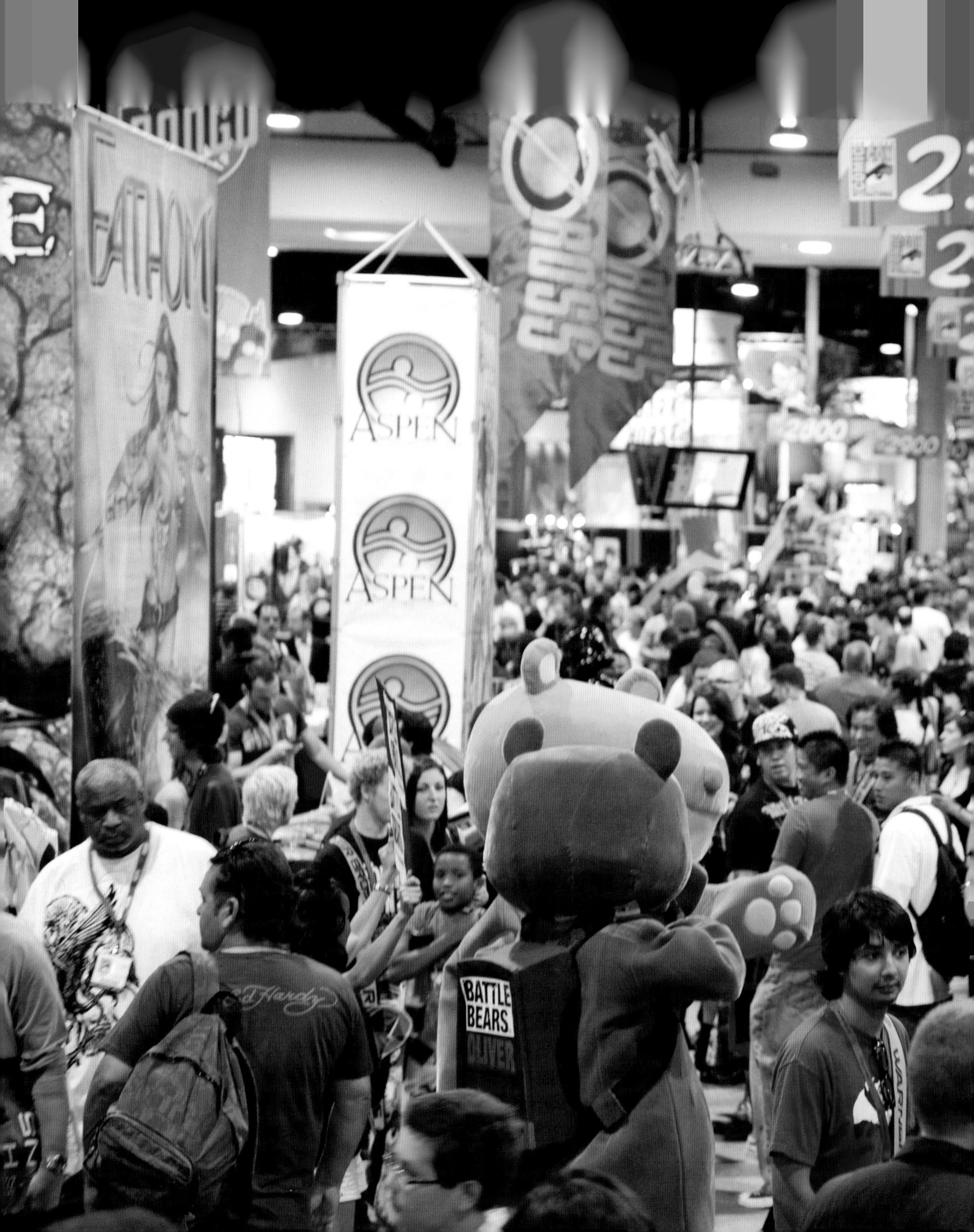
FATHOM
ASPEN
ASPEN
BATTLE BEARS
OLIVER
Ed Hardy

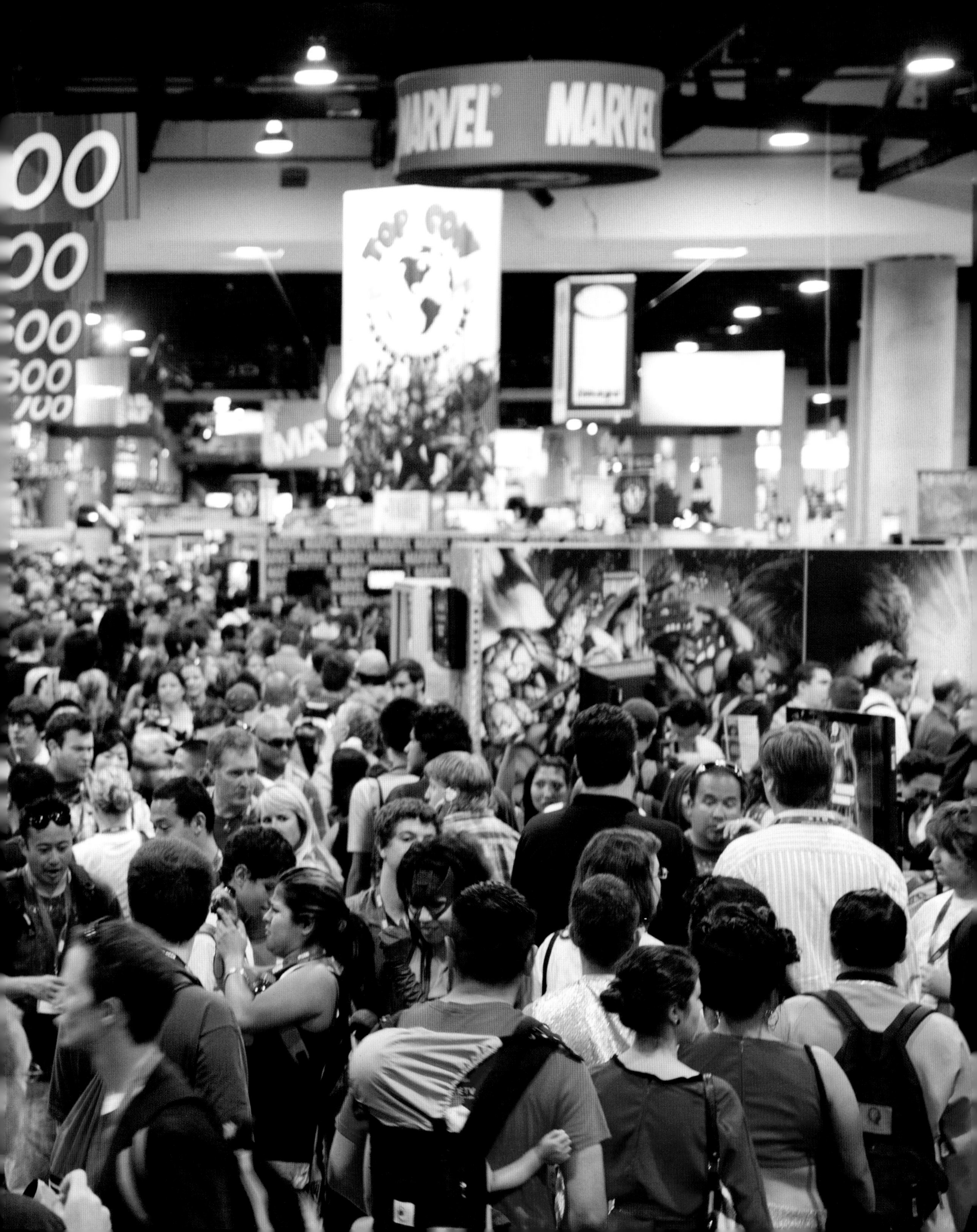
MARVEL
MARVEL

nicholas gurewitch

artist, creator | The Perry Bible Fellowship

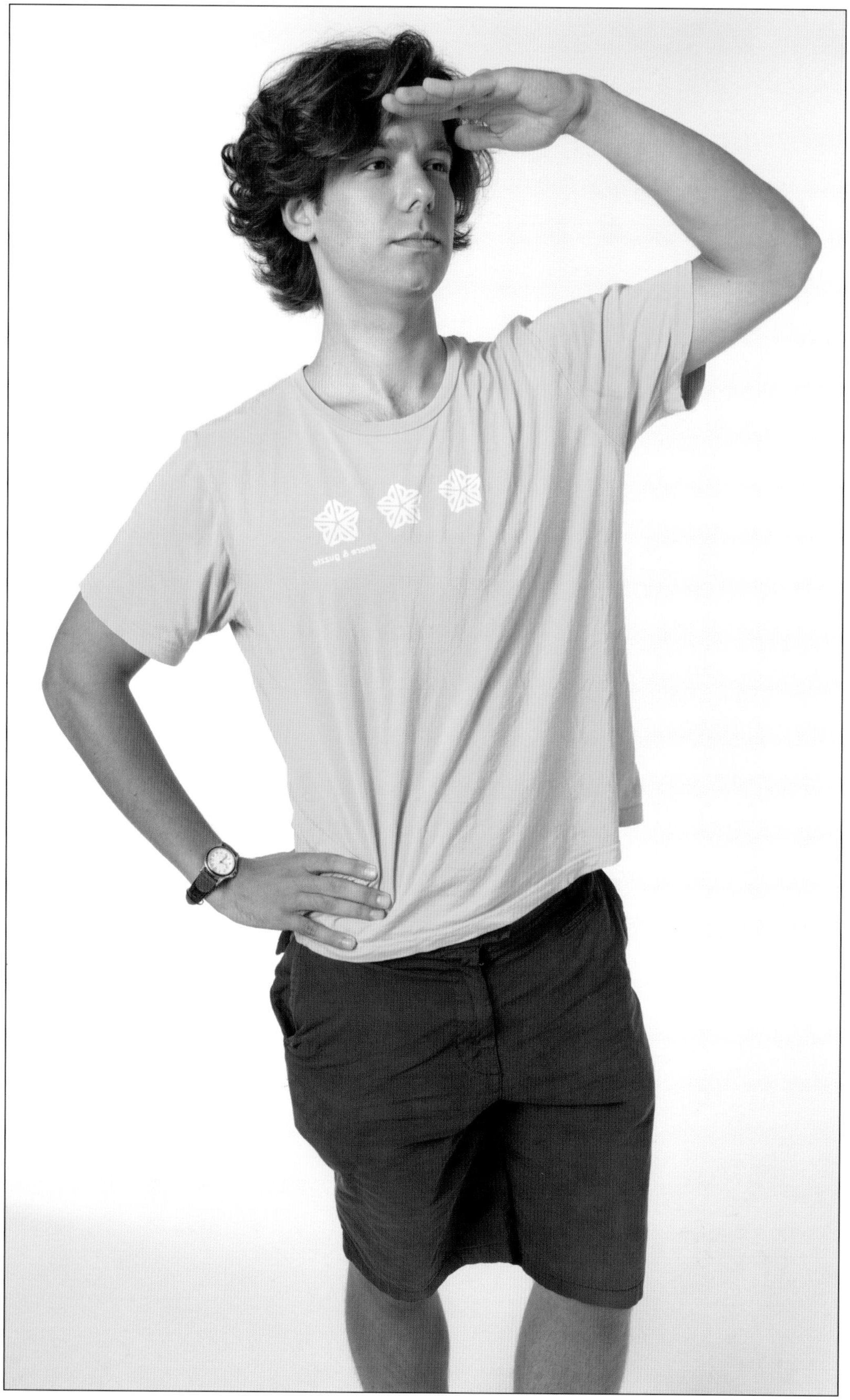

“It's a lot like Disneyland, only the people who populate it are not innocent. They are not innocent children.”

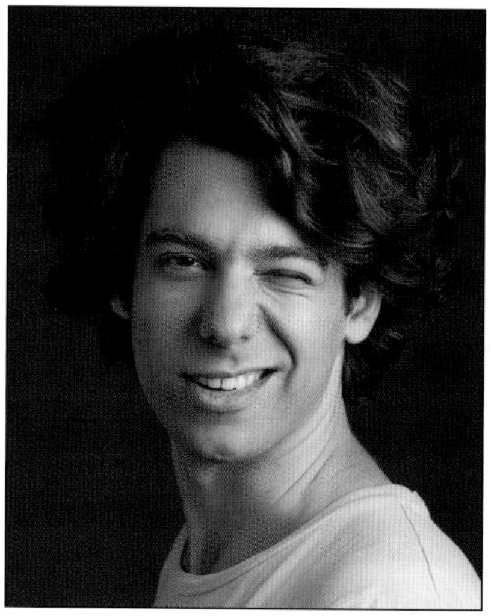

felicia day

actor, creator | The Guild

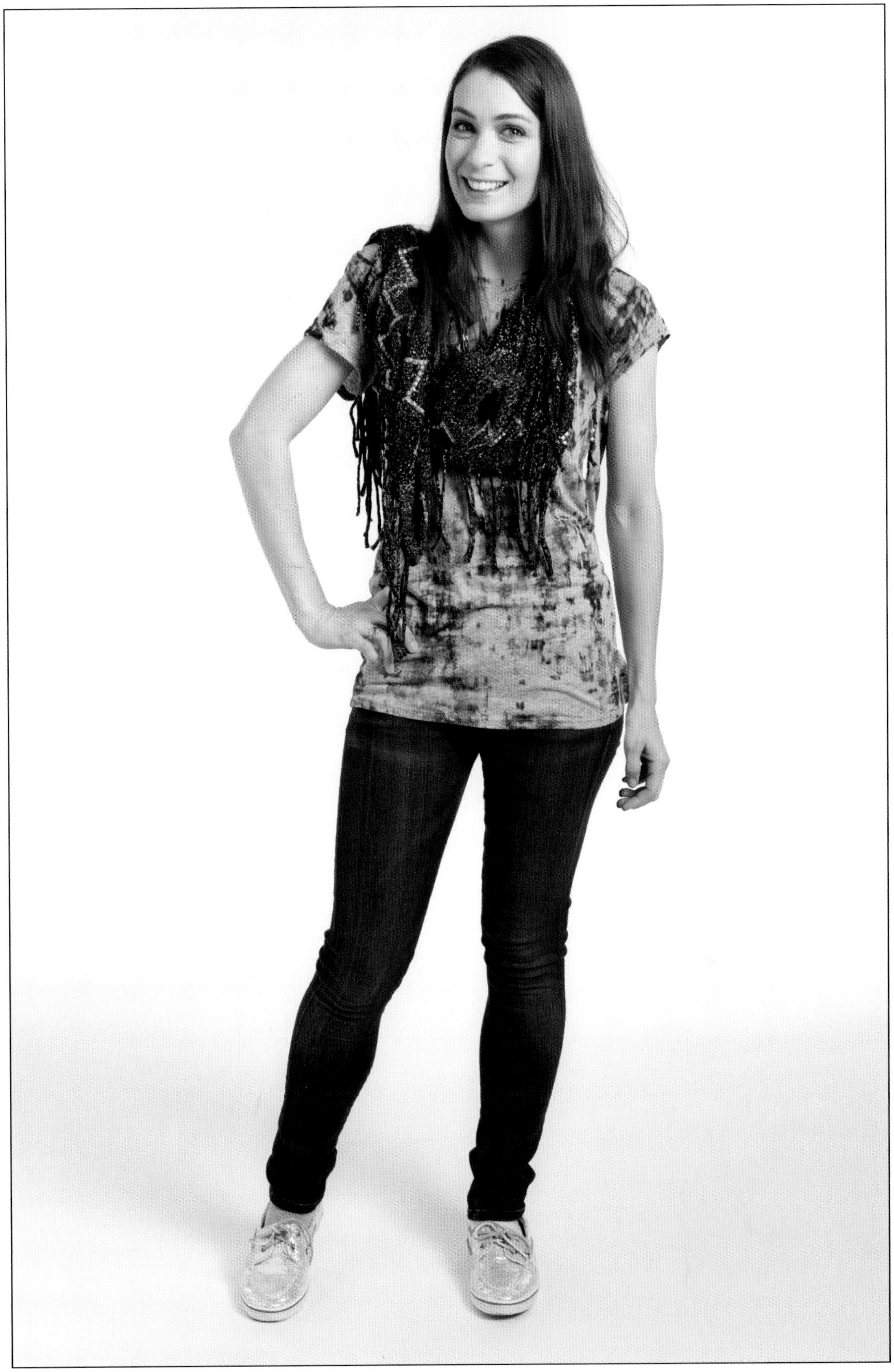

"All I do every day, all day, is try to tell everyone about my show. And I think that's kind of what geeks are—they're willing to be out there about things that they're passionate about without being ashamed about it. And it makes me really proud to be a part of it."

max brooks

writer | World War Z and The Zombie Survival Guide

" I think the expectation of fans at Comic-Con is to simply immerse themselves in the culture, to find people like them, to feel part of something. "

" I wasn't expecting this kind of enthusiasm. I was not expecting a guy to ask me for a dental impression. I said, 'Why do you want a dental impression? Are you going to commit a murder and frame me?' He's like, 'No, no, no. Here's what I'm gonna do: I'm gonna make an impression of your teeth, then tattoo those teeth onto my arm. Then I can say I was bitten by Zombie Max Brooks.' "

> You can kind of goof off and be whatever you want. And it doesn't really matter. It's one of the only times you can walk around downtown like this and everyone just kind of laughs and it doesn't matter.

Matthew Michael Spencer,
Kristen Gwen Perez,
Dasan James Taitano

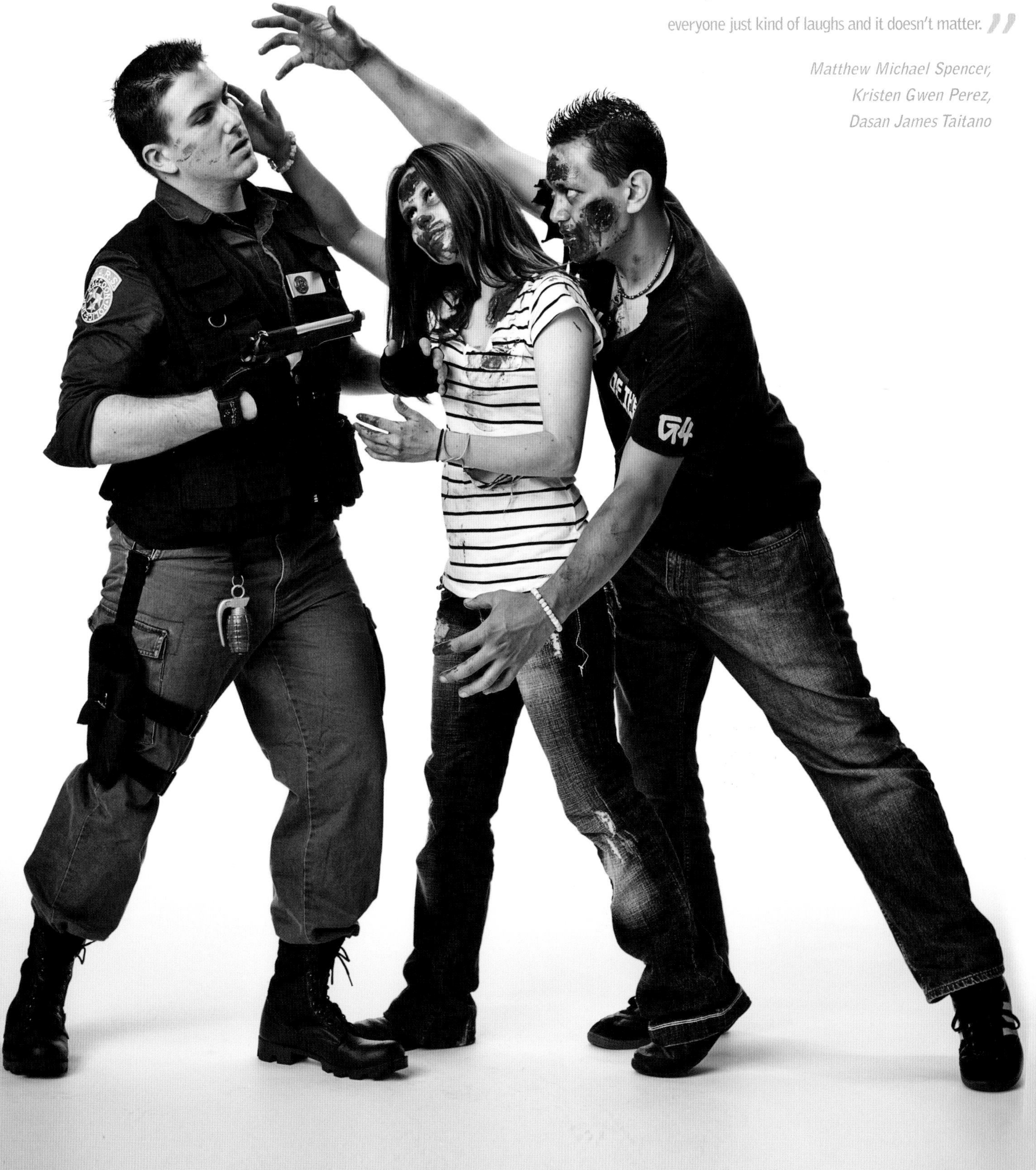
G4

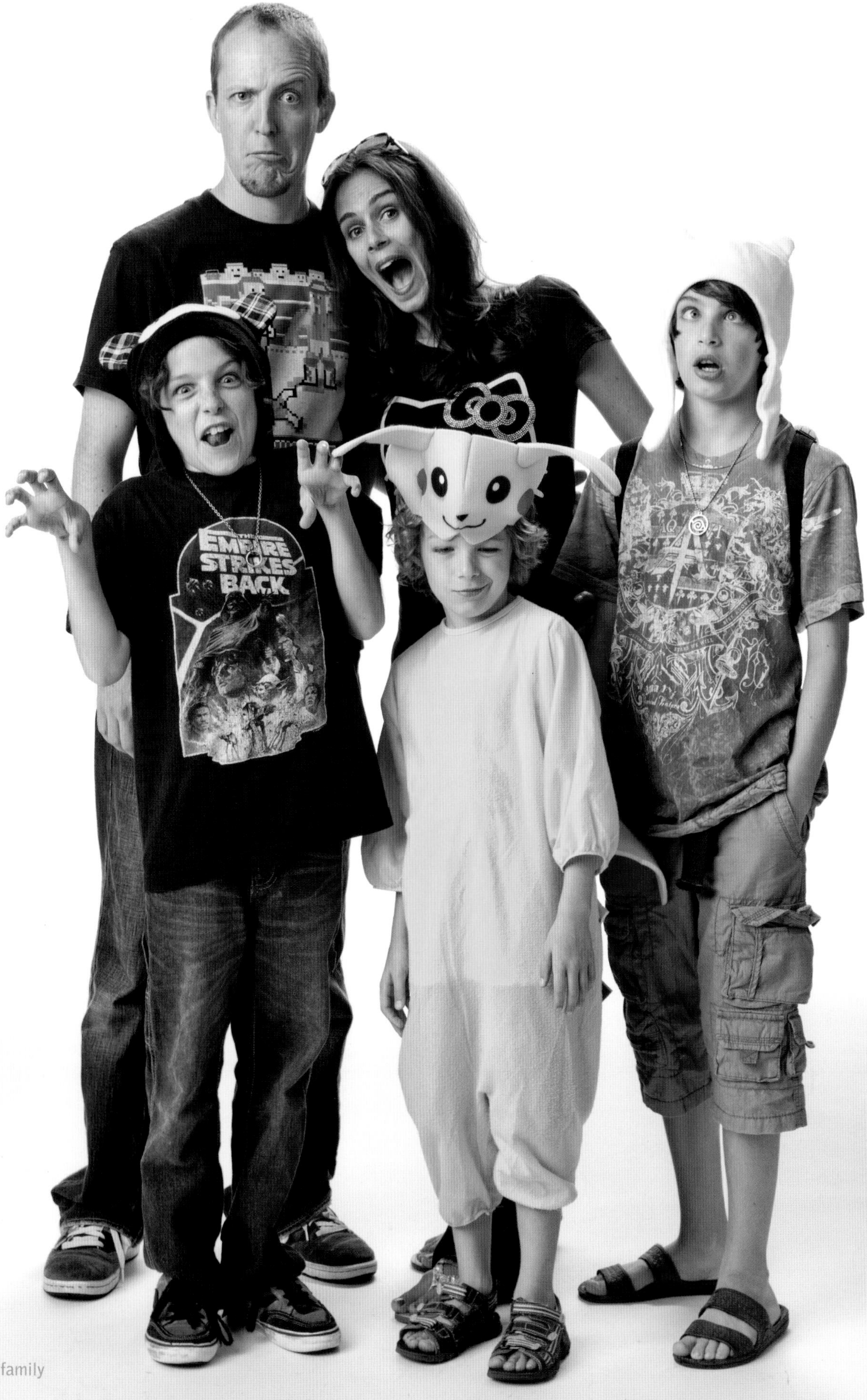
EMPIRE
STRIKES
BACK

The Guillory family

“Comic-Con isn’t just about comics or movies. It’s about community, and it’s about finding each other and being able to express yourself and what you love without any kind of hate.”

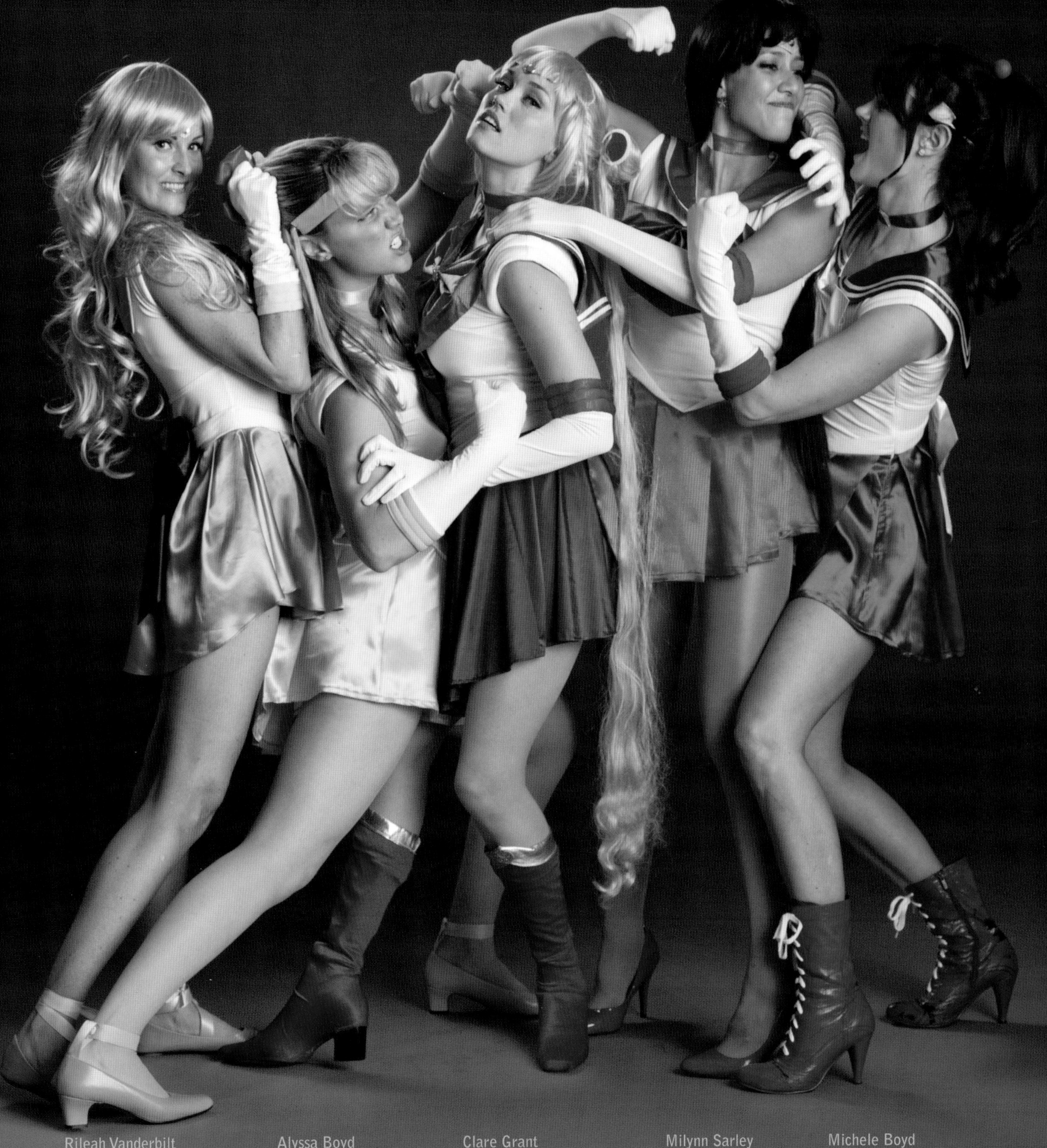

Rileah Vanderbilt Alyssa Boyd Clare Grant Milynn Sarley Michele Boyd

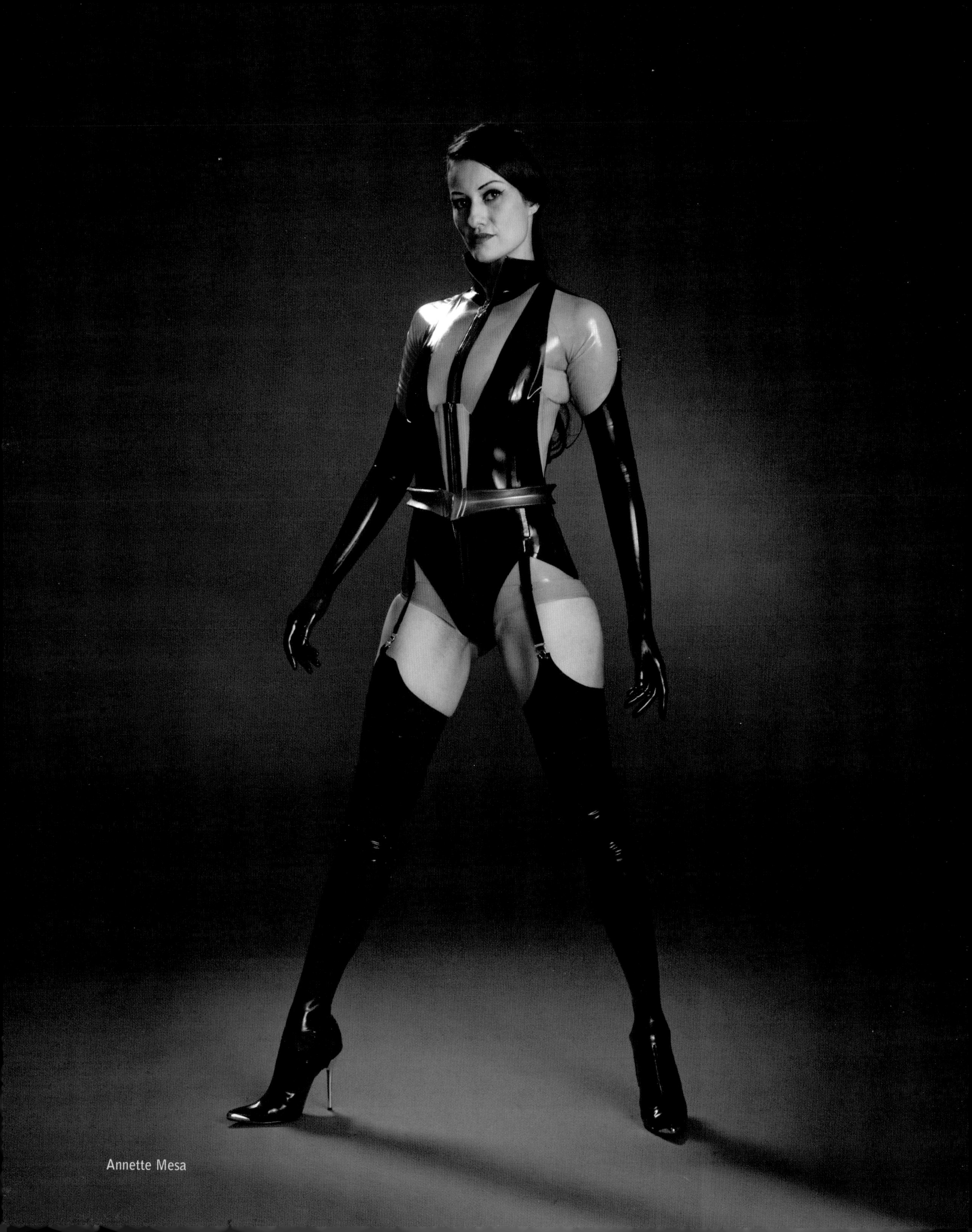

Annette Mesa

morgan webb

tv personality | G4 Network

"The craziest things you see here are women dressed in very strange and revealing outfits. And you know it's from a comic book or an anime or a video game, but you can't quite place it, and all you know is that girl forgot her pants."

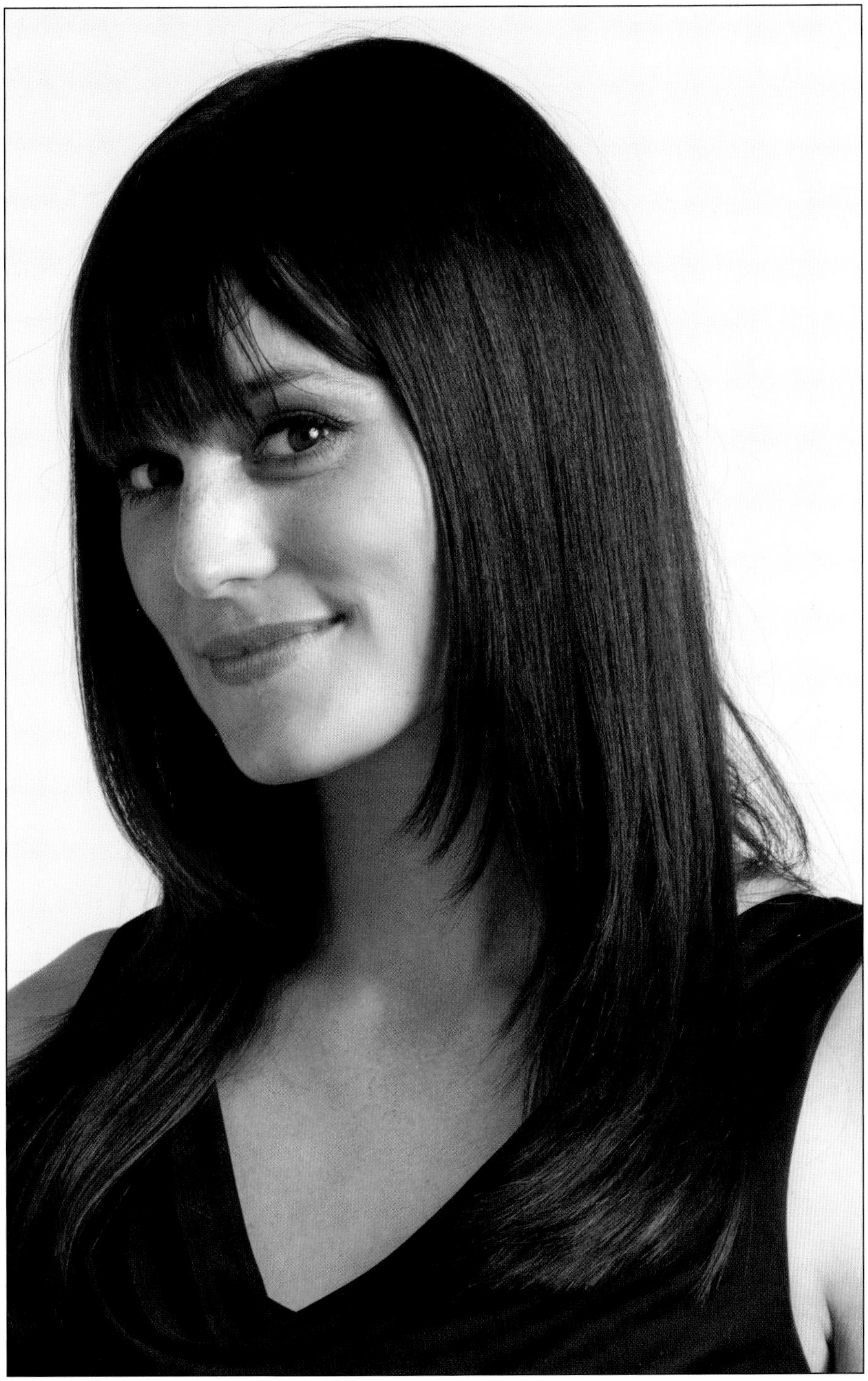

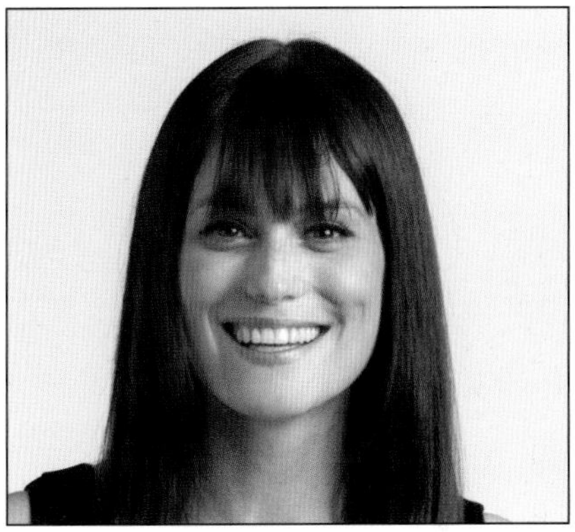

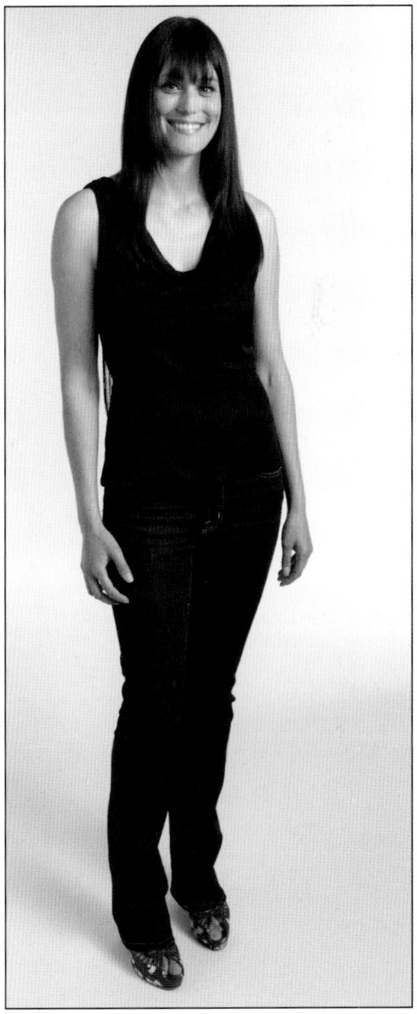

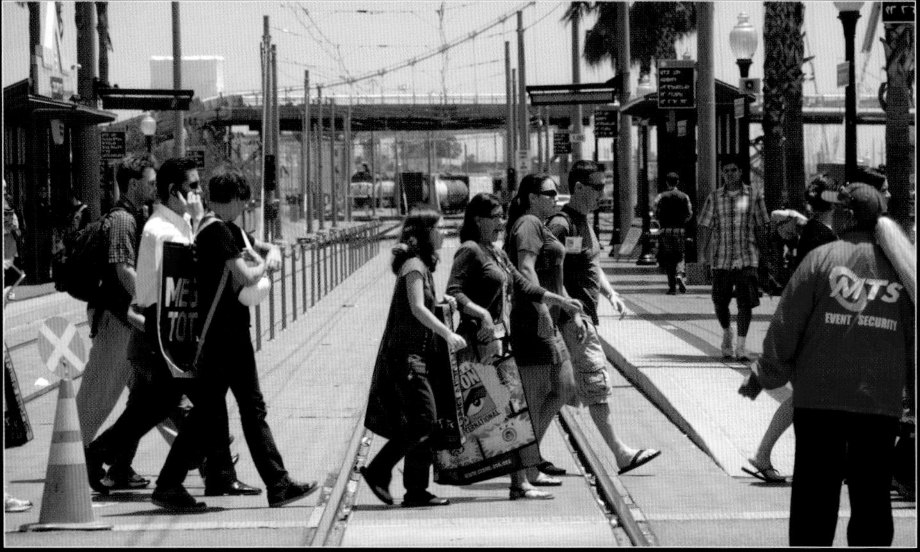
MTS
EVENT SECURITY

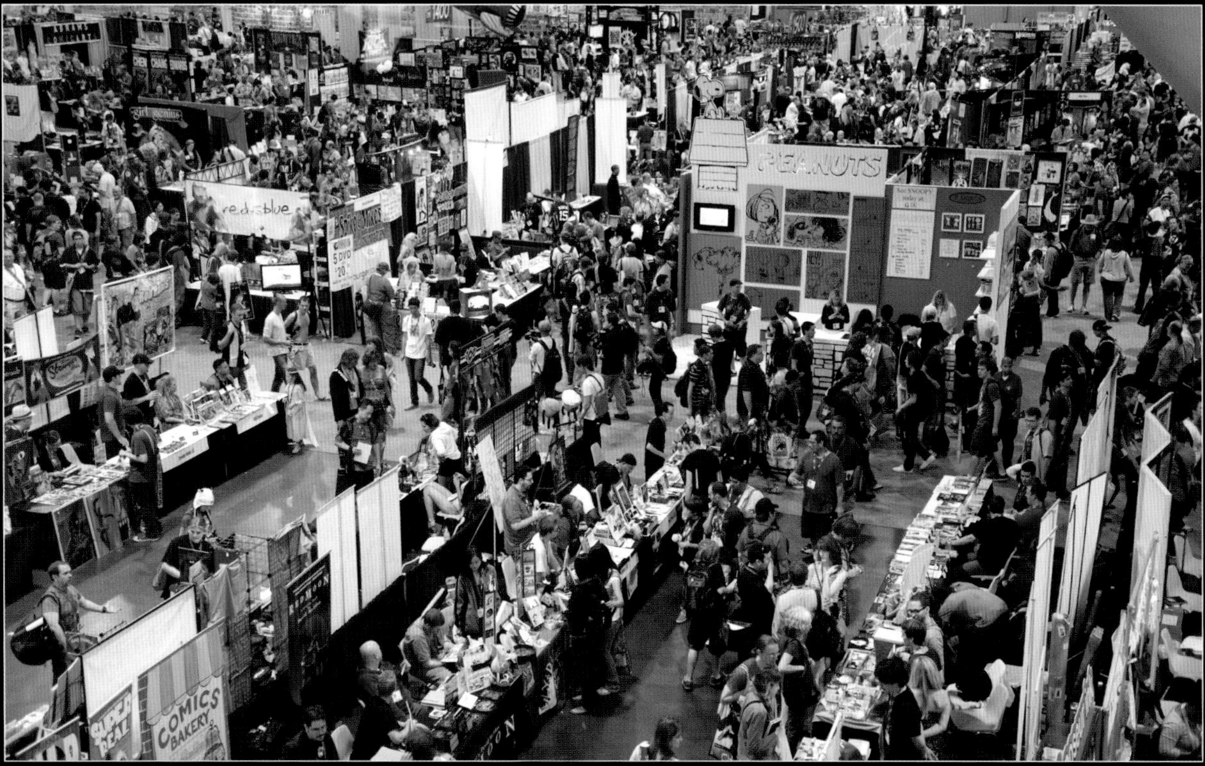
PEANUTS
red vs blue
COMICS
BAKERY

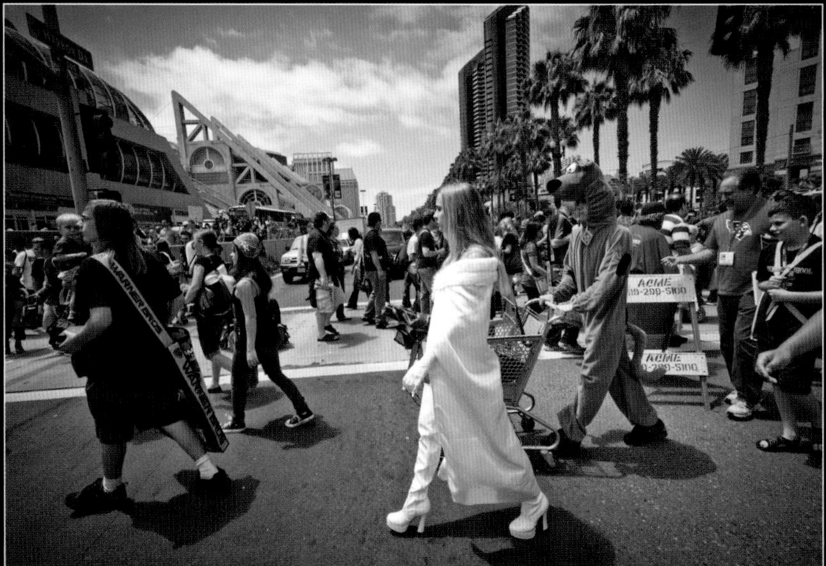
ACME

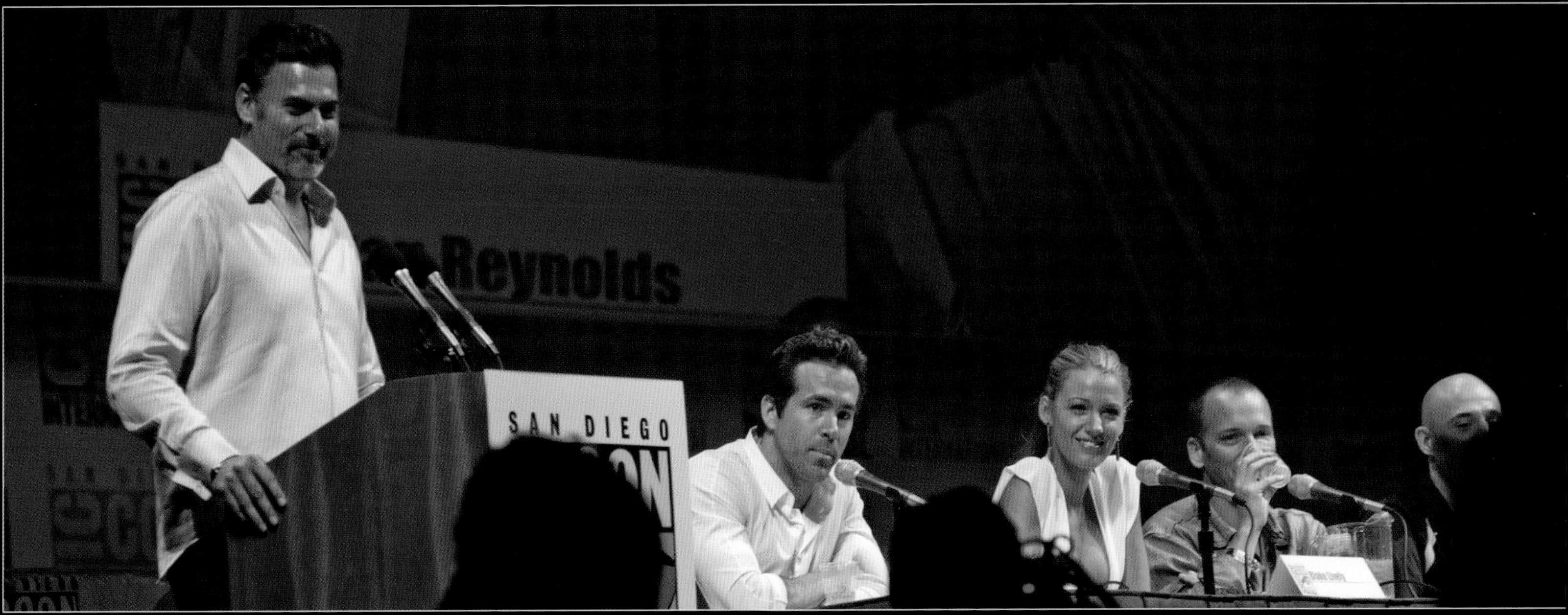
Reynolds
SAN DIEGO
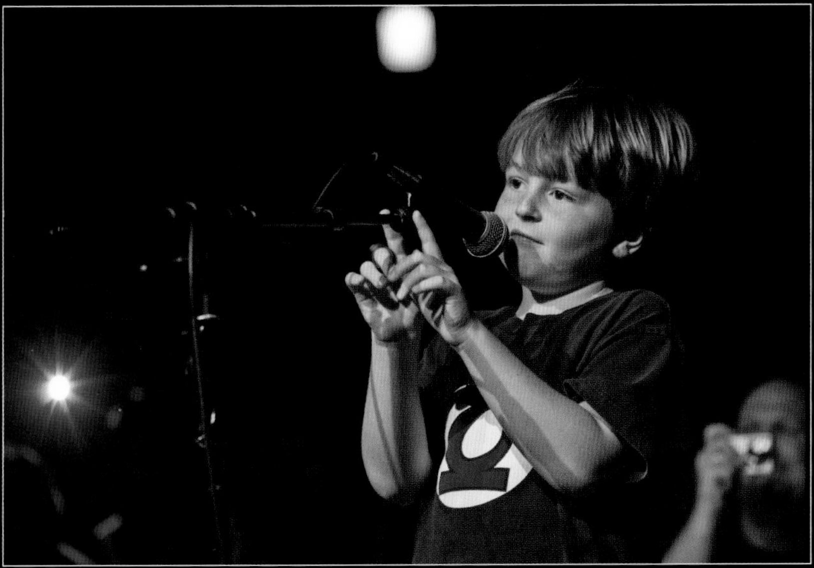
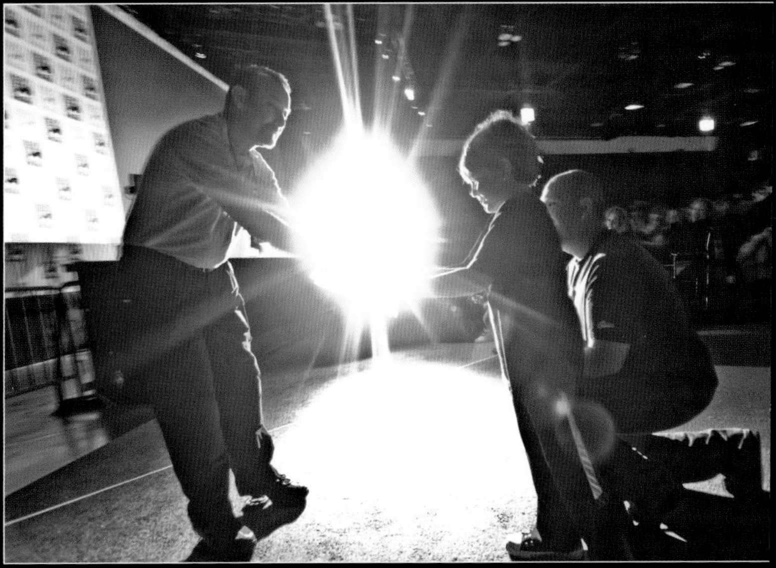
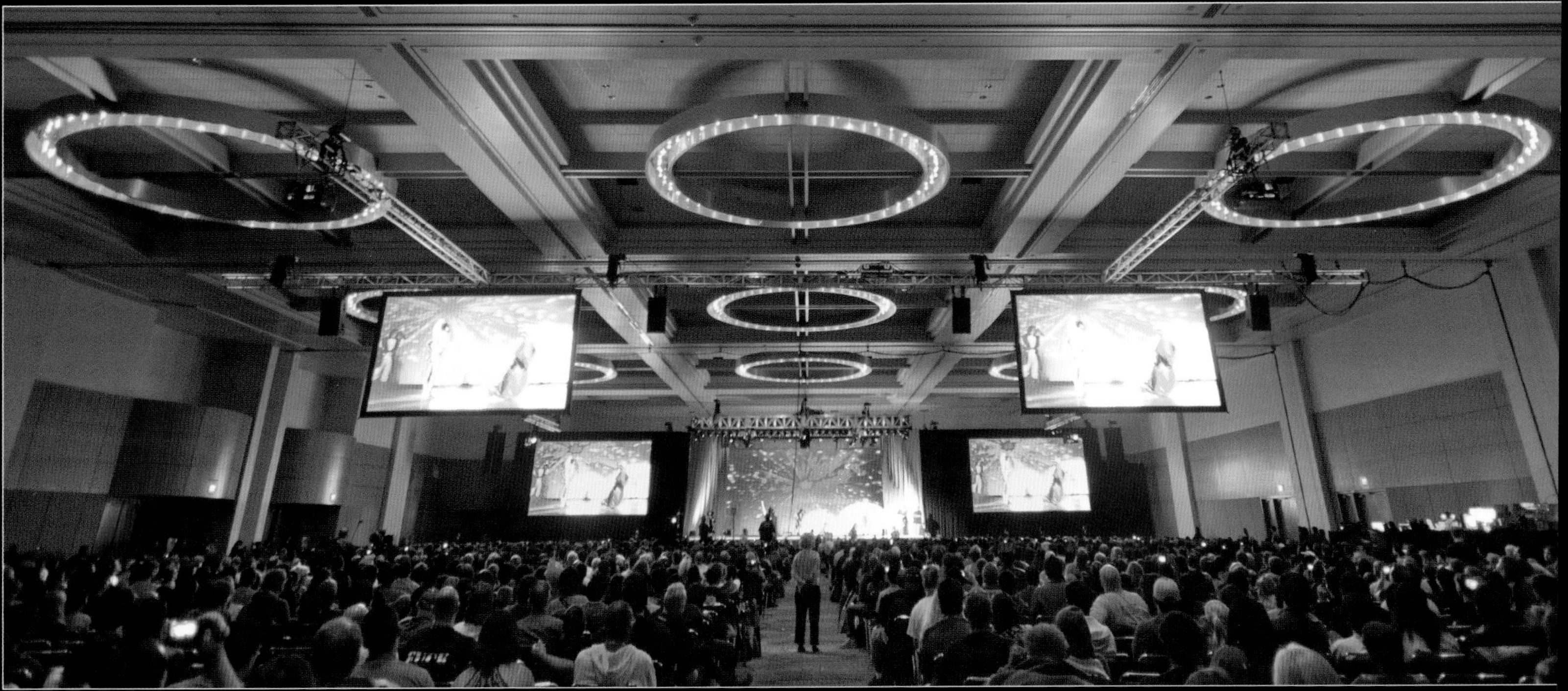

> "The first Comic-Con I came to back in 1990 was very small; it was inside a little hotel. If you looked out the window, you'd maybe see one guy dressed as Green Lantern being chased down the street by a bunch of Marines."

Grant Morrison

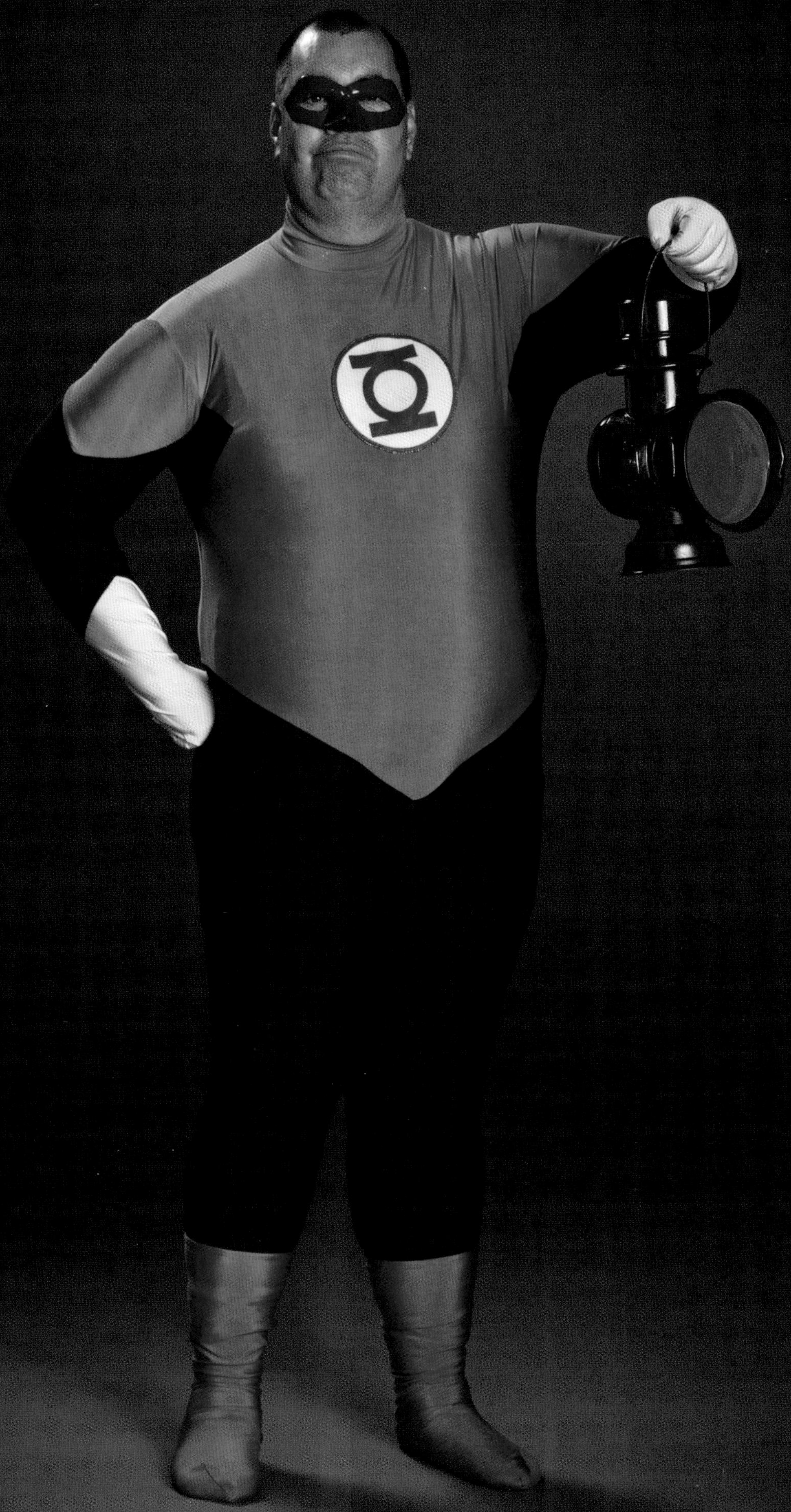

Tom Lee Christian

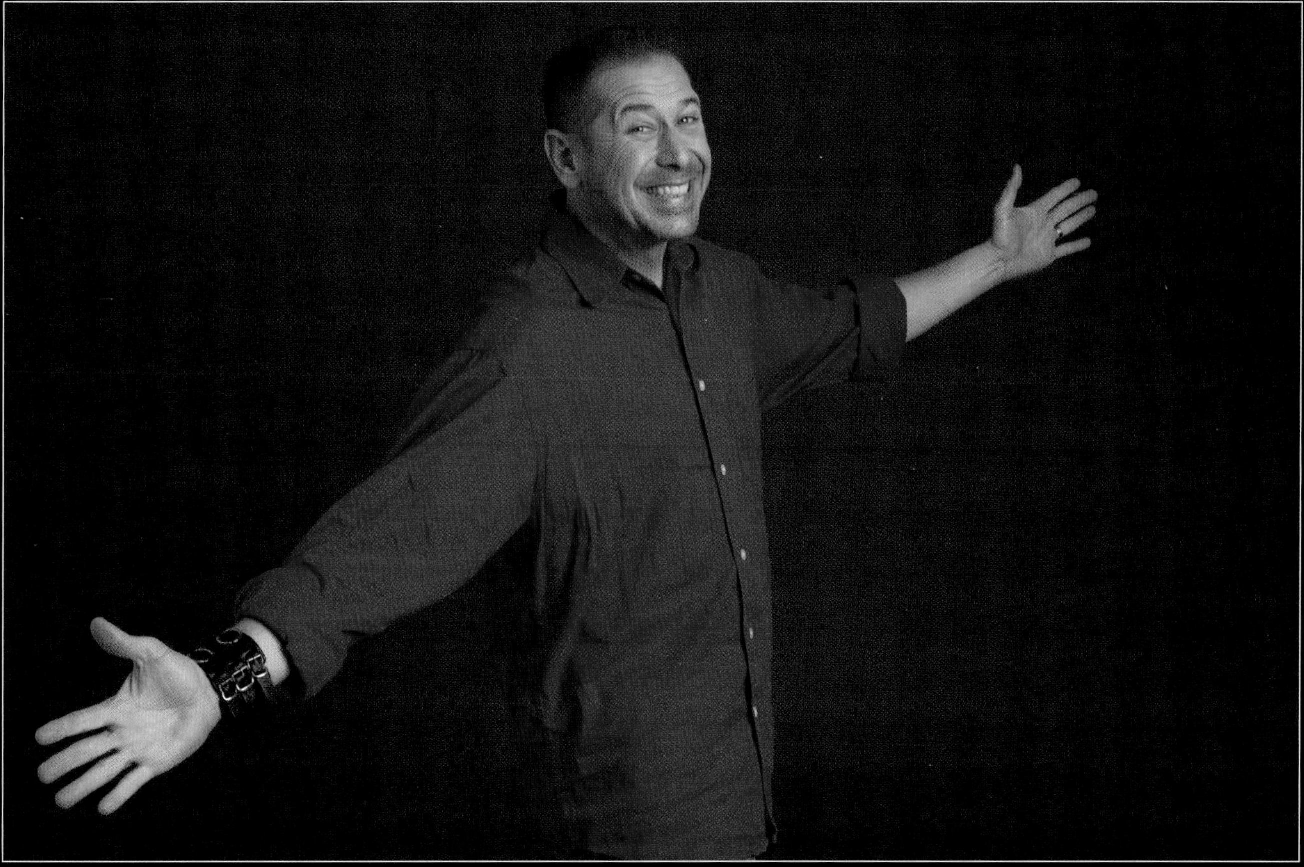

billy tucci

self-publisher, creator | Shi

“This place has really put our industry, our little funny book industry, into the spotlight and on the front page of mainstream America. And I love it for that.”

“When I was a kid, comic books were sort of this illegitimate art form, and didn't have any mainstream appeal. If you read comic books, you were in this really tiny minority. I feel like this place is a great example of how comic books have gained legitimacy. I mean, there's people from all over the world here now at Comic-Con.”

marc guggenheim

writer | Eli Stone, The Flash, Young X-Men

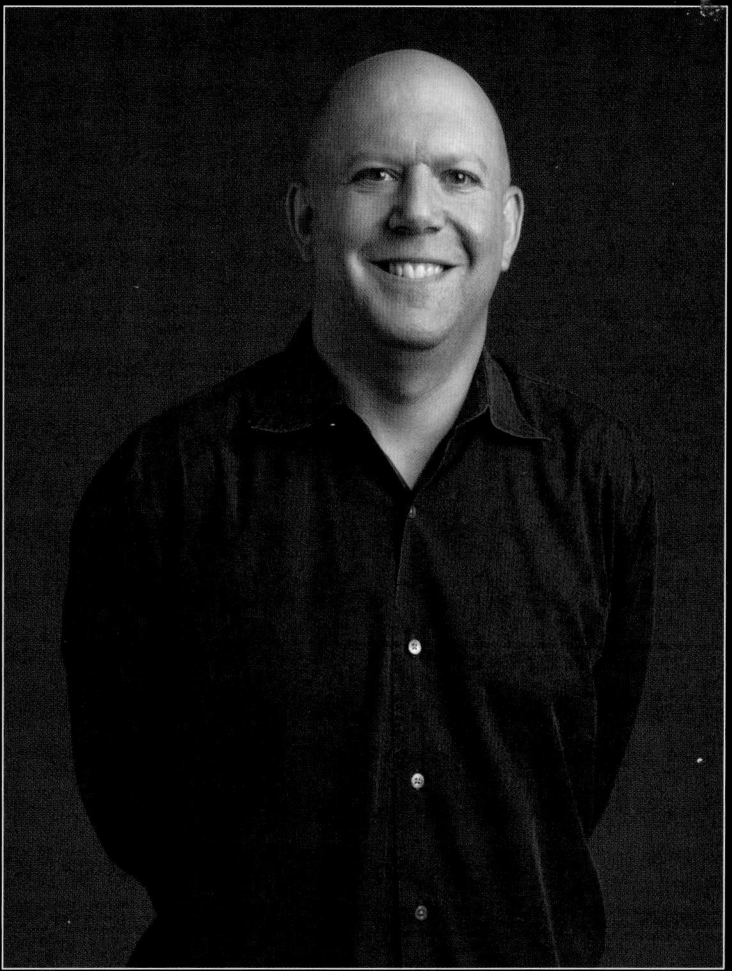

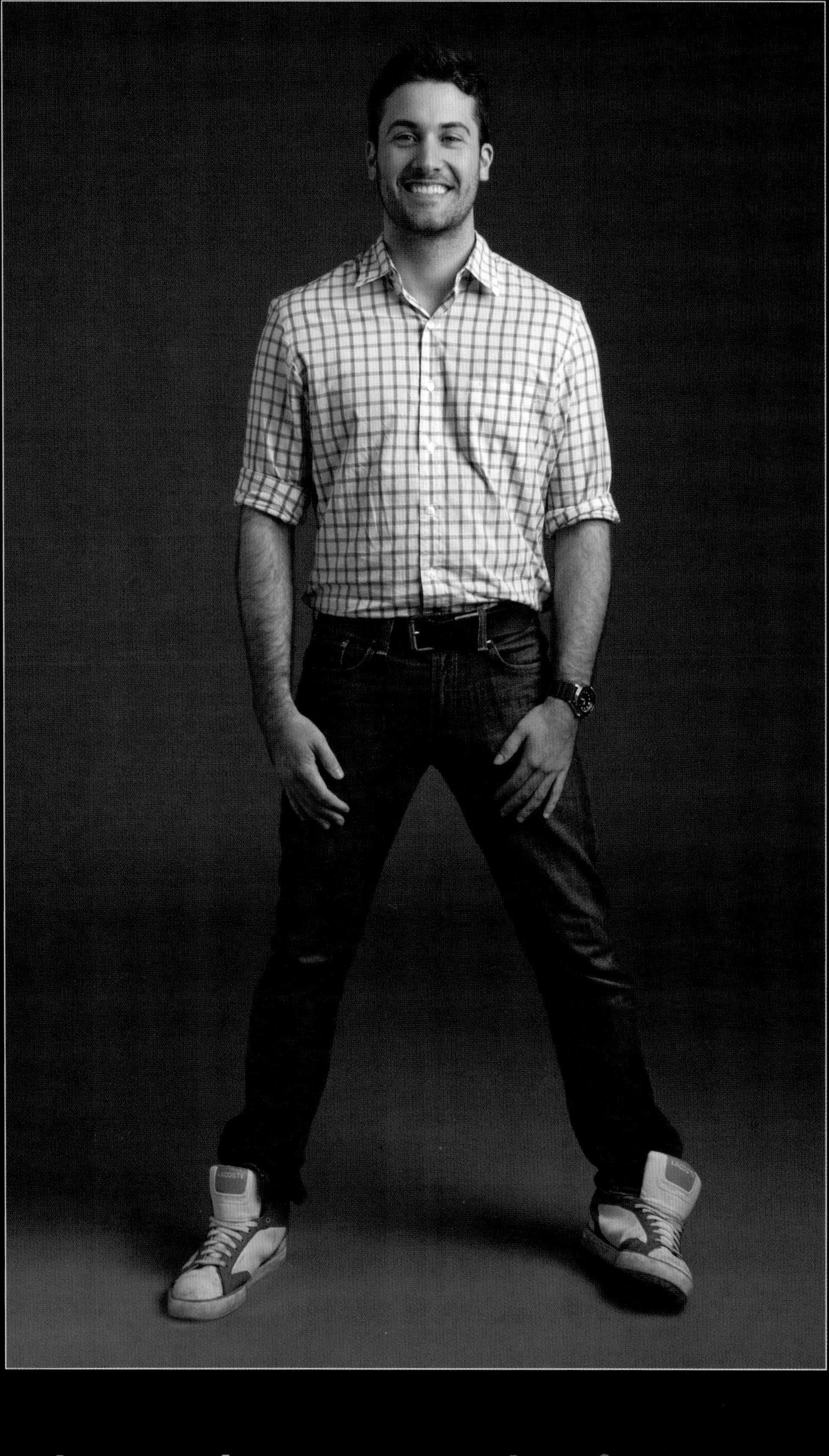

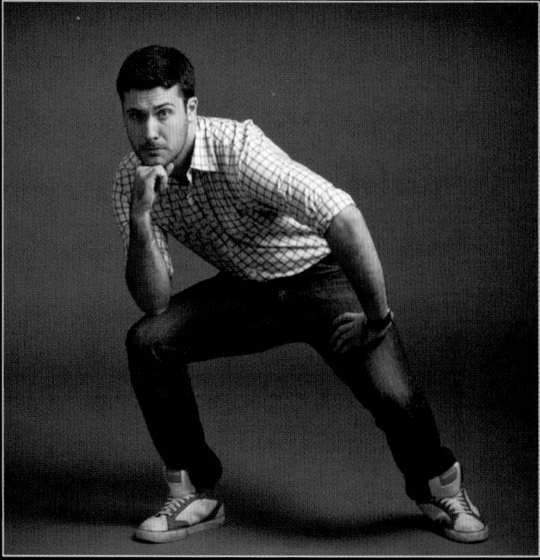

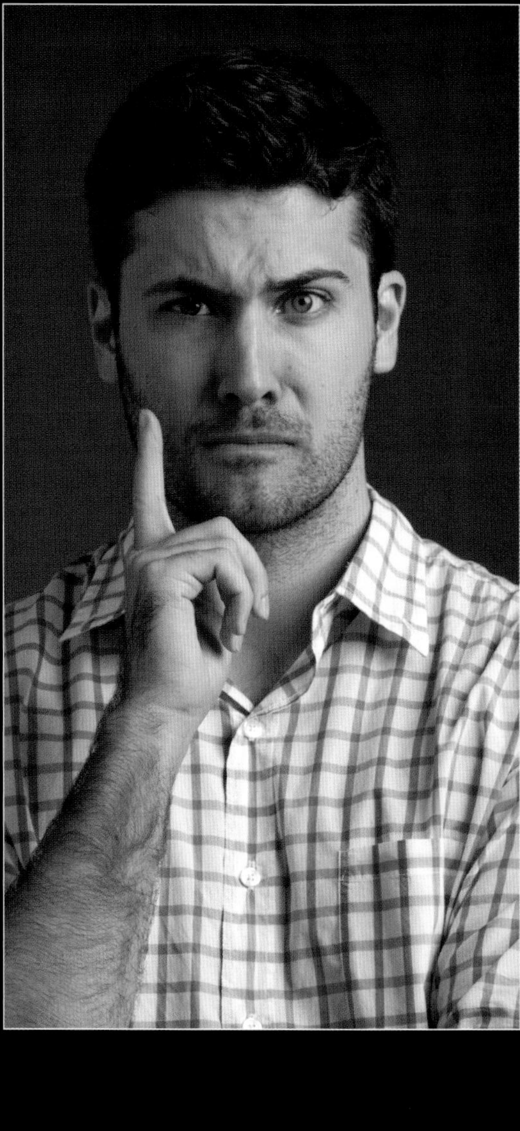

stephen christy

editor-in-chief | Archaia Comics

“It's literally just a giant summer camp for grown-ups. With alcohol.”

“When I was flying in, I bumped the seat of a guy in front of me a couple times. I thought he was annoyed—he kept looking at me. But when we landed in San Diego, he turned around and said, ‘I just have to tell you how much your site has meant to me. I'm entering into the Catholic priesthood, and this is one of my last free acts as a man—I had to come to Comic-Con.’ I think he had to come here because he can't worship what he wants to once he's ordained. Because it's sacrilegious to him. ”

Harry Knowles

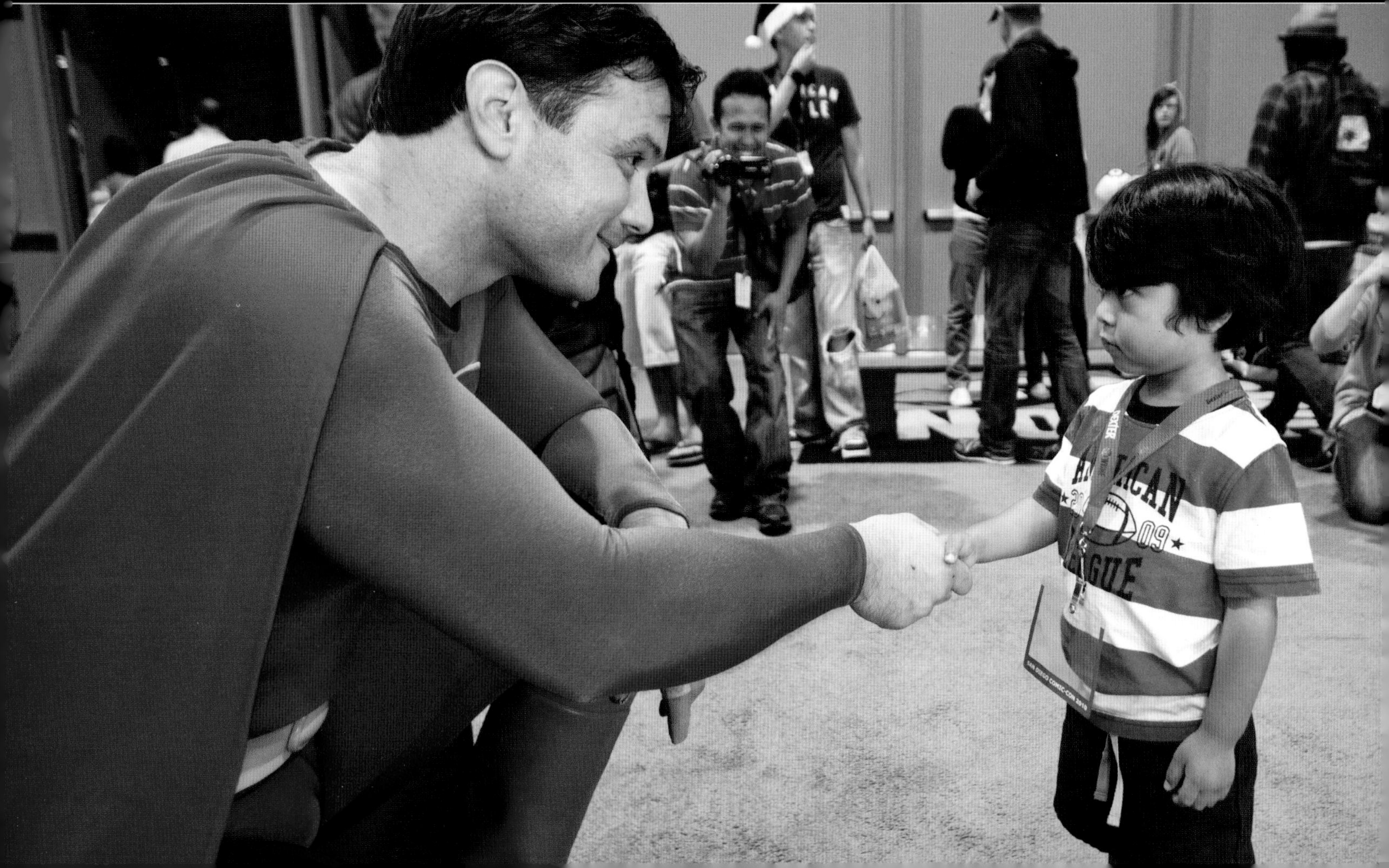

cliff bleszinski

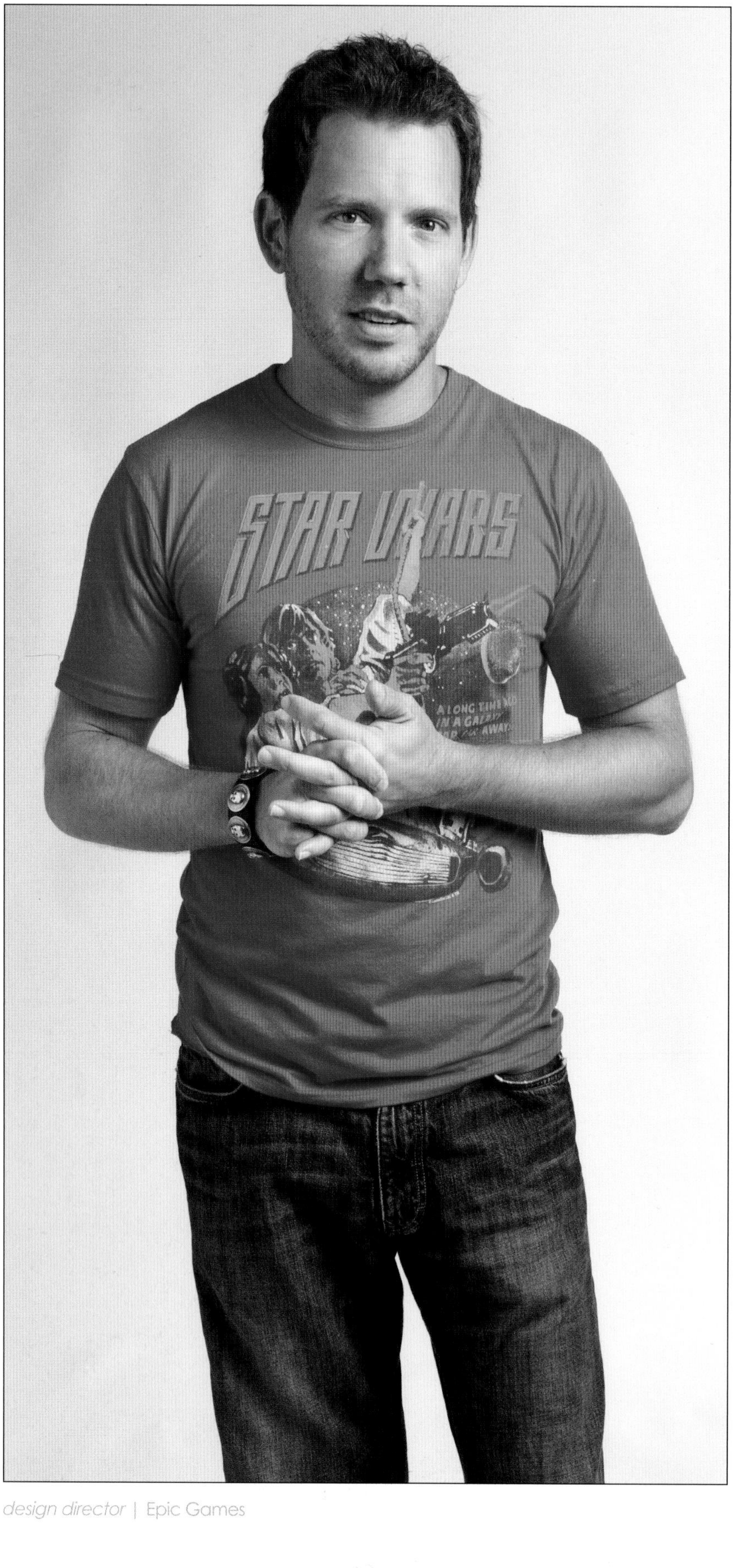

design director | Epic Games

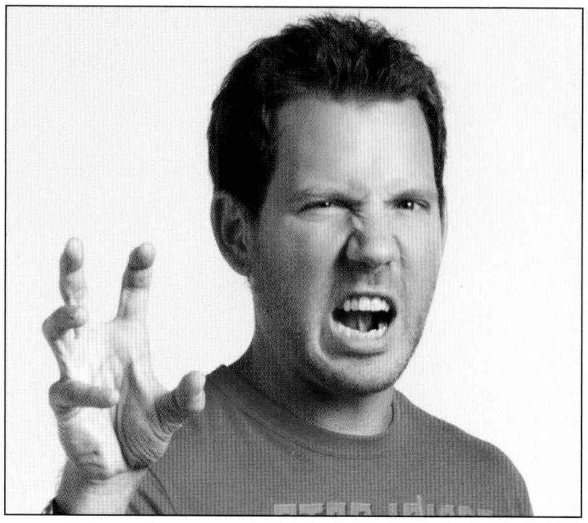

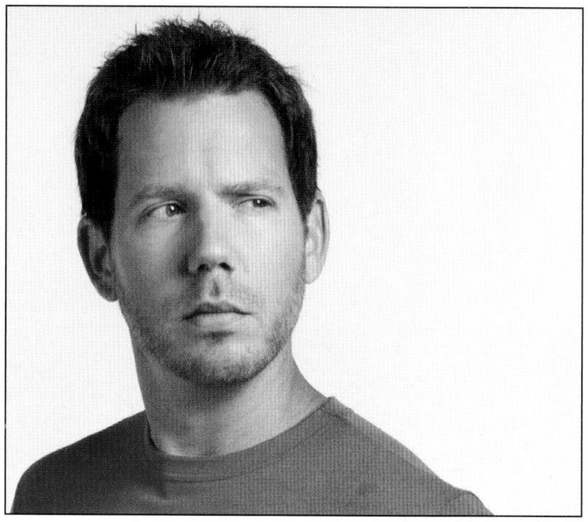

"Walking the show floor, I get people stopping me and telling me how *Gears of War* changed their life or they met their fiancée playing the game on Xbox Live. You get to shake their hand, look them in the eye, and say, 'Thank you. Thank you for being a fan.' That's part of the magic, I think, at this convention."

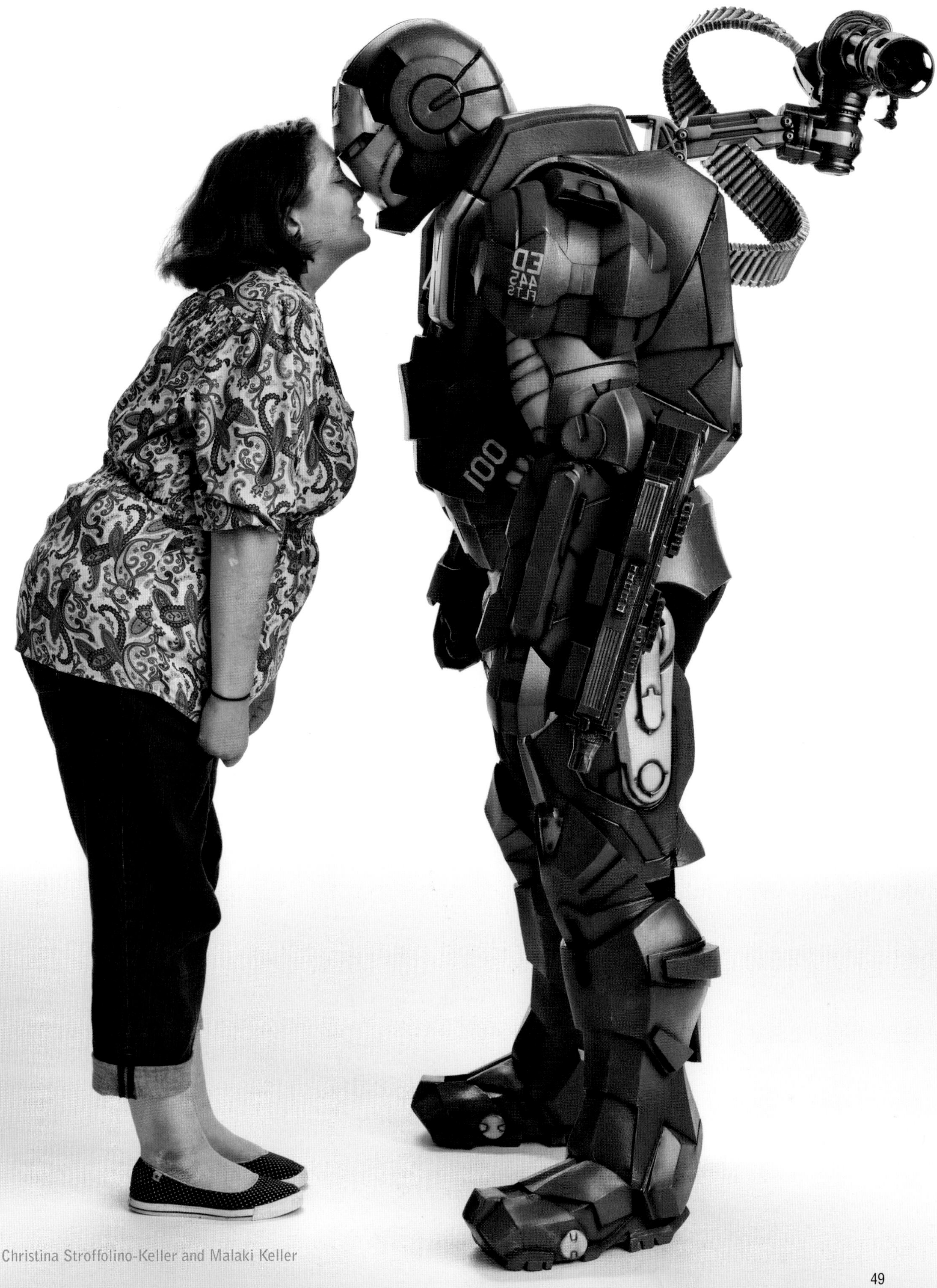

Christina Stroffolino-Keller and Malaki Keller

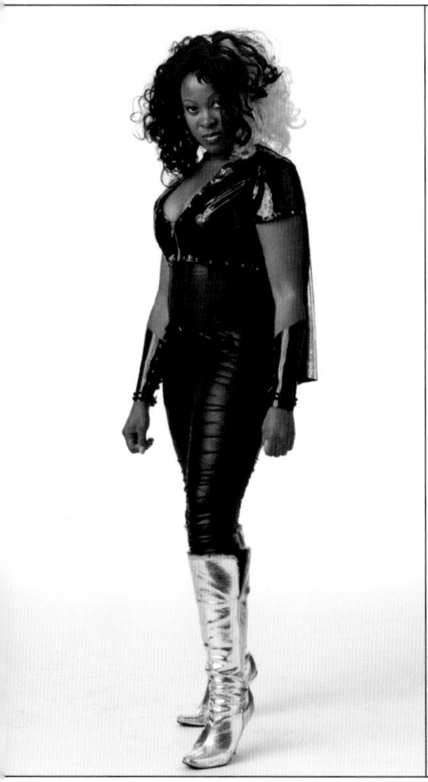

Nikki Brown

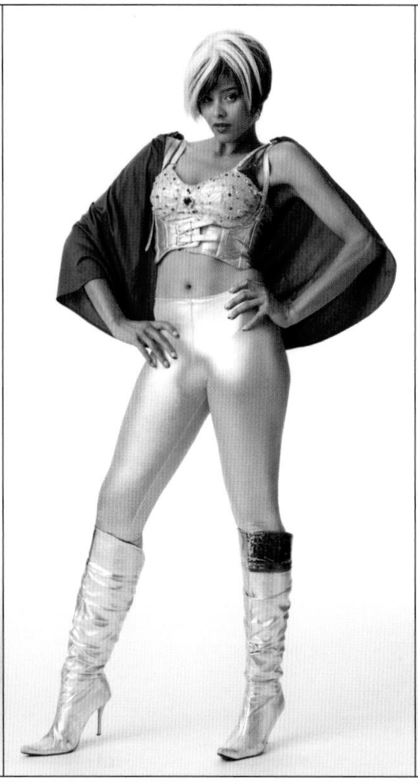

Teri Benjamin

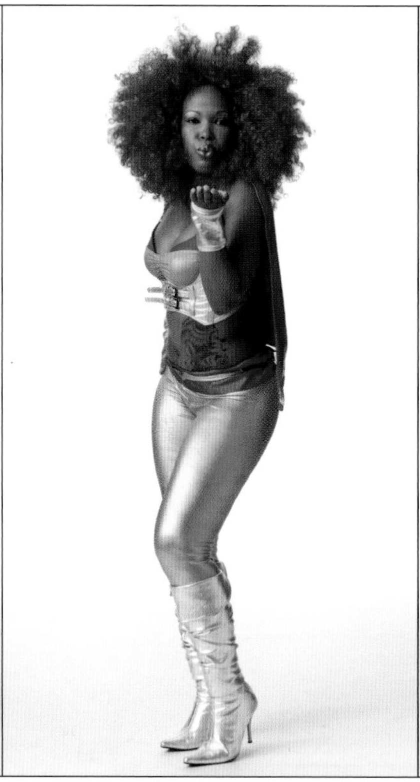

Celeste Sullivan

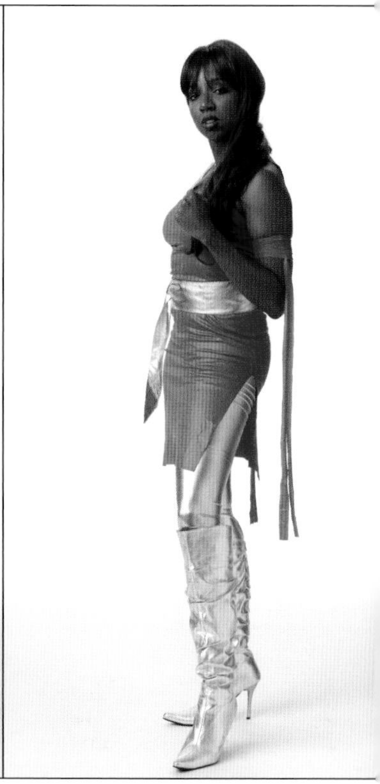

Landi Maduro

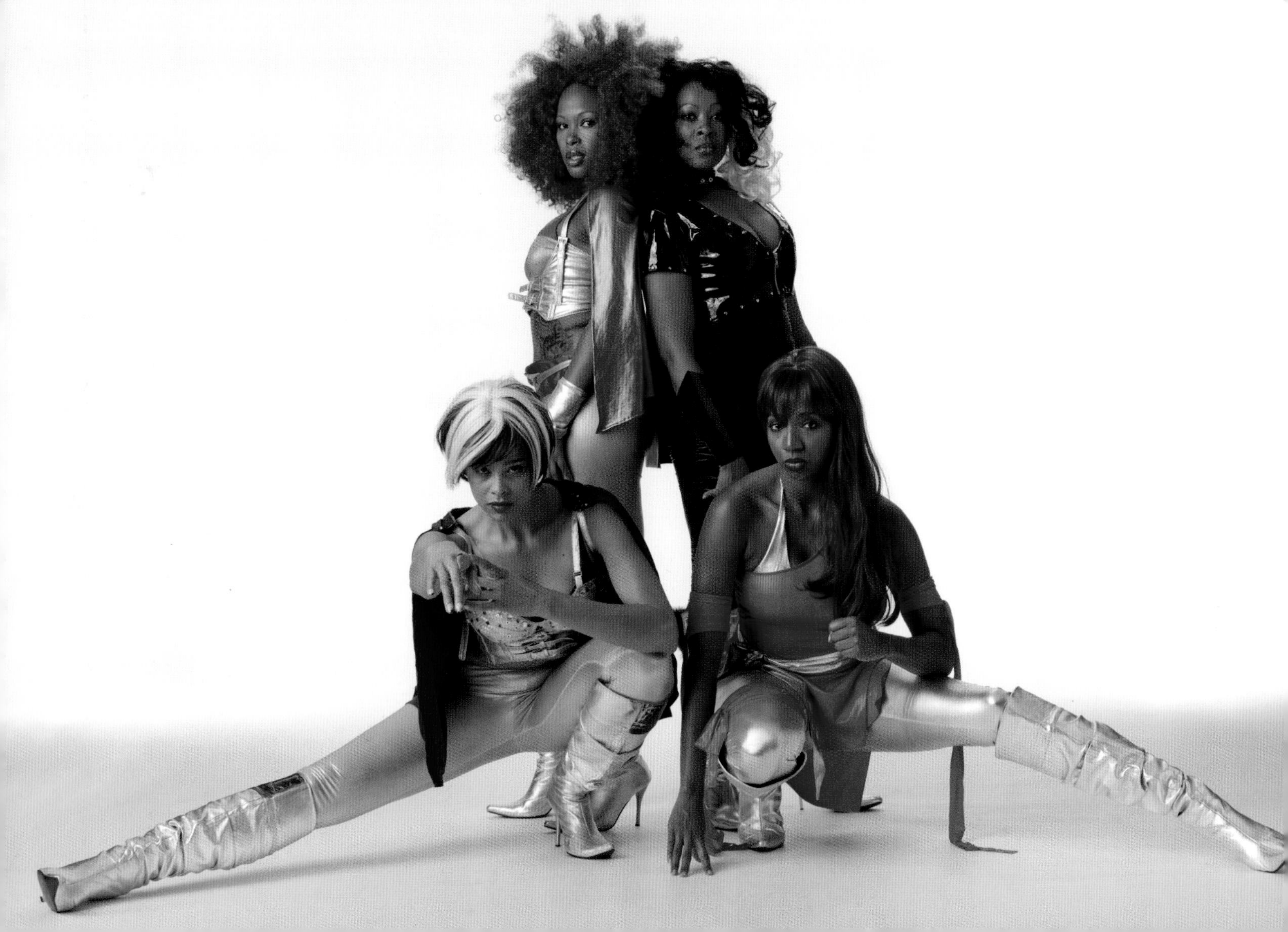

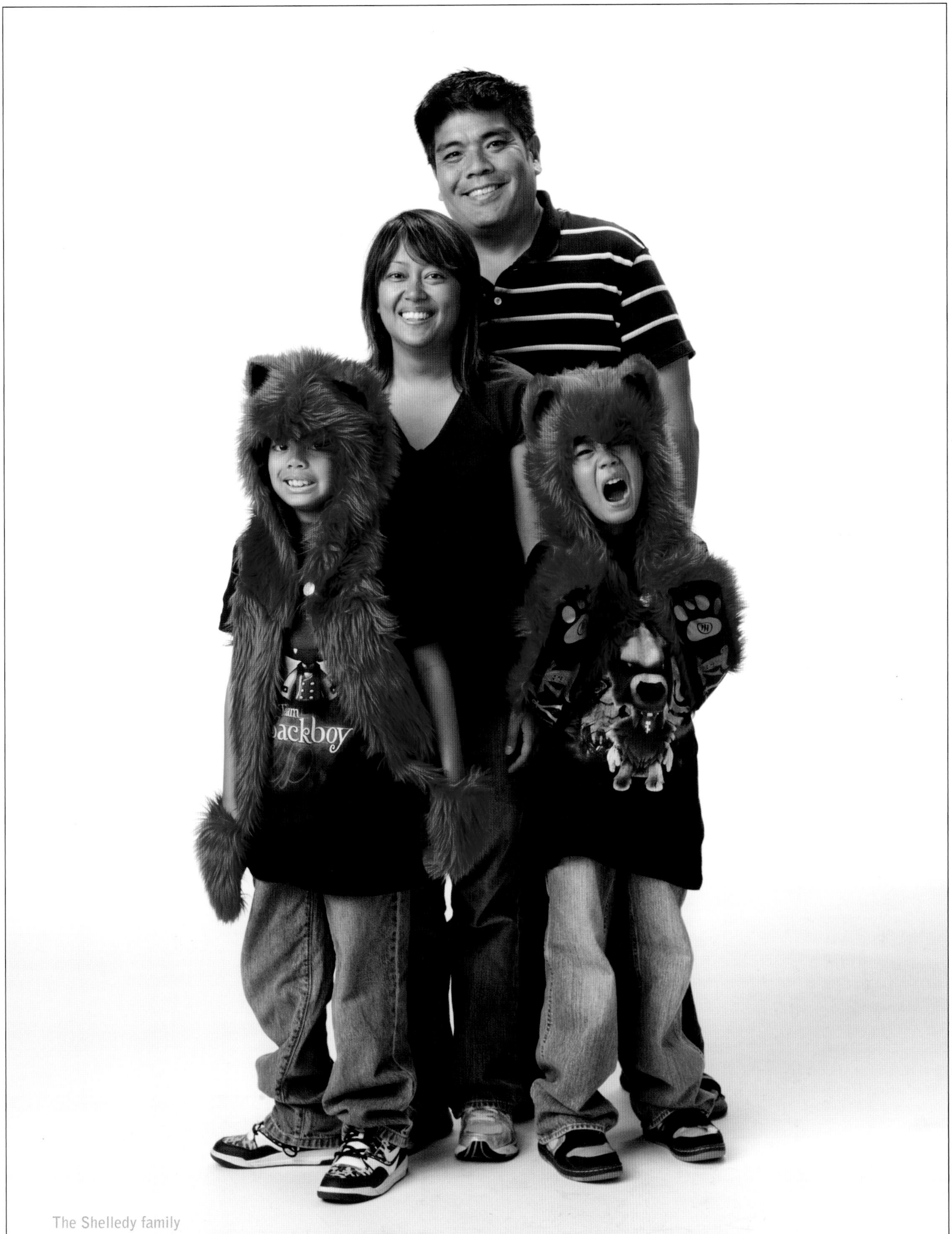

The Shelledy family

seth green

actor, voice actor | Robot Chicken, Buffy the Vampire Slayer, Family Guy

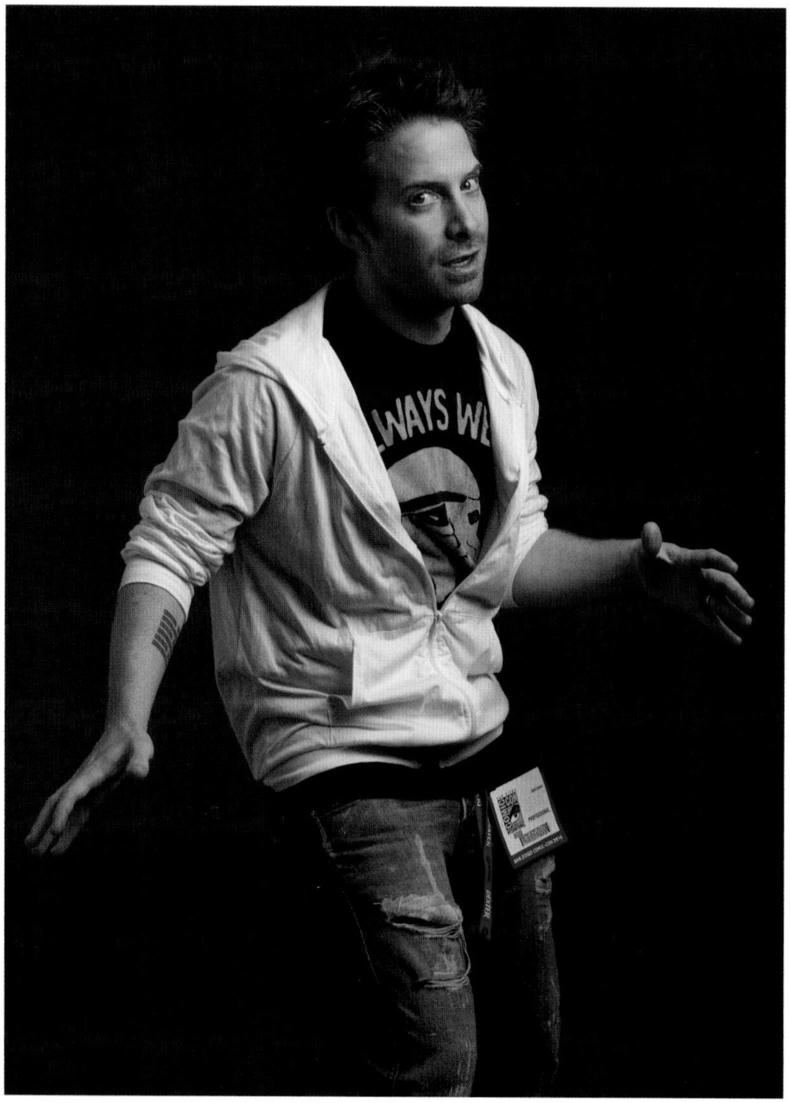

"Comic-Con has evolved dramatically in the time that I've been coming here, just because the culture has changed so significantly. It used to be just a great place for nerds to commune in a natural habitat without fear of persecution, and now it's become this kind of free-trade marketplace that also has a tourism element."

"I actually met my wife at Comic-Con. So that was pretty exciting. We had a crazy night, two people who just sort of knew each other and had a bunch of friends in common—we were practically kidnapped and taken across this bridge in San Diego that I didn't know existed and apparently is only one way. And we wound up having the adventure of a lifetime and bonded in a way that made us husband and wife. How about that?"

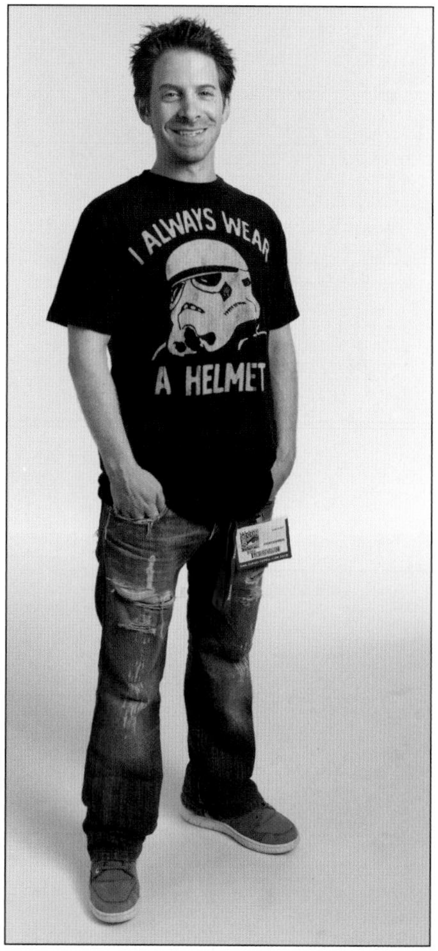
I ALWAYS WEAR
A HELMET

> “Everyone’s sort of embraced it now, and there’s a hip factor that there never was before. And I kind of like that.”

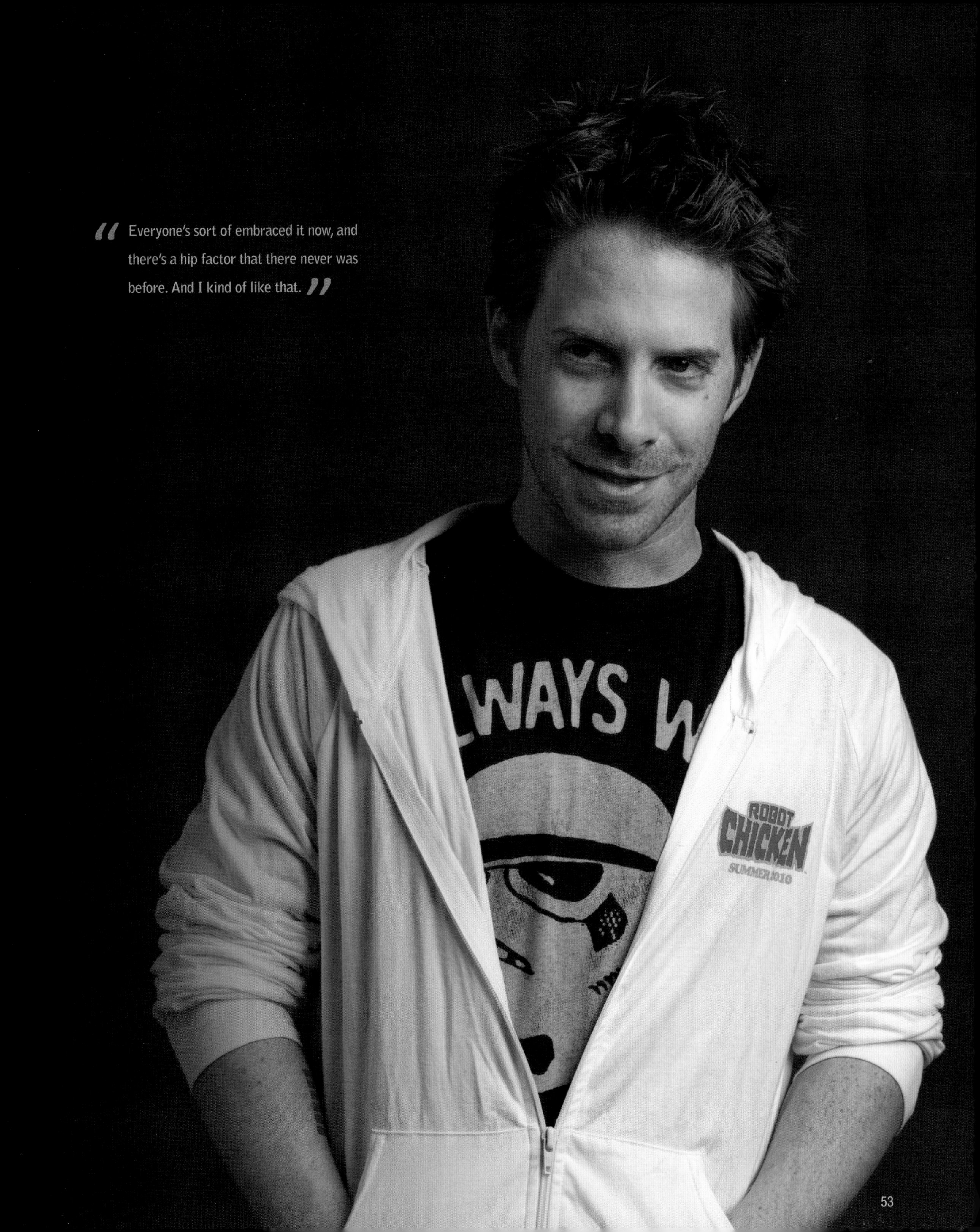

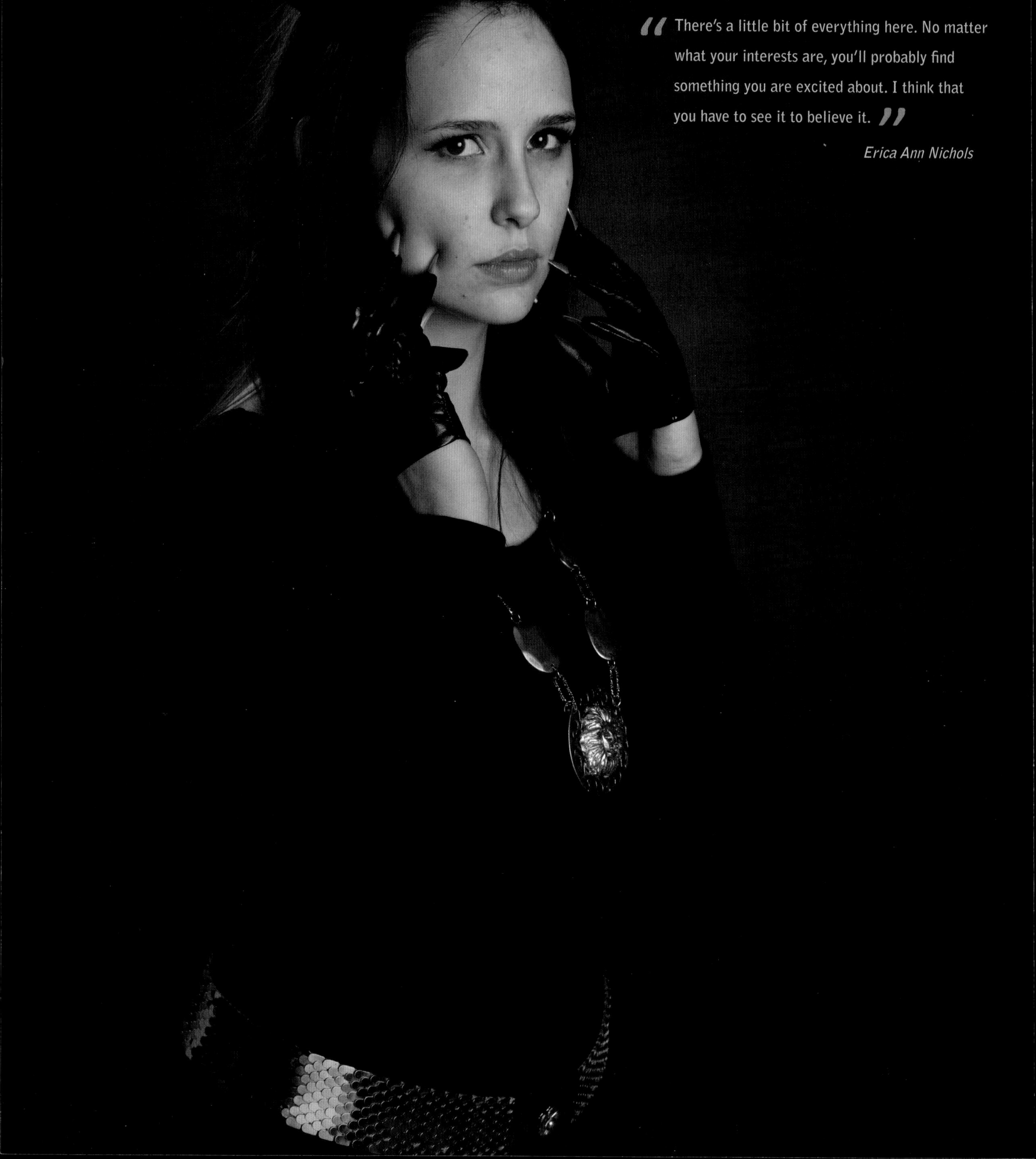

“There’s a little bit of everything here. No matter what your interests are, you’ll probably find something you are excited about. I think that you have to see it to believe it.”

Erica Ann Nichols

edgar wright

writer, director | Shaun of the Dead, Scott Pilgrim vs. the World

" When we did *Shaun of the Dead* screenings, we looked for Ken Foree, who is the star of *Dawn of the Dead*. And we were able to go up to his booth and say, 'We're the guys who made *Shaun of the Dead*—do you want to come see it tonight?' Crazy things like that would not happen in any other walk of life. "

marv wolfman

writer, creator | Blade, The New Teen Titans

" What we've been loving since we were kids is now everywhere. We've actually co-opted the whole mainstream. So we won! "

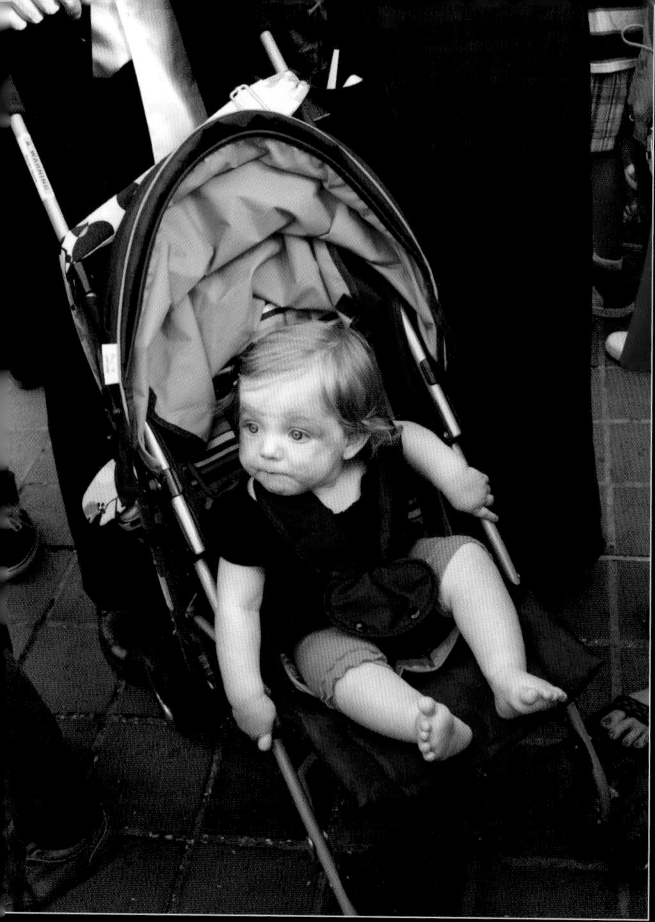

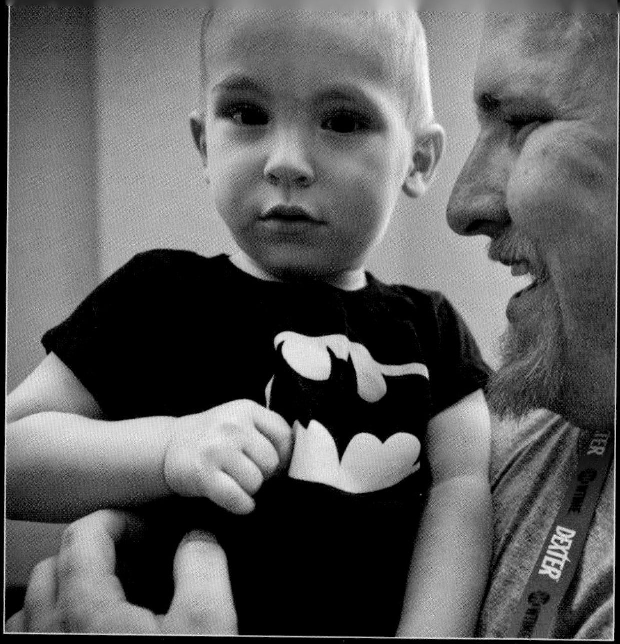
DEXTER

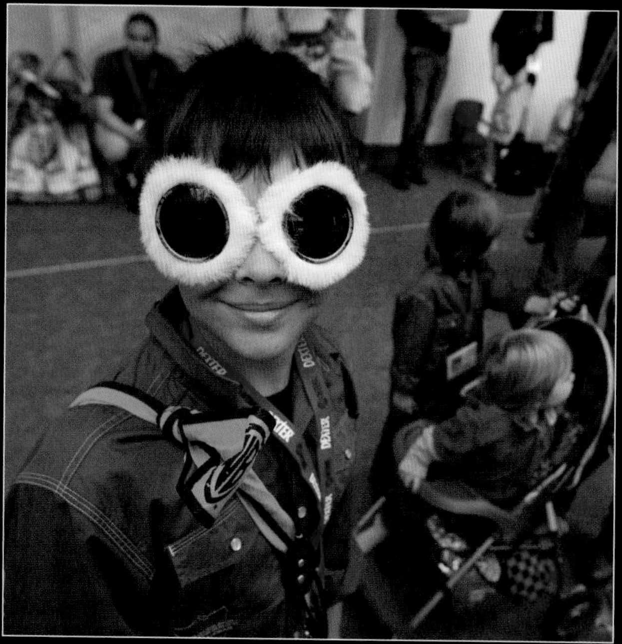
DEXTER

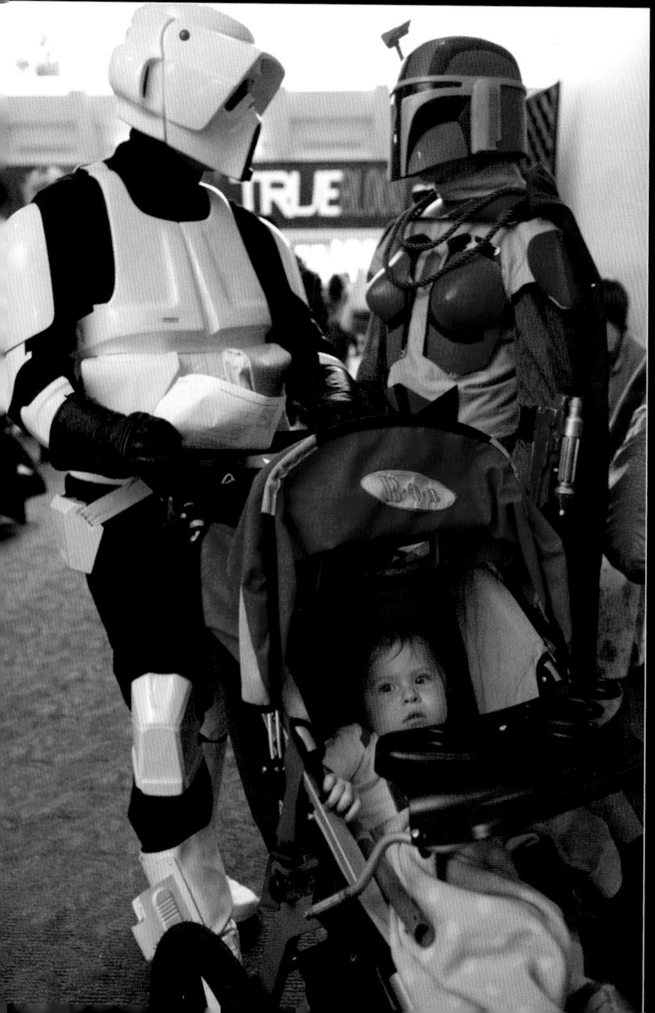
TRUE

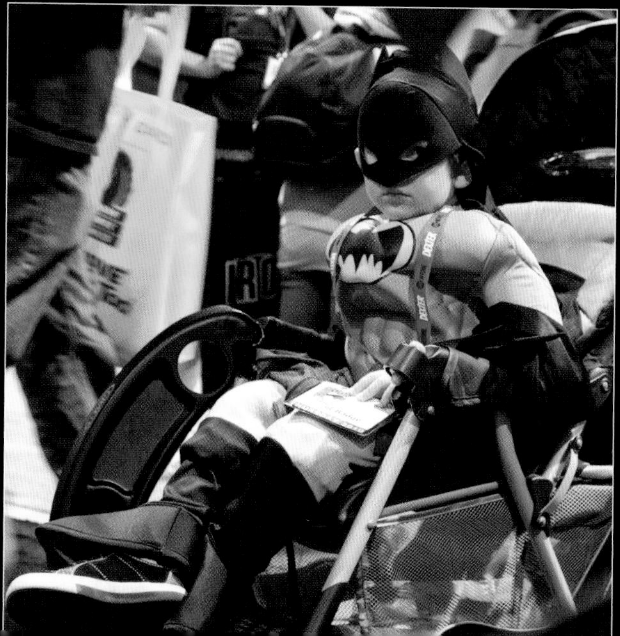

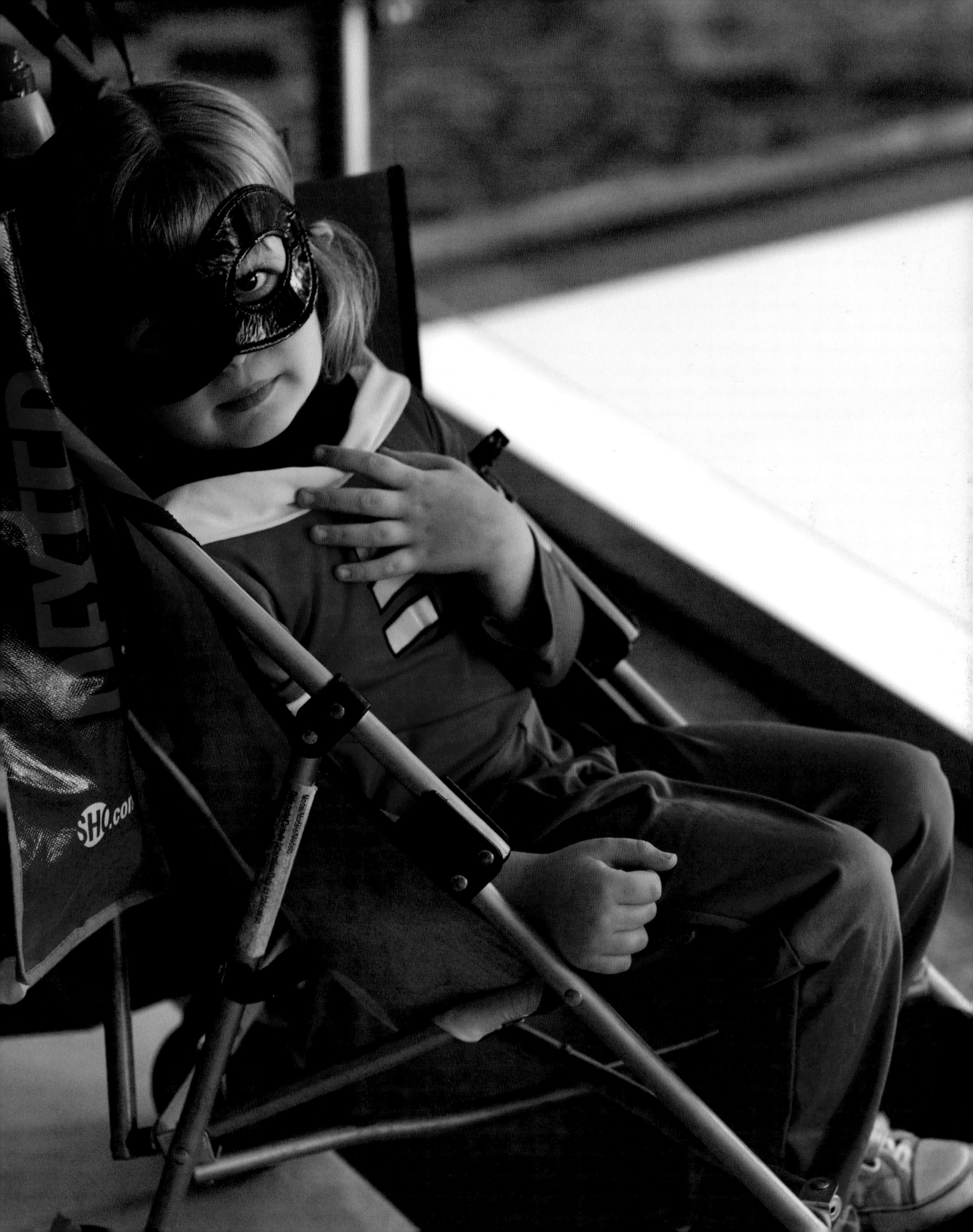

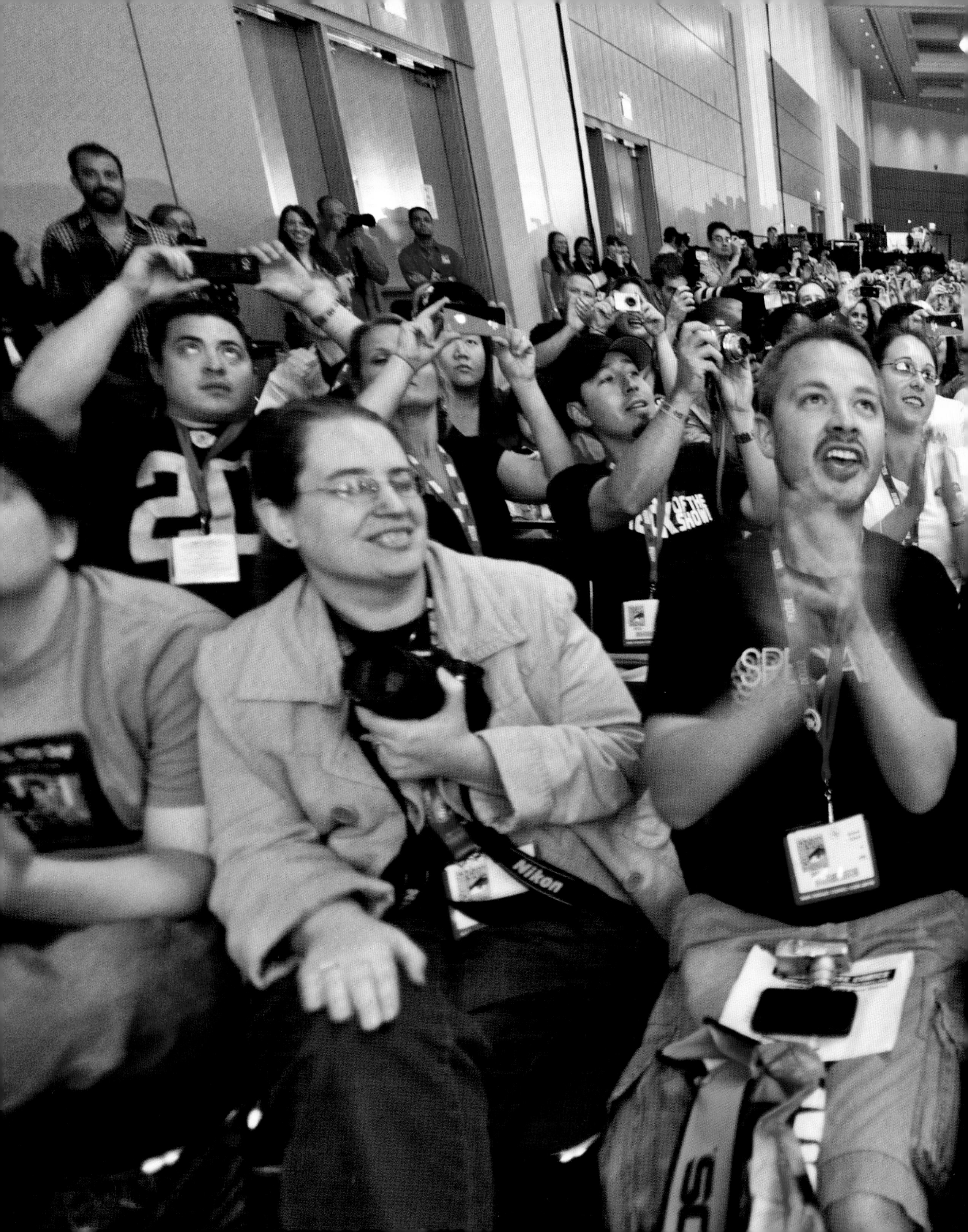
Nikon

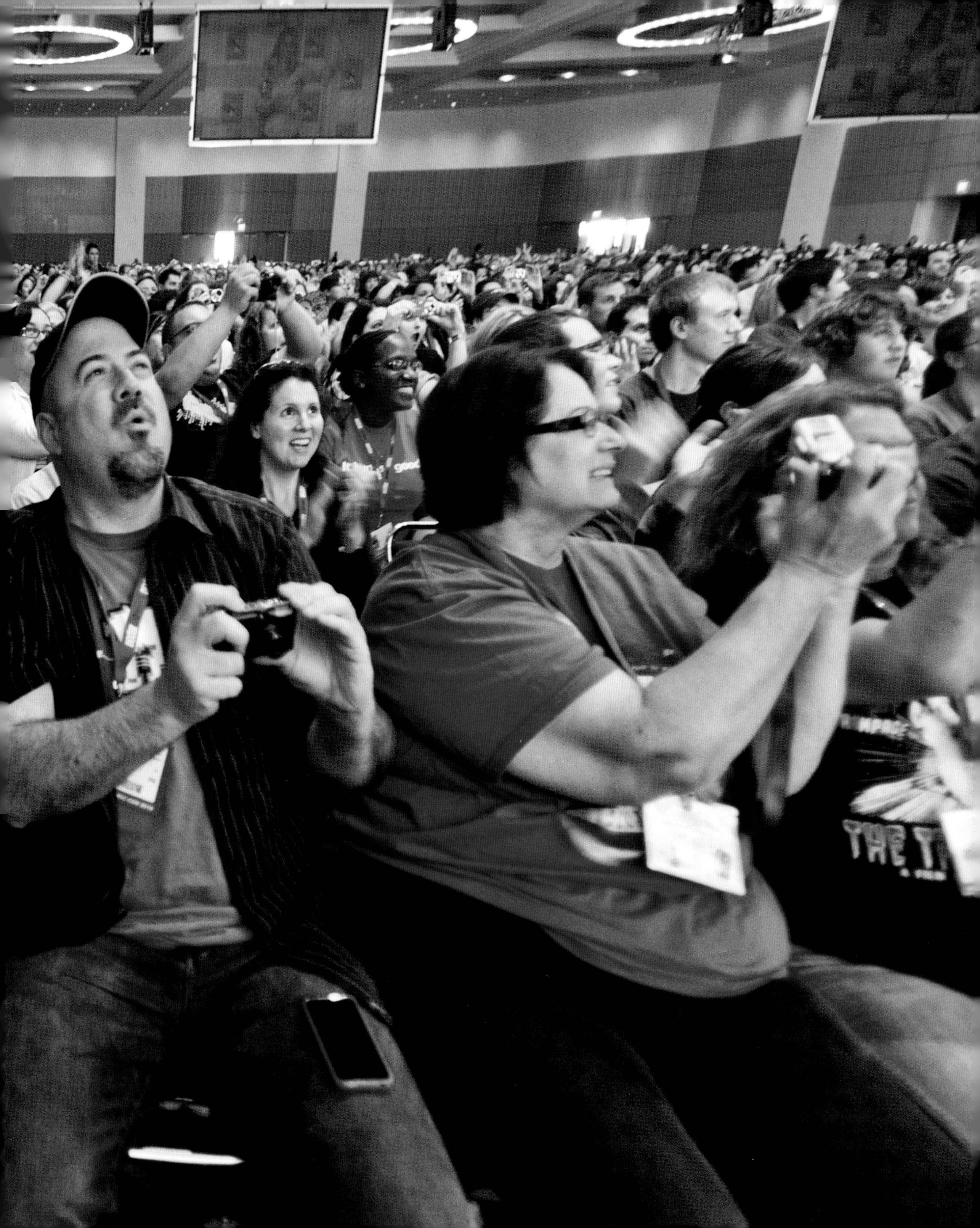

tara mcpherson

artist

> “Where else do you get to meet your fans, walk around the same area, and have a drink with them at the bar? It blurs those lines, so it’s not just artist and fan.”

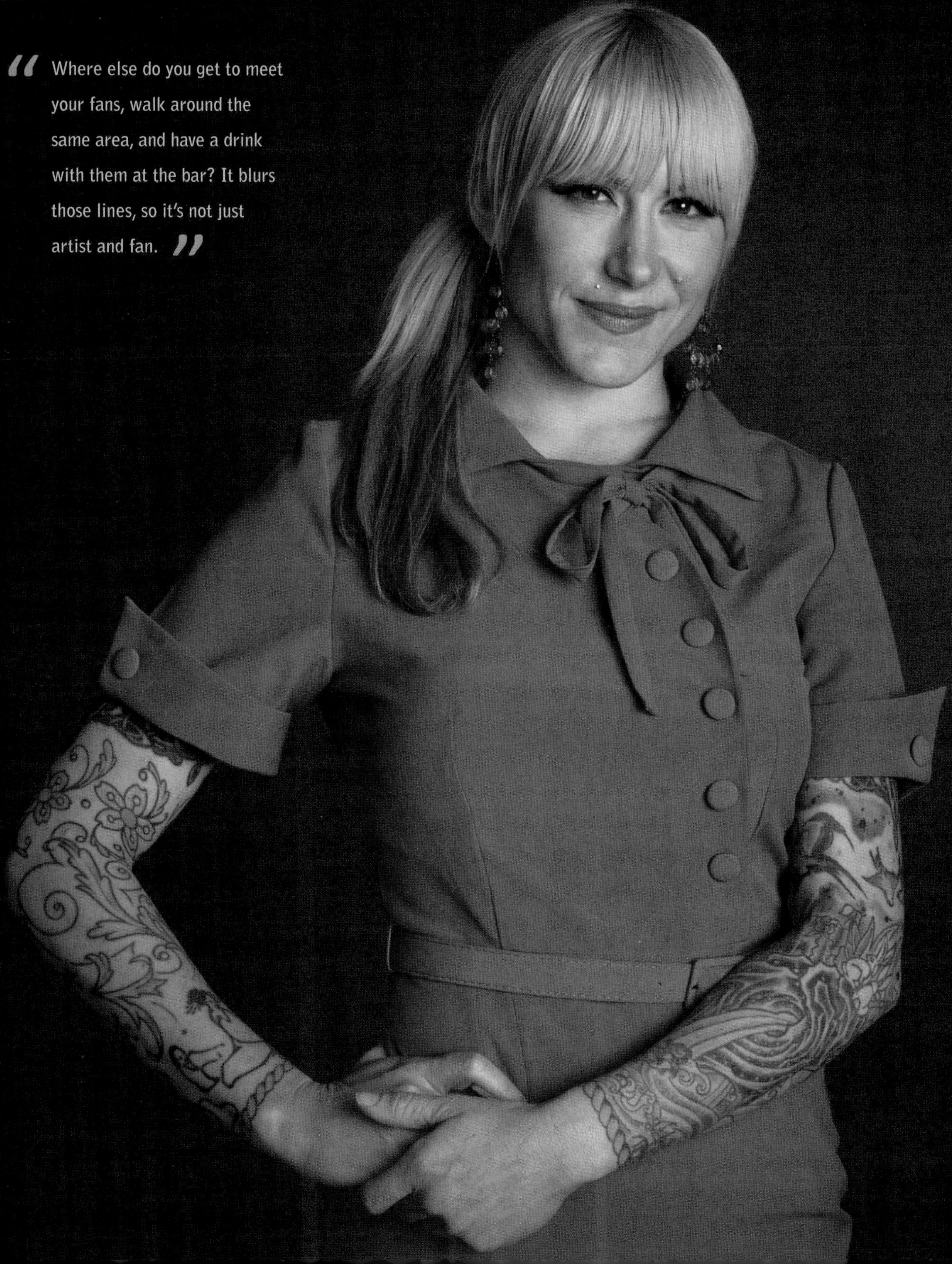

richard hatch

actor | Battlestar Galactica

“People want to come and feel part of something—feel connected to the greater world and be part of this magical industry that has kind of been a savior, I think, for a lot of people's lives.”

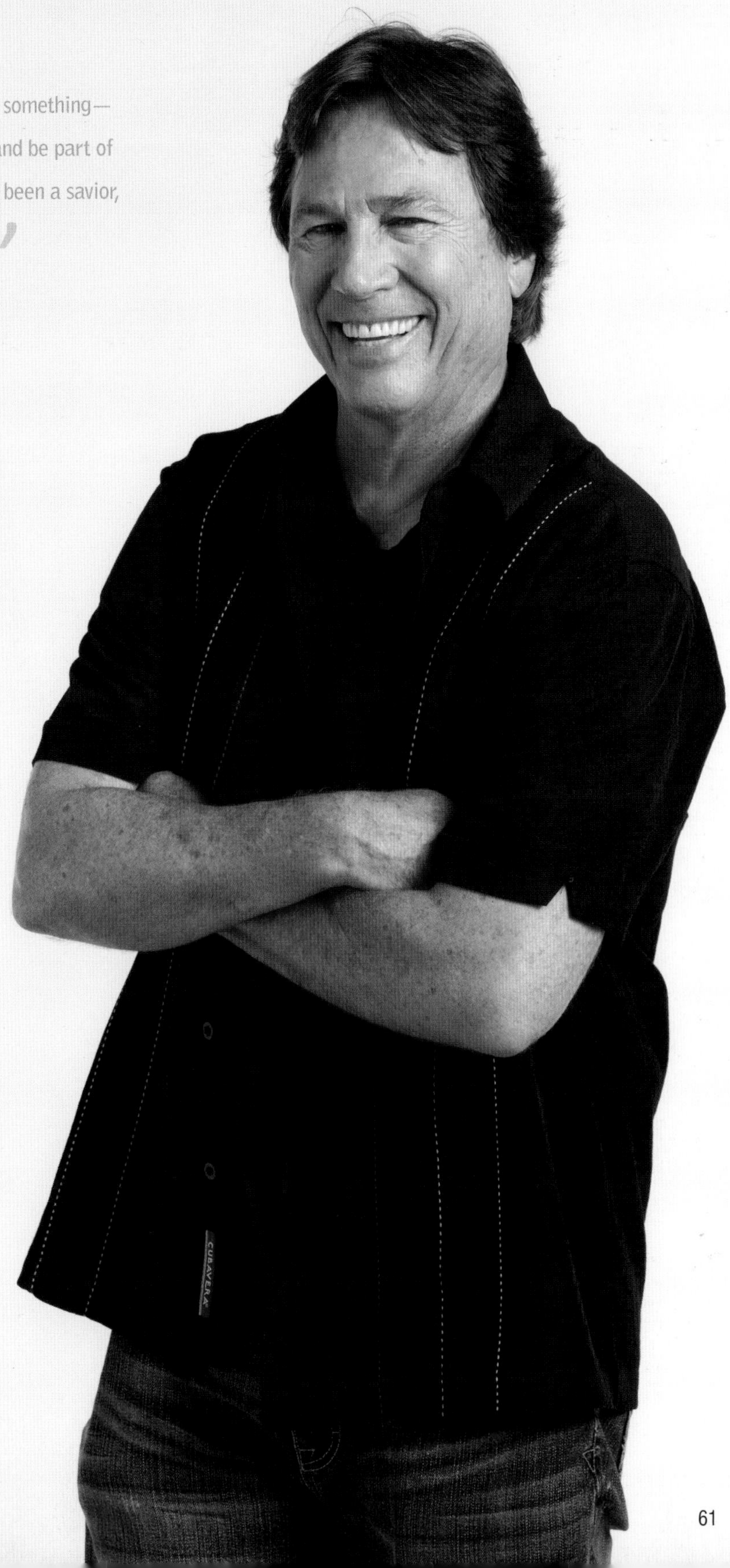
CUBAVERA

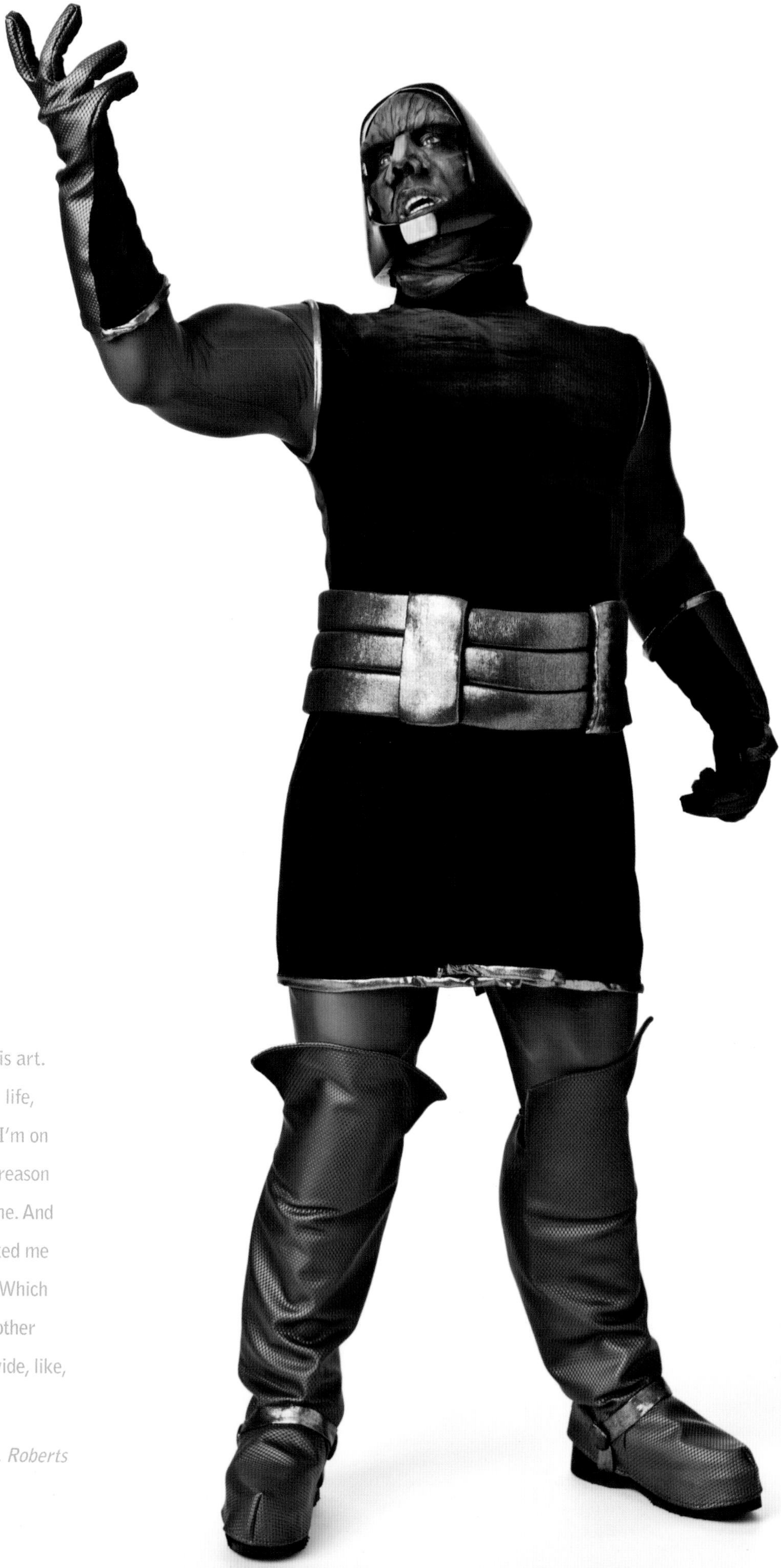

“Jack Kirby is always larger than life in his art. So I wanted to do something larger than life, which is like Kirby, and that's the reason I'm on two-inch lifts in my shoes. And that's the reason why I spent over $800 getting all this done. And the people at DC Comics love it. They asked me to go onstage during some of the panels. Which I love doing. It's just so much fun seeing other people's reactions. Kids have their eyes wide, like, 'Oh my God.'”

Jeffrey C. Roberts

The common bond is geekdom. The other day I was sitting at a table and a conversation came up: what would happen if Lord Voldemort and Darth Vader fought. And that was just like, incomprehensible—that could never happen. But it's good that people could have that conversation and not feel weird about it, and not have people look at them funny. It's just a really great atmosphere. You can talk about anything.

Ross Alan Miller

Jennifer K. Staller

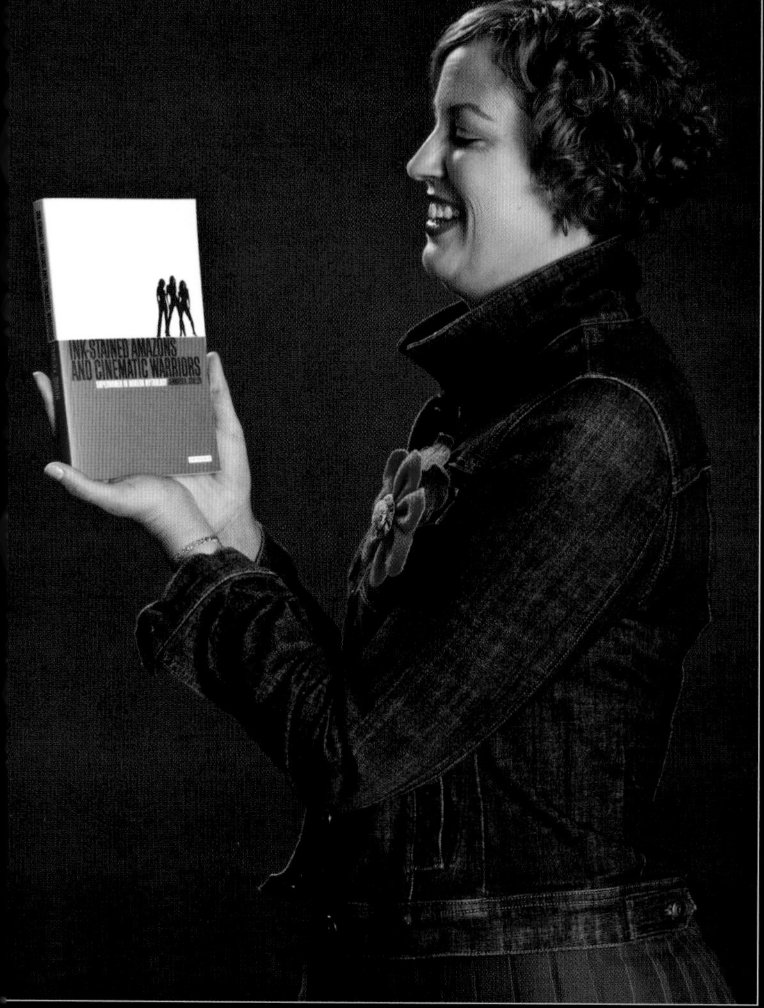
INK-STAINED AMAZONS
AND CINEMATIC WARRIORS

Kristine Harris and Warren "Skinner" Davis

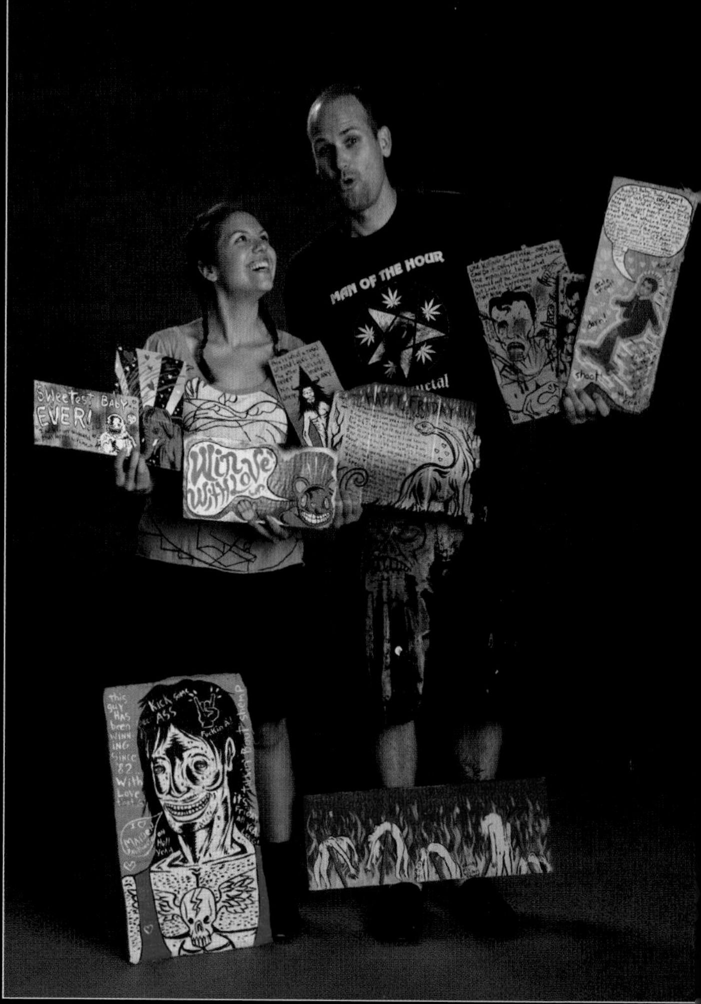
MAN OF THE HOUR

Chad Edward Blakely

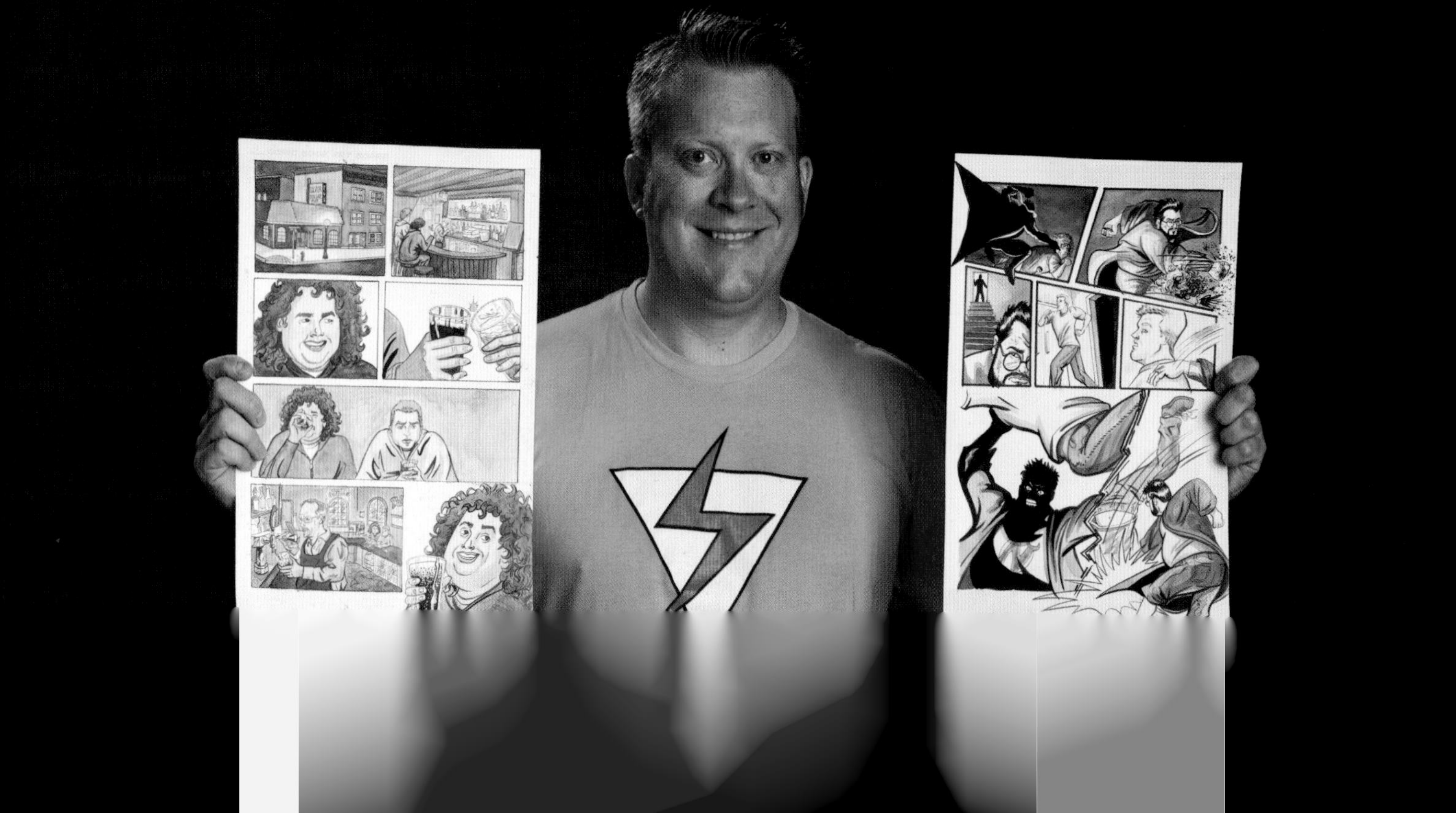

jerry robinson

creator of The Joker and the man who gave Robin, the Boy Wonder, his name

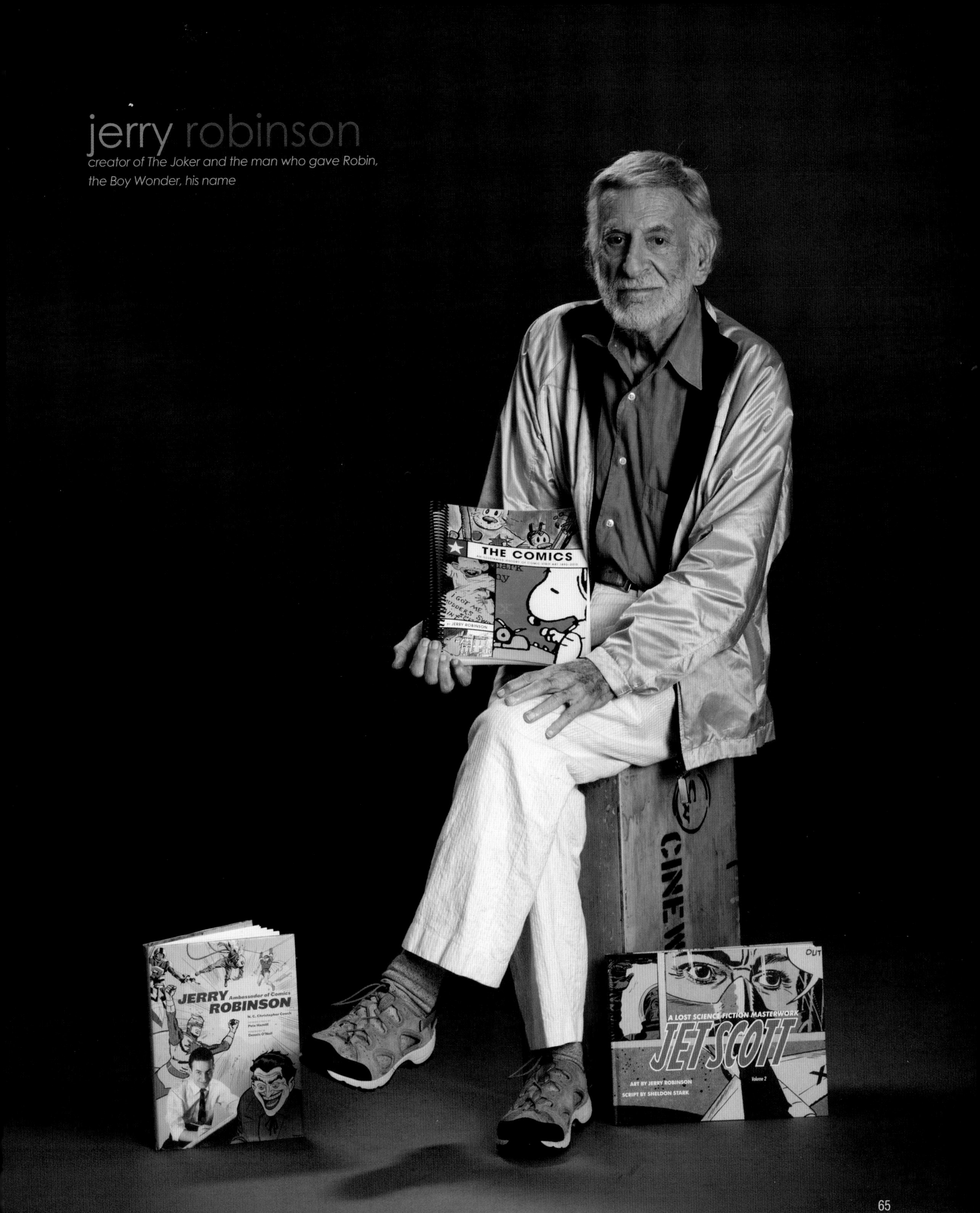
THE COMICS
BY JERRY ROBINSON
JERRY ROBINSON
Ambassador of Comics
A LOST SCIENCE FICTION MASTERWORK
JET SCOTT
ART BY JERRY ROBINSON
SCRIPT BY SHELDON STARK
Volume 2
CINE

olivia wilde

actress | Tron: Legacy

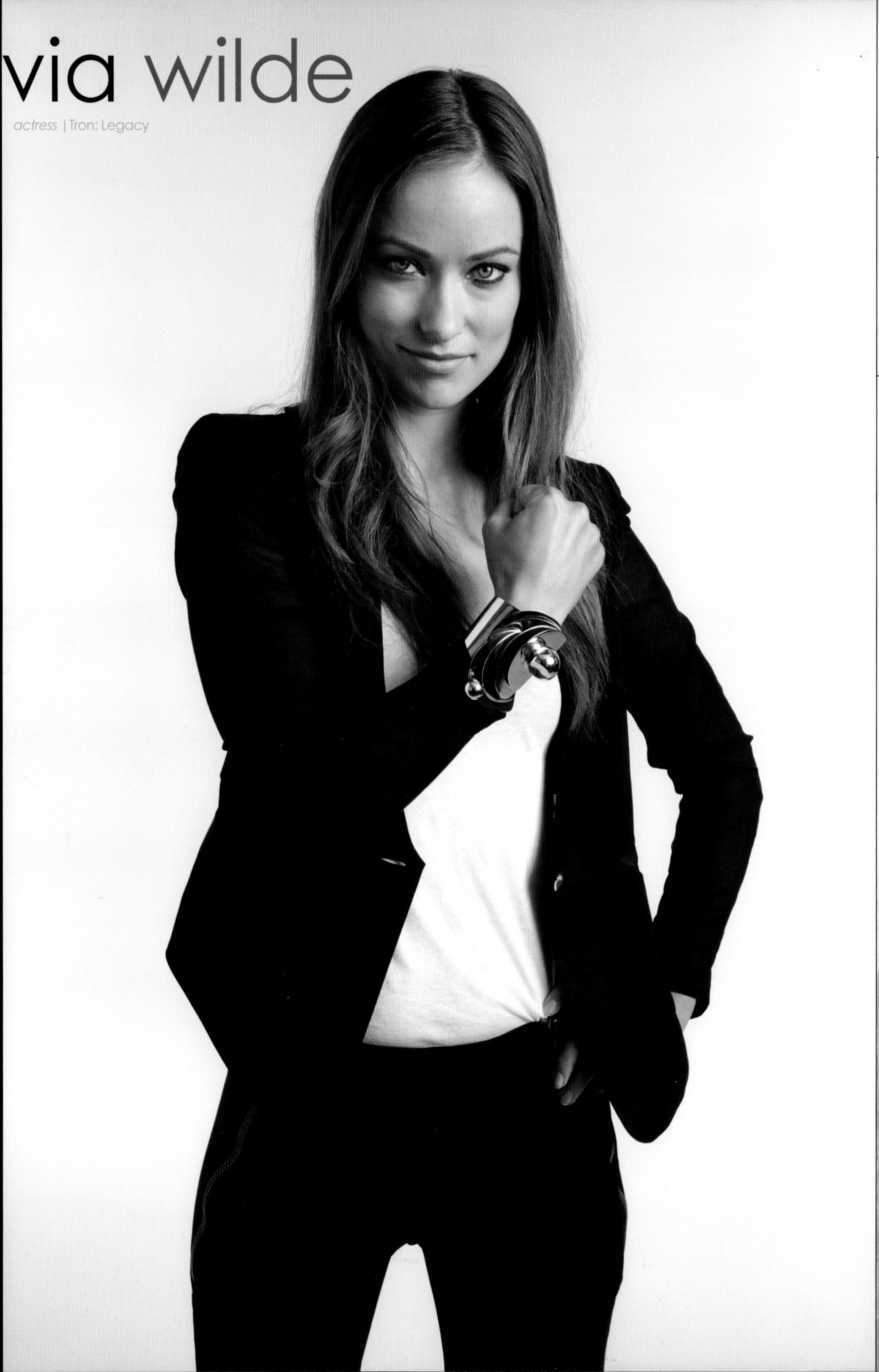

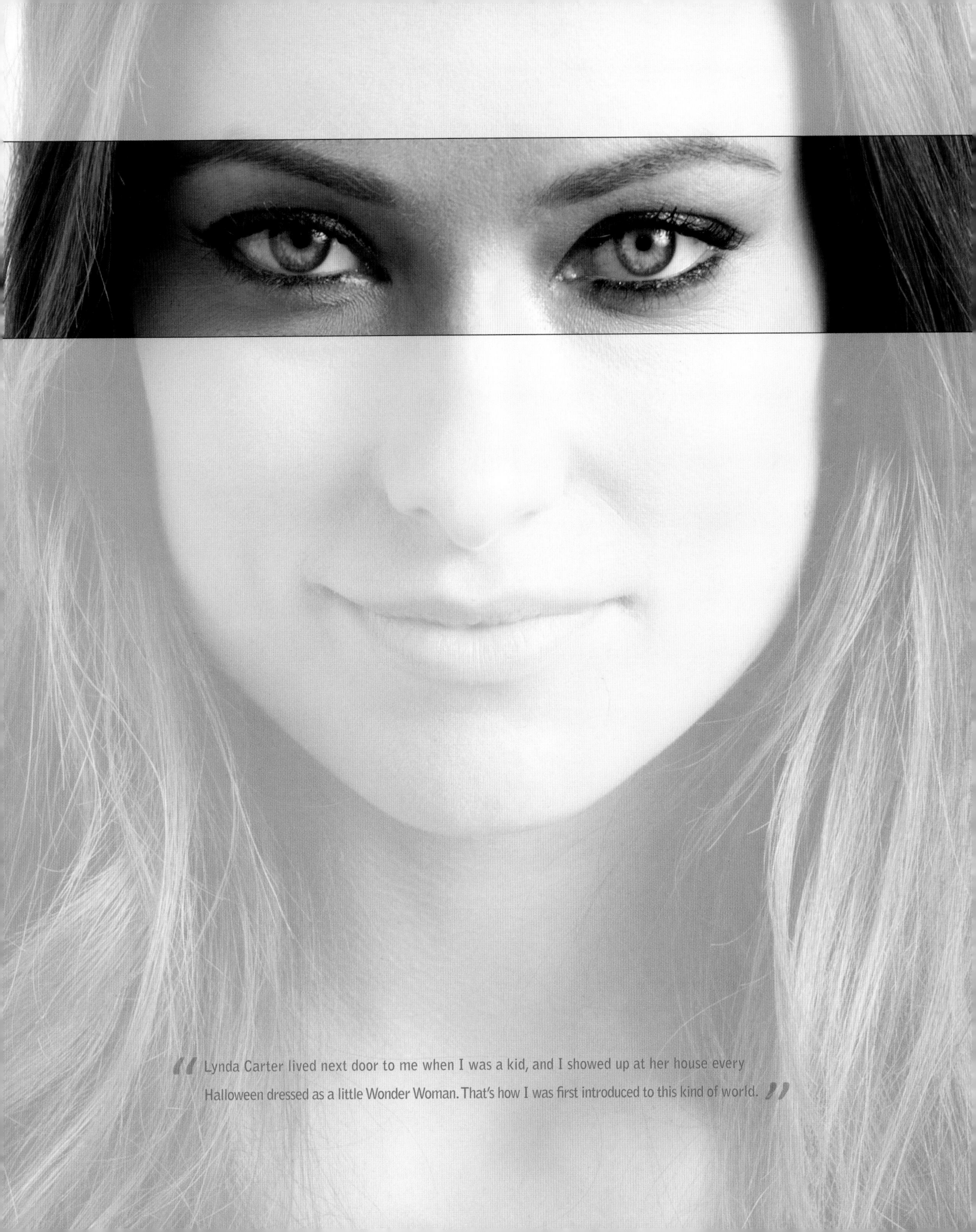

“Lynda Carter lived next door to me when I was a kid, and I showed up at her house every Halloween dressed as a little Wonder Woman. That's how I was first introduced to this kind of world.”

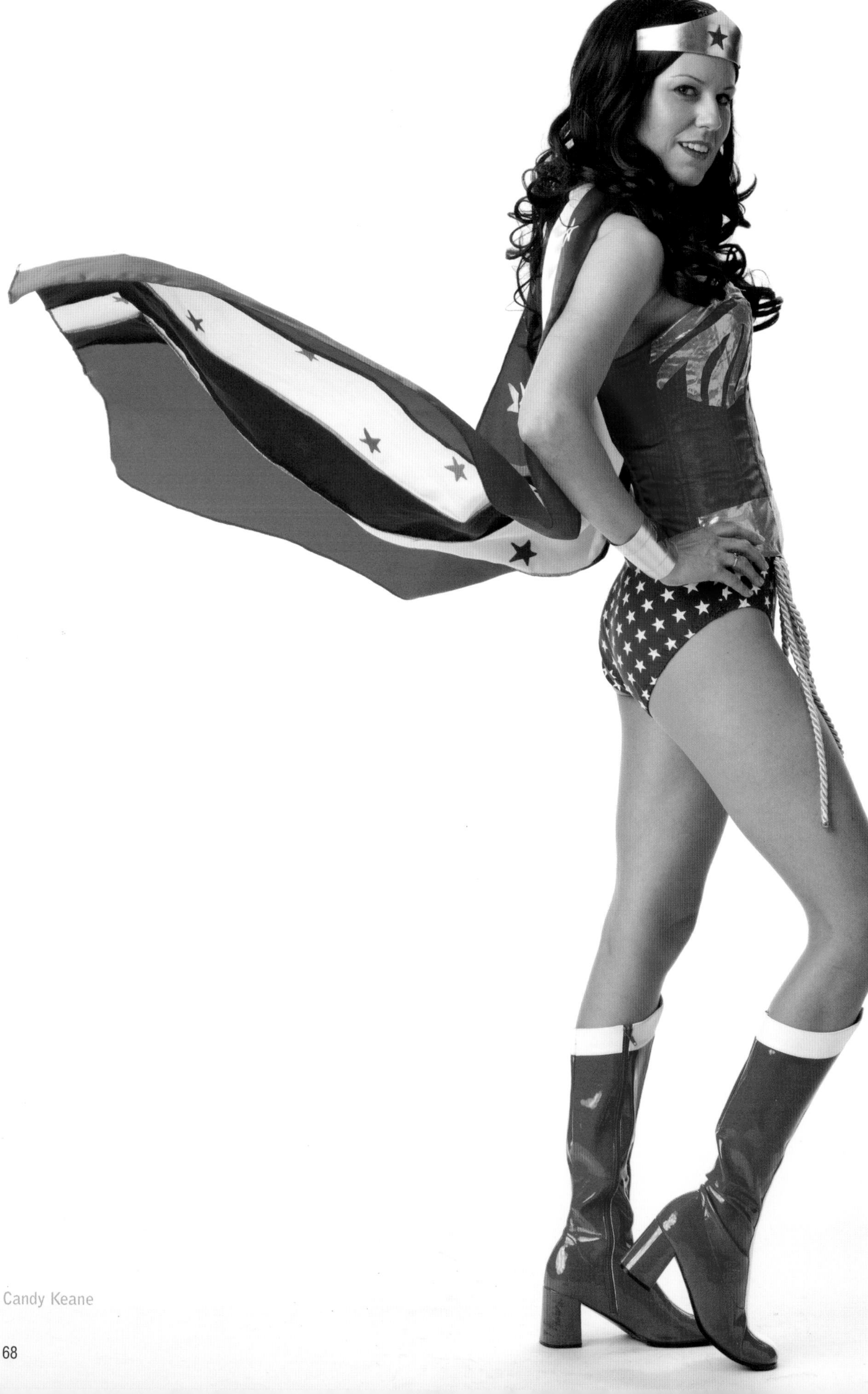

Candy Keane

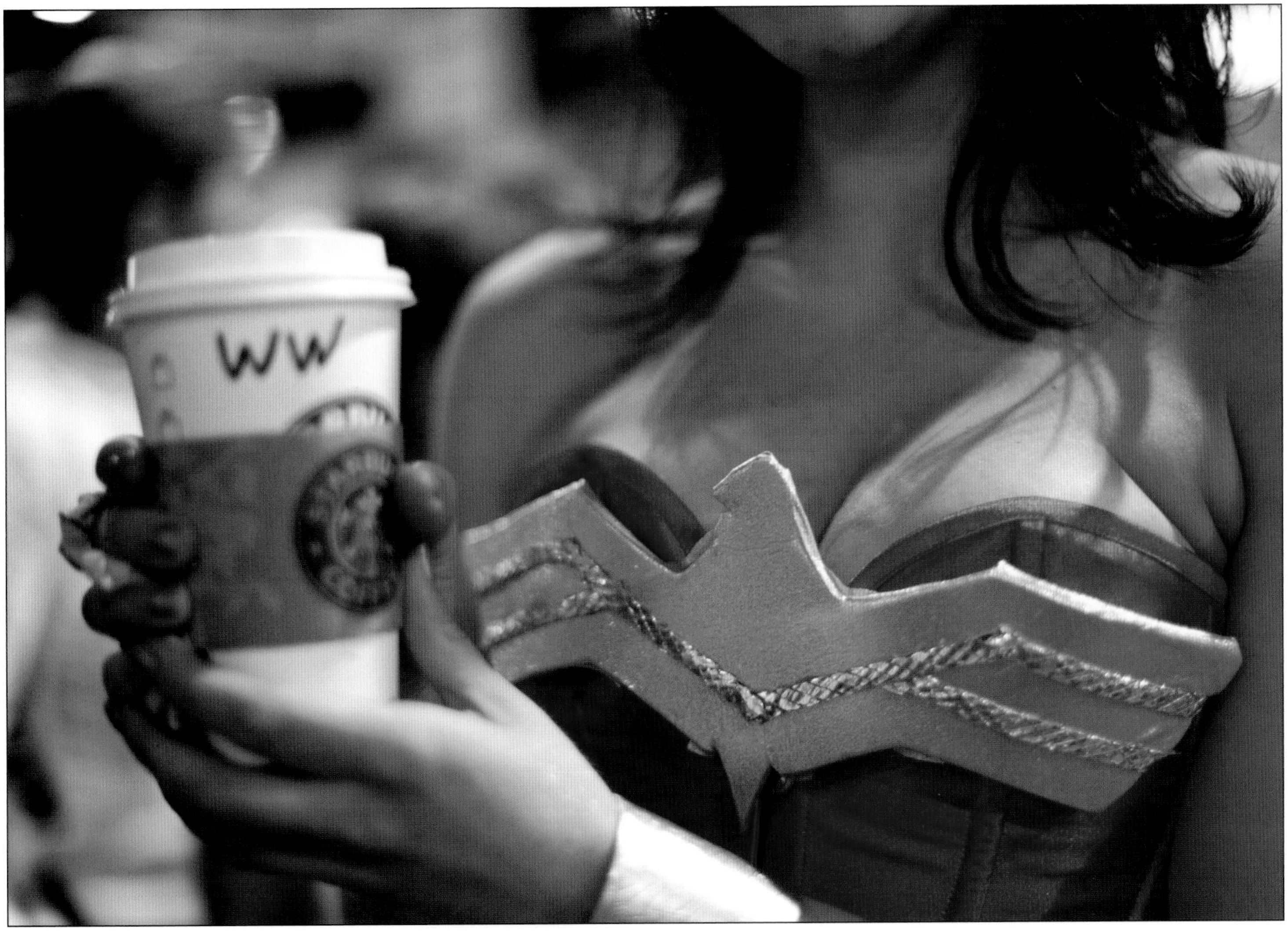
WW

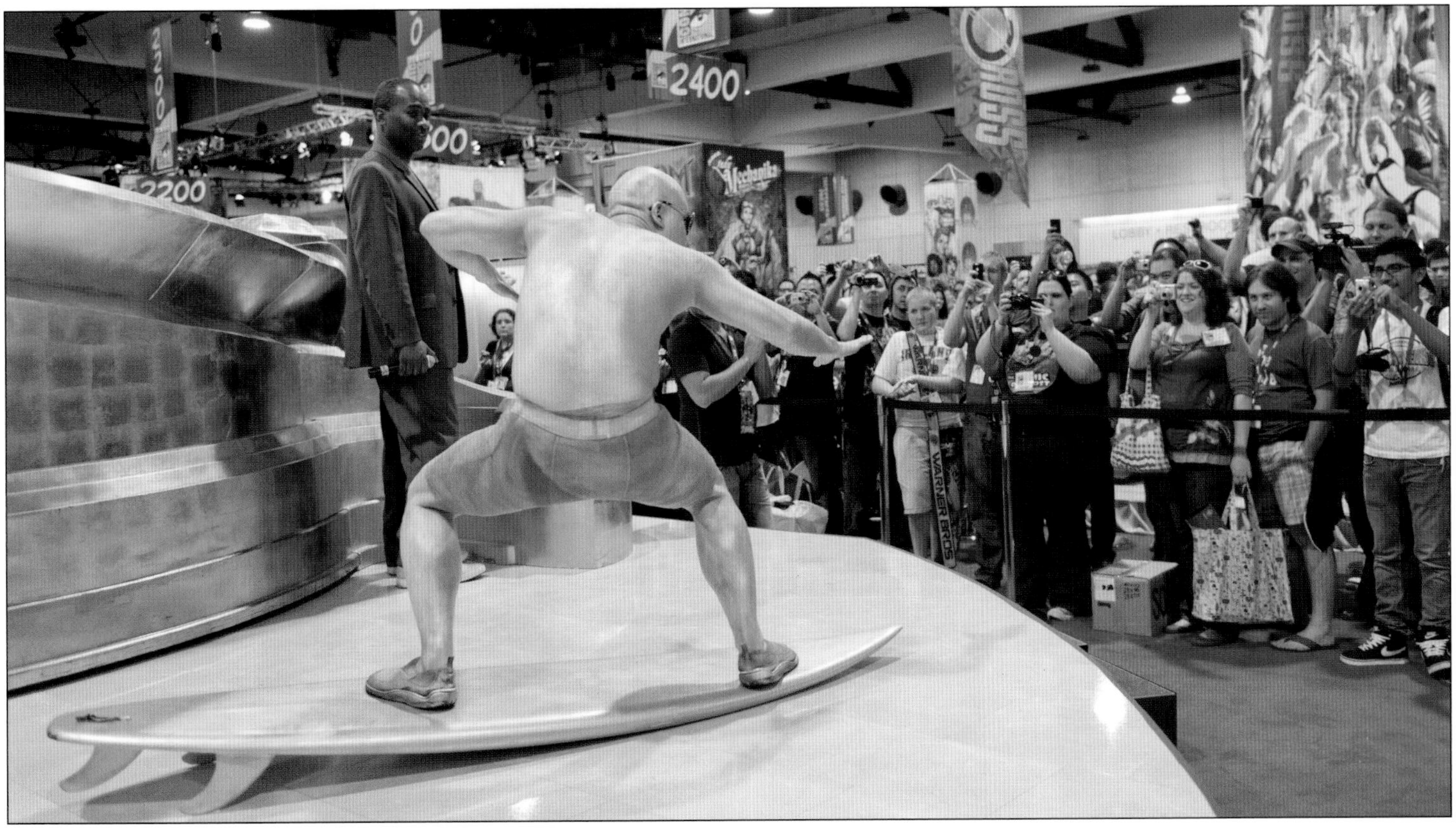
2400
2200

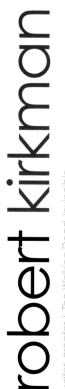

robert kirkman

writer, creator | The Walking Dead, Invincible

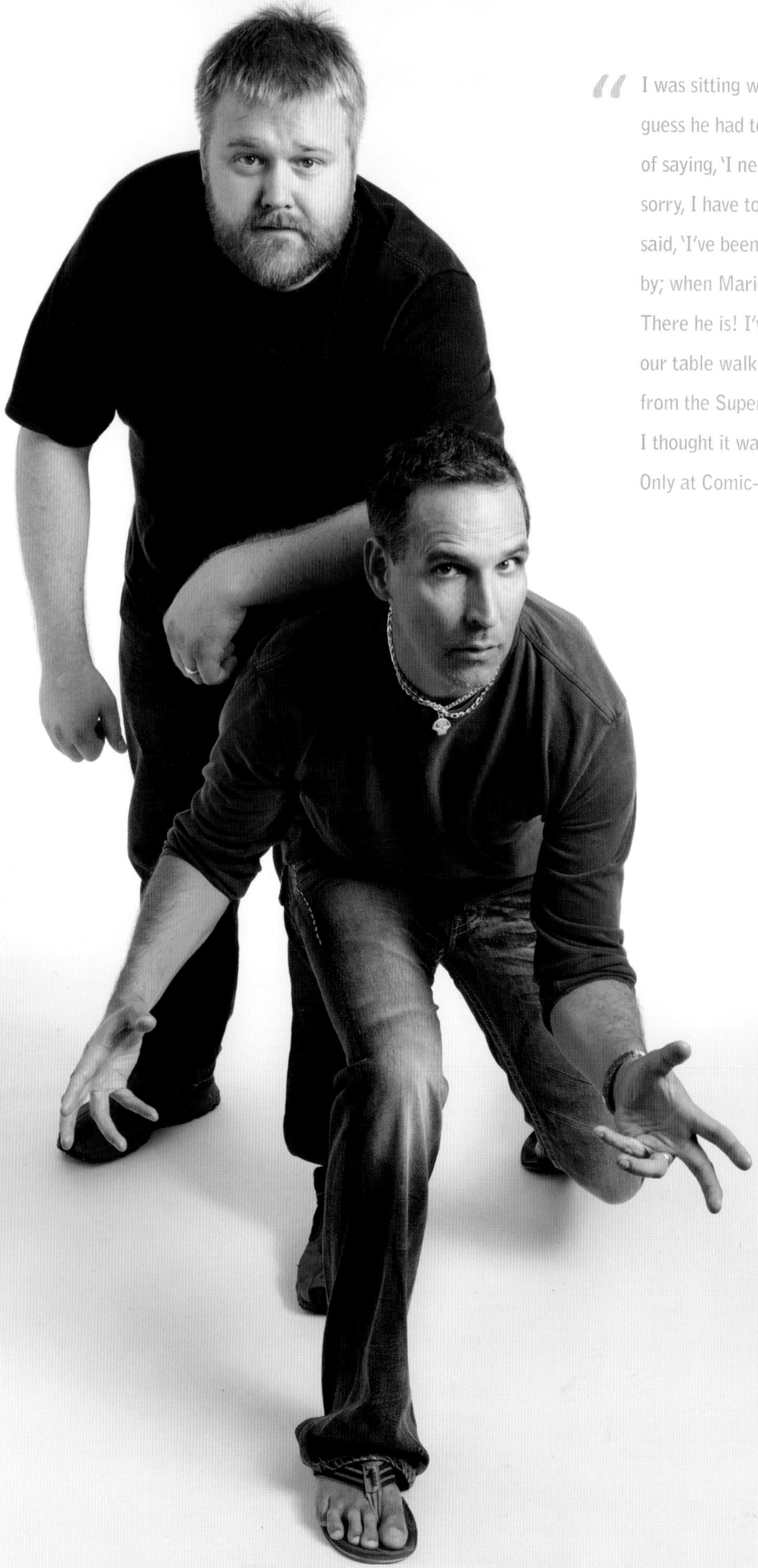

“I was sitting with Patton Oswalt, and I guess he had to catch a flight, but instead of saying, ‘I need to catch my fight, I’m sorry, I have to go,’ he looked up and said, ‘I’ve been waiting for Mario to walk by; when Mario walks by I leave. Oh! There he is! I’ve got to go.’ And then by our table walked a guy dressed as Mario from the Super Mario Bros. game, and I thought it was the funniest thing ever. Only at Comic-Con.”

todd mcfarlane

writer, creator | Spawn, McFarlane Toys

“Every single one of those fans has taken hard-earned money out of their pockets and somehow pushed it in my direction. They help feed my family, they help put a roof over my head, and they allow me to continue to do my artwork. If that person is going to take time enough to support what I do, if they've got a question, I owe them an honest answer.”

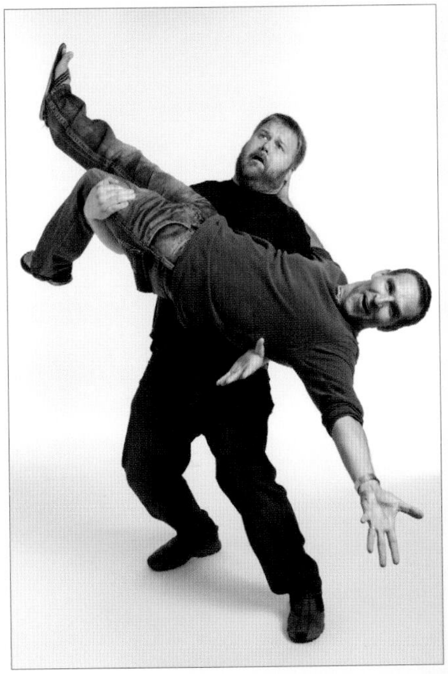

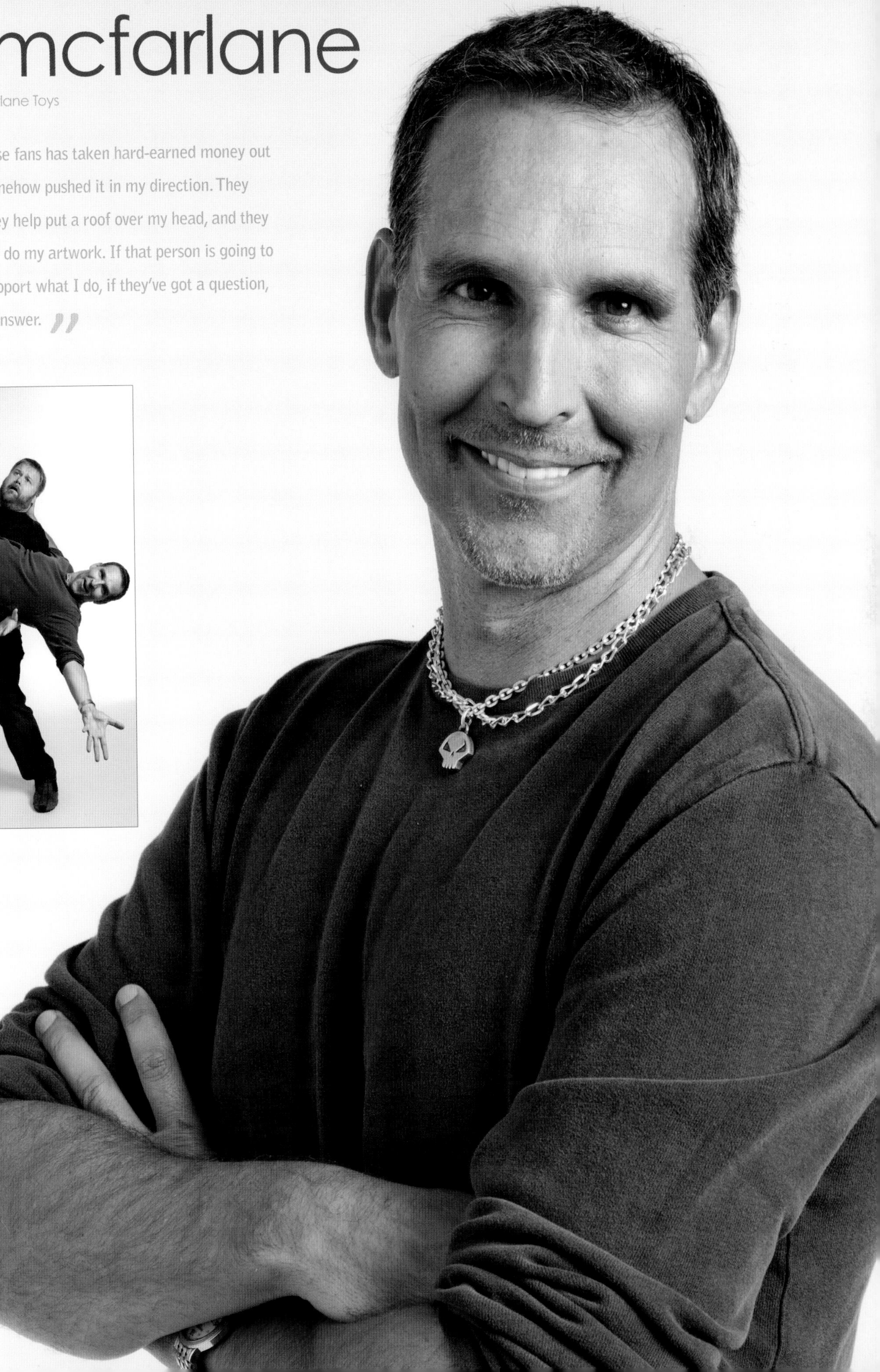

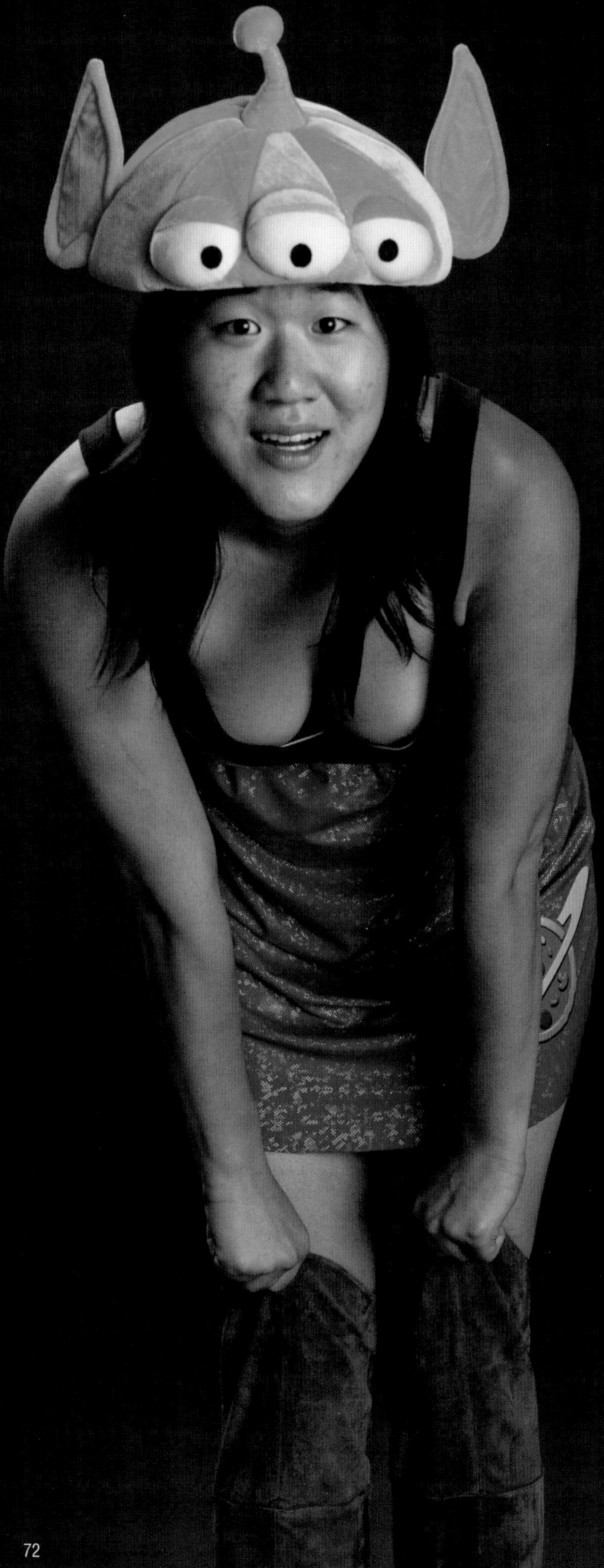

“There’s such a great camaraderie here. People will offer to help you out when they can, and everyone here is just kind of like a really big nerd at heart. And we have such a passion for toys and comics and movies and popular culture, and this is just like nerd heaven for all of us.”

Elaine Chang

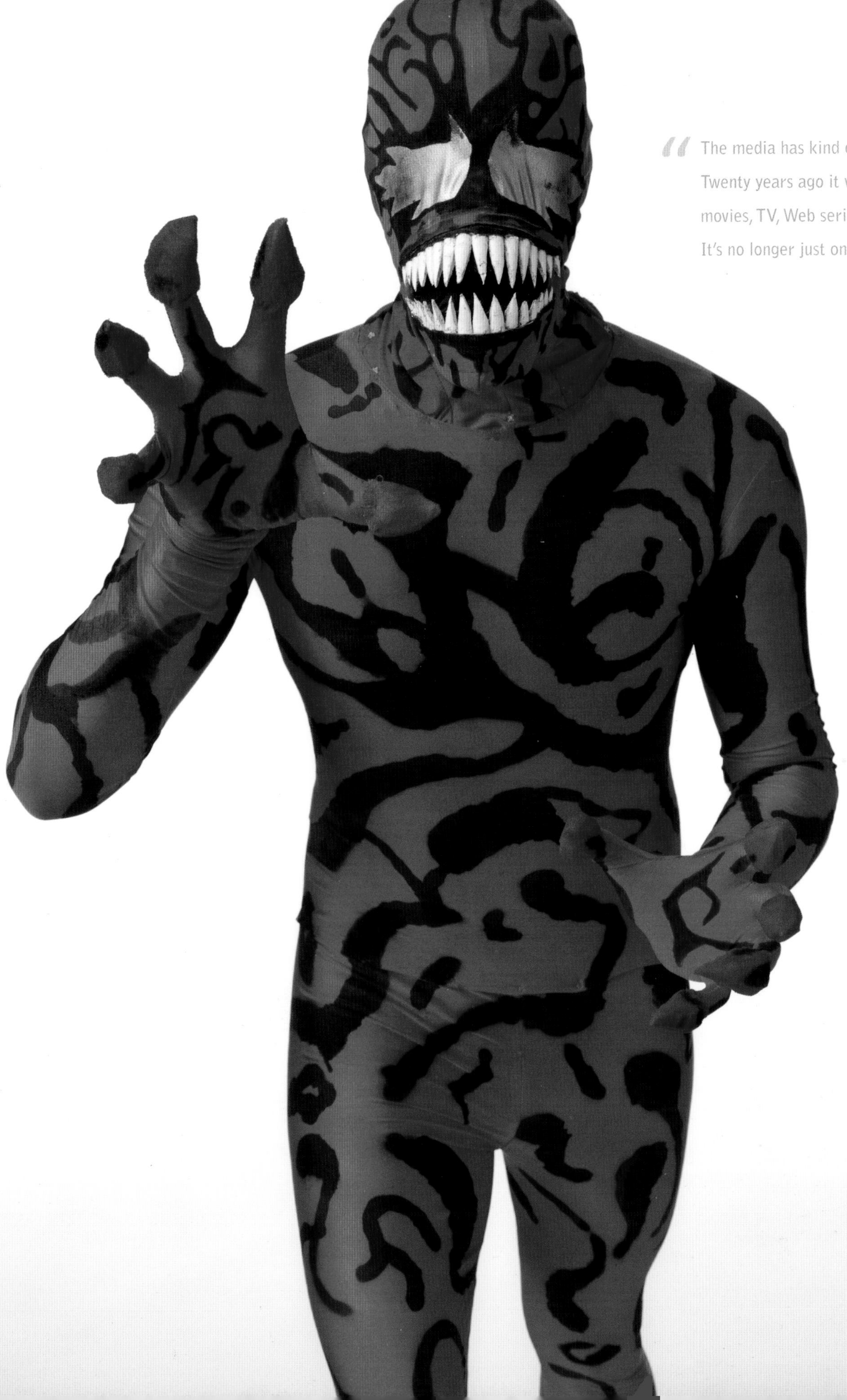

“The media has kind of taken over the event. Twenty years ago it was a lot of comics. Now it's movies, TV, Web series…it's a bit of everything. It's no longer just one specific fanbase.”

Bradley Upton

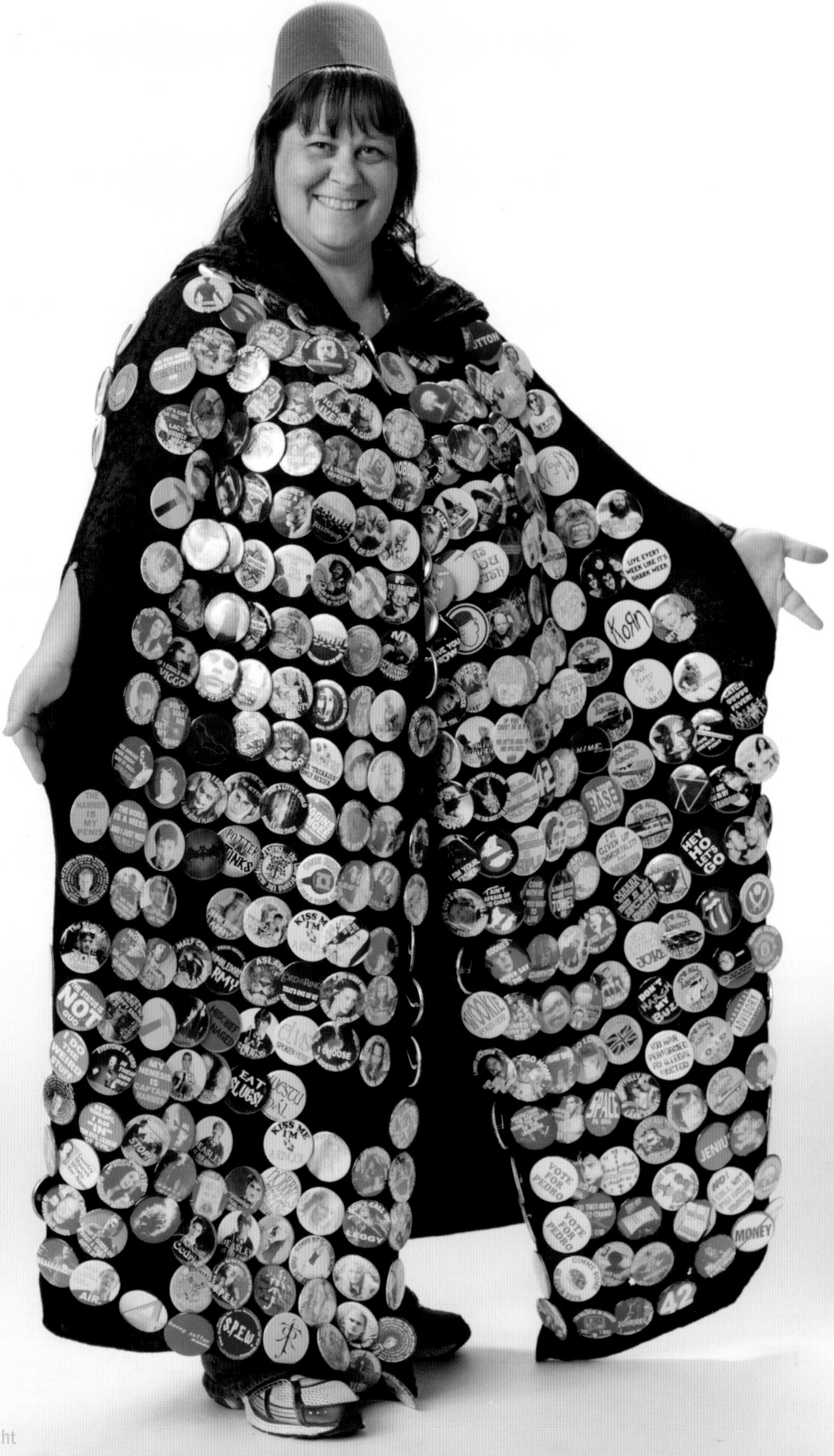
LIVE EVERY WEEK LIKE IT'S SHARK WEEK
KoRn
THE HAMMER IS MY PENIS
HEY HO LET'S GO
EAT SLUGS!
VOTE FOR PEDRO
VOTE FOR PEDRO
MONEY
42

Suzanne Eggebrecht

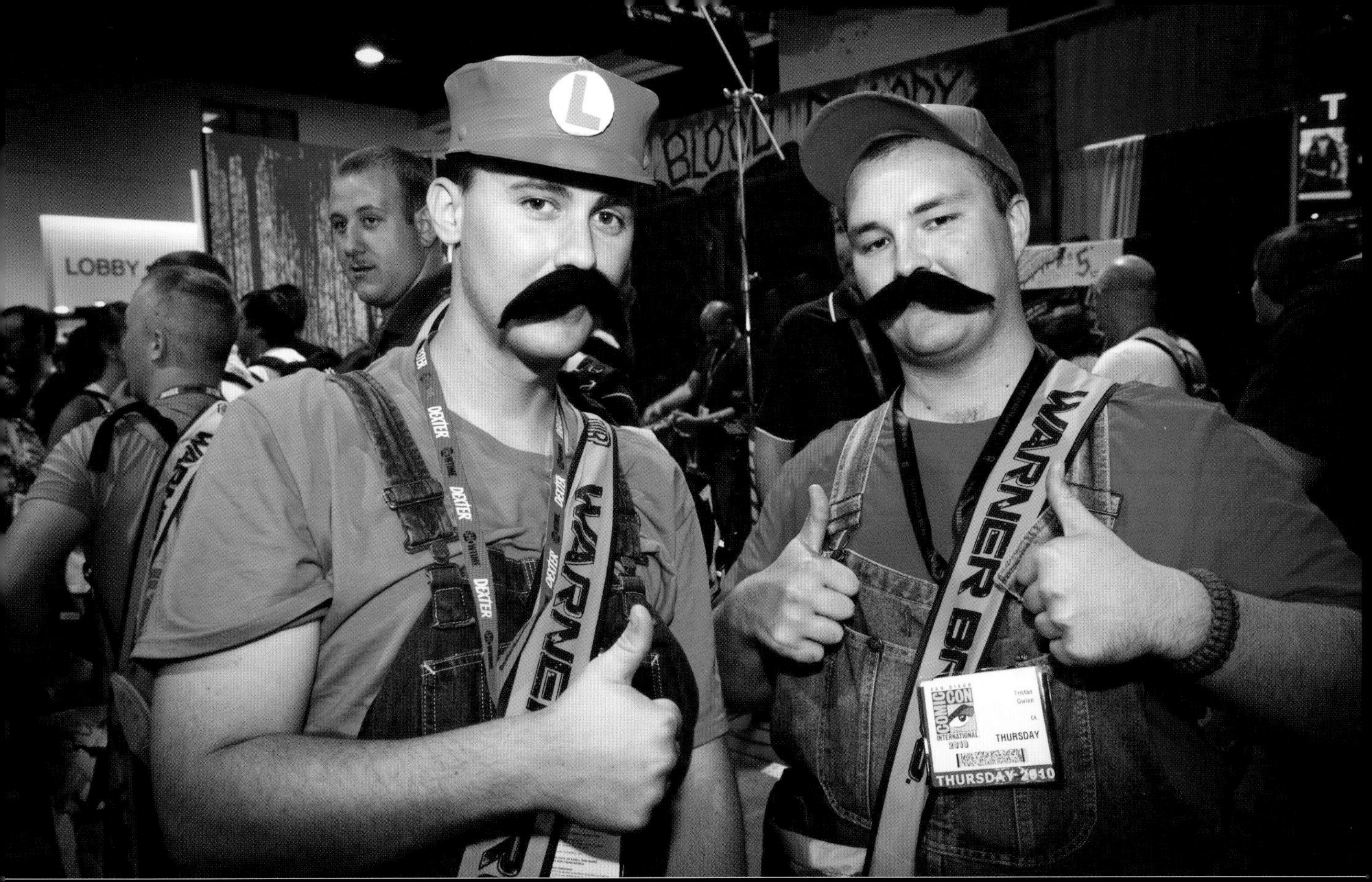
LOBBY
DEXTER
WARNER
COMIC CON
INTERNATIONAL
THURSDAY
THURSDAY 2010

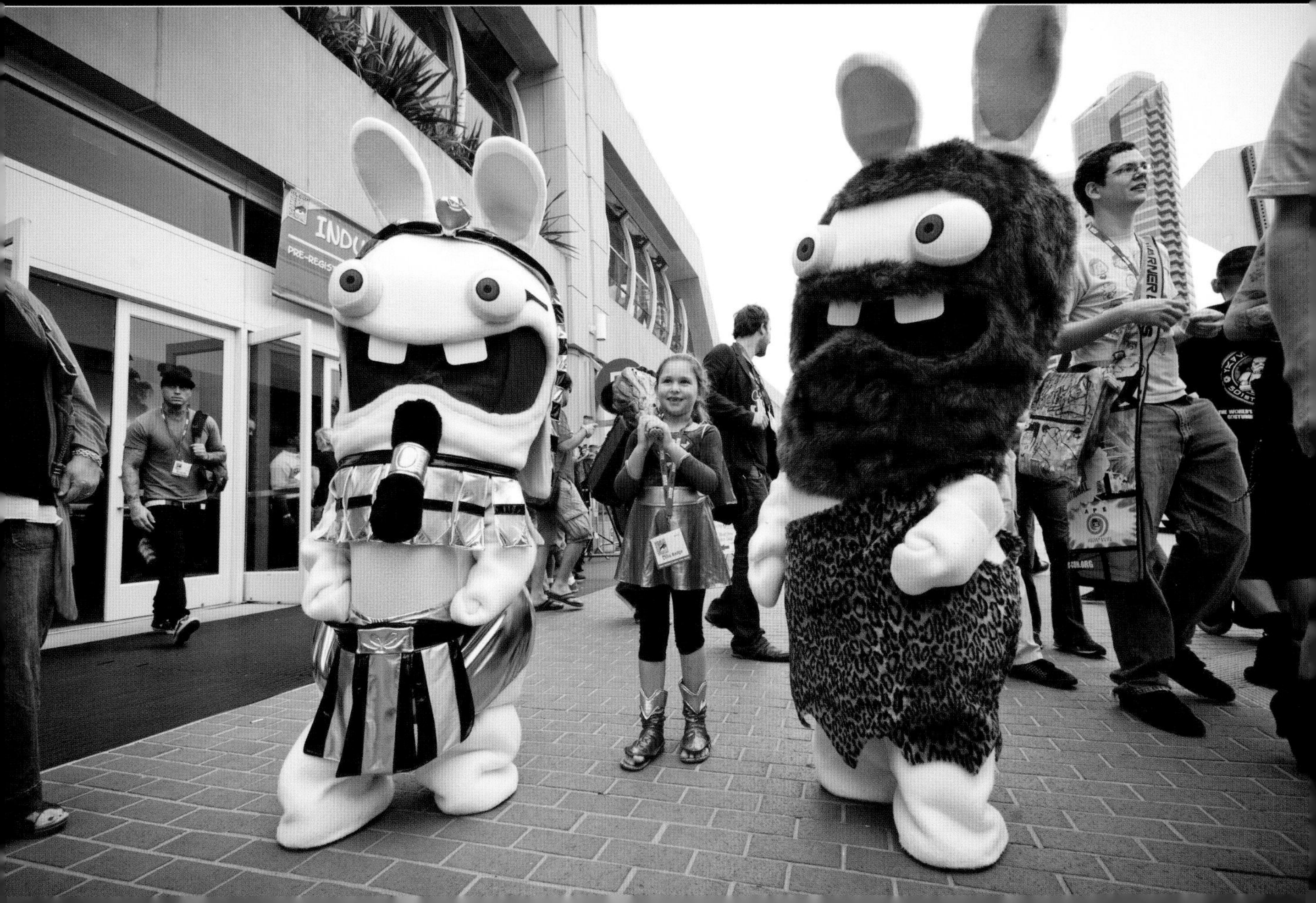
PRE-REGIST

day two

“Day two is a madhouse. It’s like the asylum dropped everyone off that morning and said, ‘I’ll pick you up at five.’ It’s insane, its packed, and it’s sweaty—but good sweaty.”

Morgan Spurlock

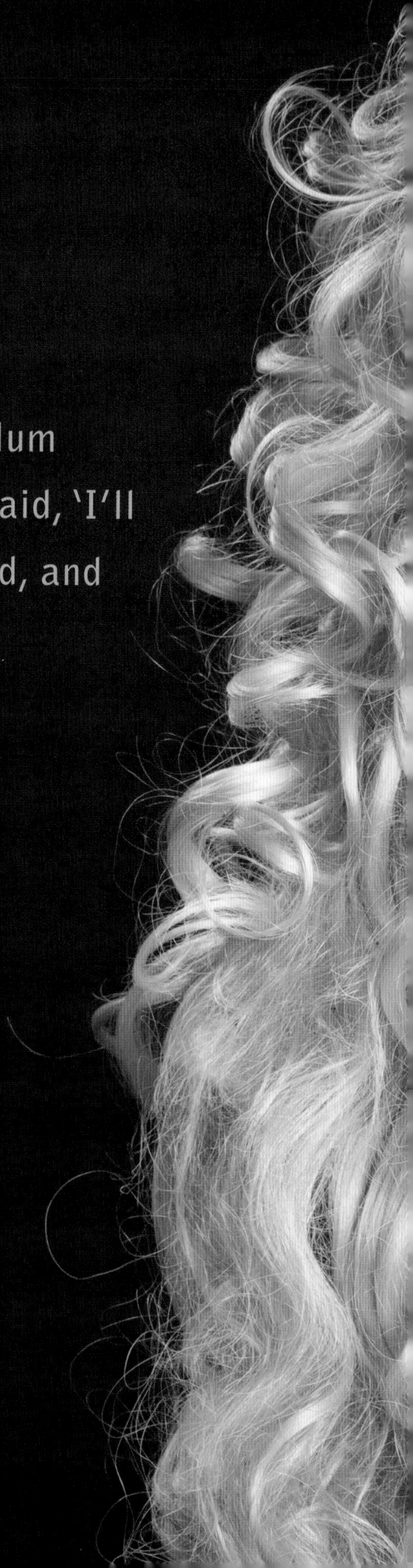

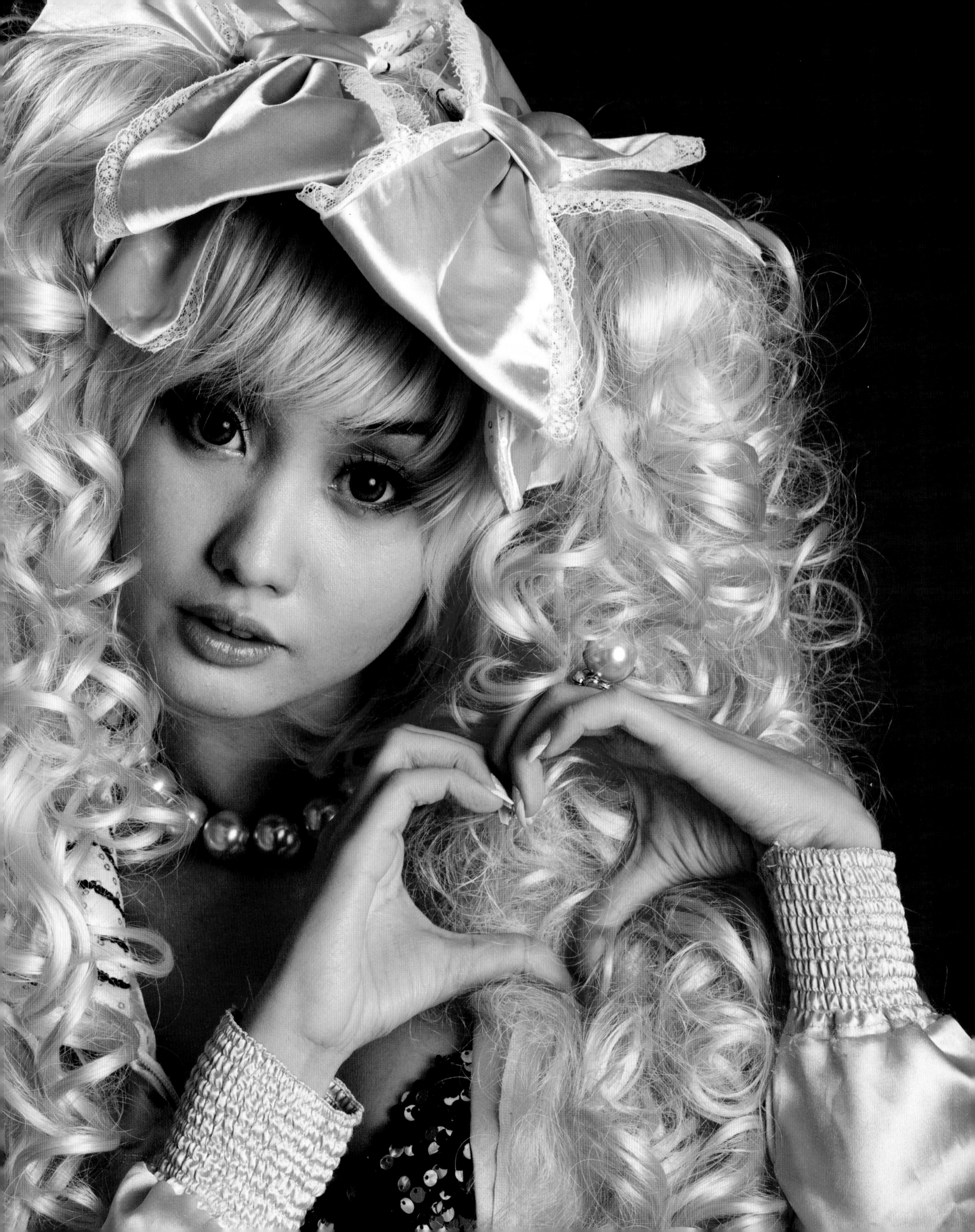

guillermo del toro

director | Pan's Labyrinth, Hellboy

" Particularly in comic books, I love the fallible guys. I love the guys who present the side of humanity that is less triumphant. Even Hellboy, as a hero, what attracted me to him was how tangible and how fallible he was in the Mignola comics. He was irascible, he was short-tempered, he was full of scars, he frequently screwed up. Things blew up in his face, and he had to resort to the most basic, two-fisted approach in fighting giant creatures. He didn't have all the resources or the power. I have never gone for the power-fantasies stuff. "

ron perlman

actor | Hellboy

“If you're fortunate enough to work in something that already has this built-in sort of revere, you want to say, 'Is this okay with you? Are we doing our job? I mean, is it everything you hoped it would be when we jumped from the medium of comic book art to three-dimensional TV or film or whatever?' At least, that's how I see it. I come down here with great humility.”

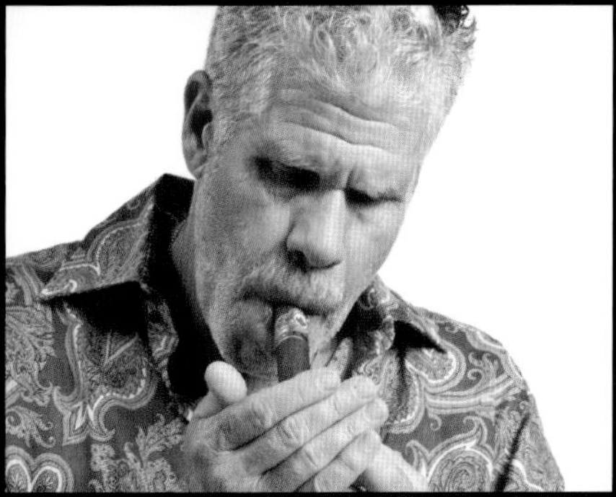

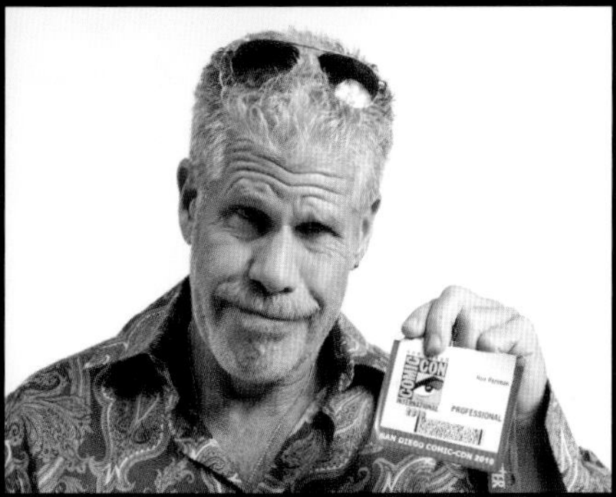
PROFESSIONAL

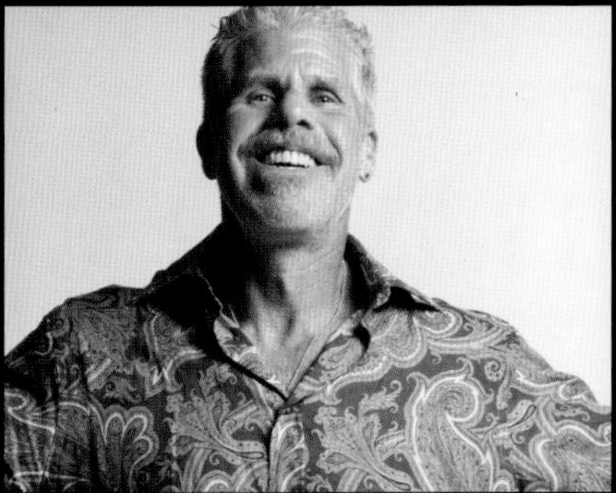

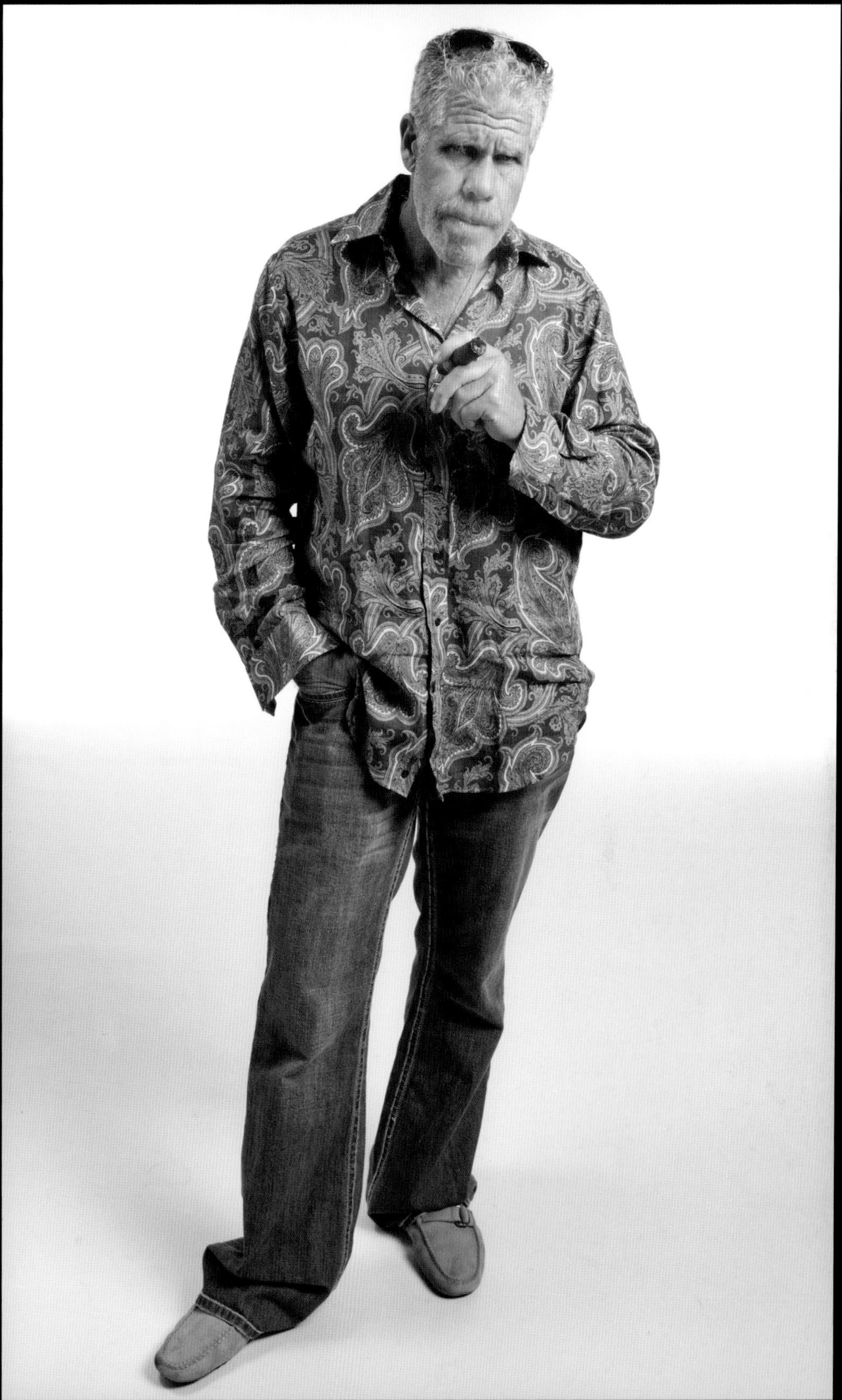

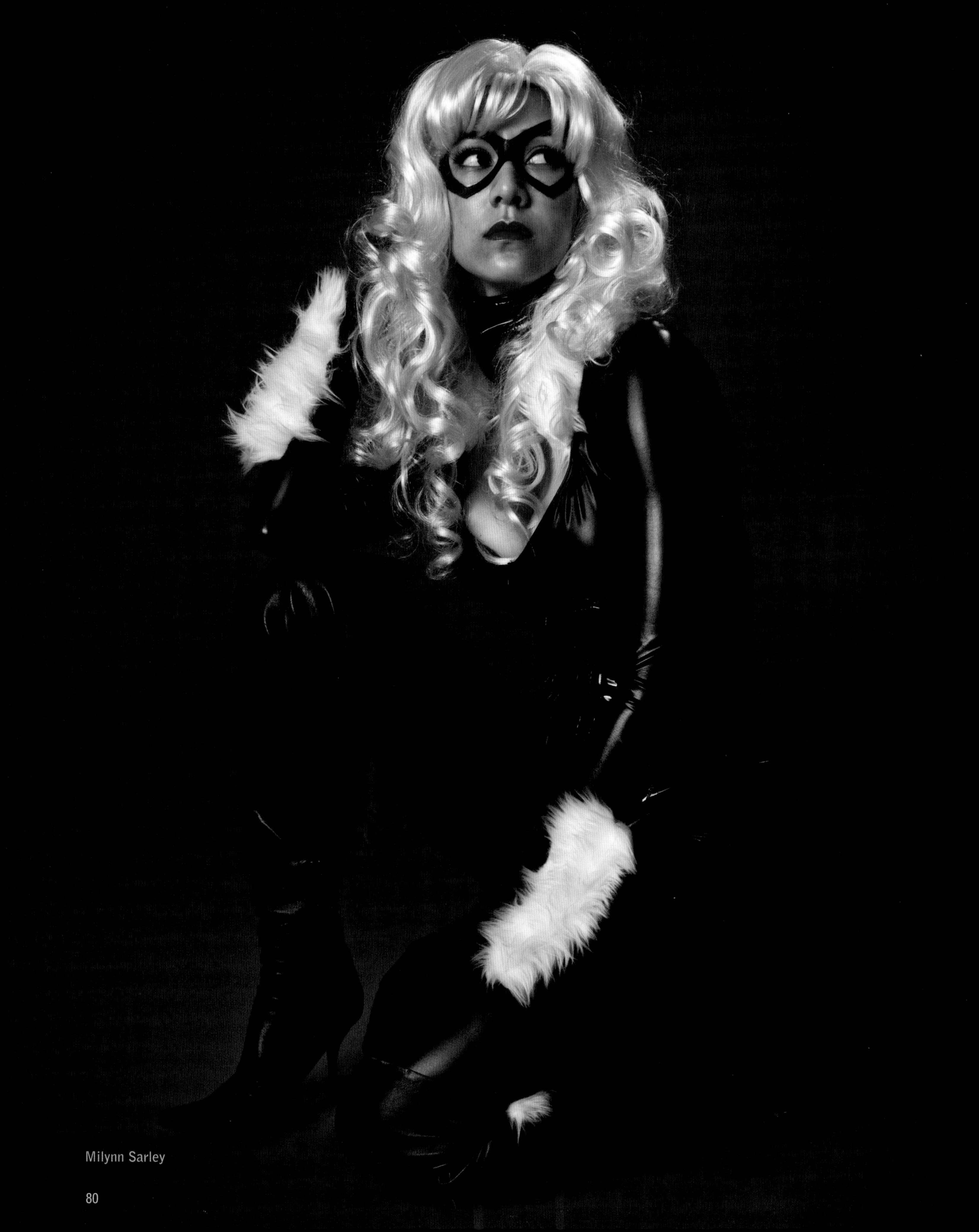

Milynn Sarley

bryan singer

director | X-Men, X2, Superman Returns

> "The convention floor reminds me of when I was a little kid and my parents took me to the New York Stock Exchange. I looked down over the floor and saw these people with the tickers, and I wondered, 'What are they all doing down there?'"

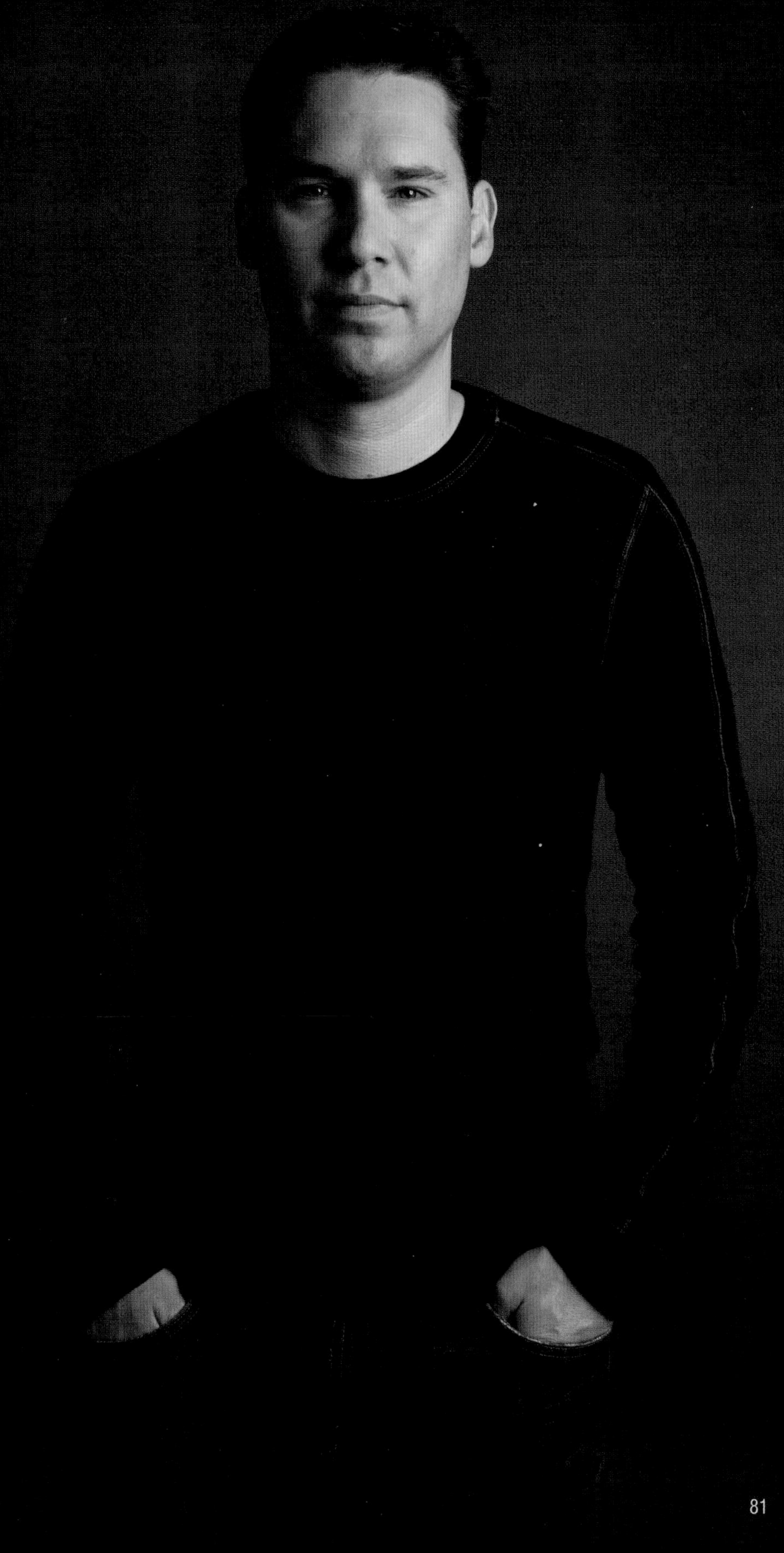

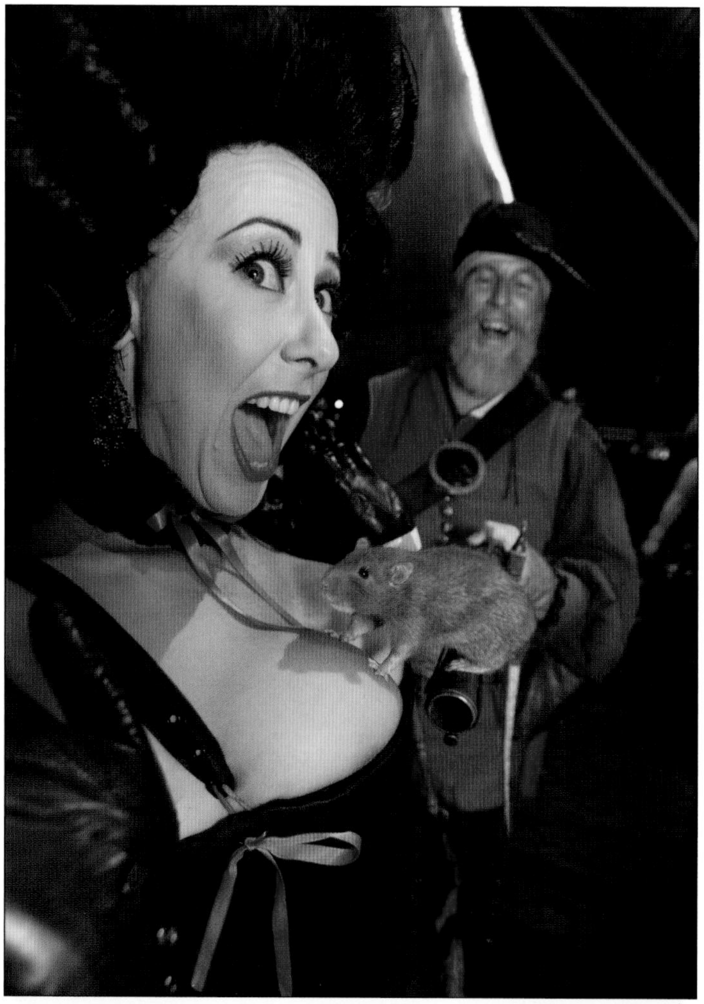

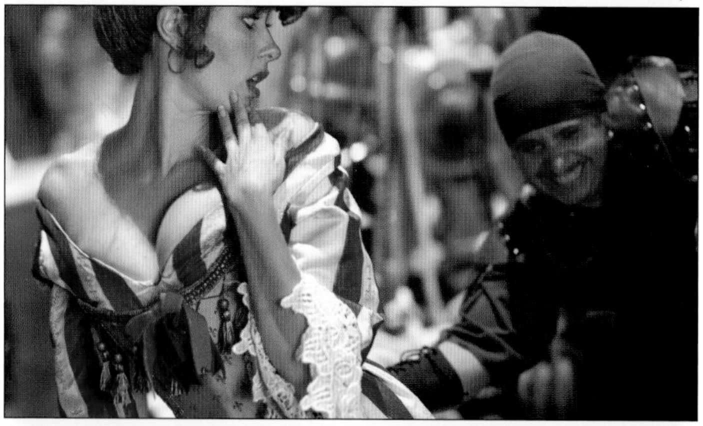

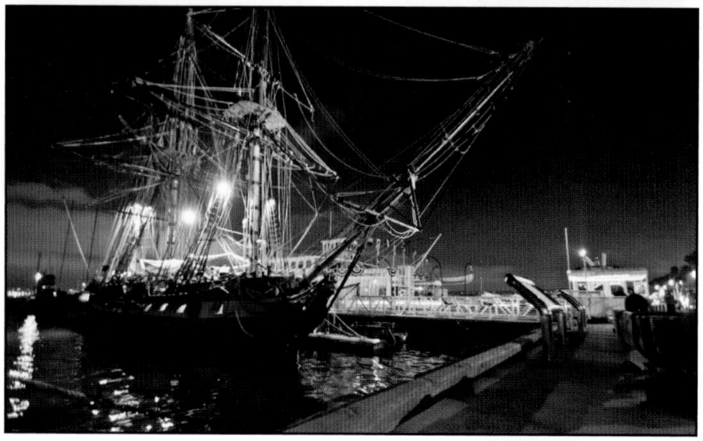

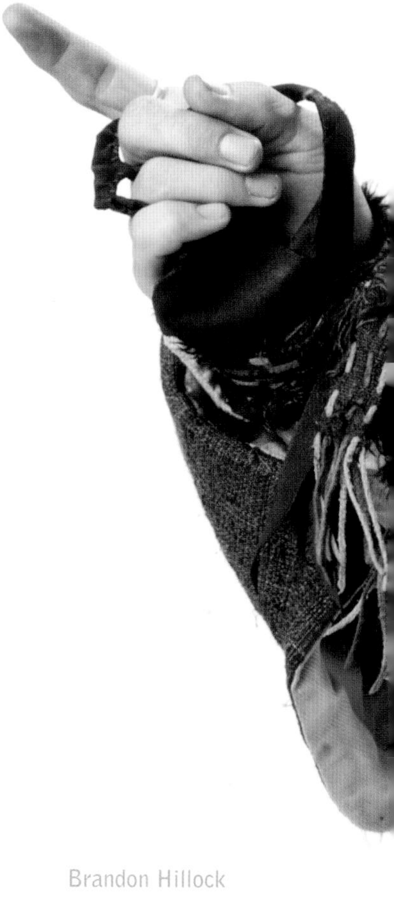

Brandon Hillock

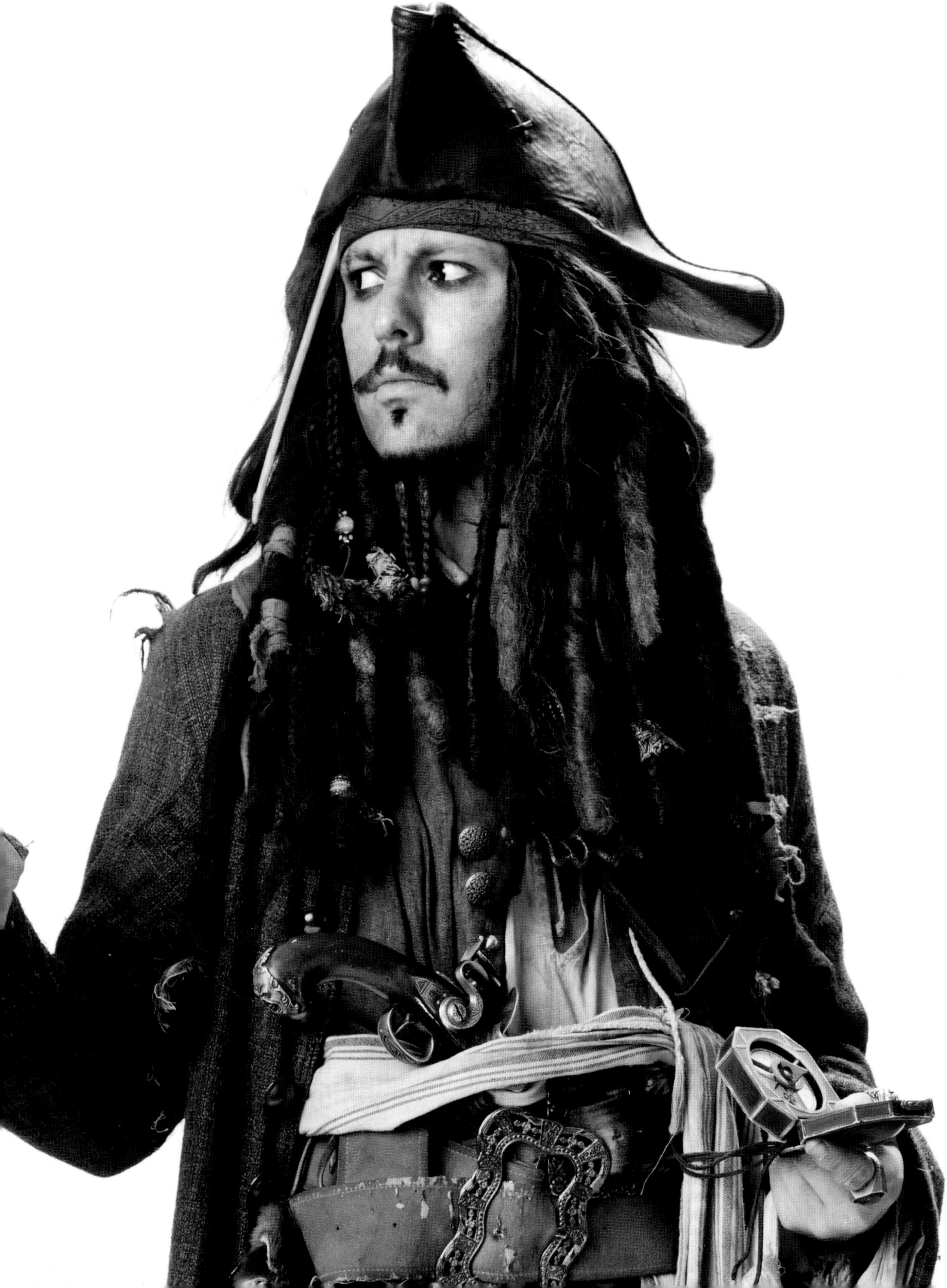

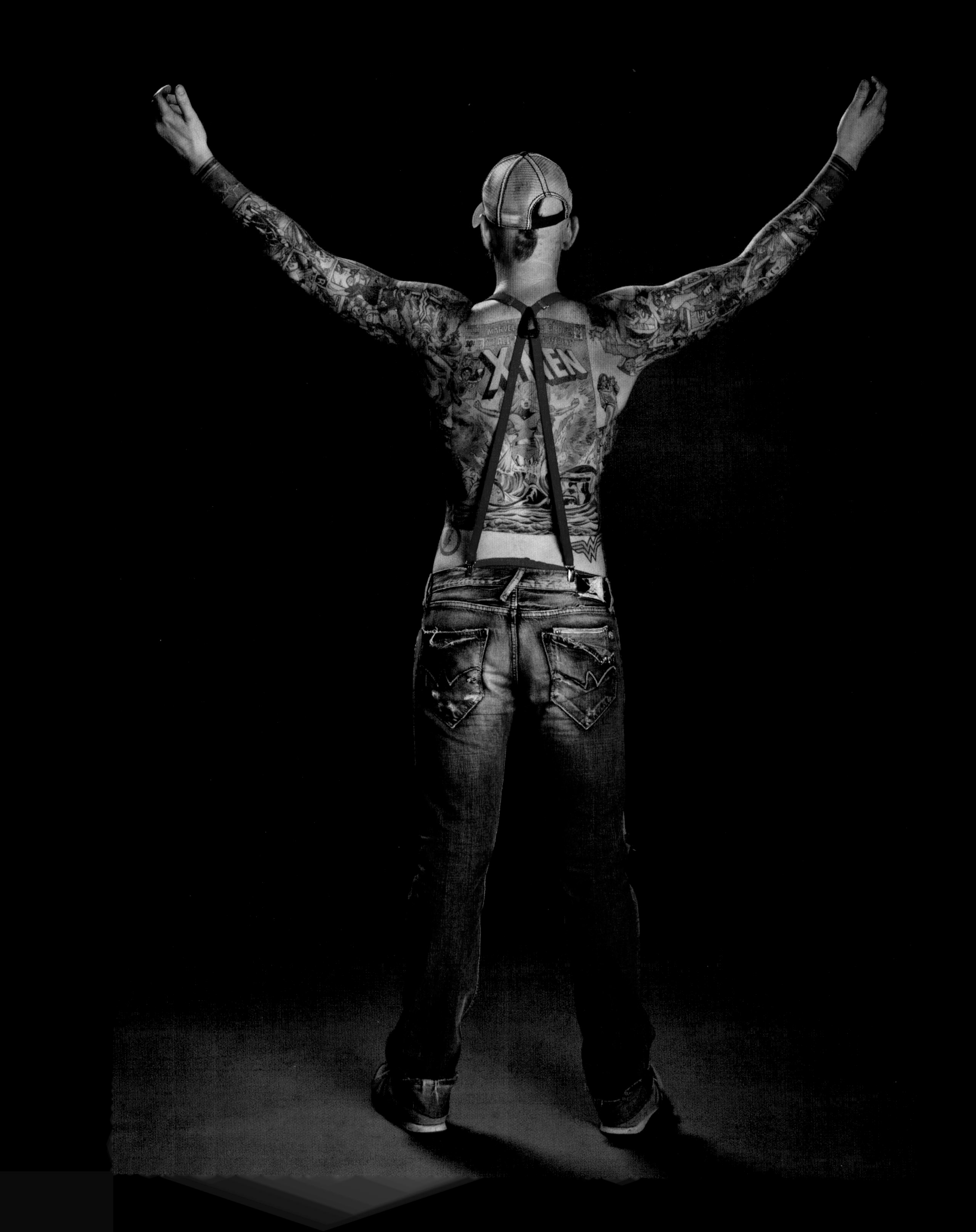
X-MEN

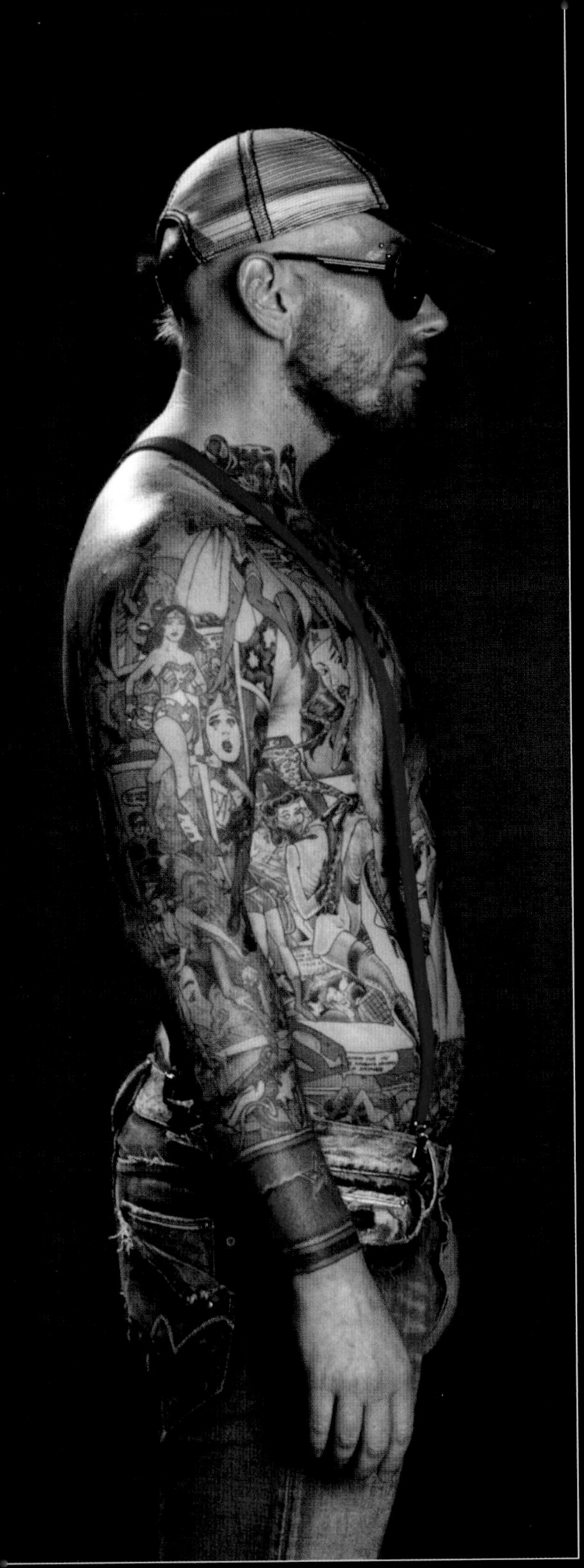

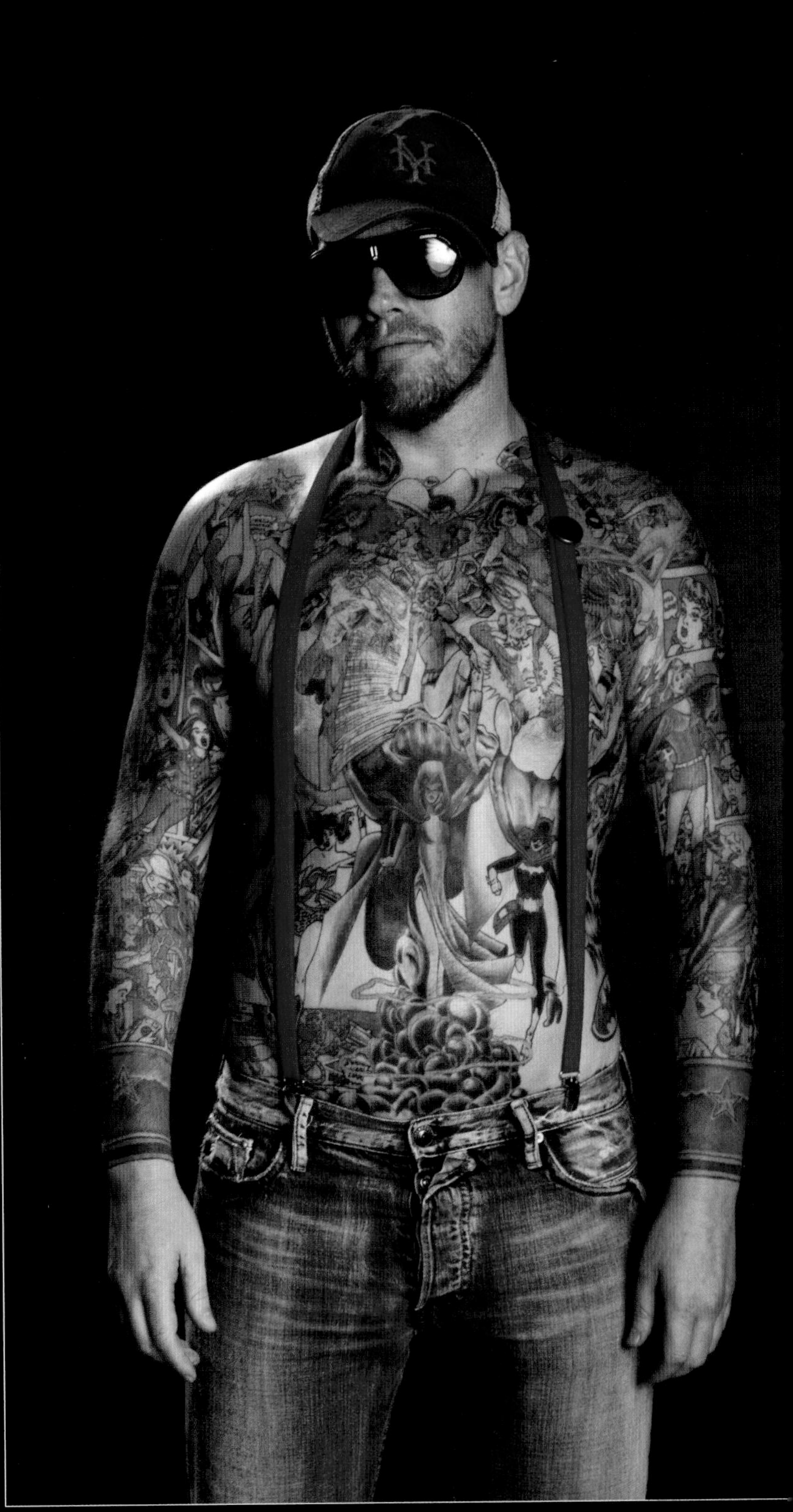

“I thought it’d be cool to do comic panels—I’d never seen that done. I’ve been working with one artist this whole time—I do the images, and I trace them, and he does the work with the needle.”

zachary quinto

actor | Heroes, Star Trek

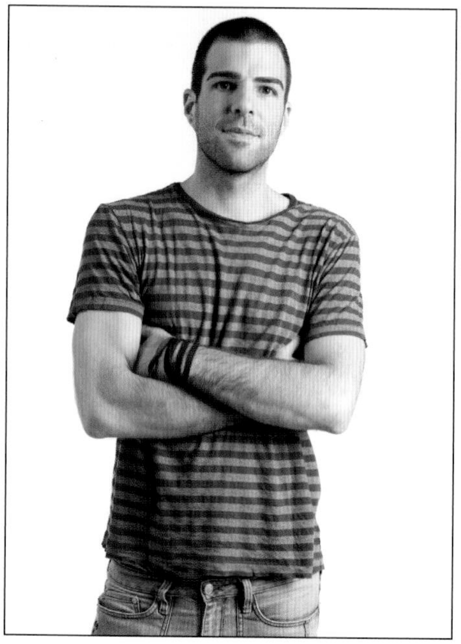

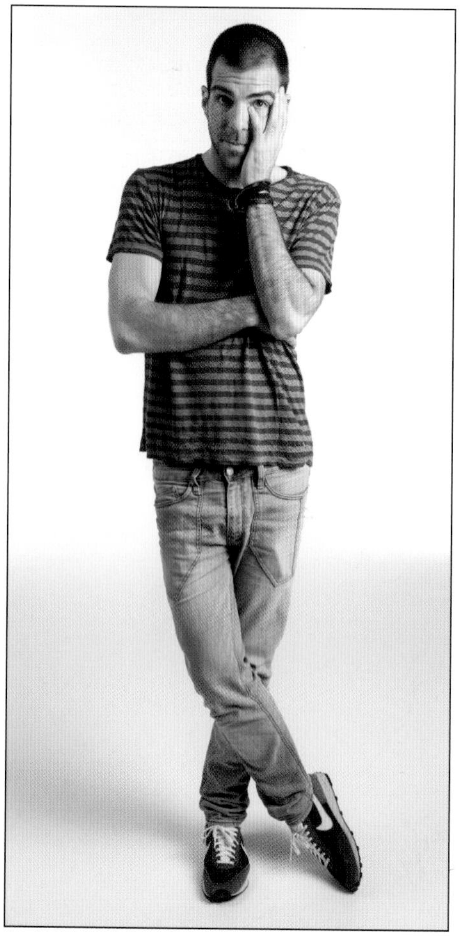

"People's devotion to science fiction, by and large, feels like it's rooted in a sense of hope. It's rooted in a sense of human potential. And I think at its best, that's the foundation of sci-fi—and it's actually something that I think we could use a lot of in this world."

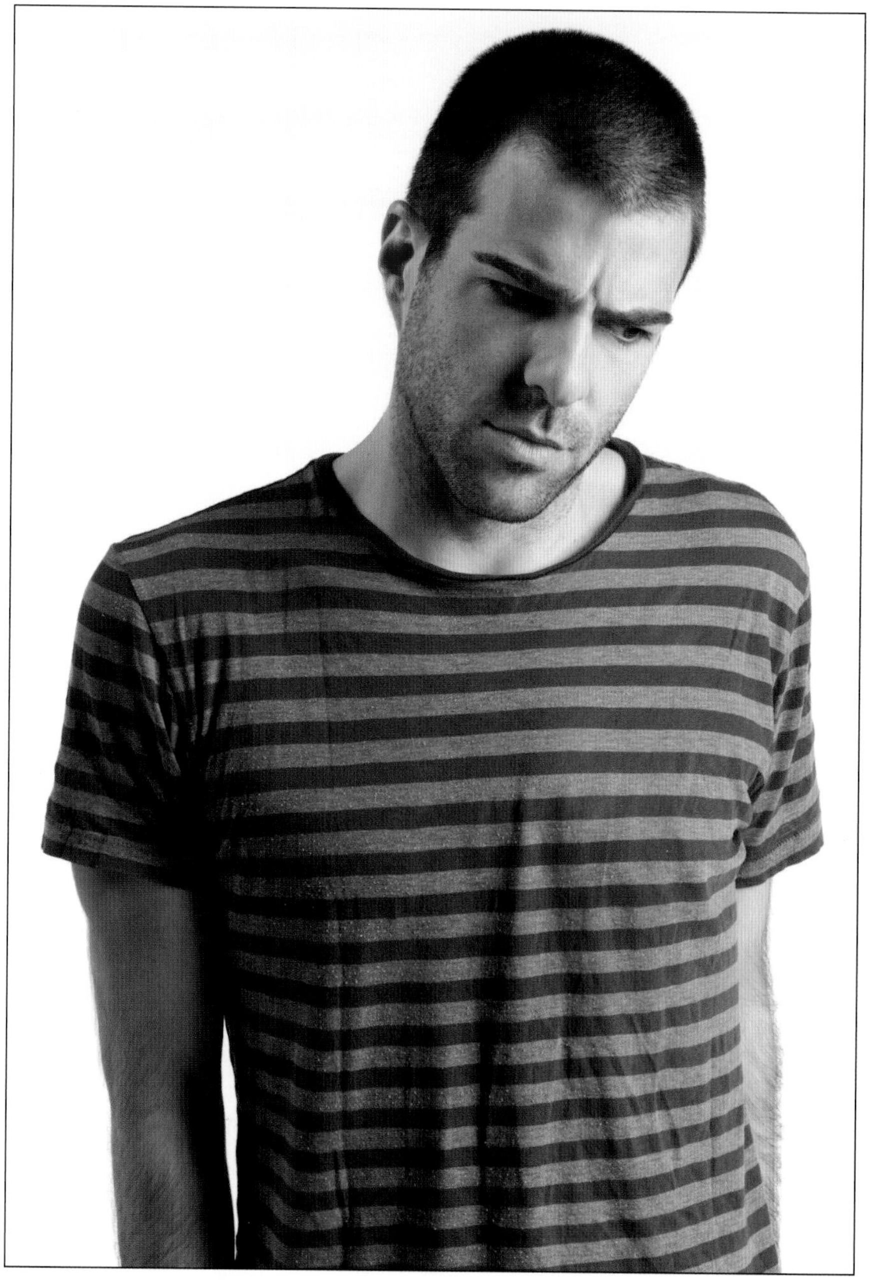

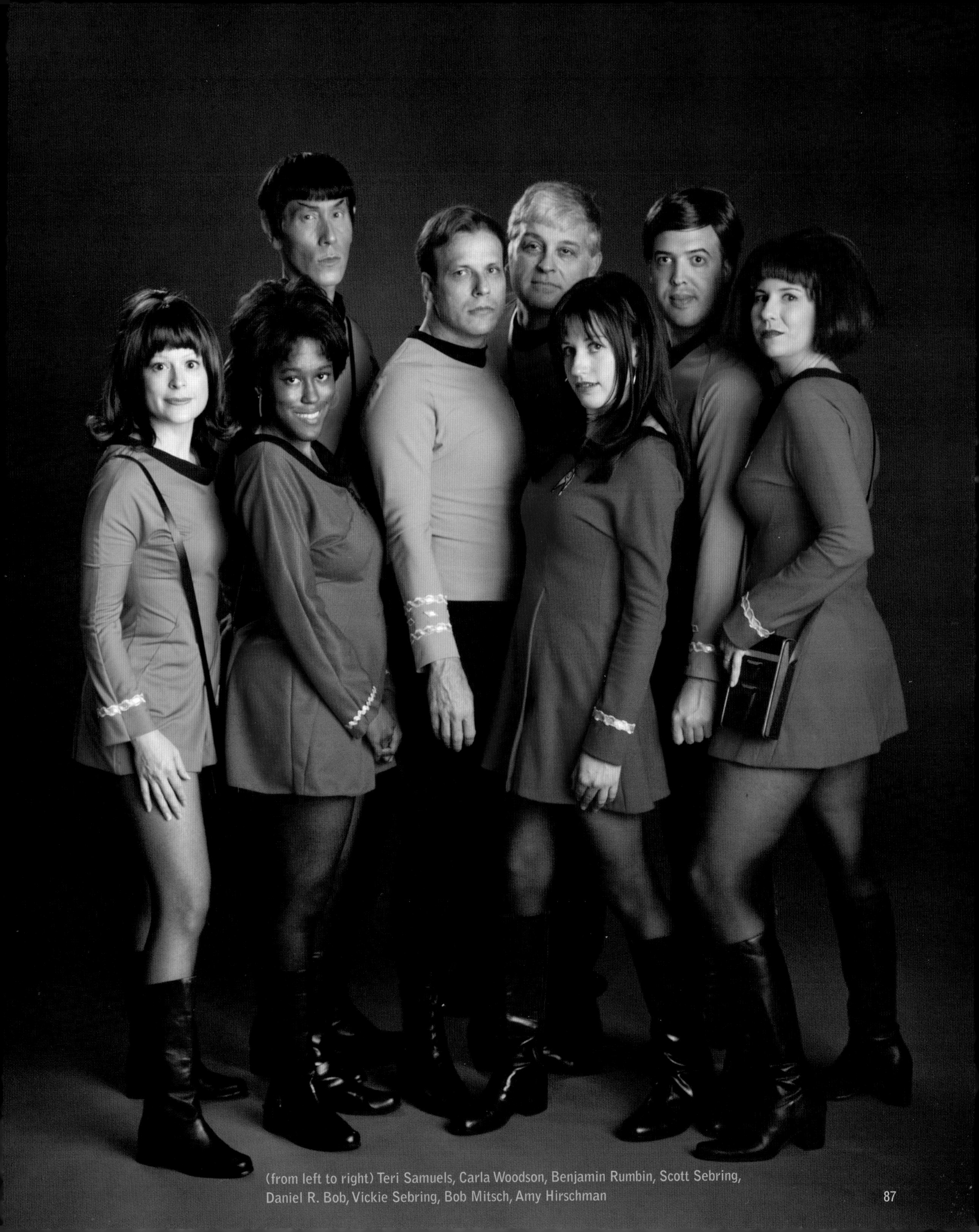

(from left to right) Teri Samuels, Carla Woodson, Benjamin Rumbin, Scott Sebring, Daniel R. Bob, Vickie Sebring, Bob Mitsch, Amy Hirschman

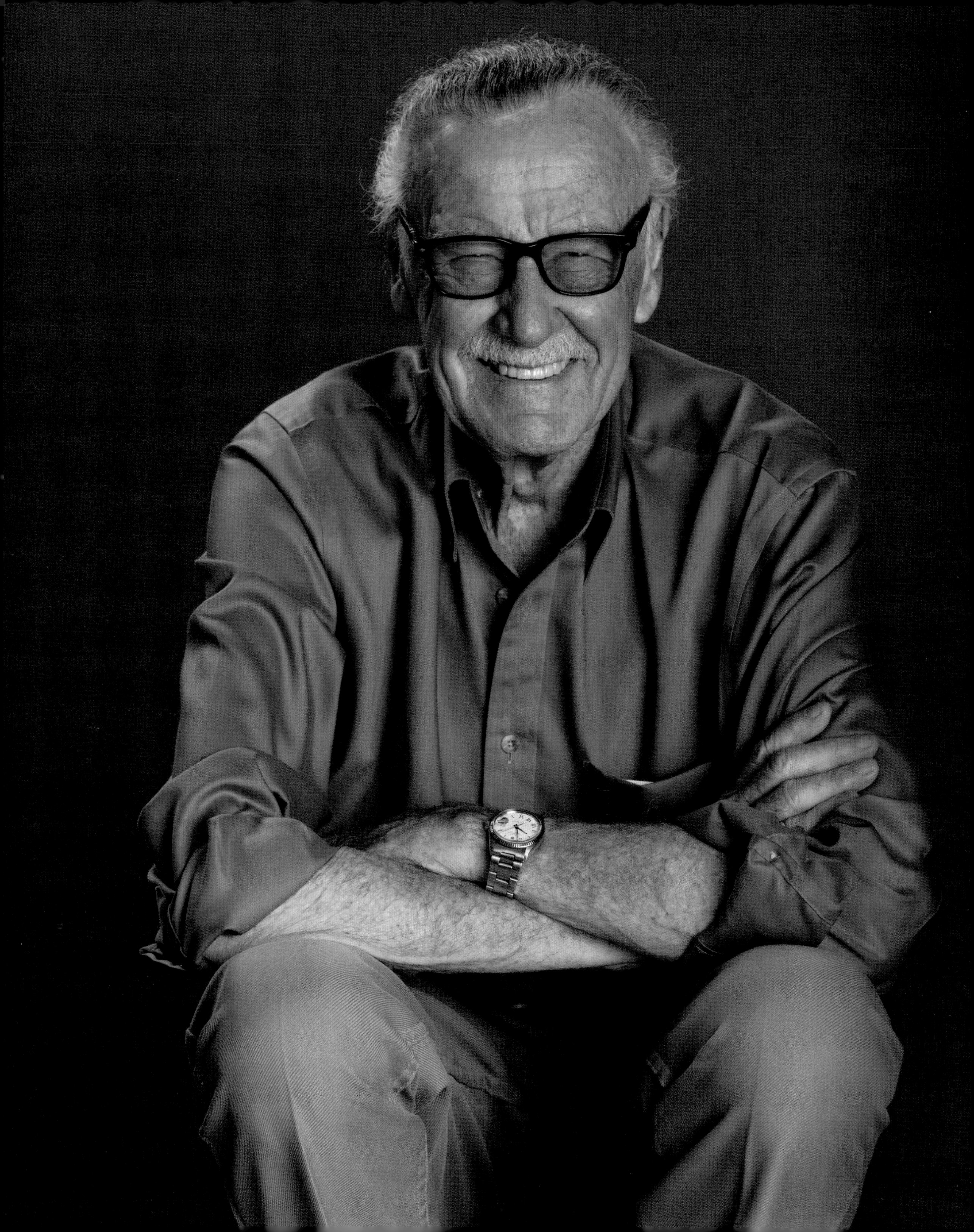

"I saw Stan Lee standing with a local, self-styled superhero named Captain Sticky. Captain Sticky was making a pitch for himself as a new superhero, saying, 'I combat evil with my peanut butter and jelly gun!' And the gun actually shot peanut butter and jelly. And Stan was saying, 'That's great! We have to put that in the comics!' Now, where else am I going to see a guy drive up in a Sticky-mobile and pull out a peanut butter and jelly gun? This is another world and I'm very happy to be a part of it."

Paul Dini

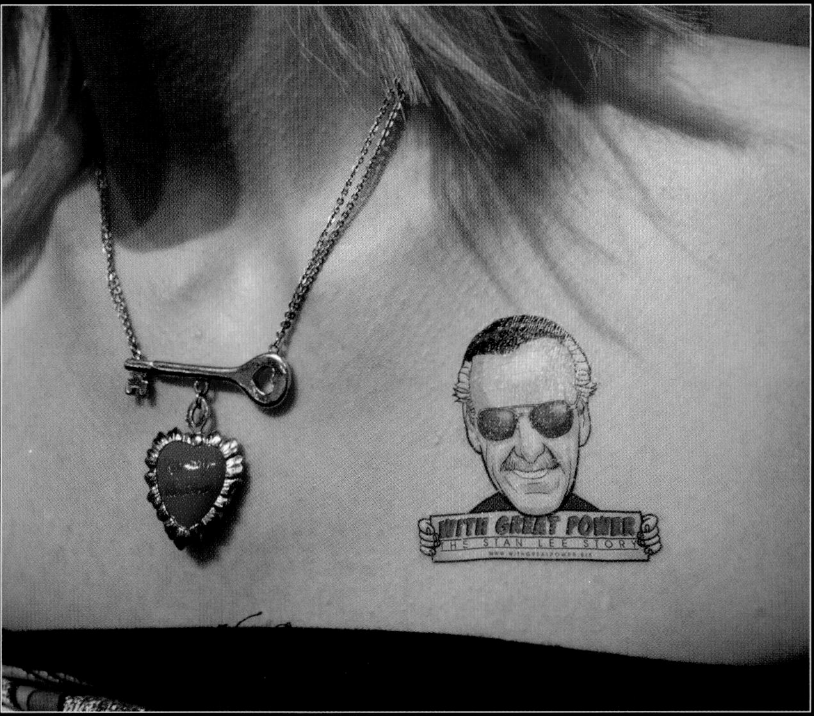
WITH GREAT POWER
THE STAN LEE STORY

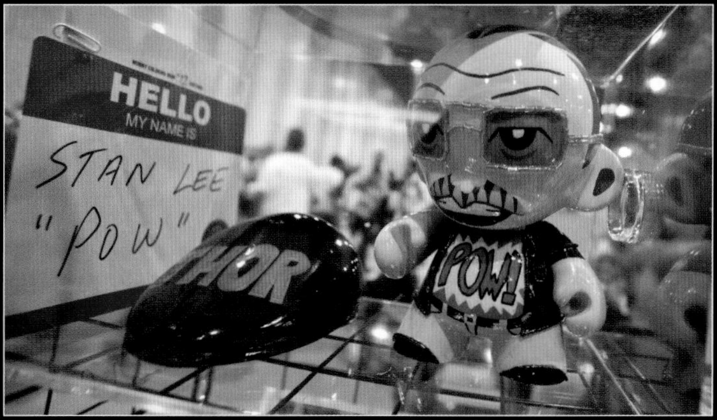
HELLO
MY NAME IS
STAN LEE
"POW"
POW!

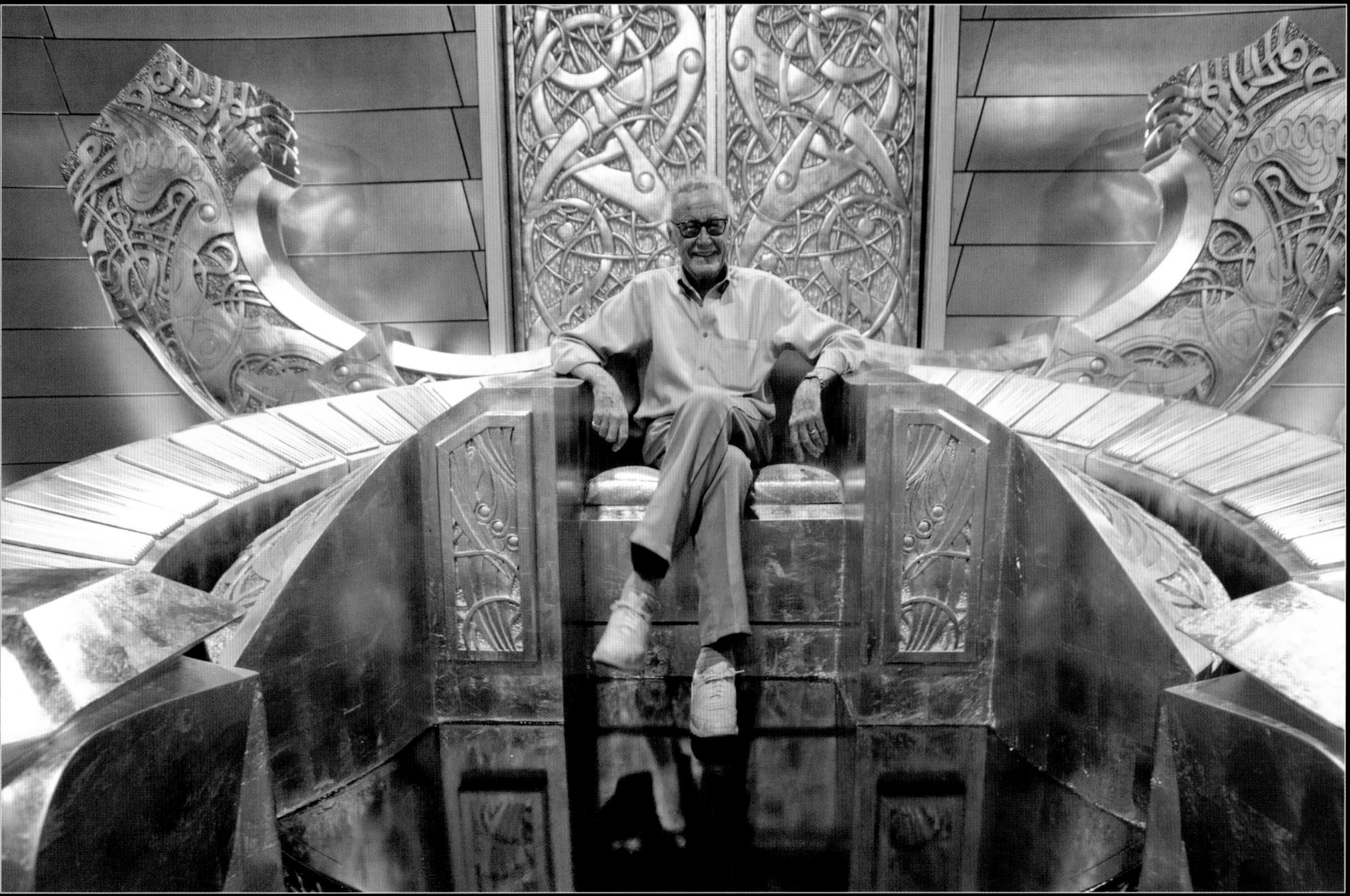

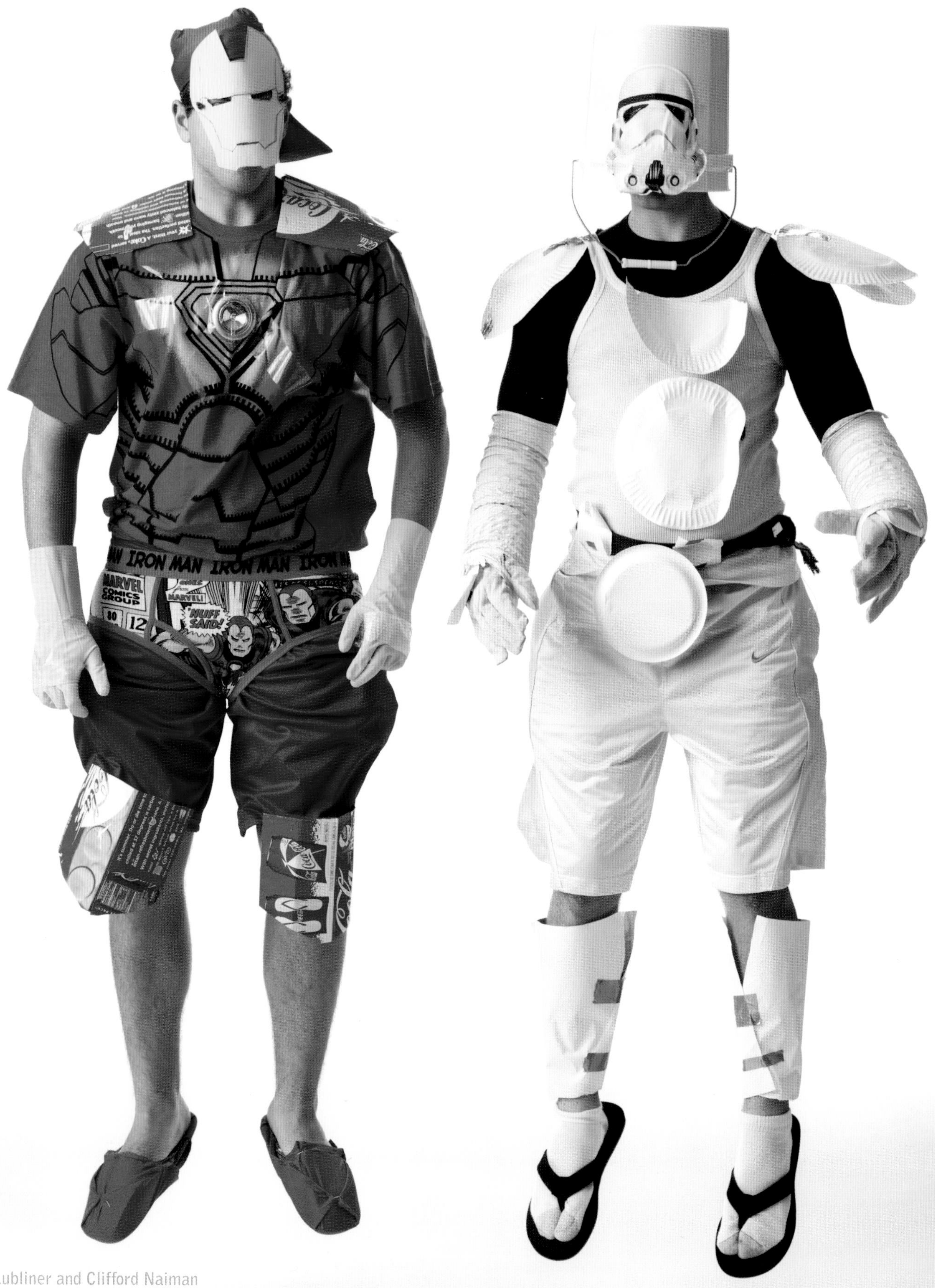
IRON MAN IRON MAN IRON
MARVEL COMICS GROUP
NUFF SAID!

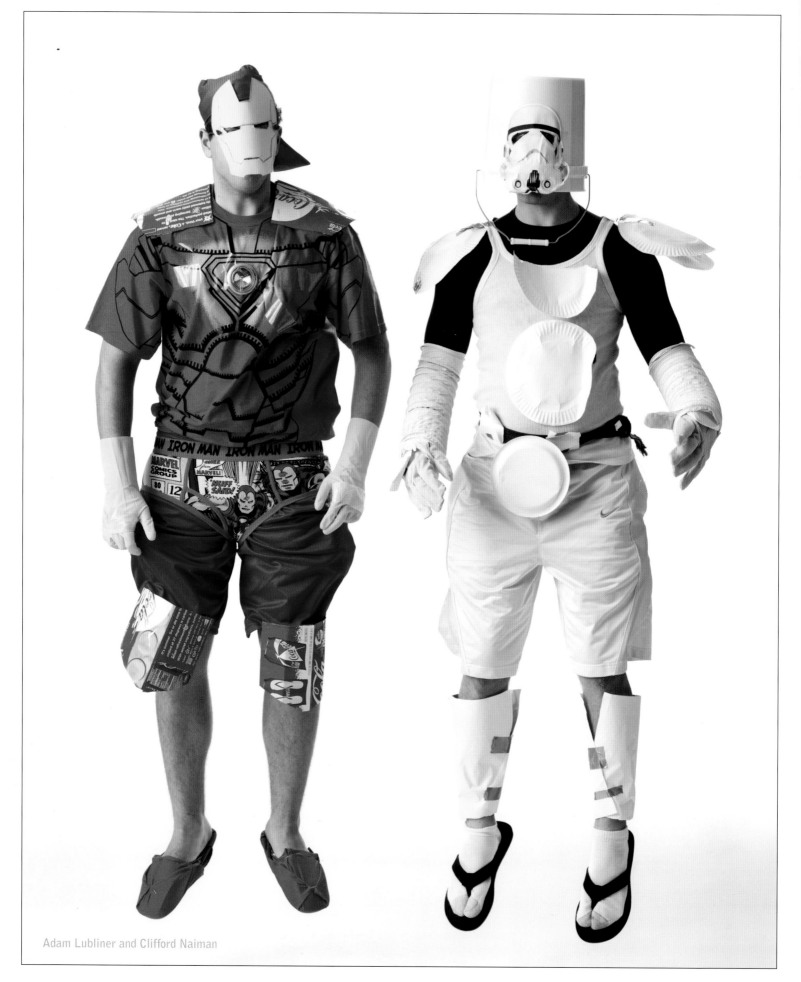

Adam Lubliner and Clifford Naiman

bill plympton

artist, animator | Your Face, Guard Dog

> "Here I can build my fan base, here I can get recognition, here I can go up against the big guys, the Pixars and the Dreamworks, and it levels the playing field. And it's a big opportunity for me to get the word out."

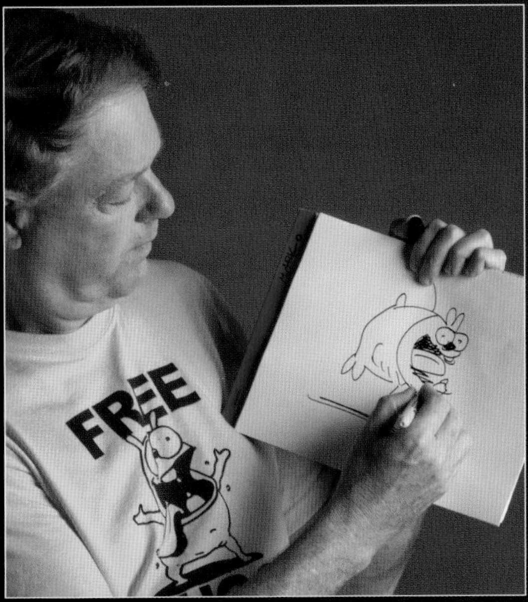
FREE

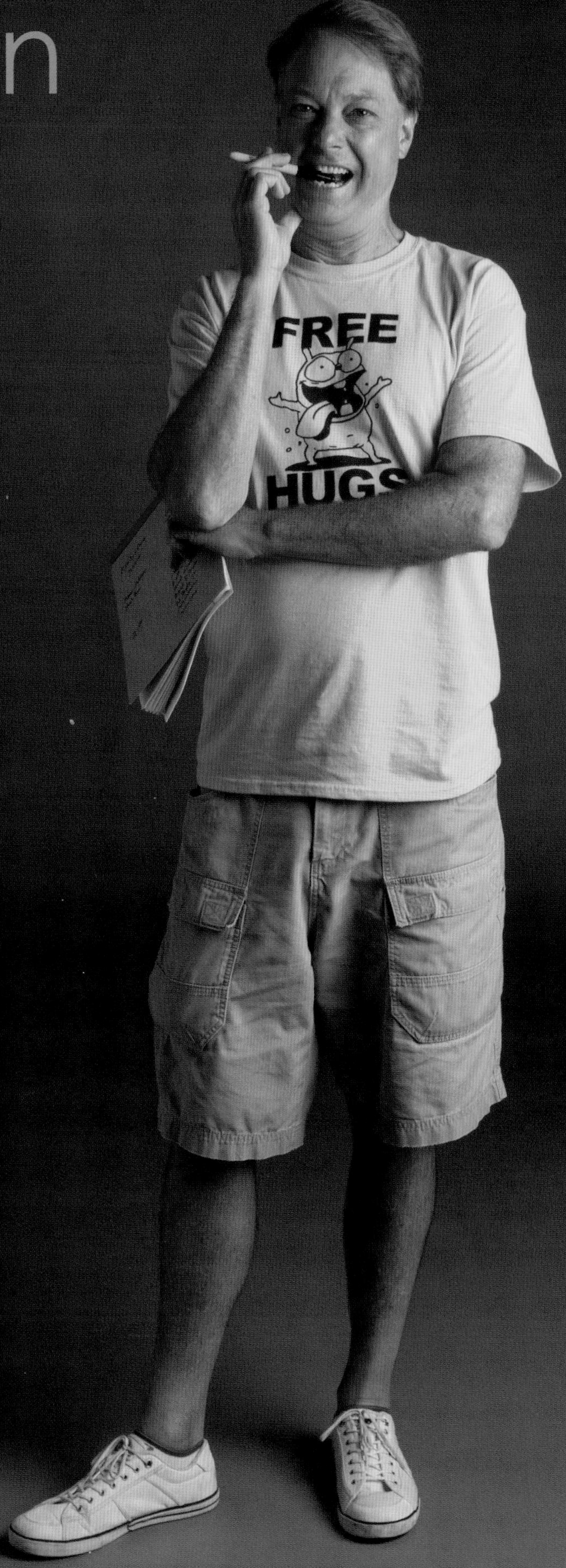
FREE
HUGS

" You get a chance to dress up; you get to disconnect from reality a little bit and be something that you always wanted to be. If justice is at the forefront of your mind, you can be Superman, Captain America, Batman…you can stand for those things here. Things you can't stand for out in the real world sometimes. "

Jeremy Andrew Cross

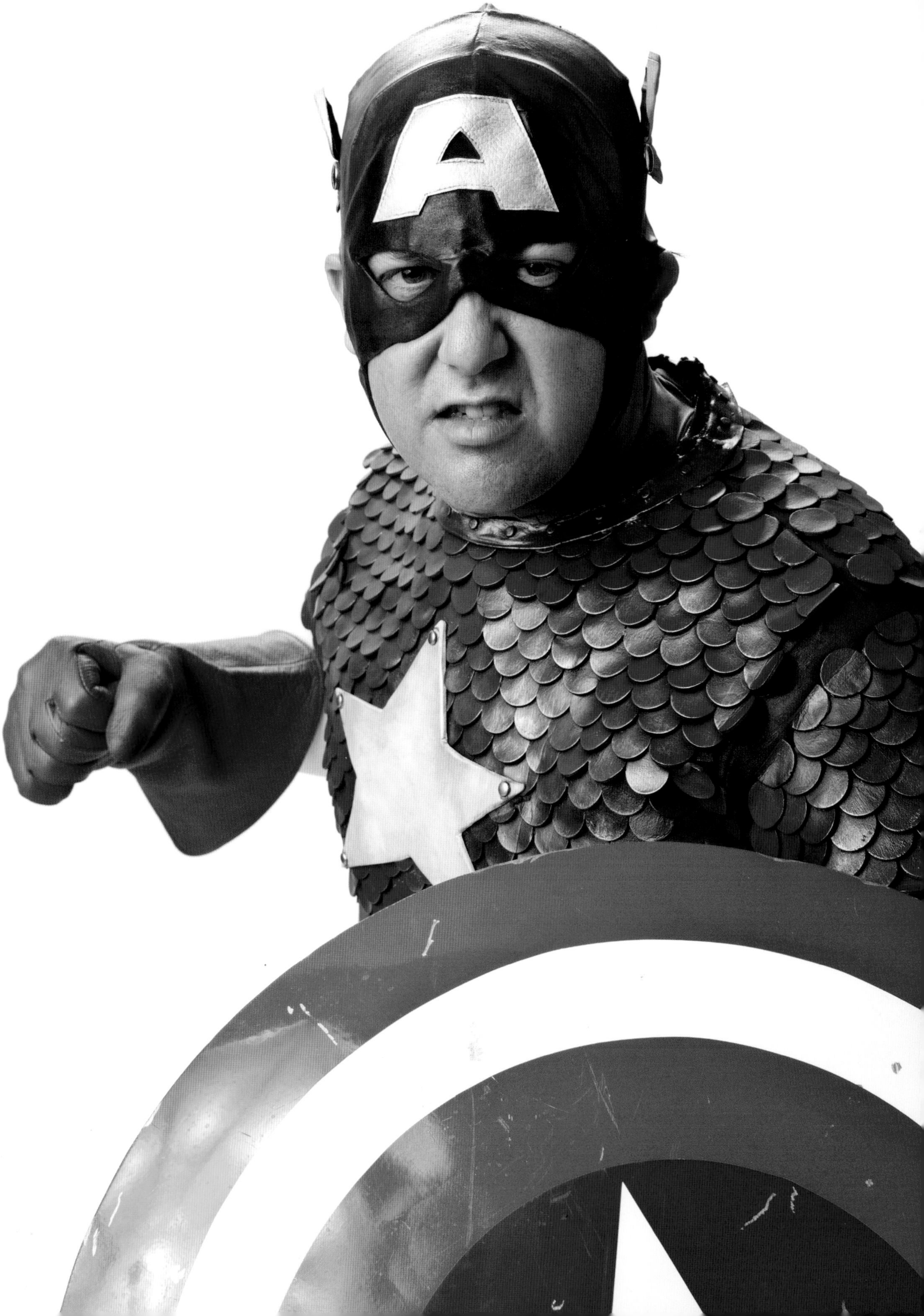

Rex Adams

Rody Knapp-Castillo

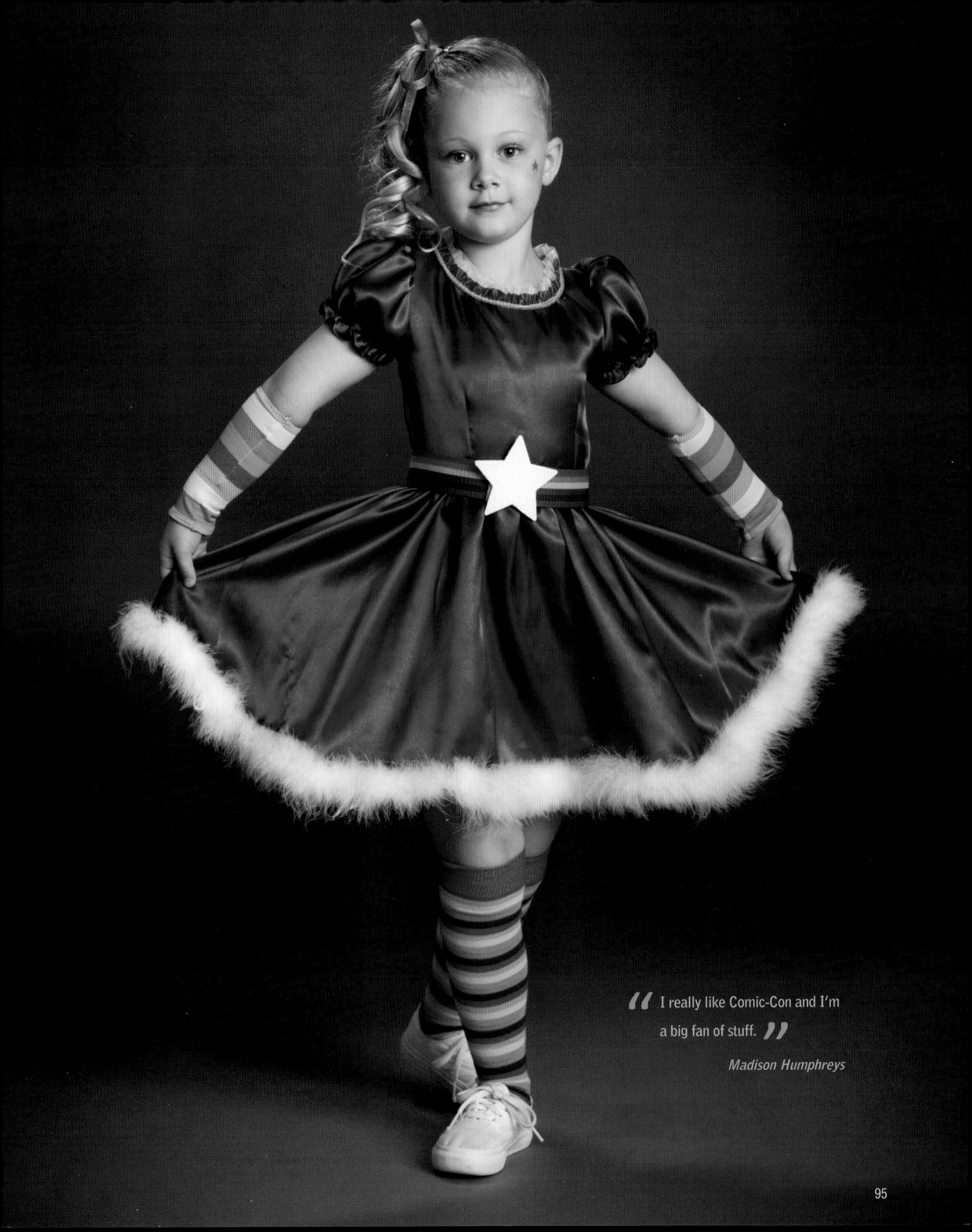

“I really like Comic-Con and I'm a big fan of stuff.”

Madison Humphreys

steve sansweet

director of content management, head of fan relations | LucasFilm

" LucasFilm always gets a great reception for Star Wars; it helps keep the brand alive. And it helps tell the fans that we are listening to them. We want to do what they want us to do. "

Daniel DeWayne Enlow

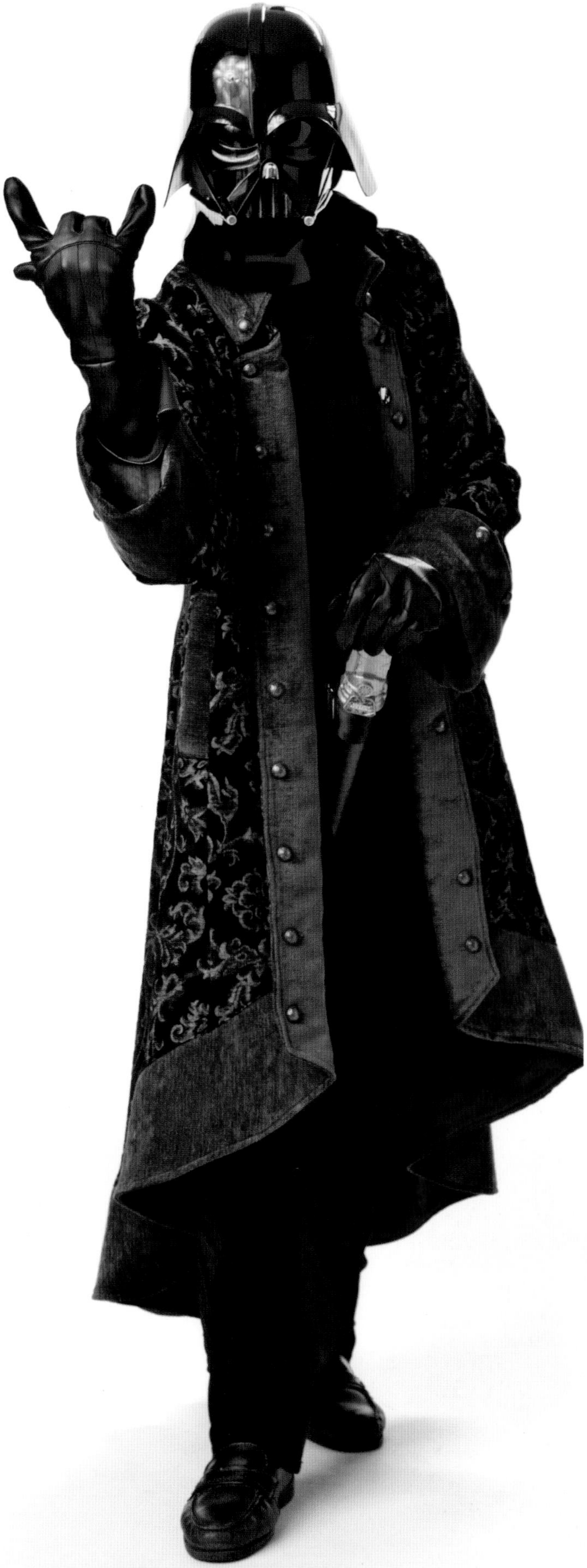

David Lawrence James

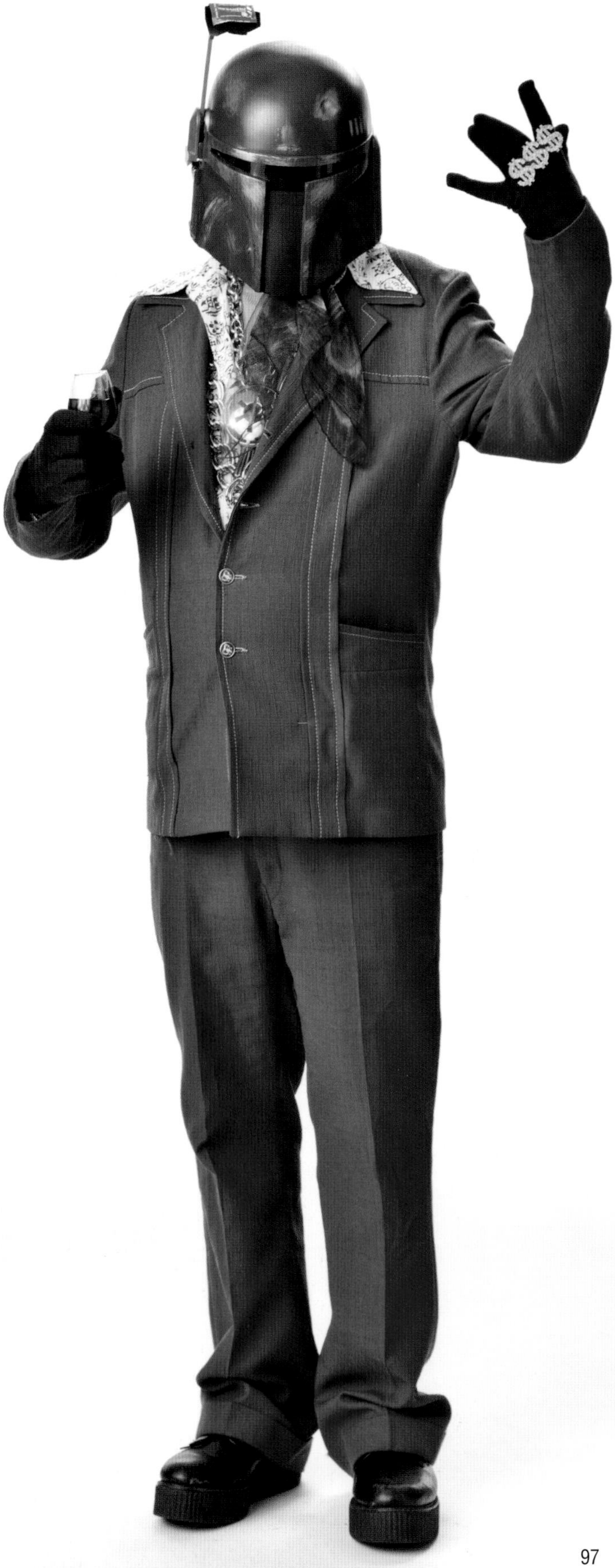

anastasia betts
comic book expert

The authors and artists here I have found to be very relatable. It's easy to connect with them and to share the experiences that we have with their books.

kearsten labrozzi
librarian

It's really just changing the perception of comics; it's not just superheroes— although those are definitely fun and they have their place. But there's so much more to comics than just that.

naysan mojgani
cosplay expert

You think of an audience as somebody who just sits there and consumes, but things like cosplay show that there's a lot more back-and-forth going on than you think.

deb aoki
manga expert

Because of manga, there are more girl creators, and more girl fans.

dave dorman

artist

It's a cross-section of humanity that I don't think you really get in any other area of a social gathering. Comics and entertainment cross the lines of age, race, and religion.

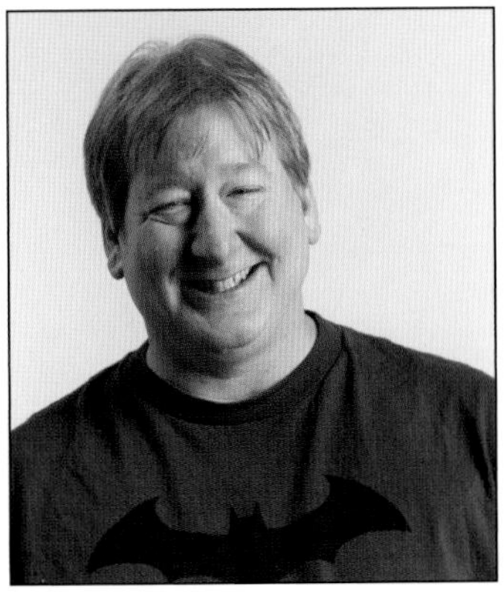

melissa rosenberg

screenwriter | Twilight series

I think it's finally come out that, the truth of the matter is, geeks are usually the smartest people in the room. So it doesn't surprise me that they are eventually talking over the world.

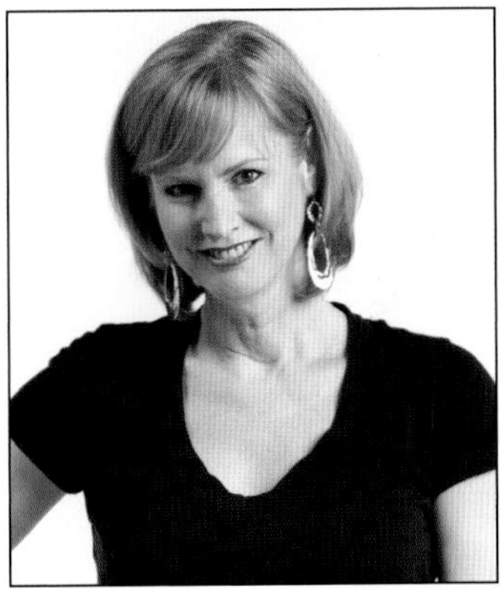

mike henry

writer, voice actor | Family Guy, The Cleveland Show

Last year, I was on the floor and saw Adam West. I know Adam West from working on *Family Guy*, and I was walking toward him—and I realized that he was talking to Lou Ferrigno. That was the quintessential Comic-Con moment for me.

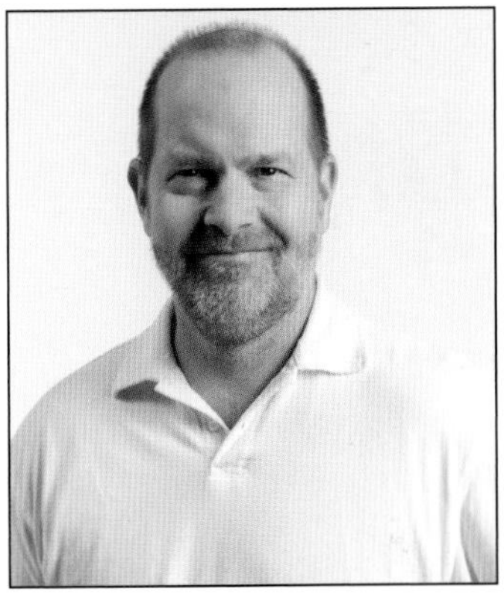

tim biskup

artist

It's this pop-culture thing that is all about what comics gave birth to and what film gave birth to—and everything in this giant creation realm.

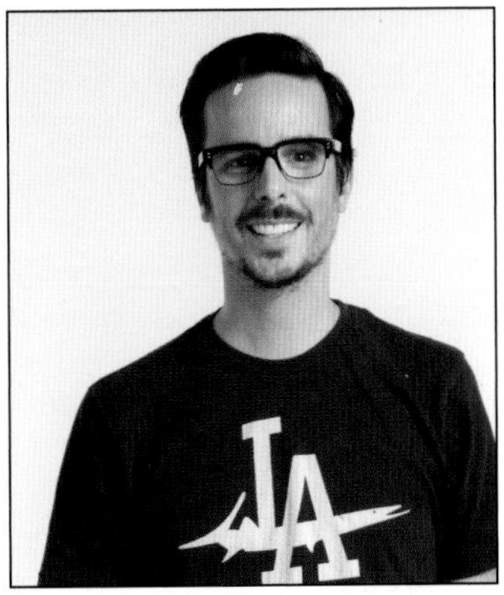
LA

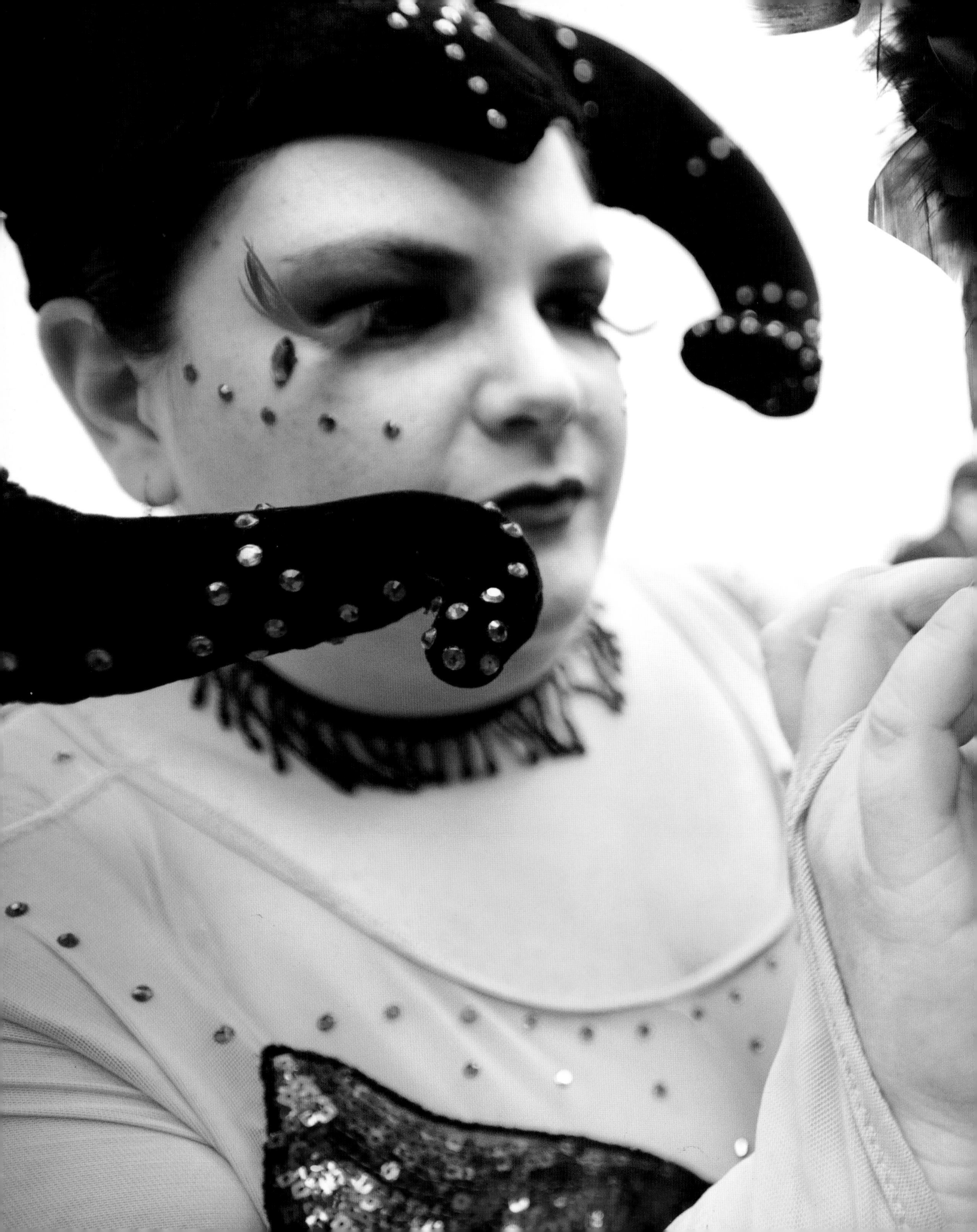

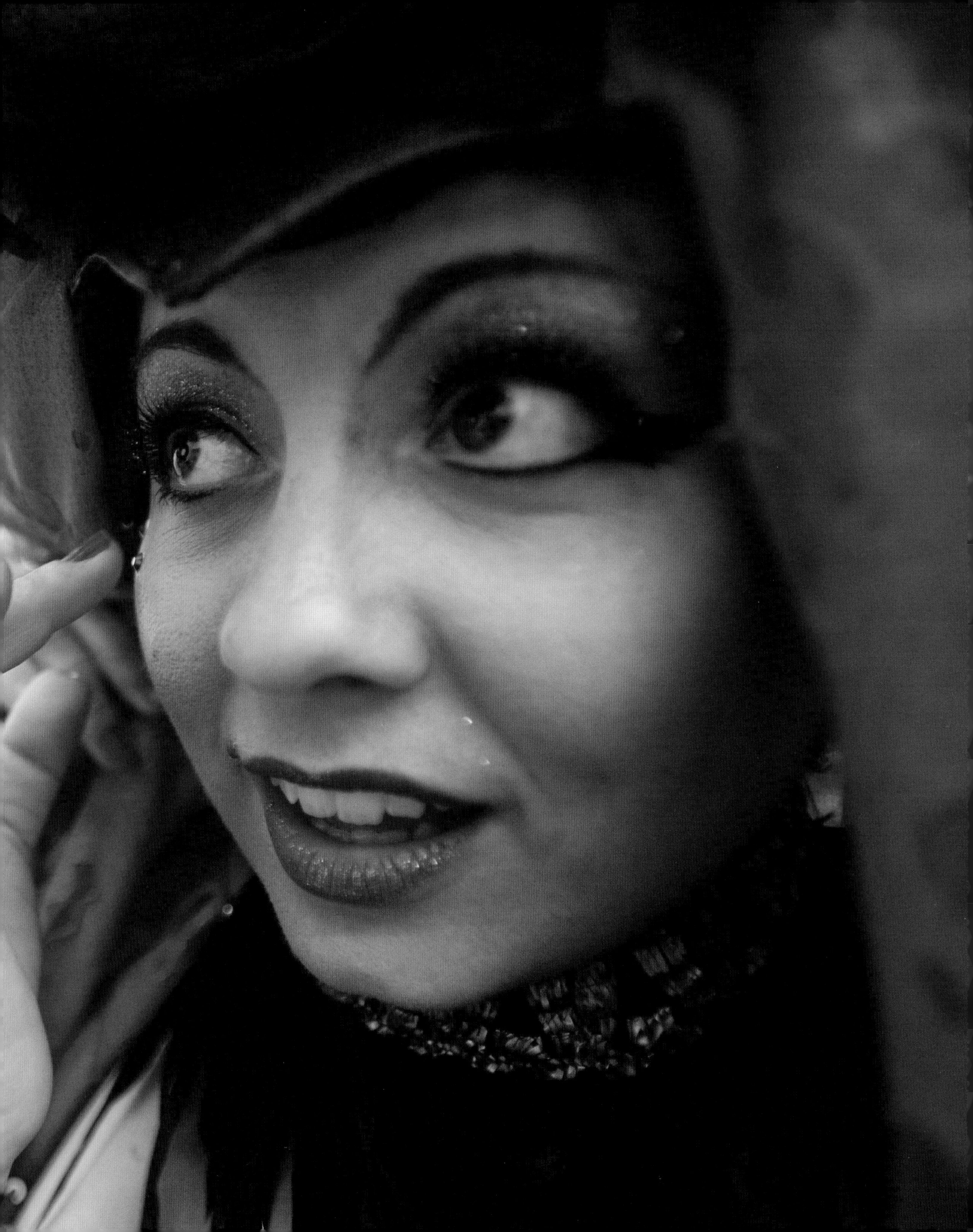

Kirk Handbury and Ramee

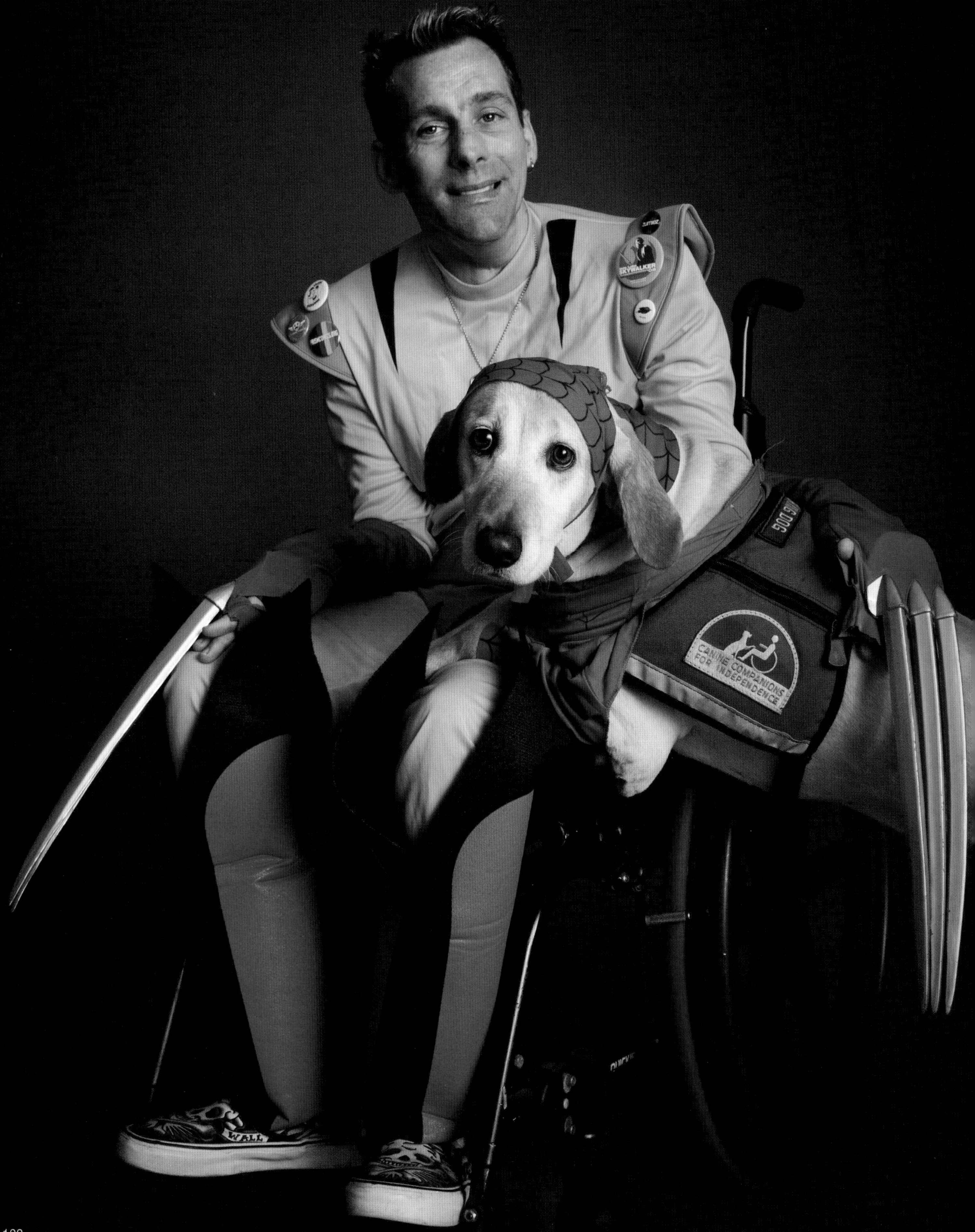
SKYWALKER
CANINE COMPANIONS FOR INDEPENDENCE
WALL

gerard way

musician, comic book creator | The Umbrella Academy

" If you can't get accepted in a
place where the unaccepted come,
where do you go? Where do you
fit in then? I think as comic fans,
we're all, to some extent, slightly
unaccepted. "

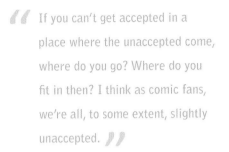

" I love the panels. I get to do this panel every year that's now starting to become a tradition. It's really just fun—we don't
have an agenda, we don't sell anything, we're not plugging anything…we just kind of make it an open forum and we talk
about whatever. That could really only happen here. I can't do that at an arena. I can't do that after a show. You can only
really do that here. "

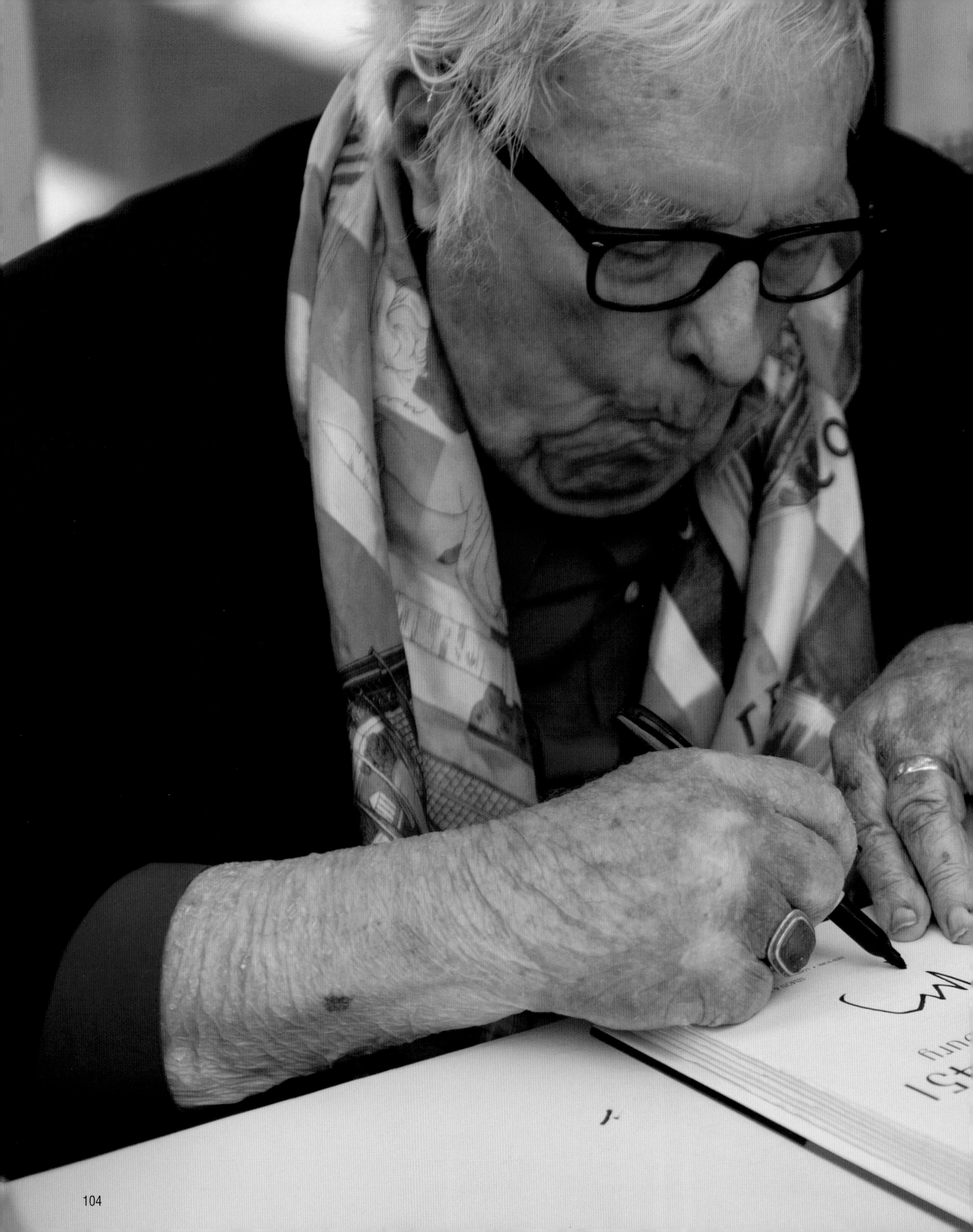

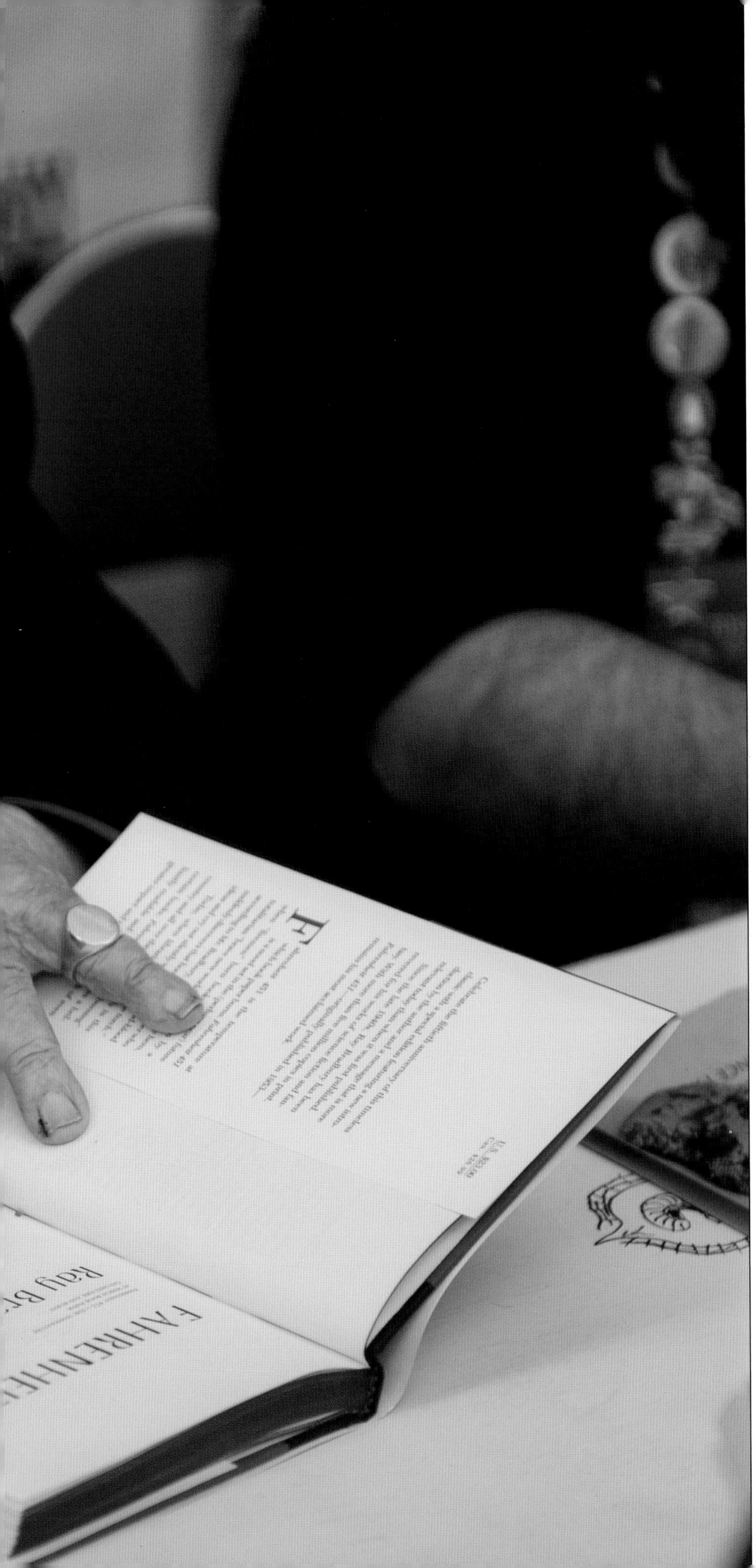

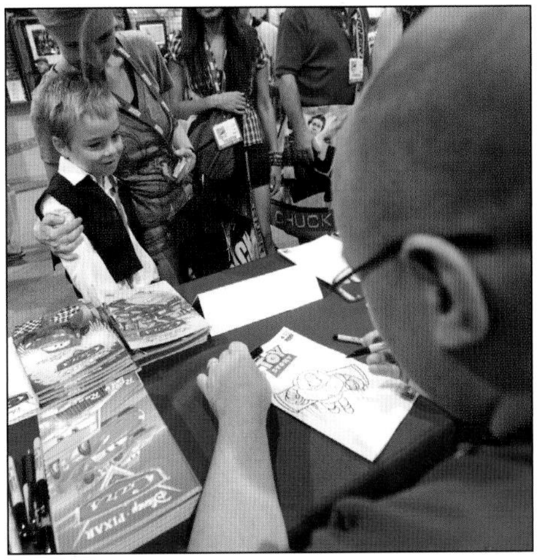
PIXAR

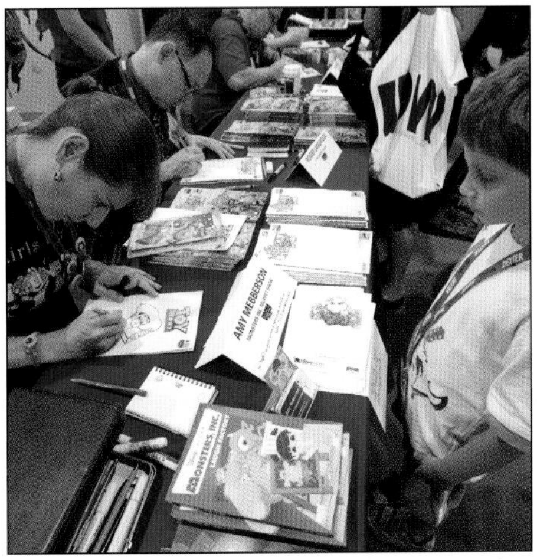
AMY MEBBERSON
MONSTERS, INC.

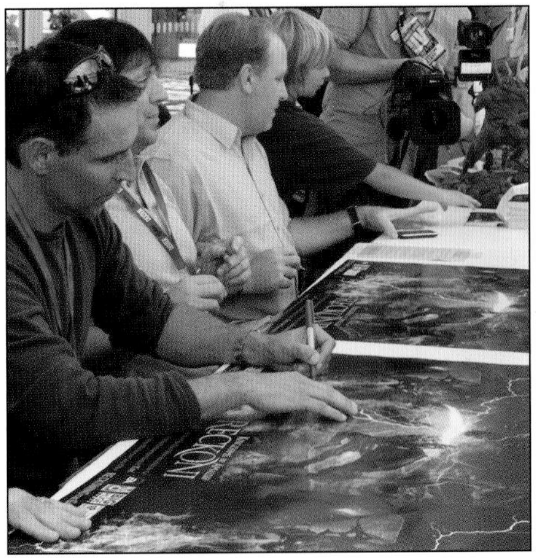

Ray Bradbury

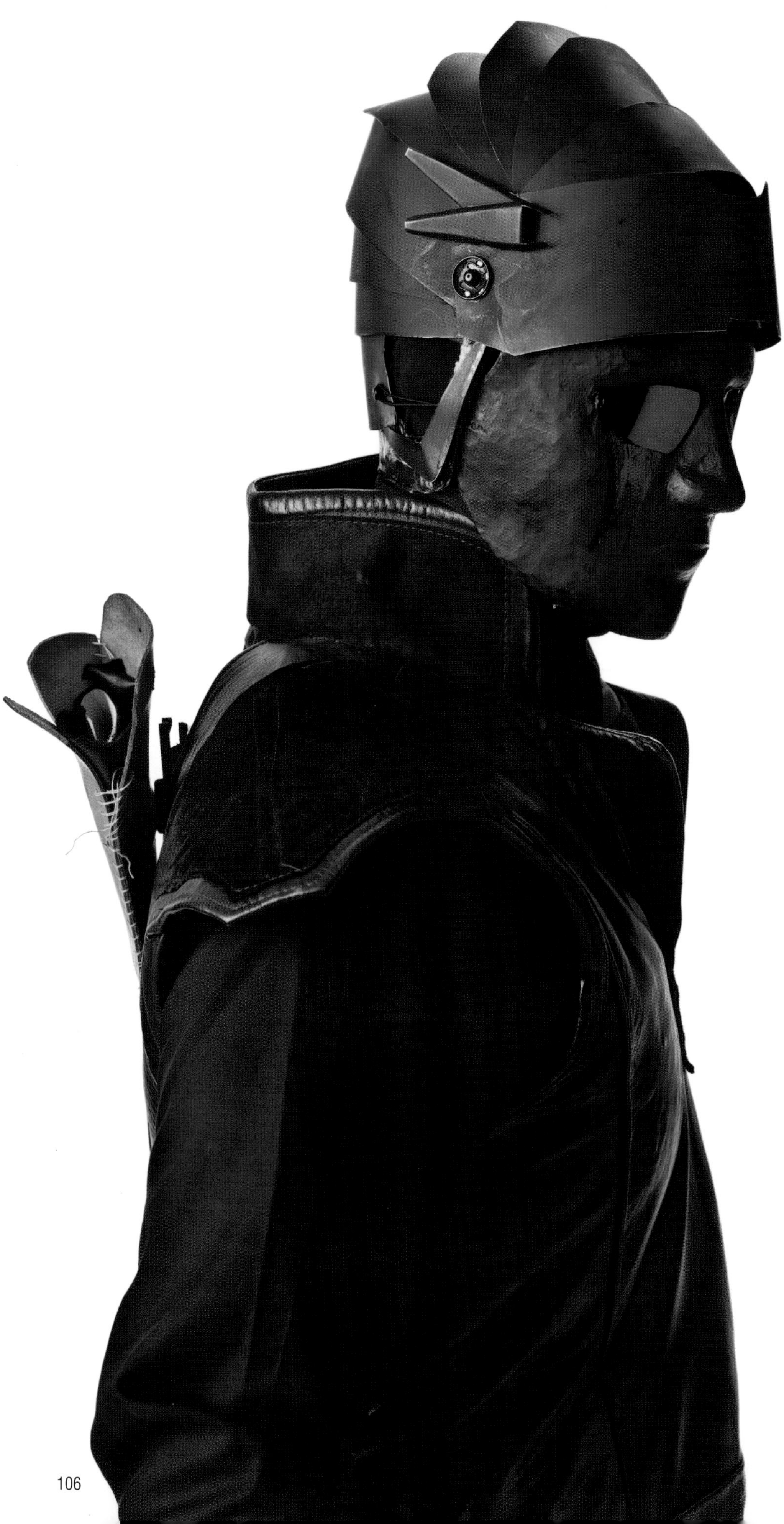

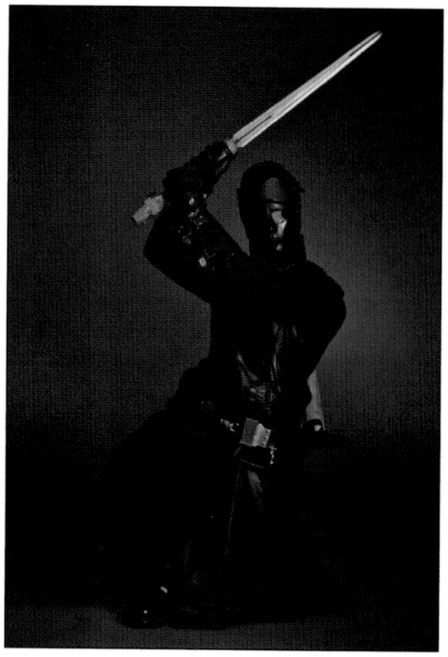

"Superheroes are who people turn to in times of despair or need, and that is certainly shown today. So I think in a way, it's kind of a symbiotic relationship that Hollywood and Comic-Con share, even though it's a little fragile at times."

Alex Serra

ellen page

actress | Hard Candy, X-Men: The Last Stand, Inception

" *Mother Come Home* floored me...I've shared it with so many people. And if I were to meet Paul Hornschemeier...I mean, his work is something that I always look out for and am just consistently blown away by. If I were to get to meet someone whose work had an impact like that on my life in a really, really sincere way, I would be just so thrilled. "

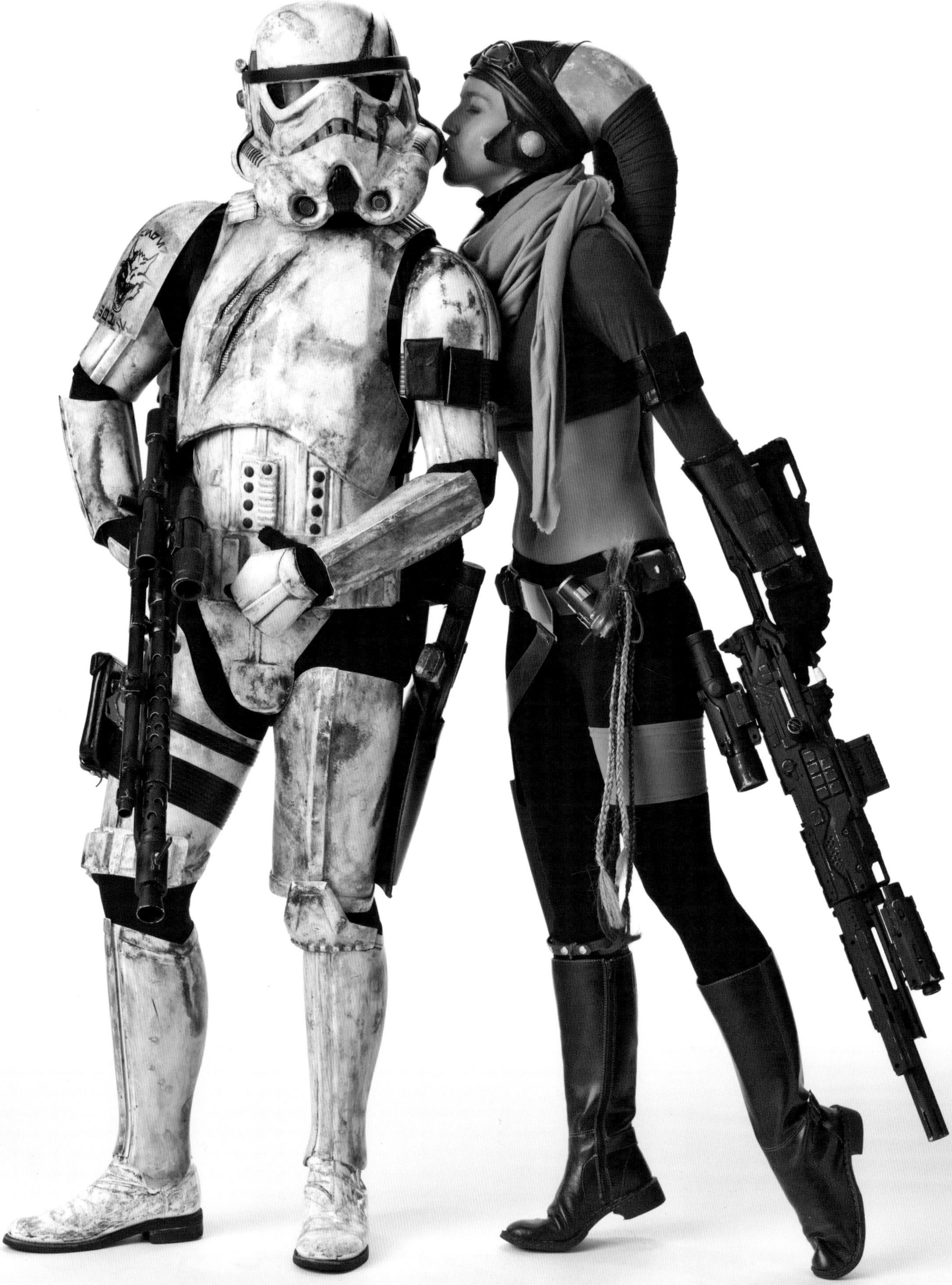

Sean Condon and Stephanie Gutowski

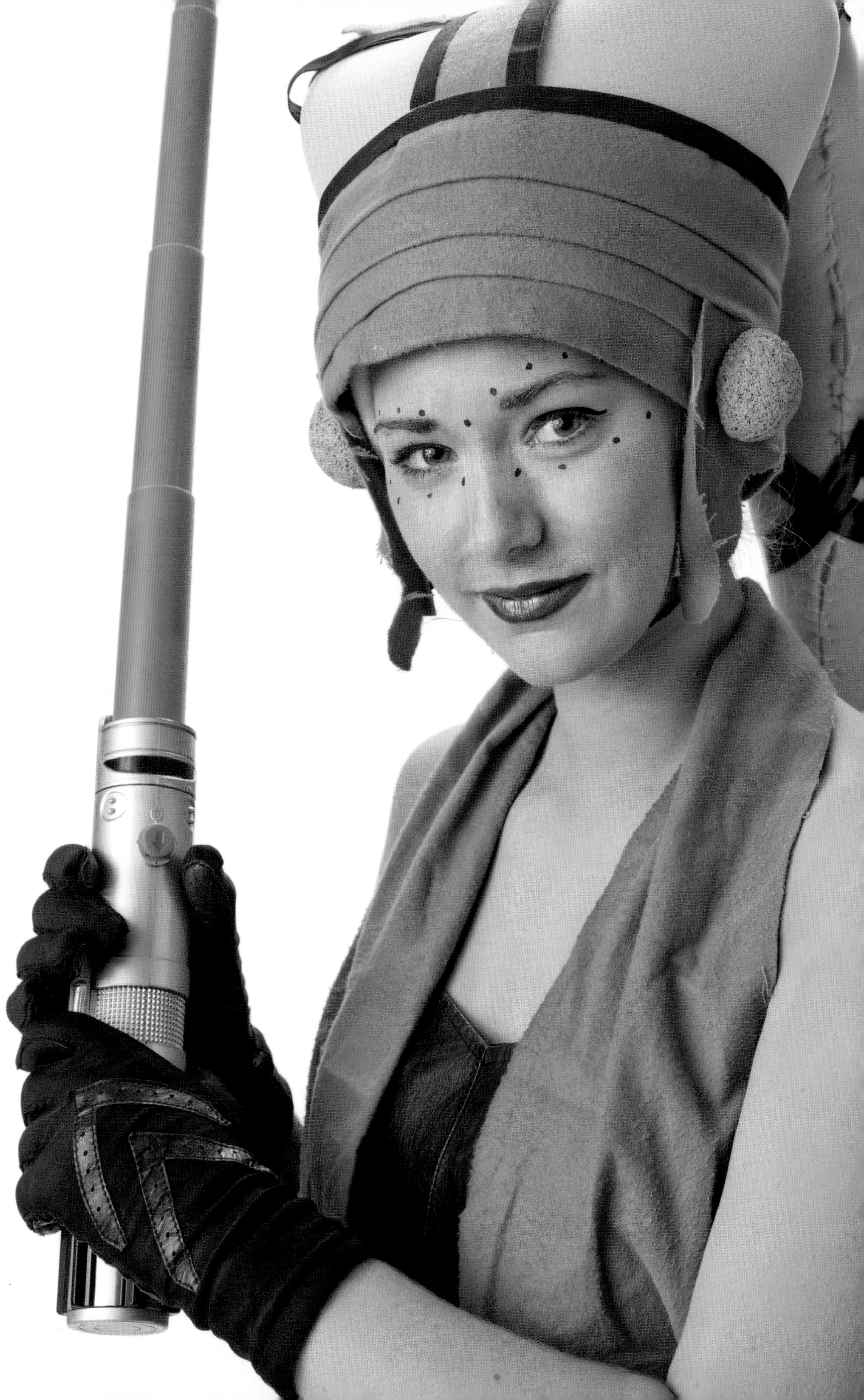

Sarah Daniels

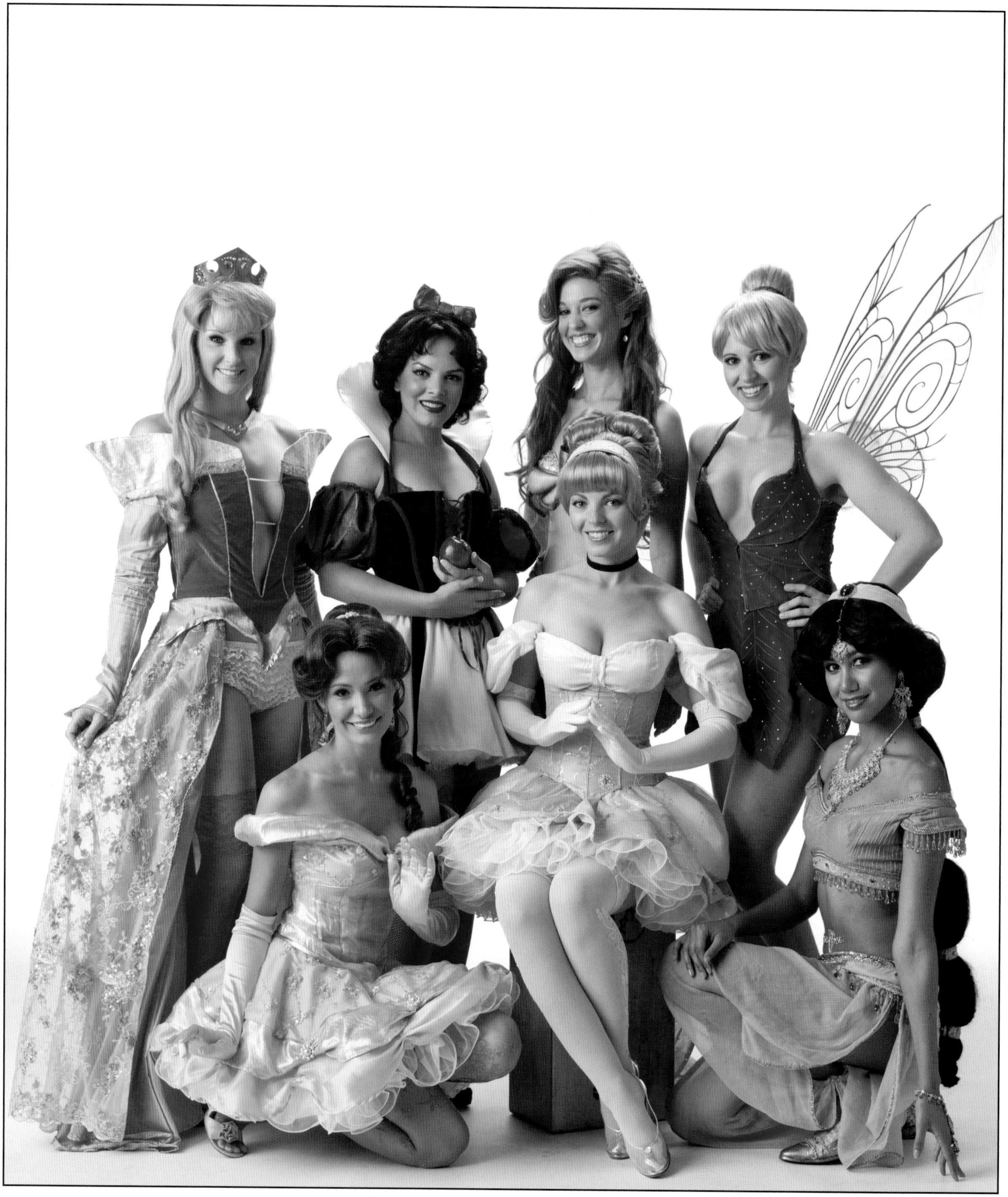

(top row, left to right) Kristen Erickson, Heather Harris, Christy Marie, Becky Young; (bottom row, left to right) Jennifer Newman, Kat Lynn, Marissa Kelly

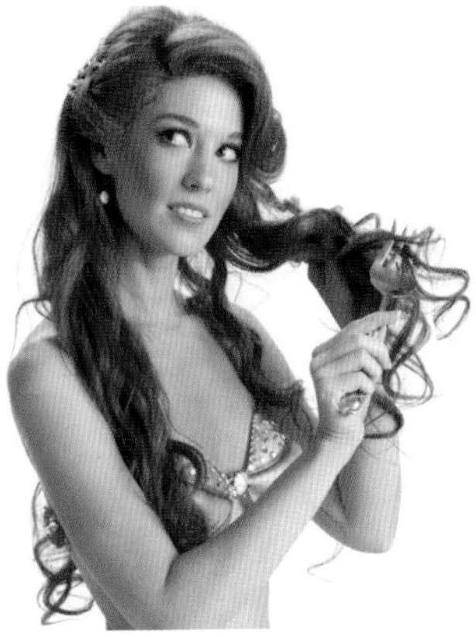

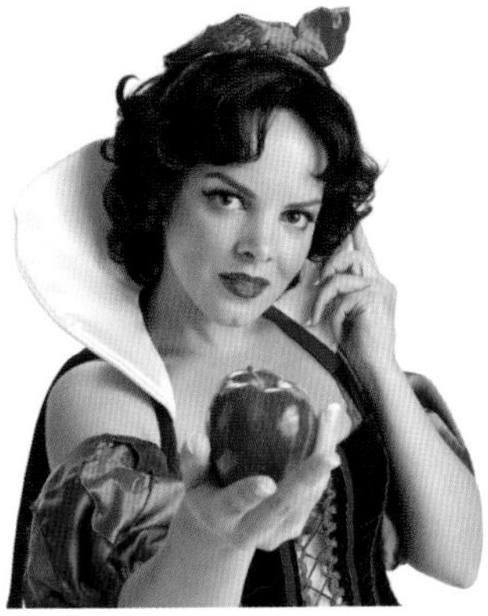

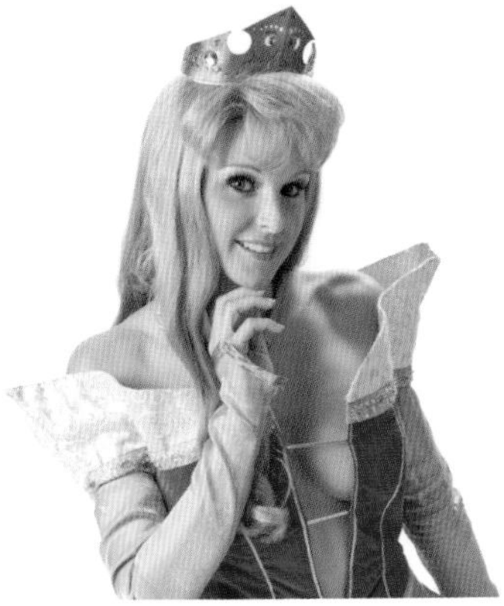

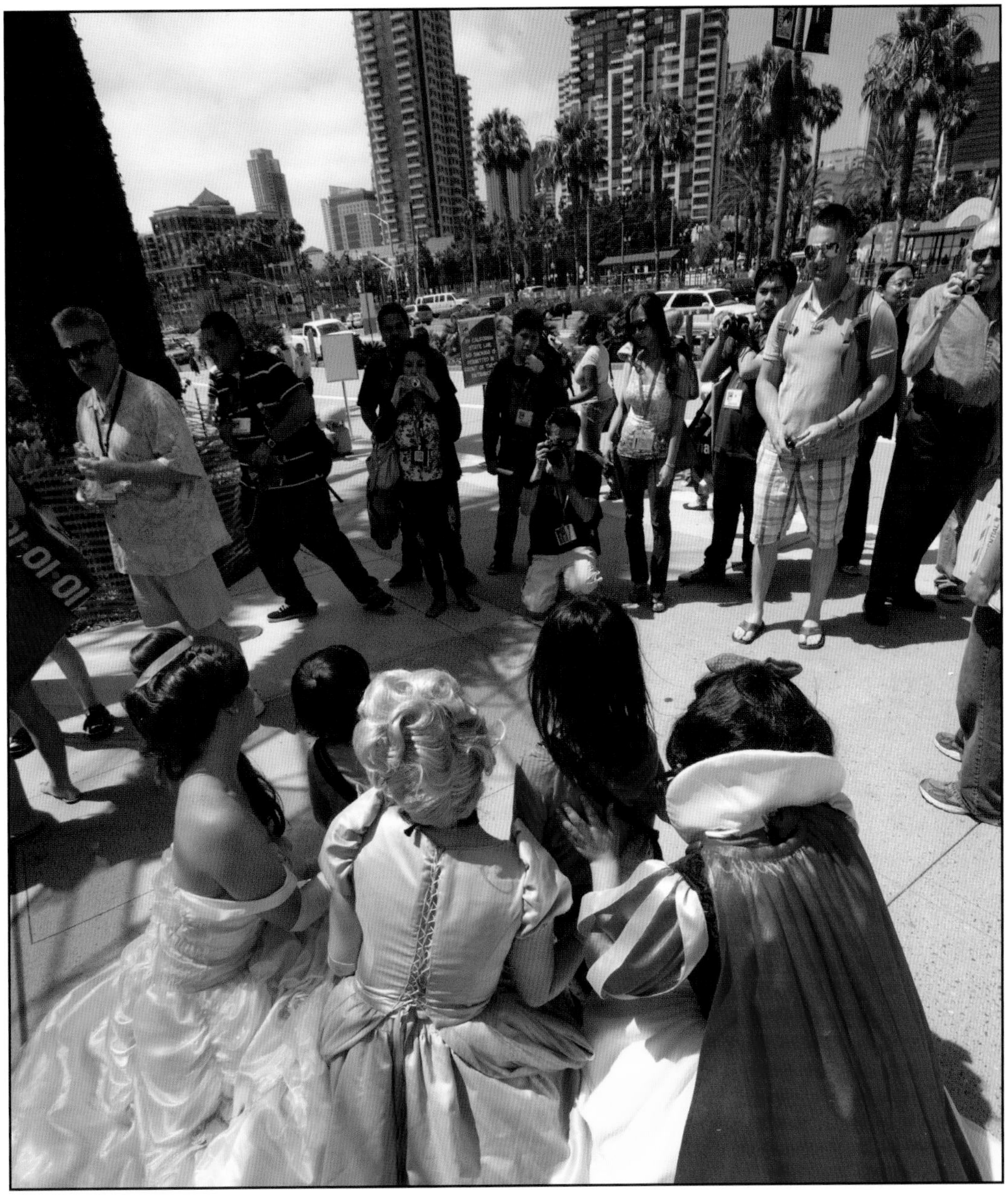

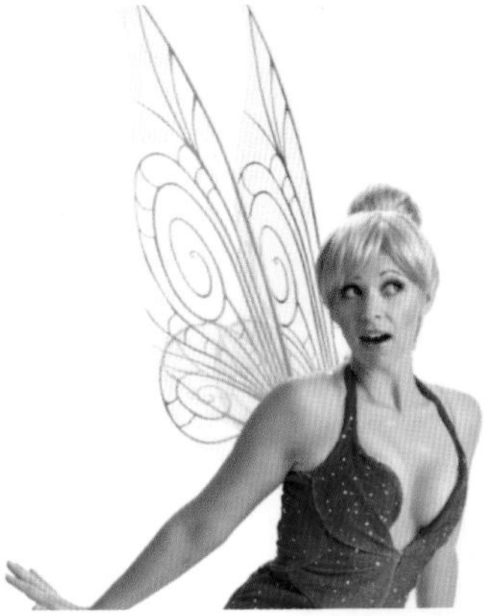

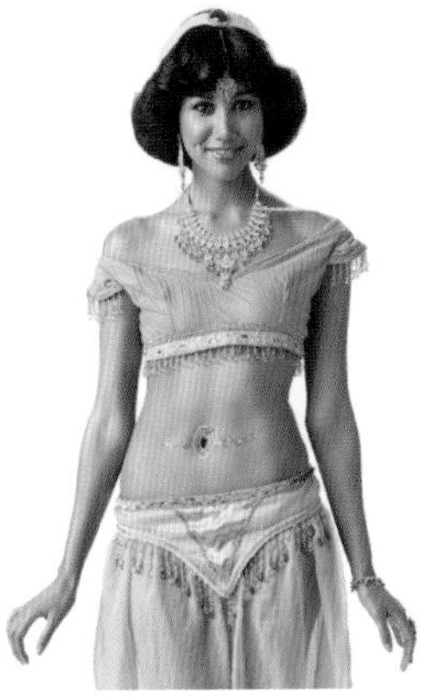

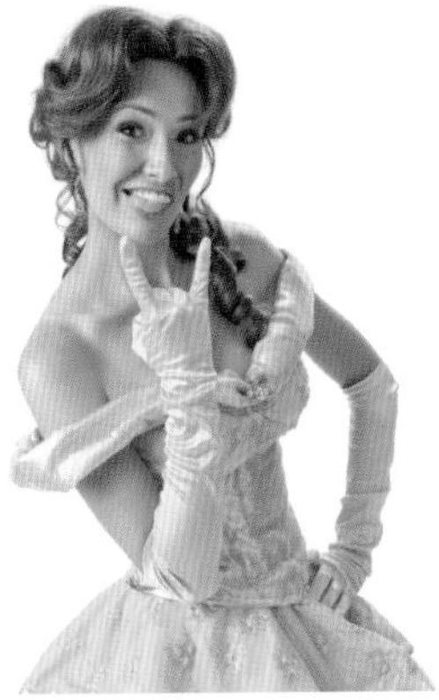

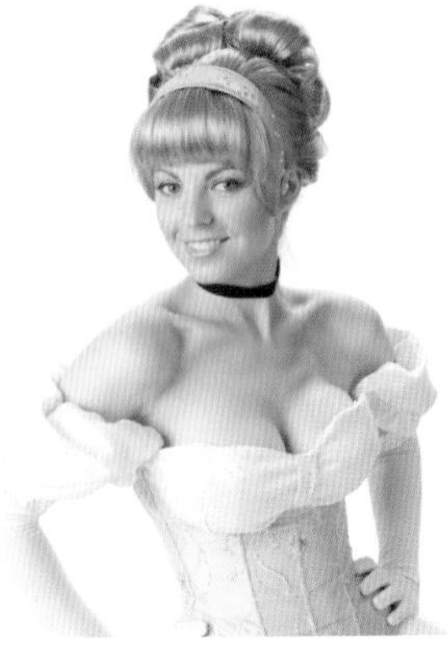

> “I love getting reactions from kids especially. It's so much fun as a character that's so easily recognizable and loved by so many kids and adults, but it's the kids' eyes. When they light up and they run after you and say, 'Tinkerbell!' You really feel that you brought some kind of magic to their day.”

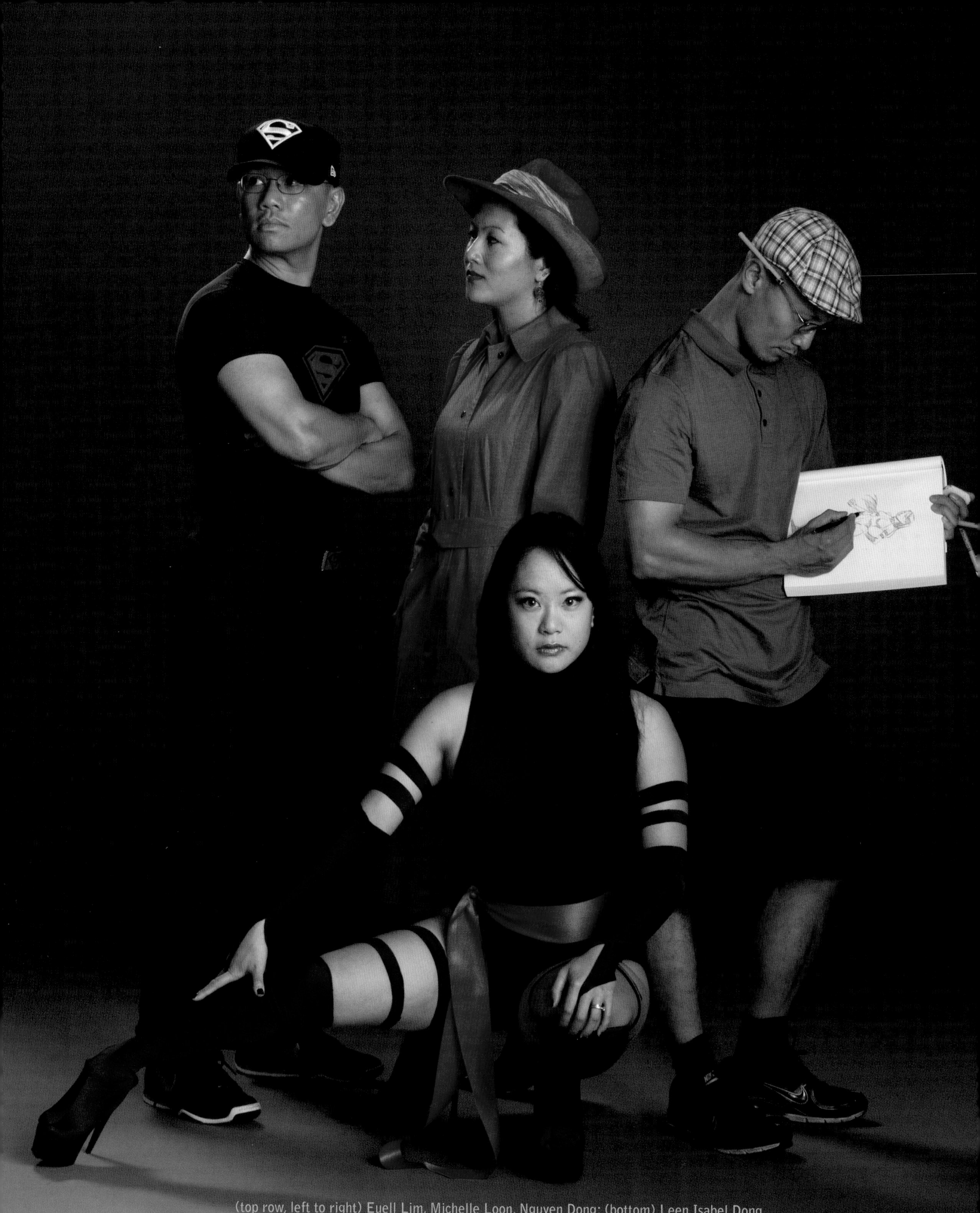

(top row, left to right) Euell Lim, Michelle Loon, Nguyen Dong; (bottom) Leen Isabel Dong

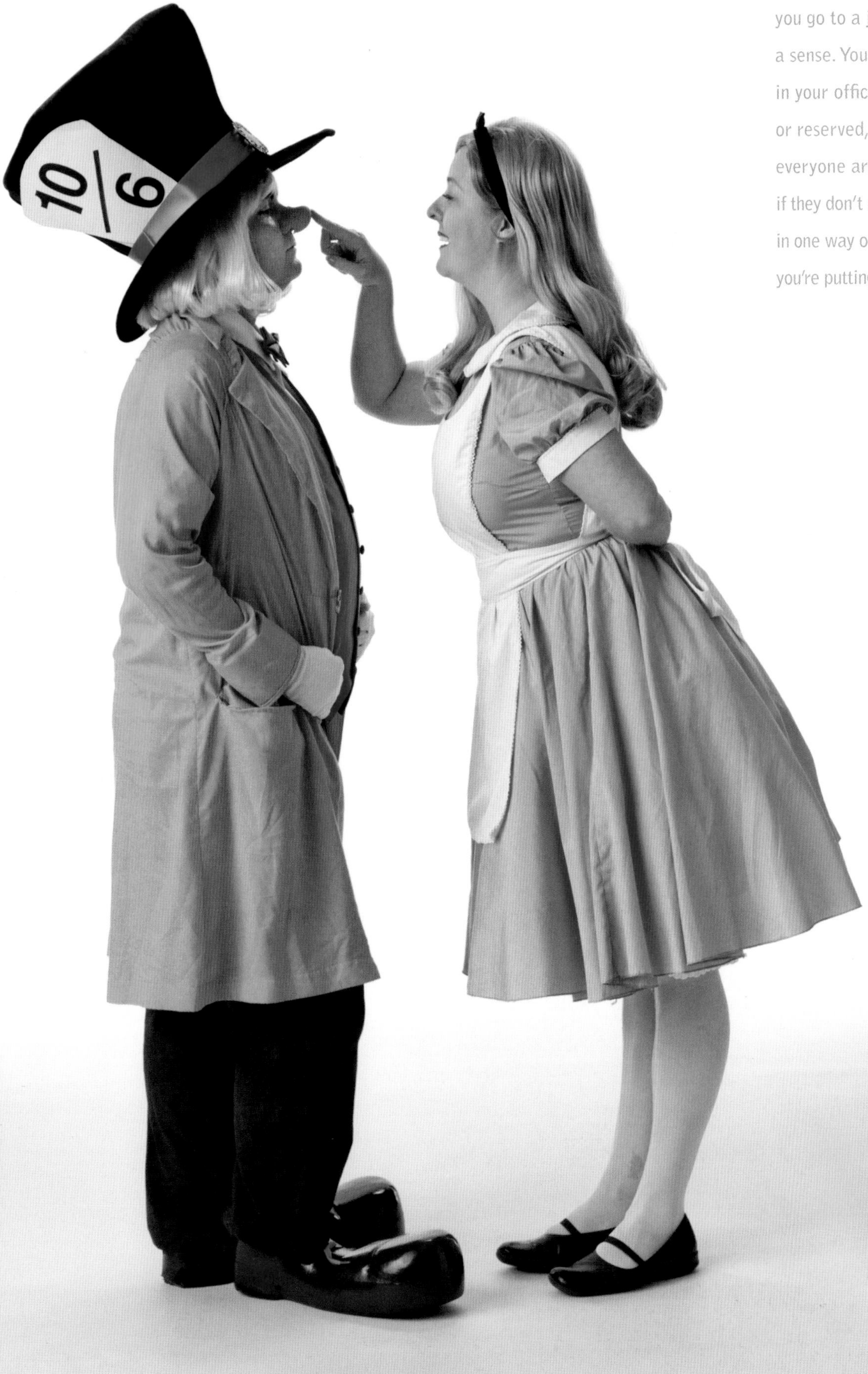

10
6

" Day to day, it's like anyone else. You get up in the morning, you put on your clothes, you go to a job. You sort of fall invisible, in a sense. You become as gray as the walls in your office...you don't feel restricted or reserved, or in any way inhibited. And everyone around you is the same way. Even if they don't necessarily know the character, in one way or another they appreciate what you're putting out there. "

Dan Rutherford and Kelly Bailey

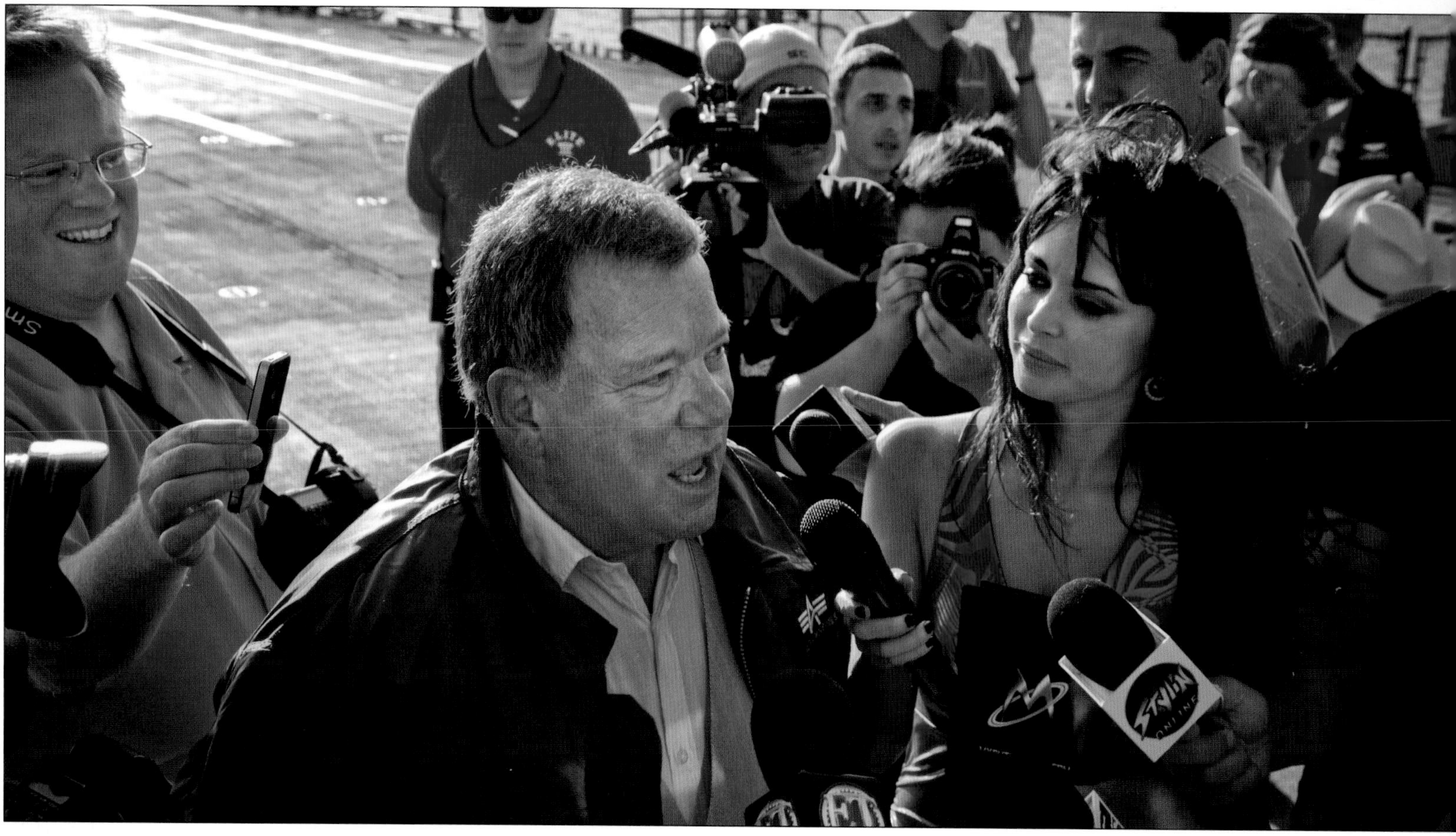

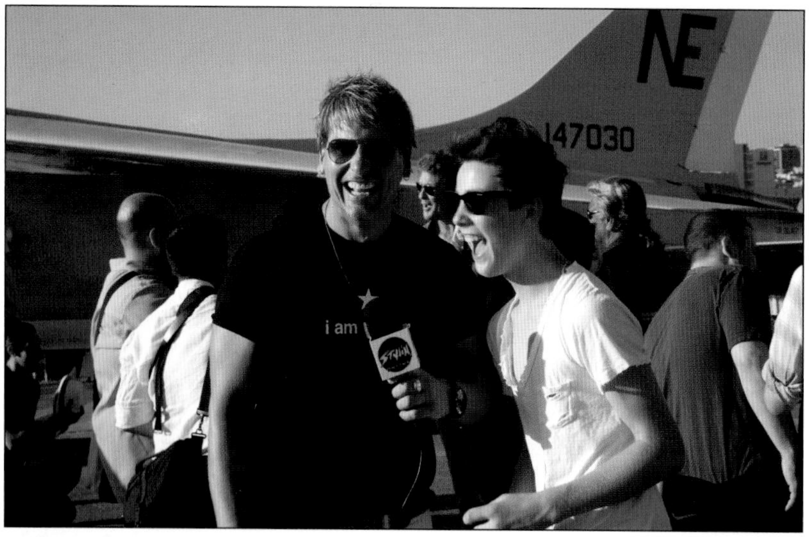
NE
147030
i am

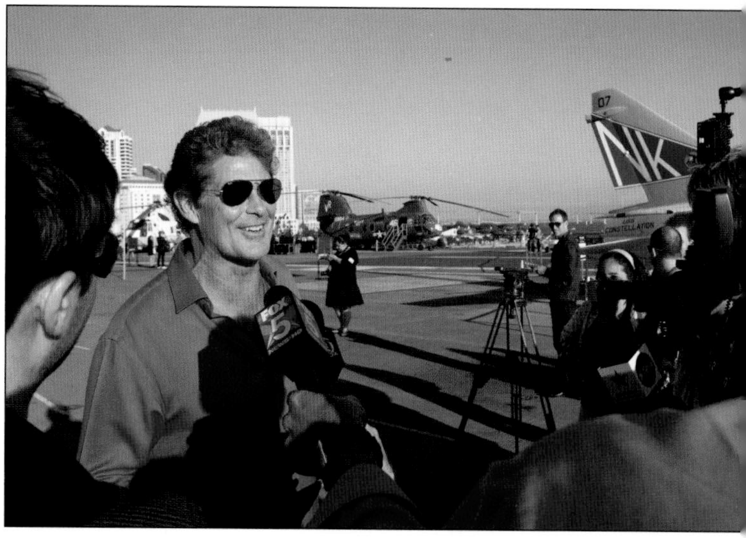
NK

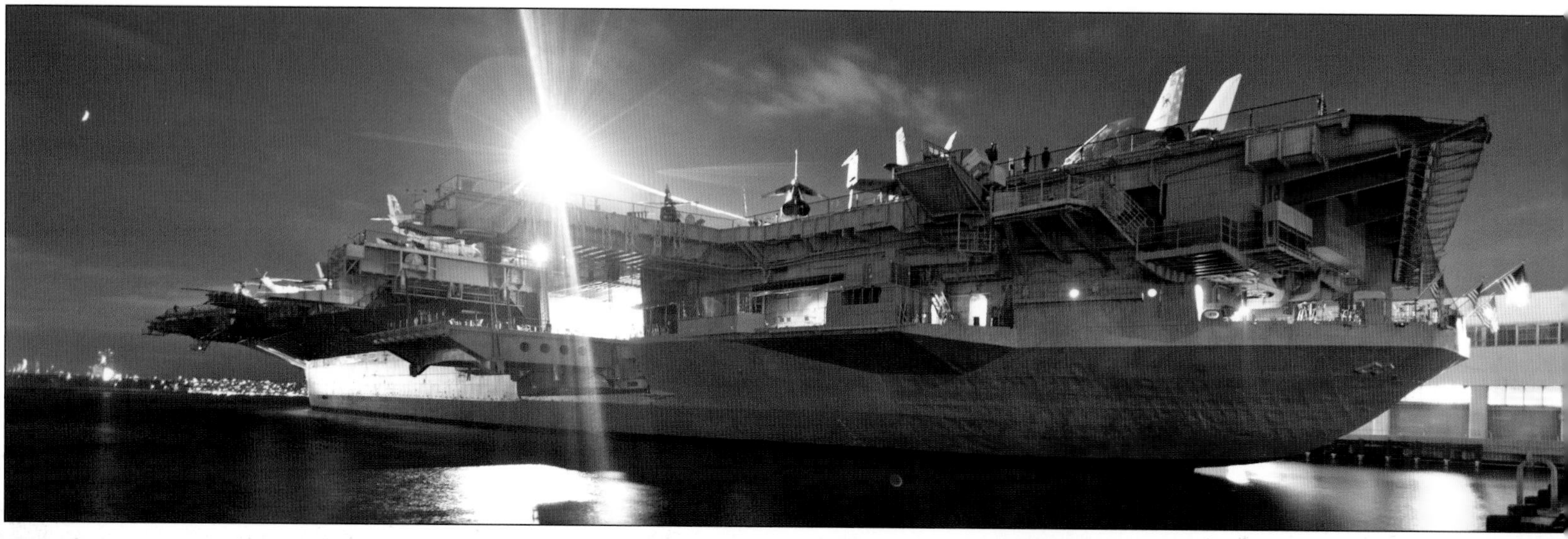

"During the question-and-answer portion after the *Iron* panel, there were identical twin fans who asked questions in tandem. One of them would start the question and the other would finish the sentence. And they had the exact same voice. It was just so surreal—but so cool, and kind of normal. I feel like eccentric people are welcome here."

Olivia Wilde

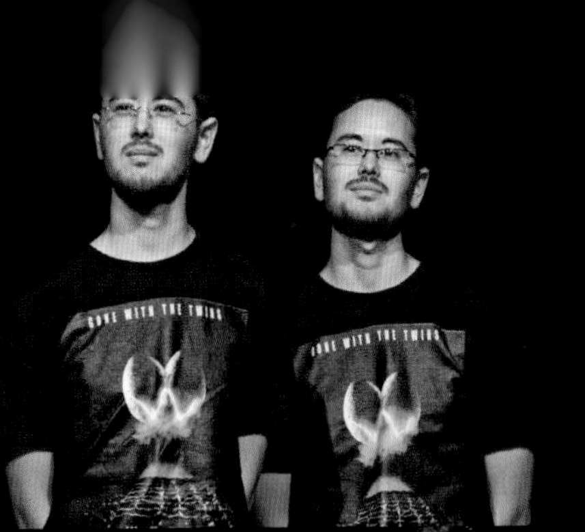
GONE WITH THE TWINS

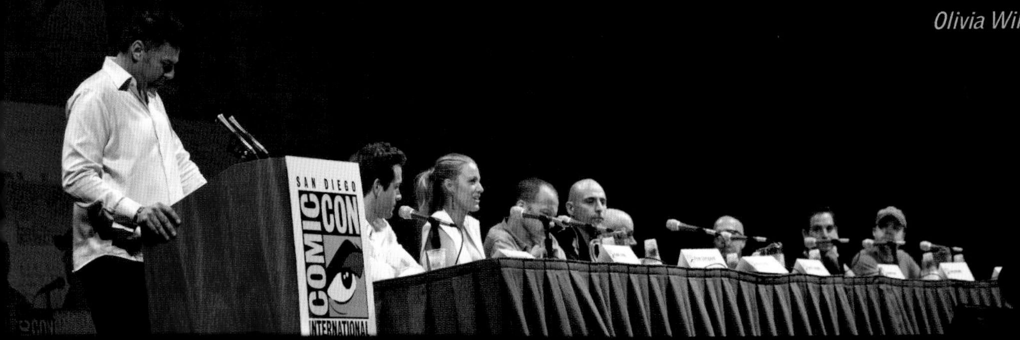
SAN DIEGO
COMIC CON
INTERNATIONAL

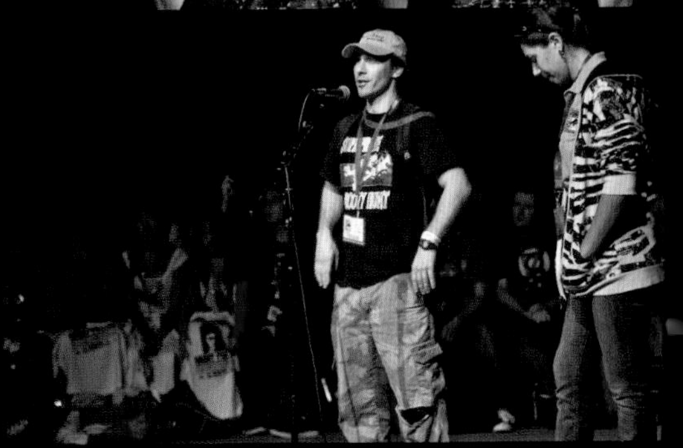

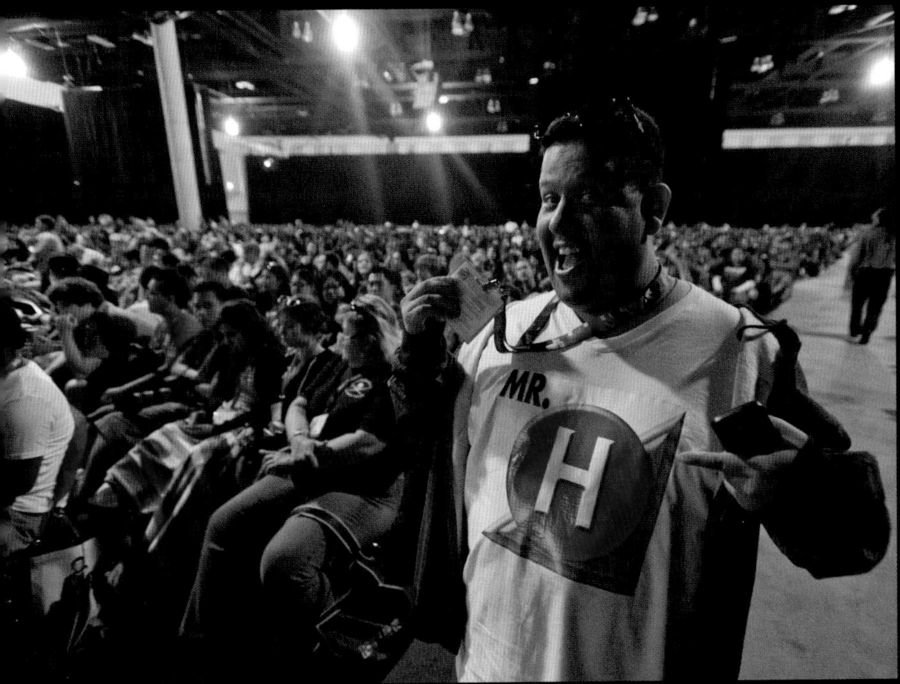
MR.
H

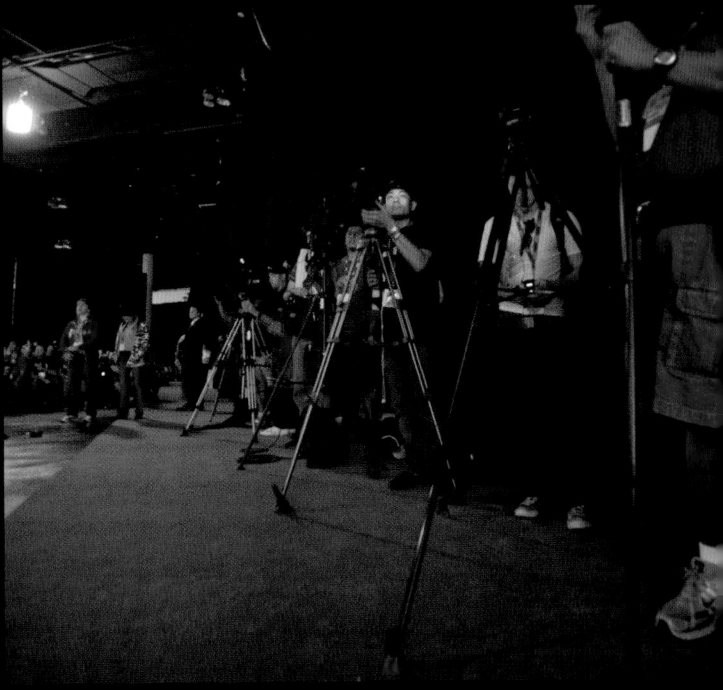

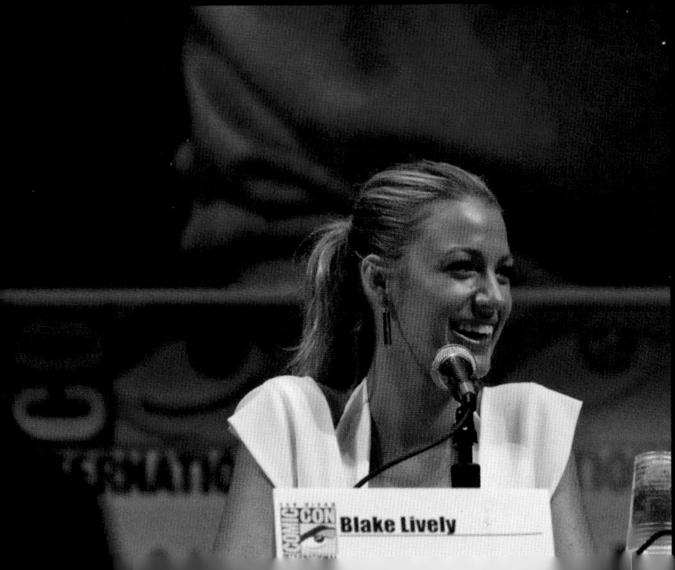
Blake Lively

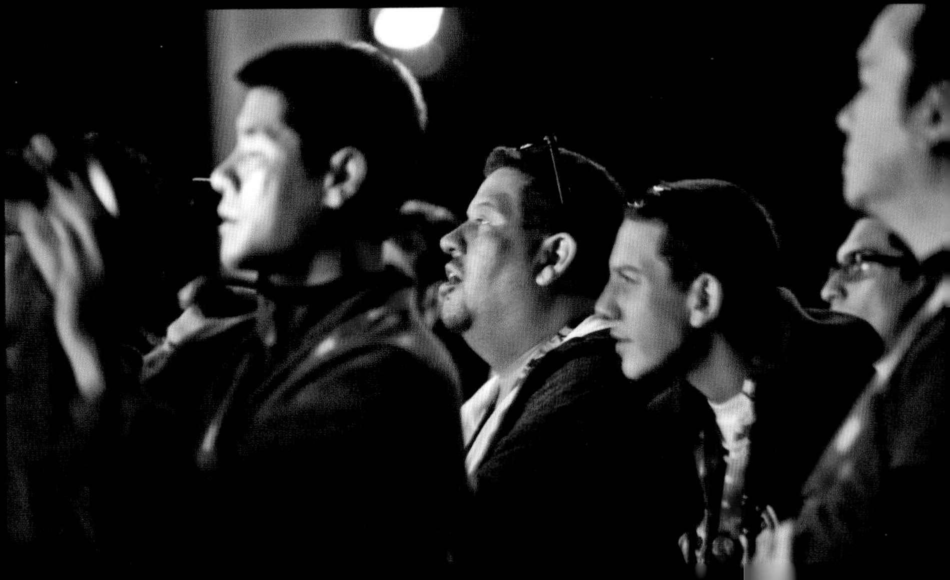

corey feldman

actor | The Lost Boys

" Where else are you going to get the opportunity to find five hundred thousand like-minded individuals in one place? "

Corey Feldman

jamison newlander

actor | The Lost Boys

" They have respect for fans here, in a way that I haven't seen in other places. And I think that the fans feel that, and that's why the fans keep coming. And it just builds and builds. "

Jamison Newlander

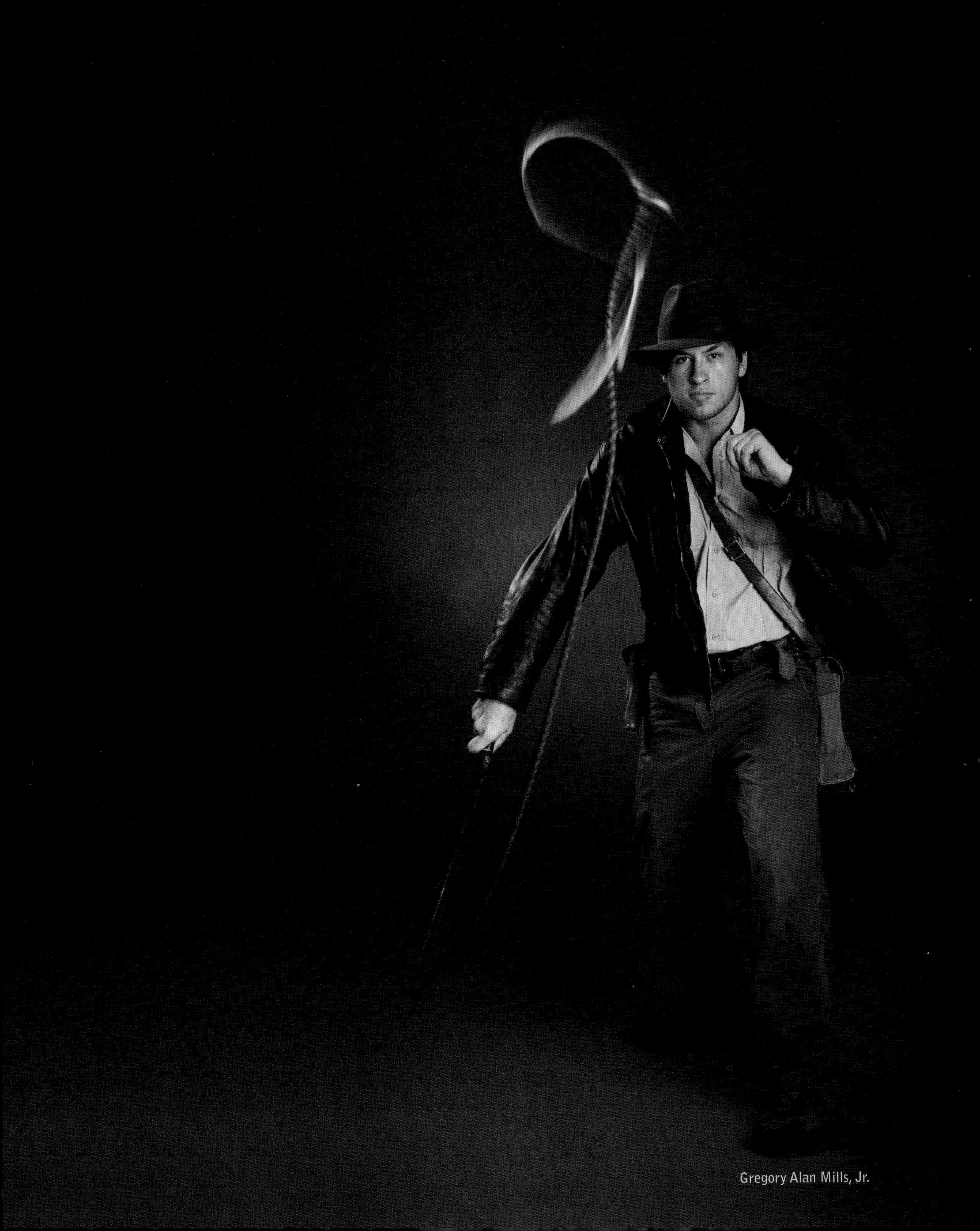

Gregory Alan Mills, Jr.

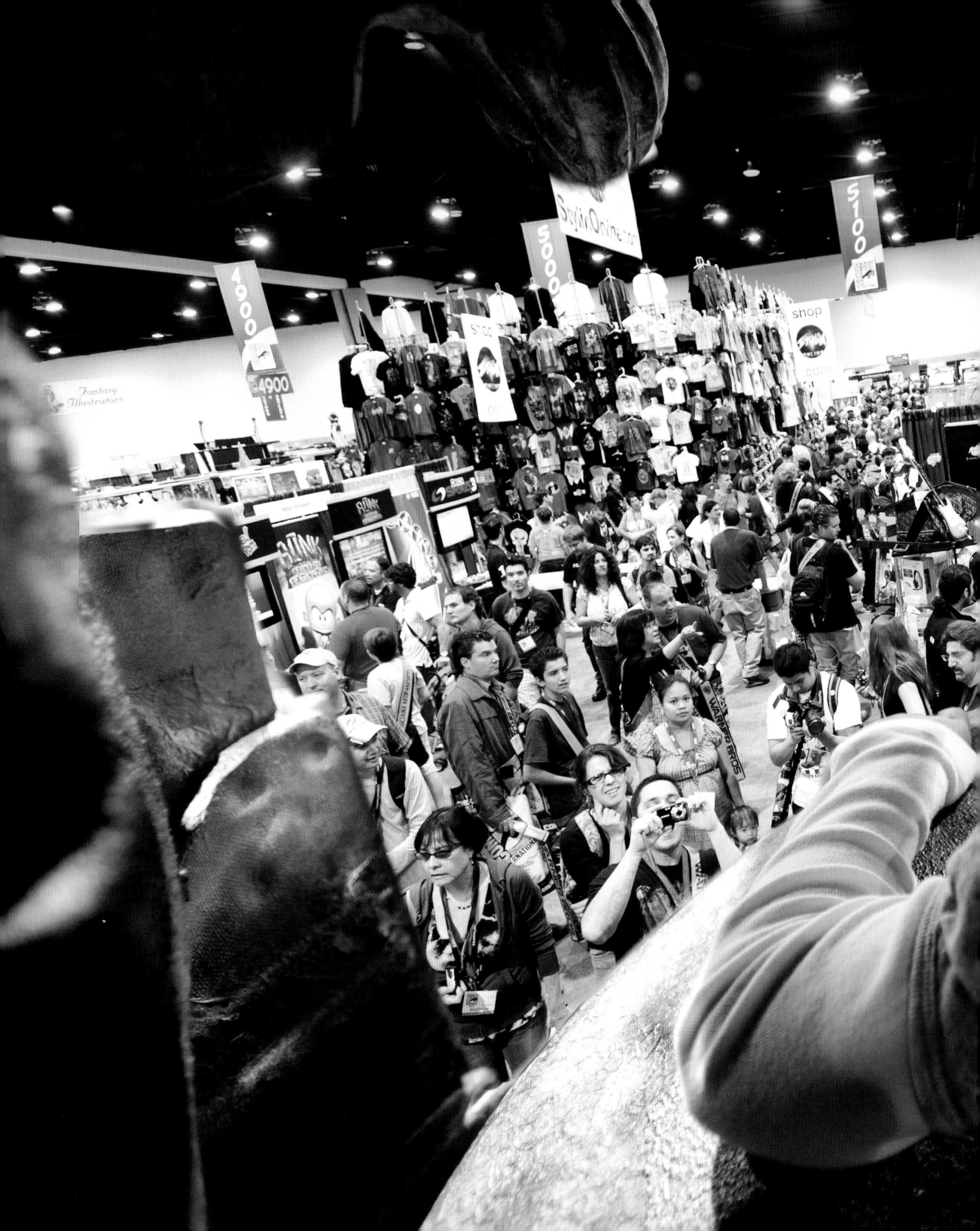
4900
5000
5100
shop
Fantasy Illustrators
WARNER BROS

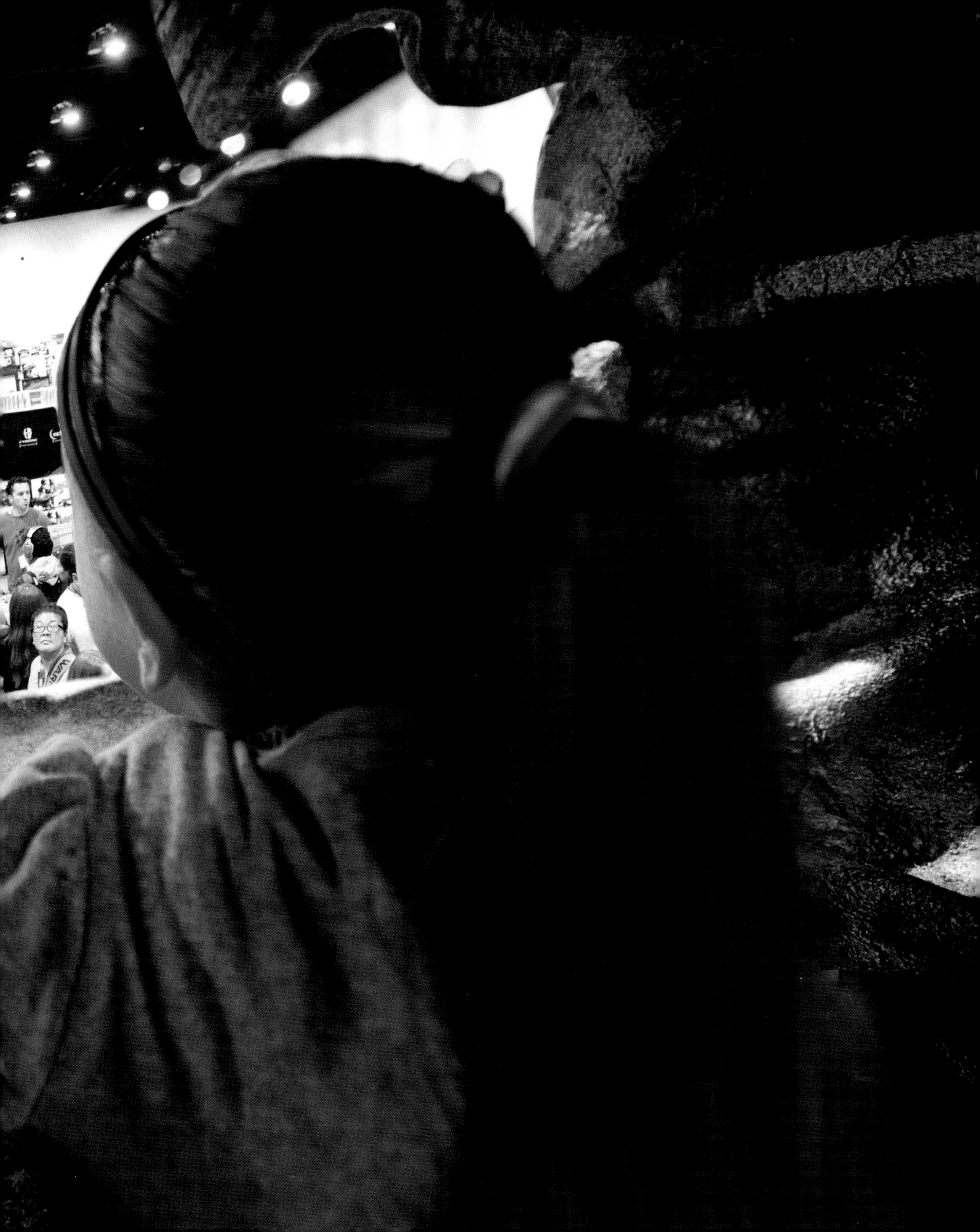

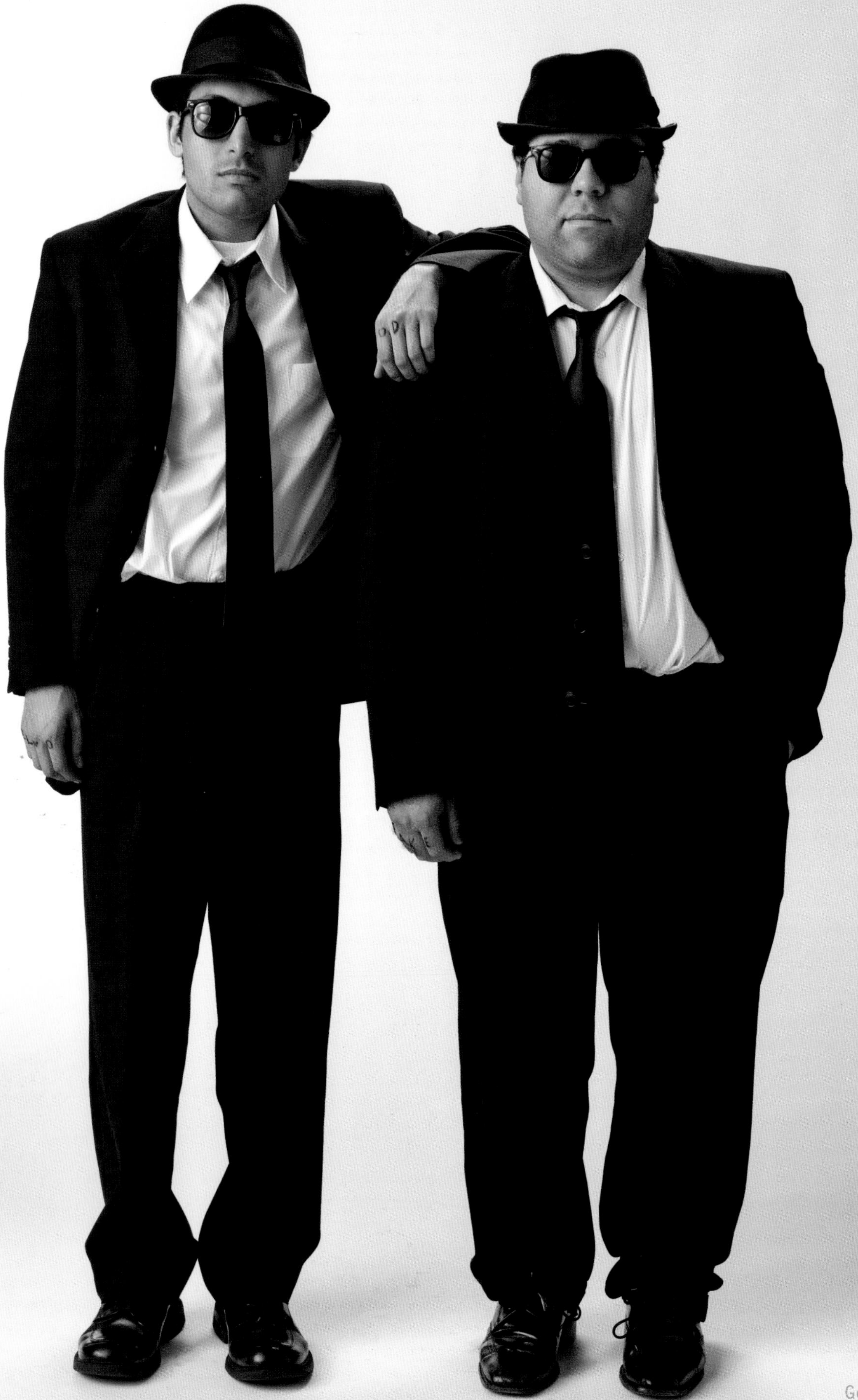

George Broomis and
Armand R. Cervera

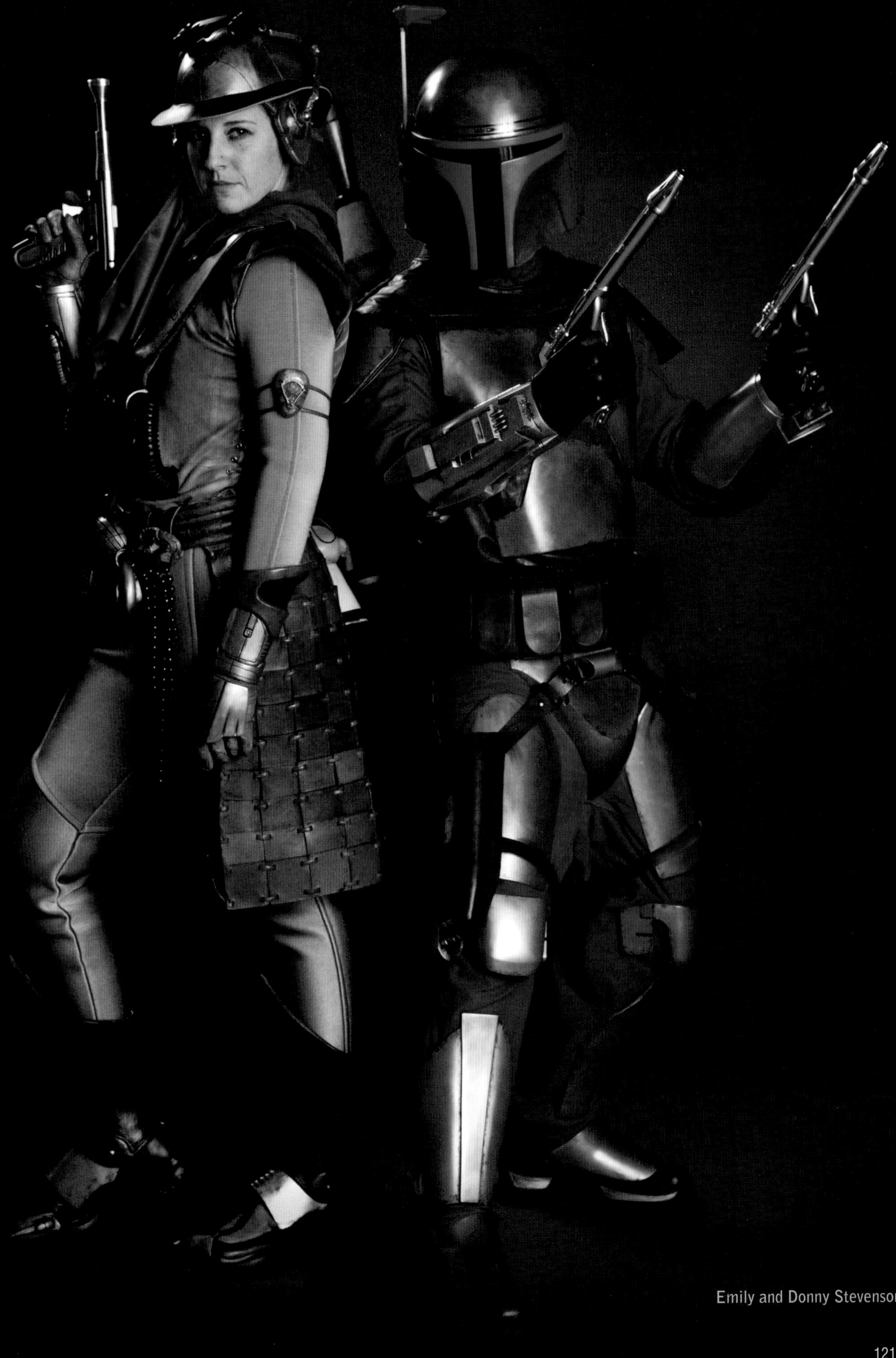

Emily and Donny Stevenson

sam trammel

actor | True Blood

"It's a very knowledgeable group of fans that end up here. And they usually know more about your character than you do. And sometimes they'll embarrass you because they will ask you really good questions that you don't have an answer to."

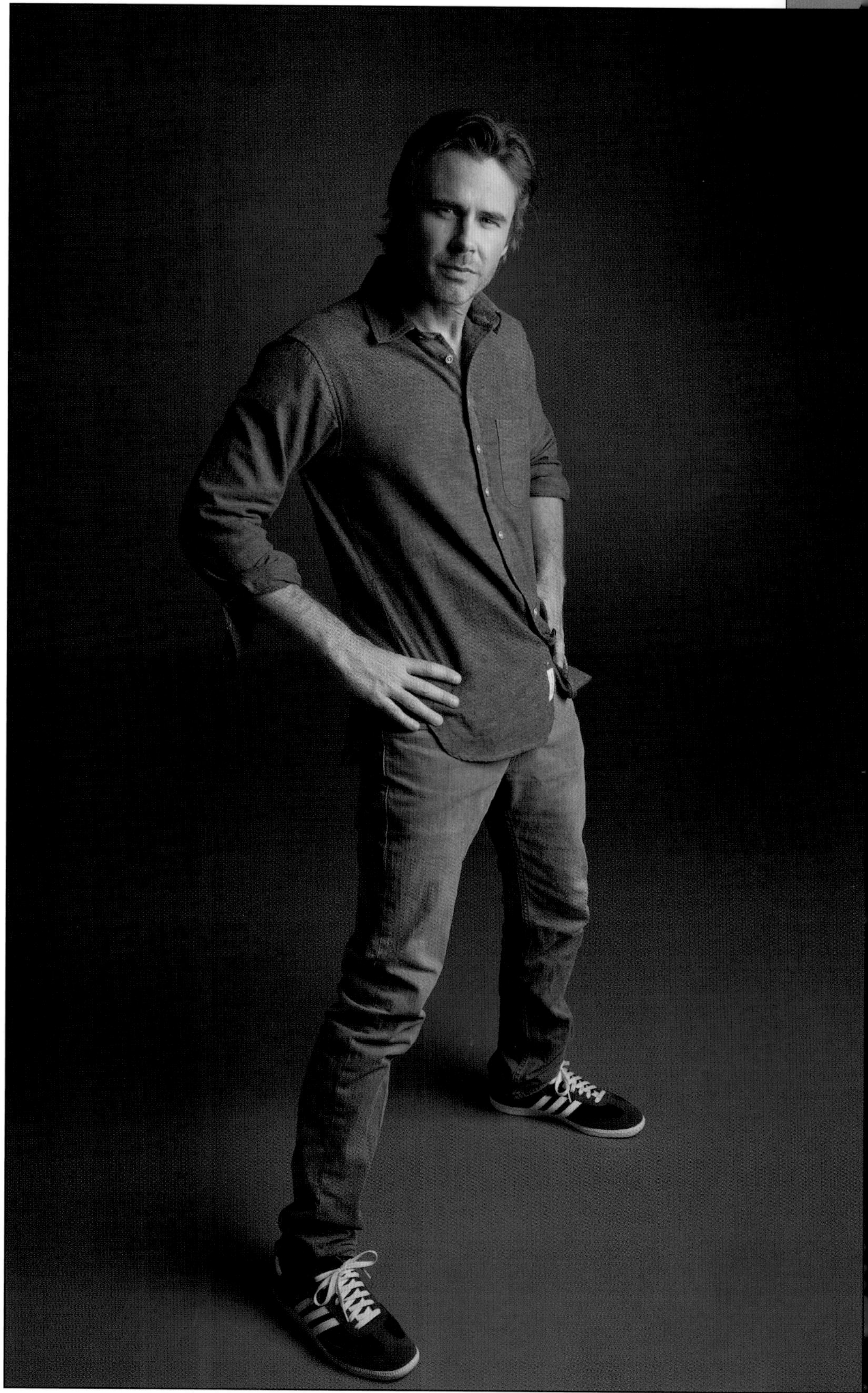

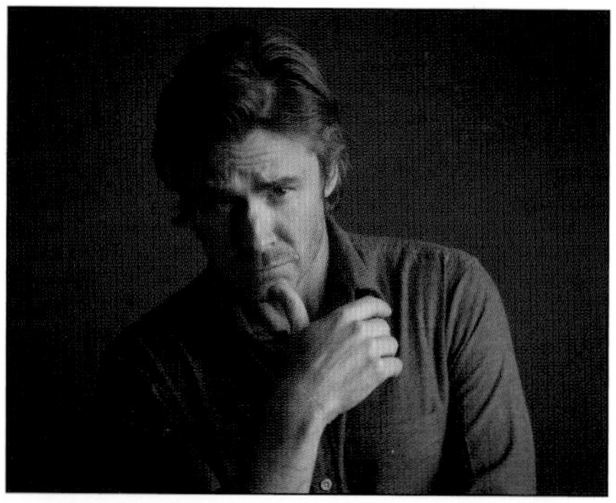

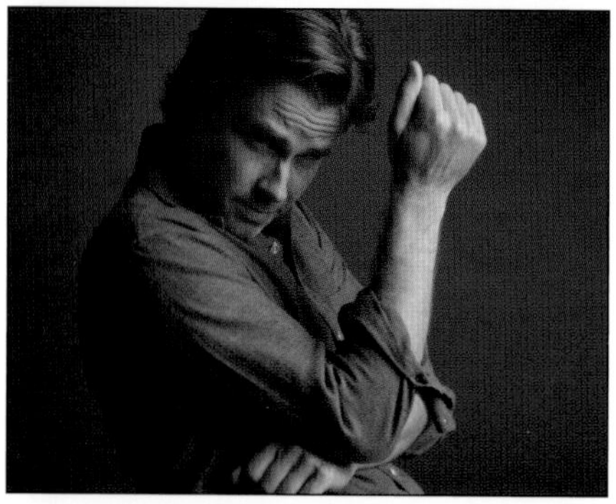

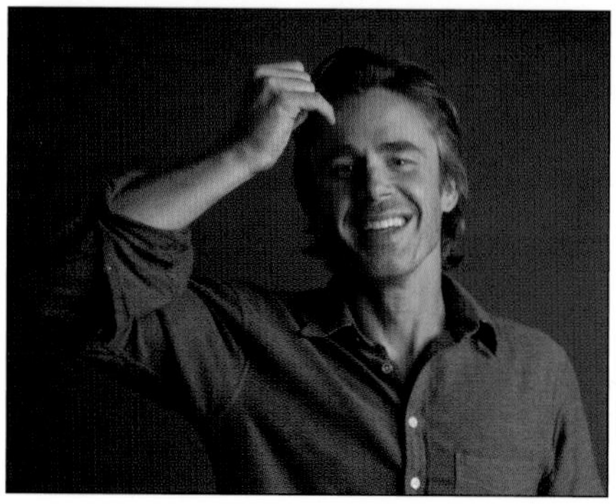

Art by Neeraj Patel

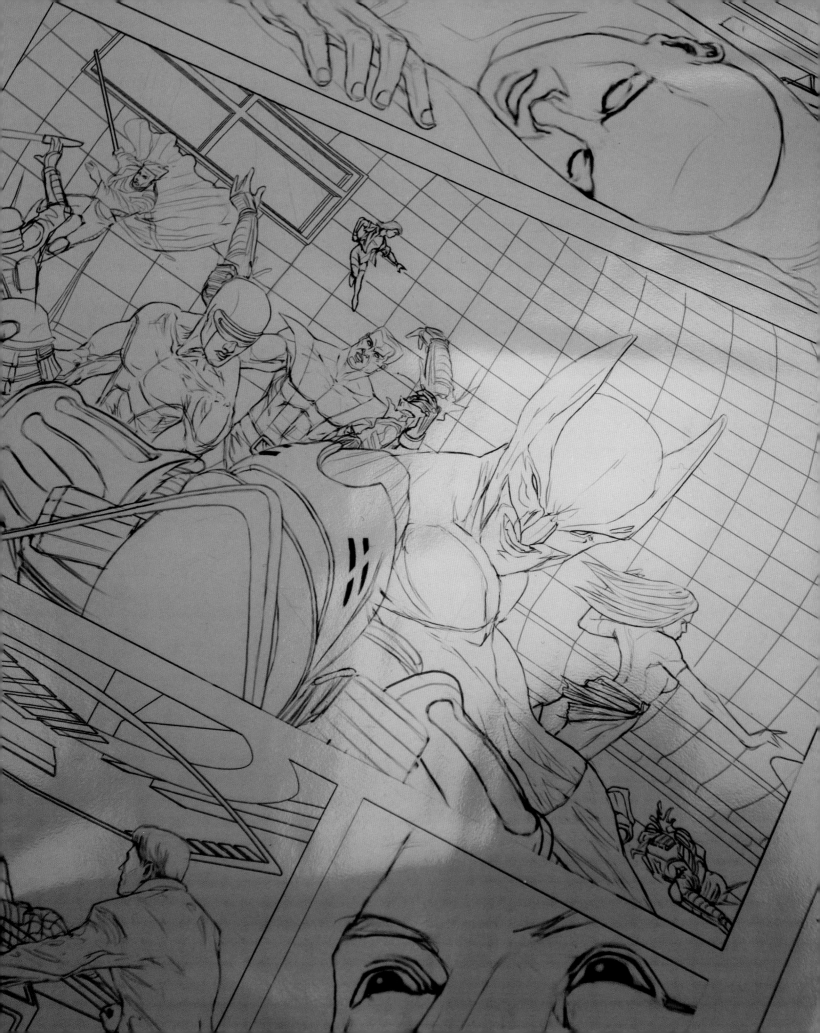

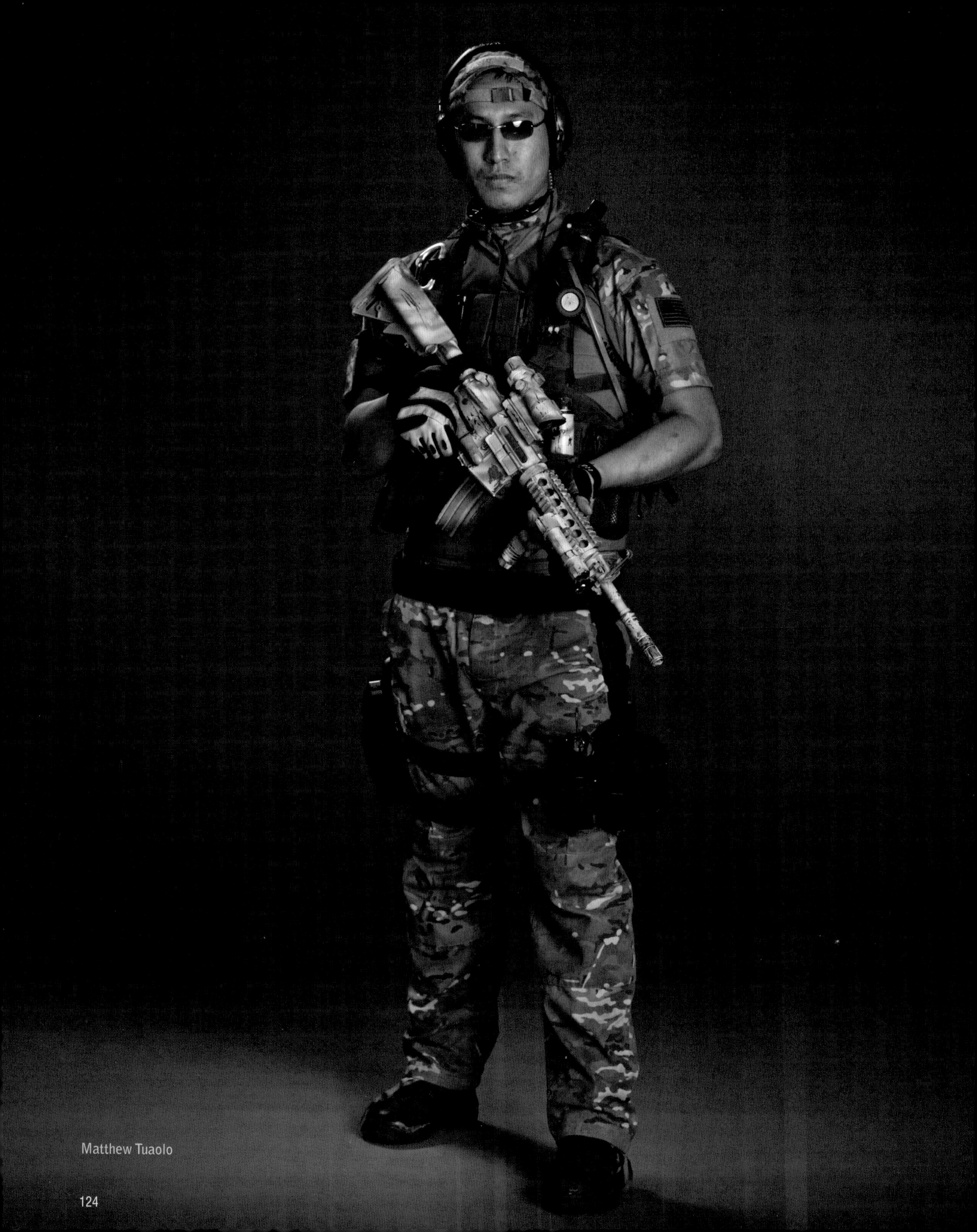

Matthew Tuaolo

Anna Ushakova

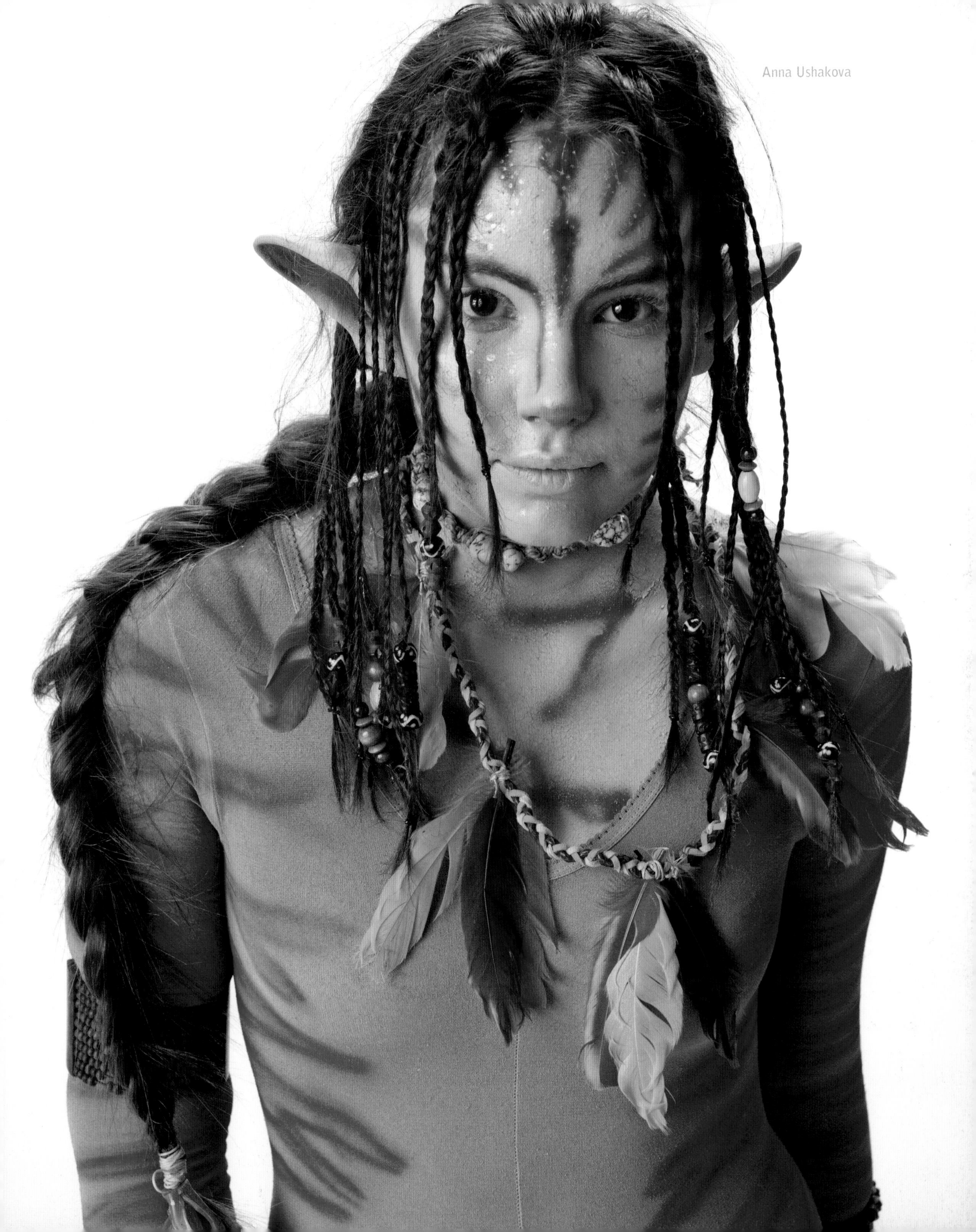

michael mcmillian

actor, writer | True Blood, Lucid

“ I wouldn't be surprised if you were walking up to the convention center and saw Batman bathing in a fountain, or a chubby Spider-Man rolling down the hill in mud. ”

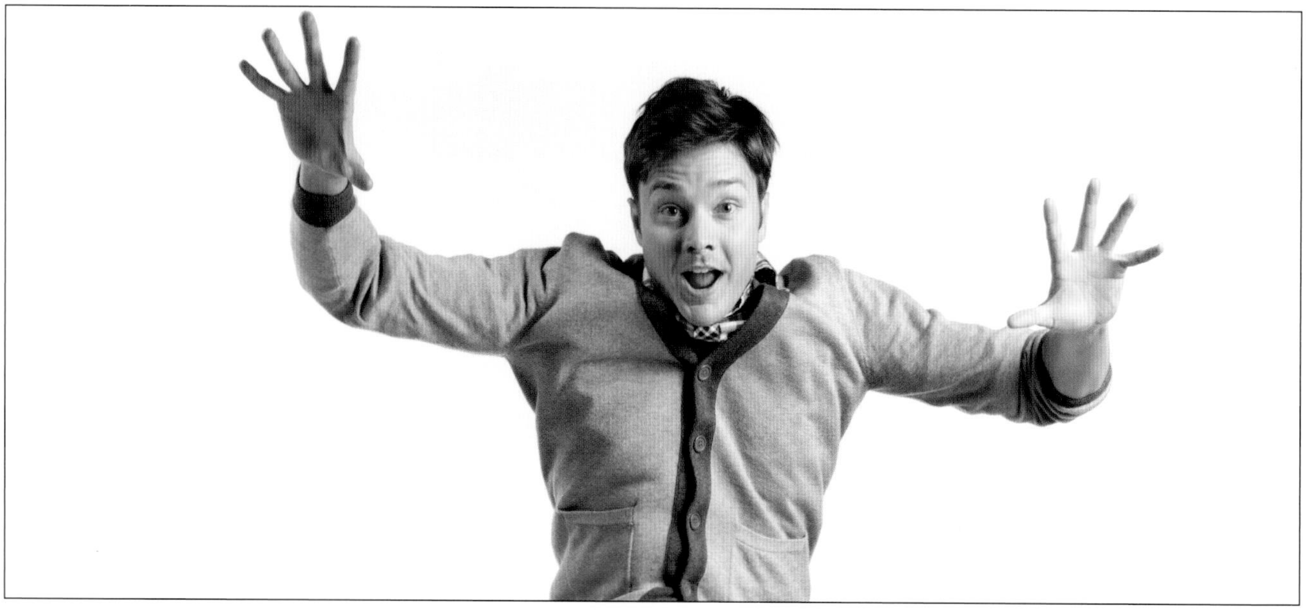

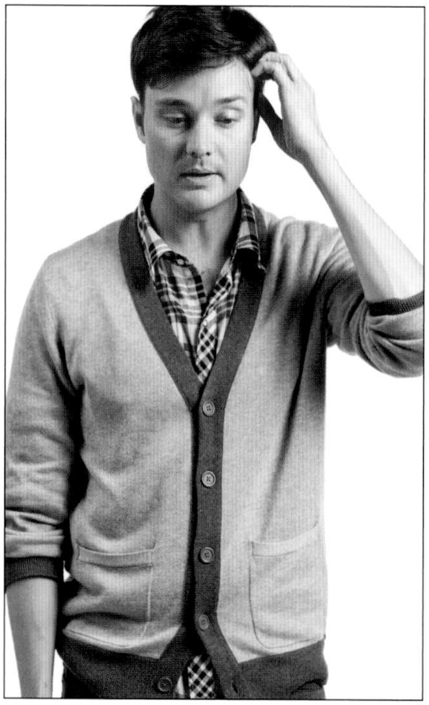

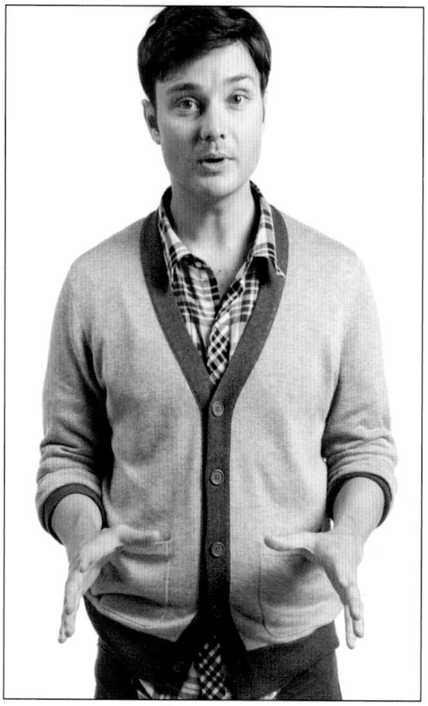

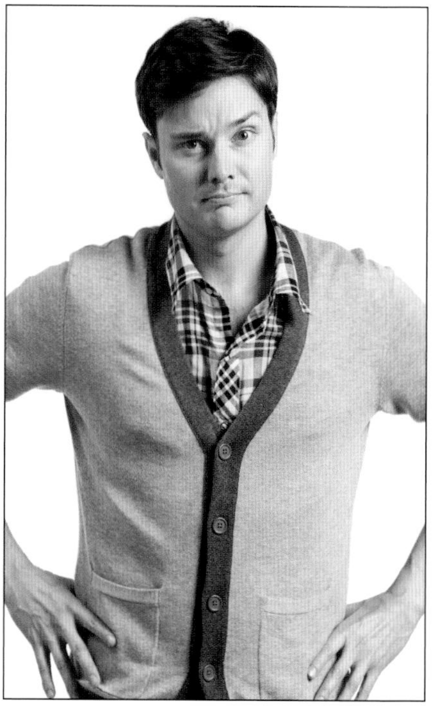

moto hagio

manga creator

" Comics as an art form are very close to the heart. Comics can move you emotionally, and in that sense they're very much like songs. "

gareb shamus

CEO | Wizard magazine

" I'm standing out front of the Hard Rock and I see this mob of people walking to the front of the hotel and I'm like, 'Oh my god, what celebrity is this going to be? Brad Pitt, Angelina Jolie, Tom Cruise, who is that?' And I look and in the middle of it is Frank Miller. "

day three

"By the third day, I've spent a bunch of money, I've gotten almost no sleep, and my legs are like pipe cleaners under a barbell. But somehow, I still manage to zombie-drag my way through…and I love it."

Morgan Spurlock

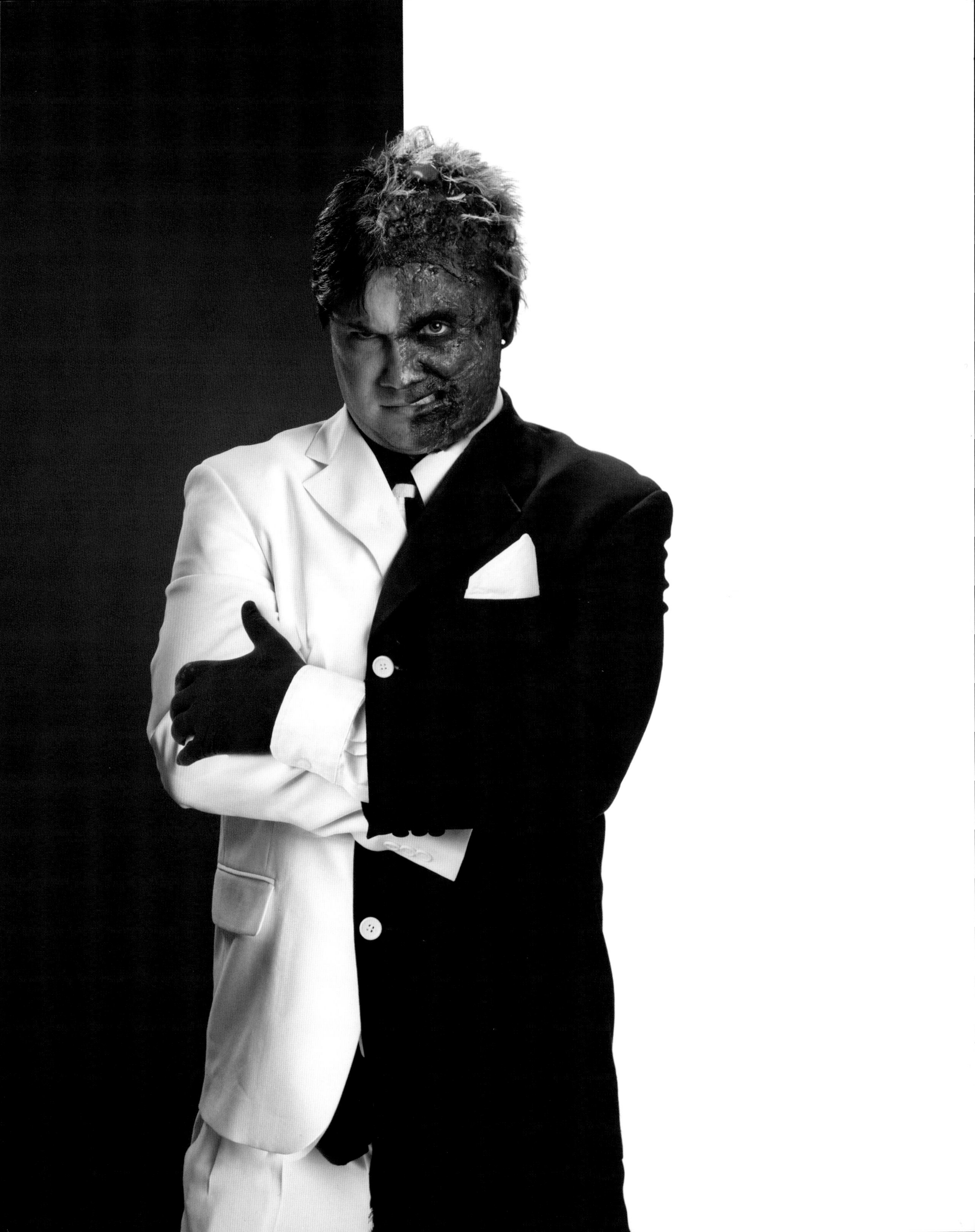

> People want to escape their everyday lives, for just a little while. It's just fun. A little bit of an escape.

Richard and Paul Rossi

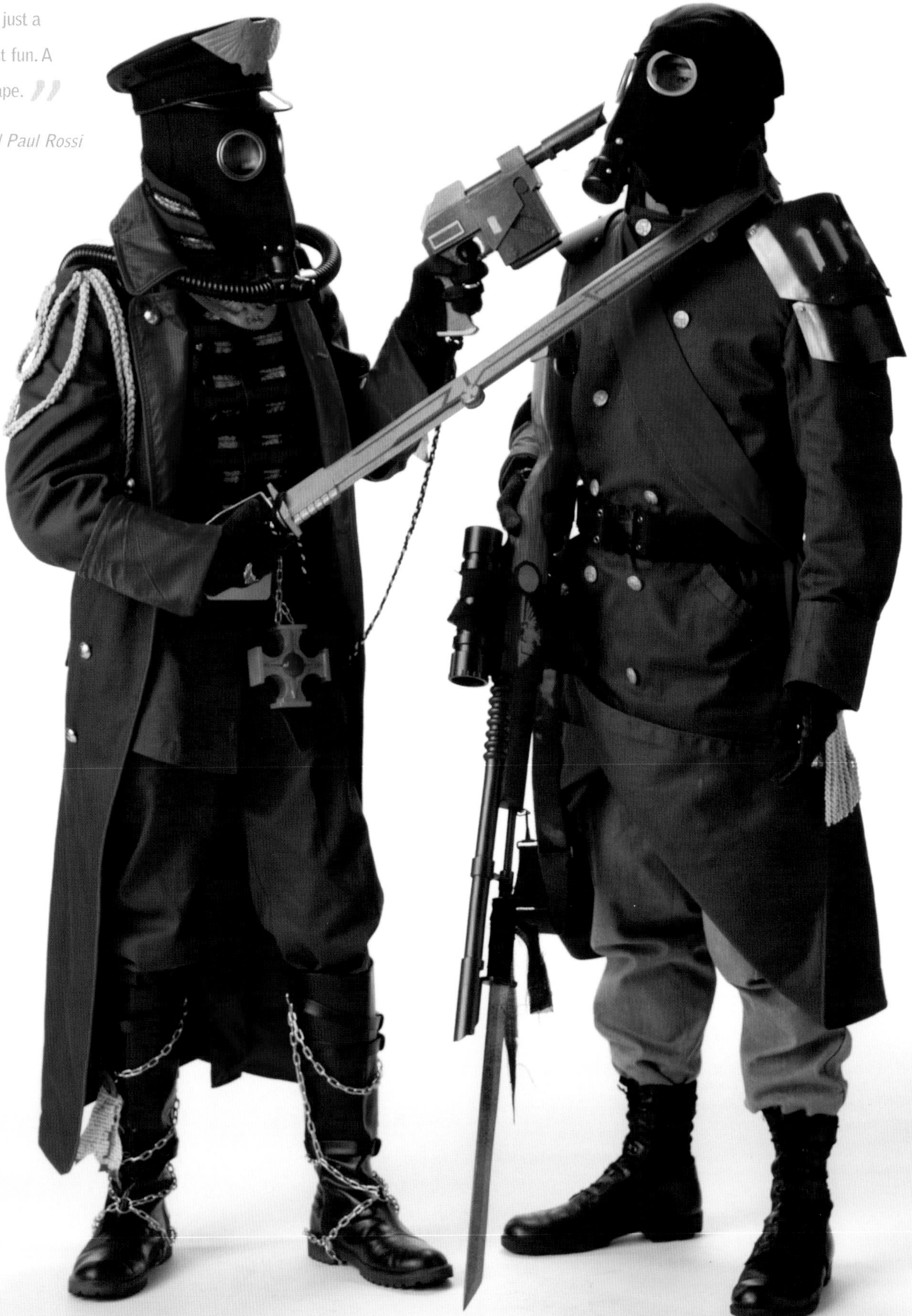

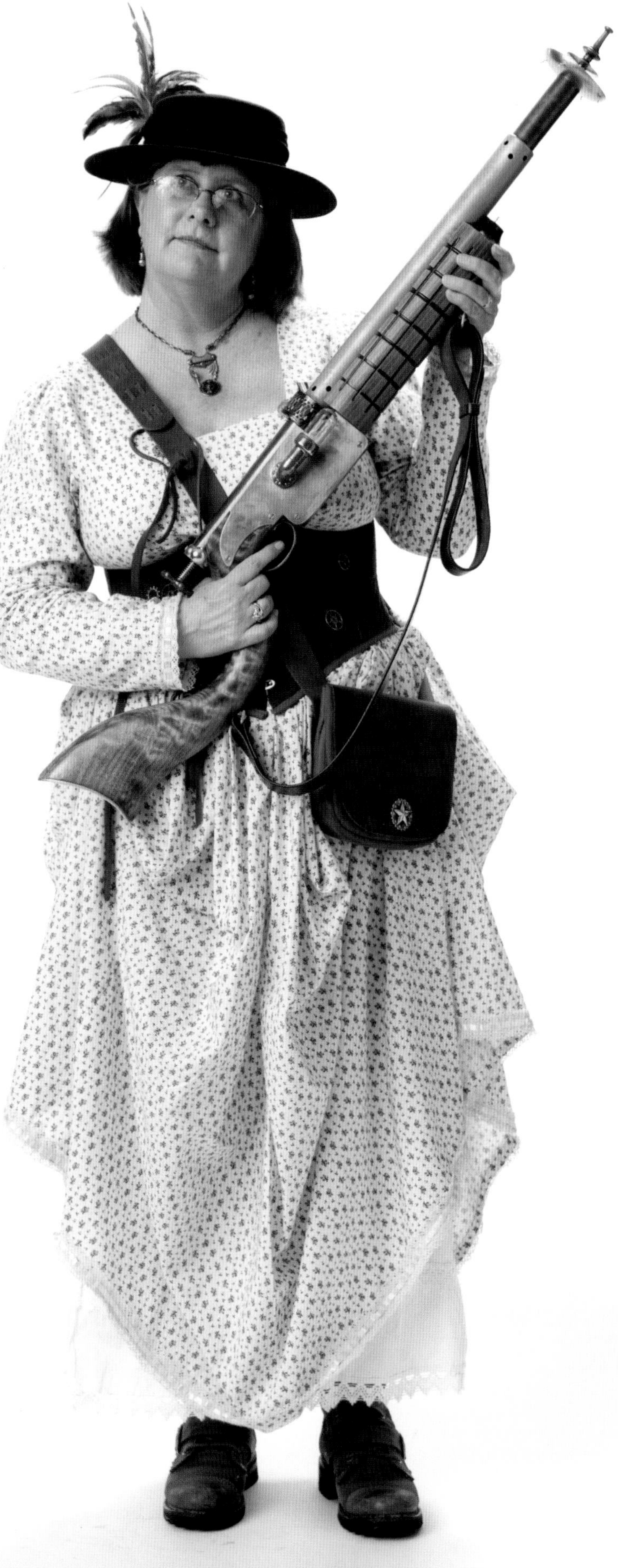

"Everyone—there is no difference in whether they're young, whether they're old, whether they're from another country—they all seem to enjoy it."

Linda Hutsell and Kim C. Hutsell

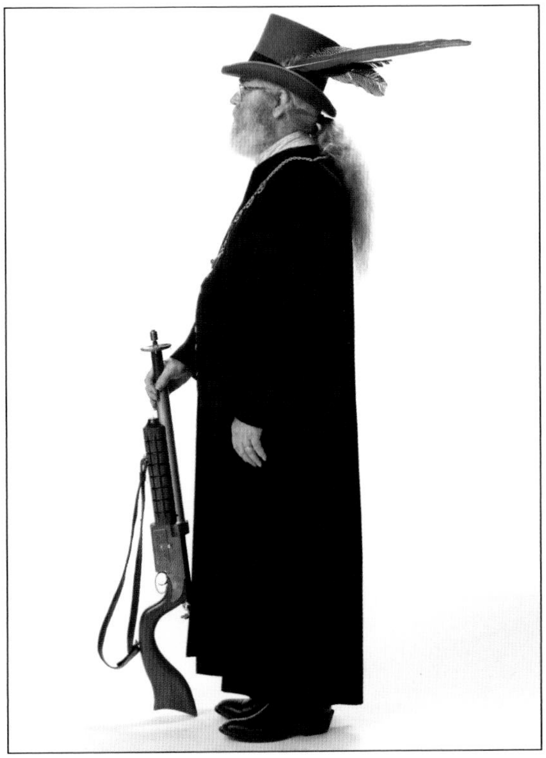

kenneth branagh

actor, director | Harry Potter and the Chamber of Secrets, Thor

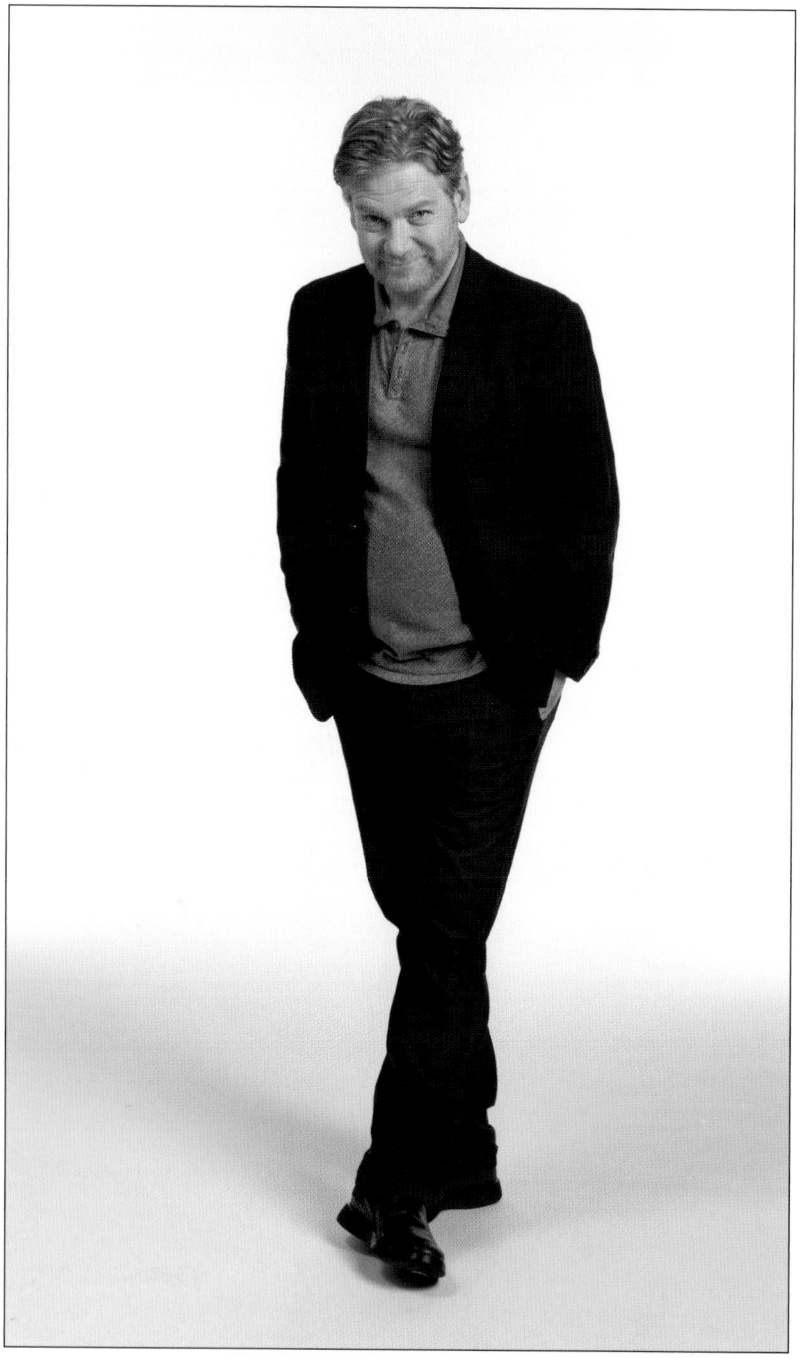

"I feel very proud to be the temporary guardian of stories that people feel are very precious."

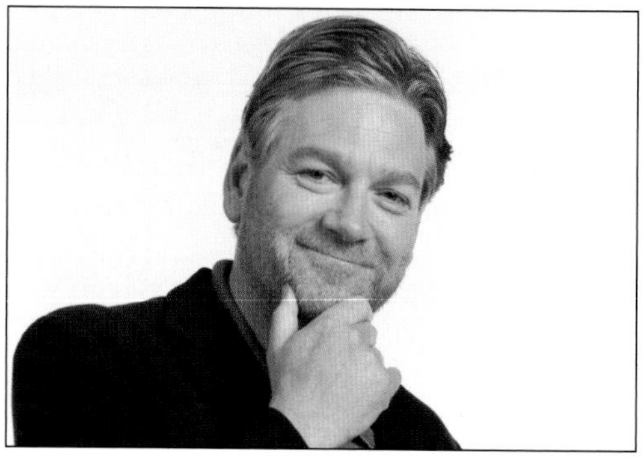

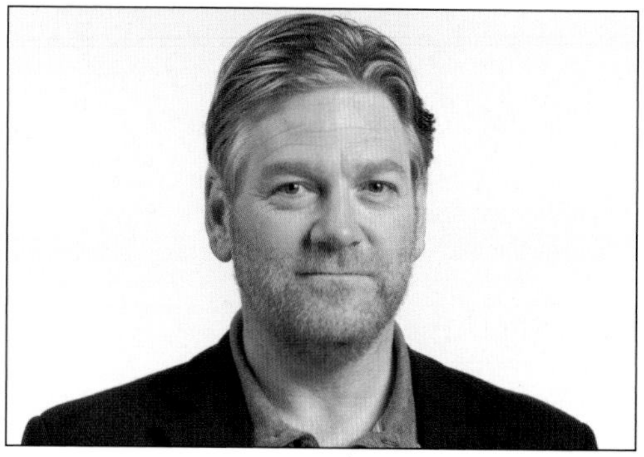

"You talk about heroes and there's excitement, there's vitality, there's sexiness. And so heroism in one's own life, I think, can be considered consciously or unconsciously as a result of looking up to, alongside, or even being critical of a hero that you see presented in a comic or a film."

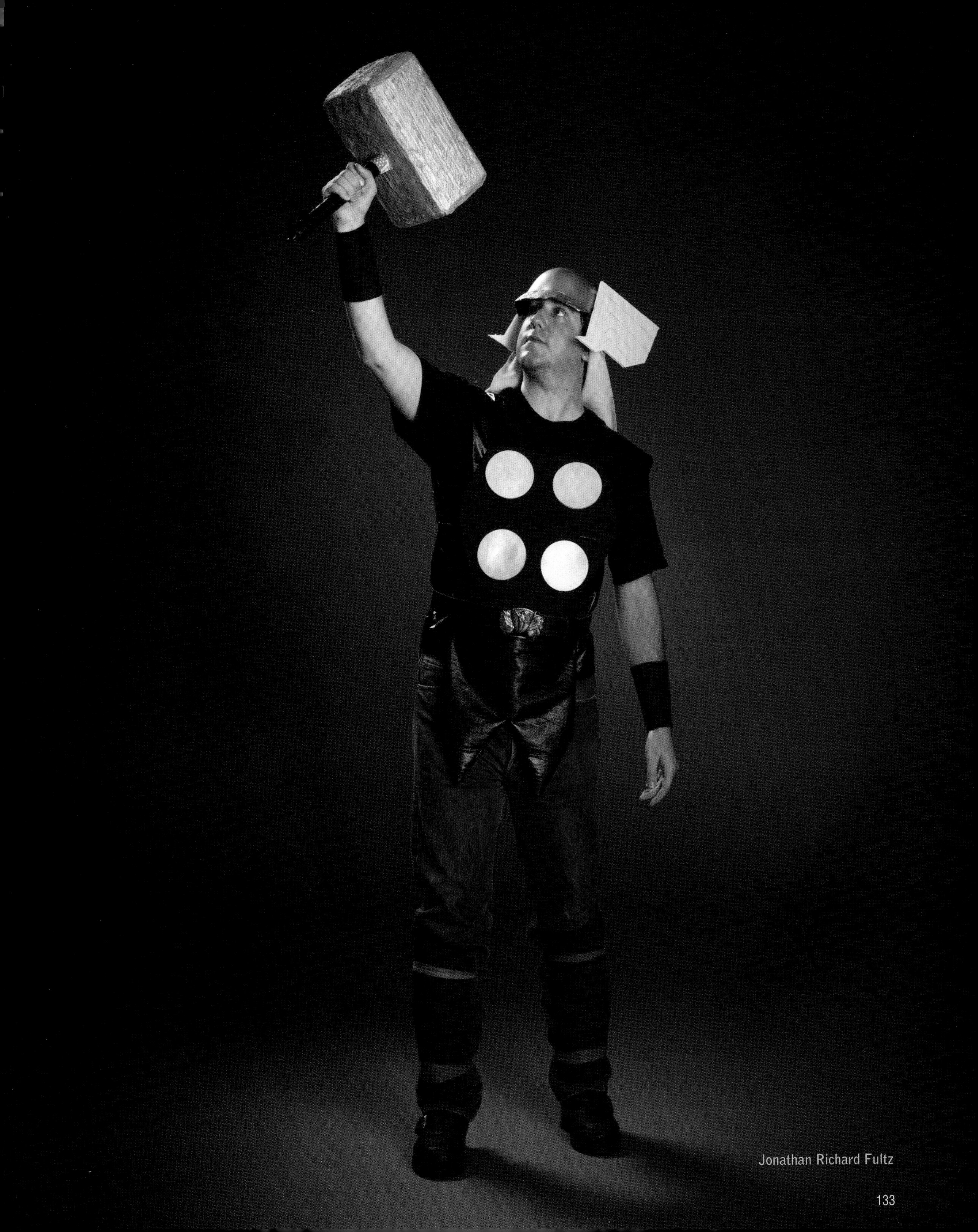

Jonathan Richard Fultz

eli roth

director | Cabin Fever, Hostel

" Comic-Con is like the Cannes Film Festival. Except in Cannes, if everyone wears tuxedoes to the screenings, here everyone wears Storm Trooper outfits and Jedi outfits. It's like Comic-Cannes. It's like being at a film festival, except you actually want to see the movies that are here. "

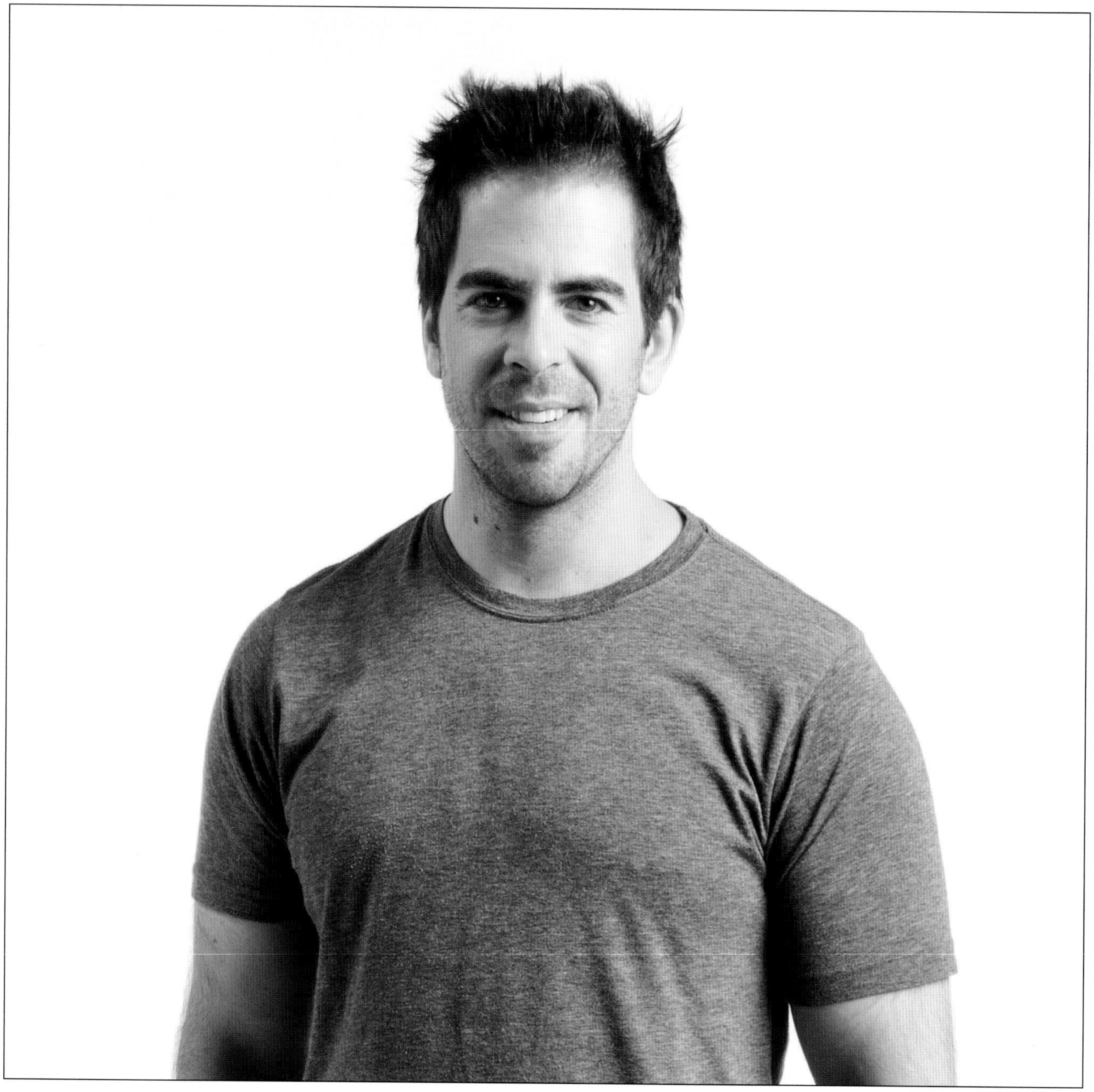

daniel stamm

director | The Last Exorcism

> "I was blown away at the devotion of people—that look in people's eyes, which you know from sex shops. You know? They have that kind of focus—it's beautiful. There seems to be no cynicism here. People are proud to be fans and it's a beautiful feeling."

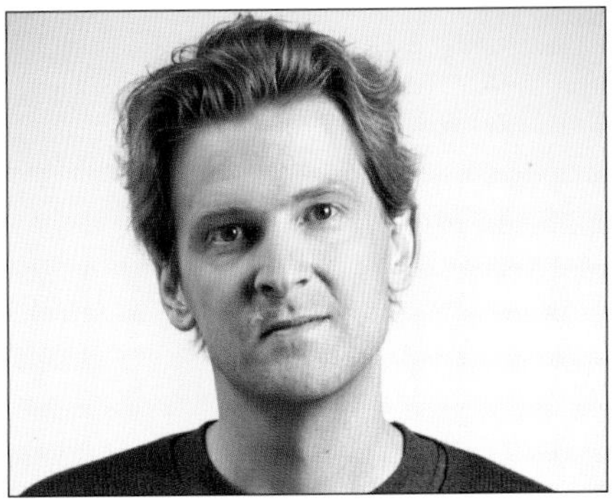

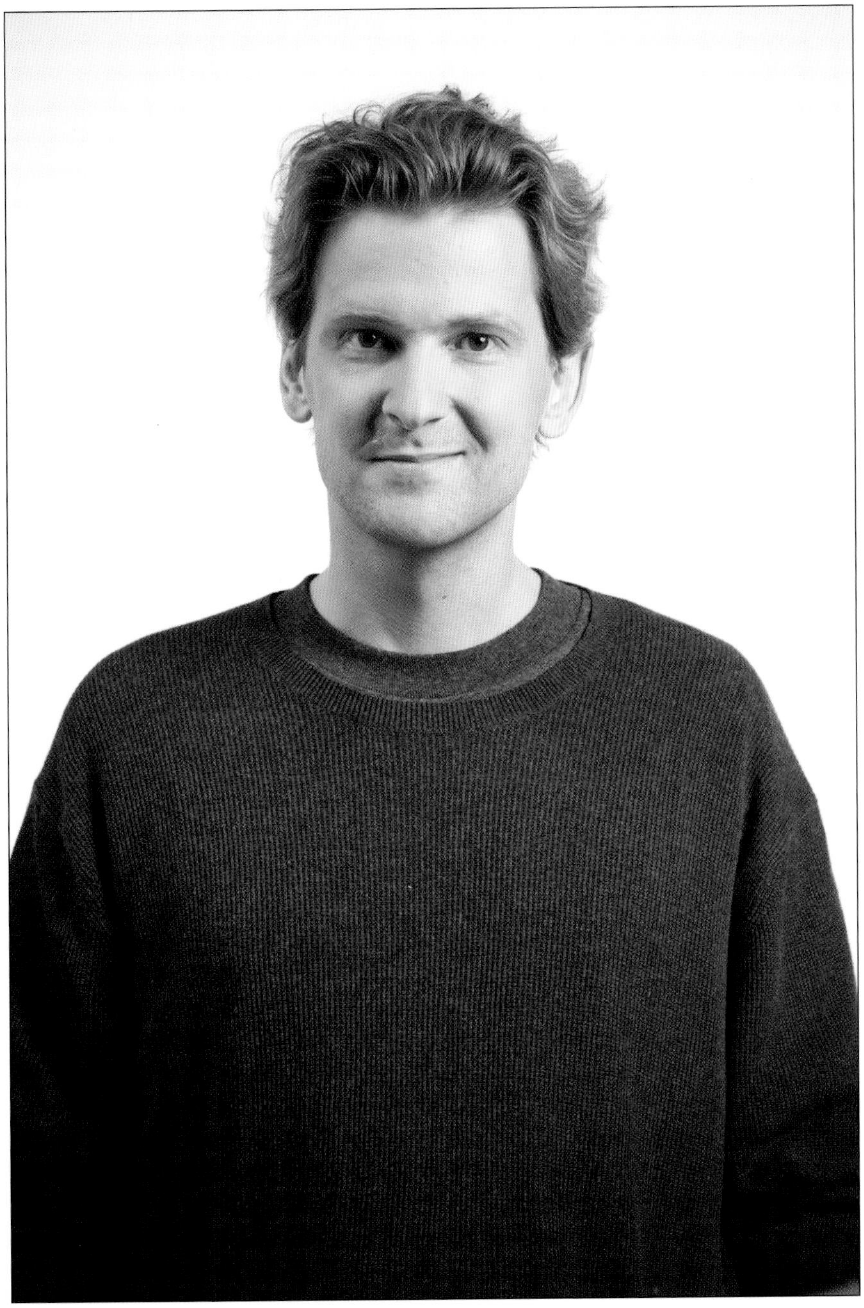

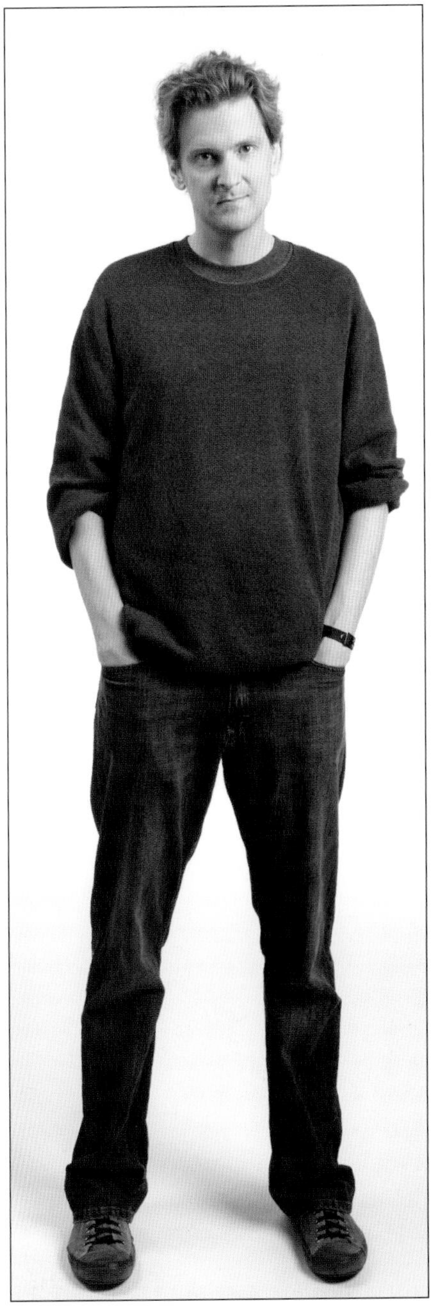

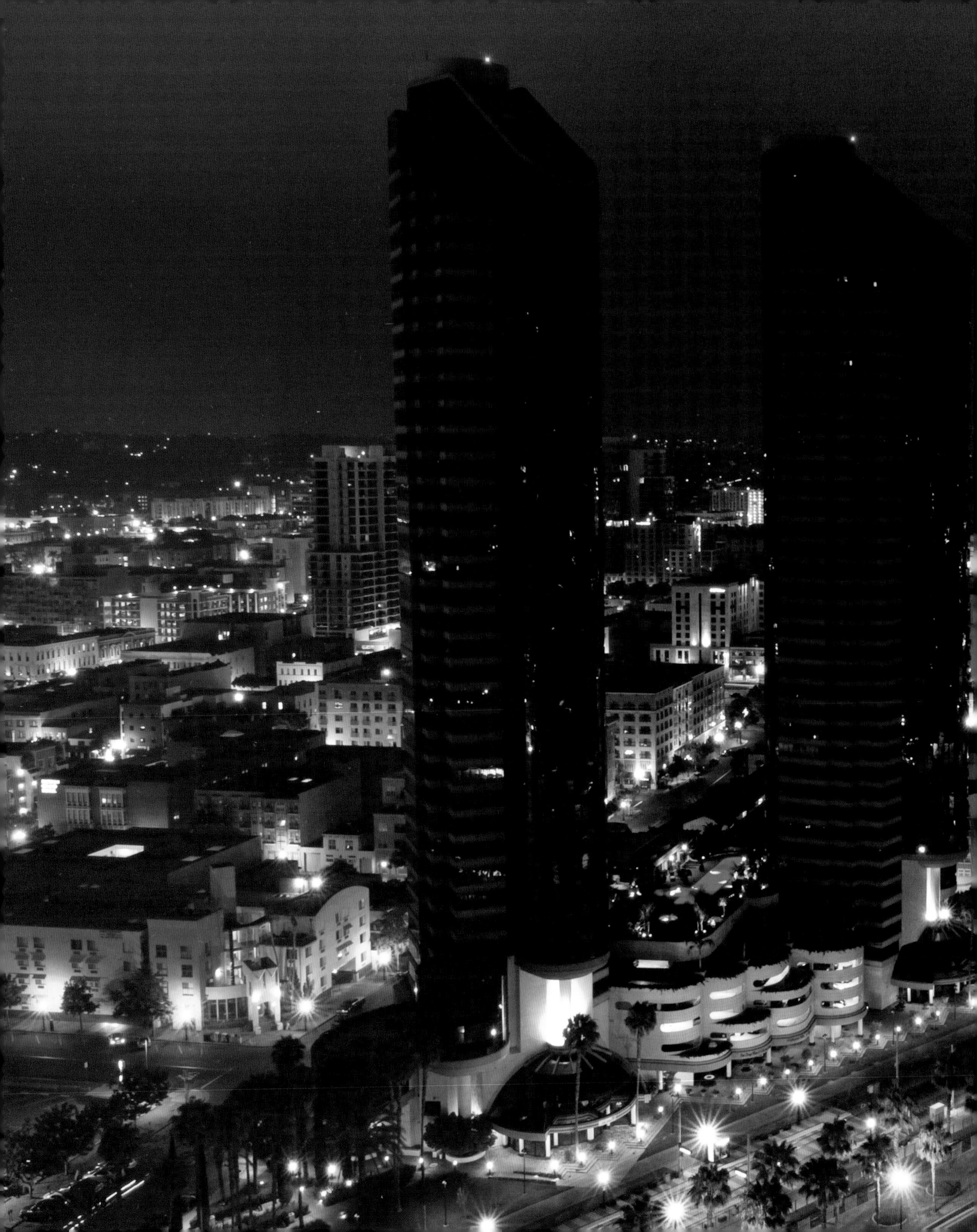

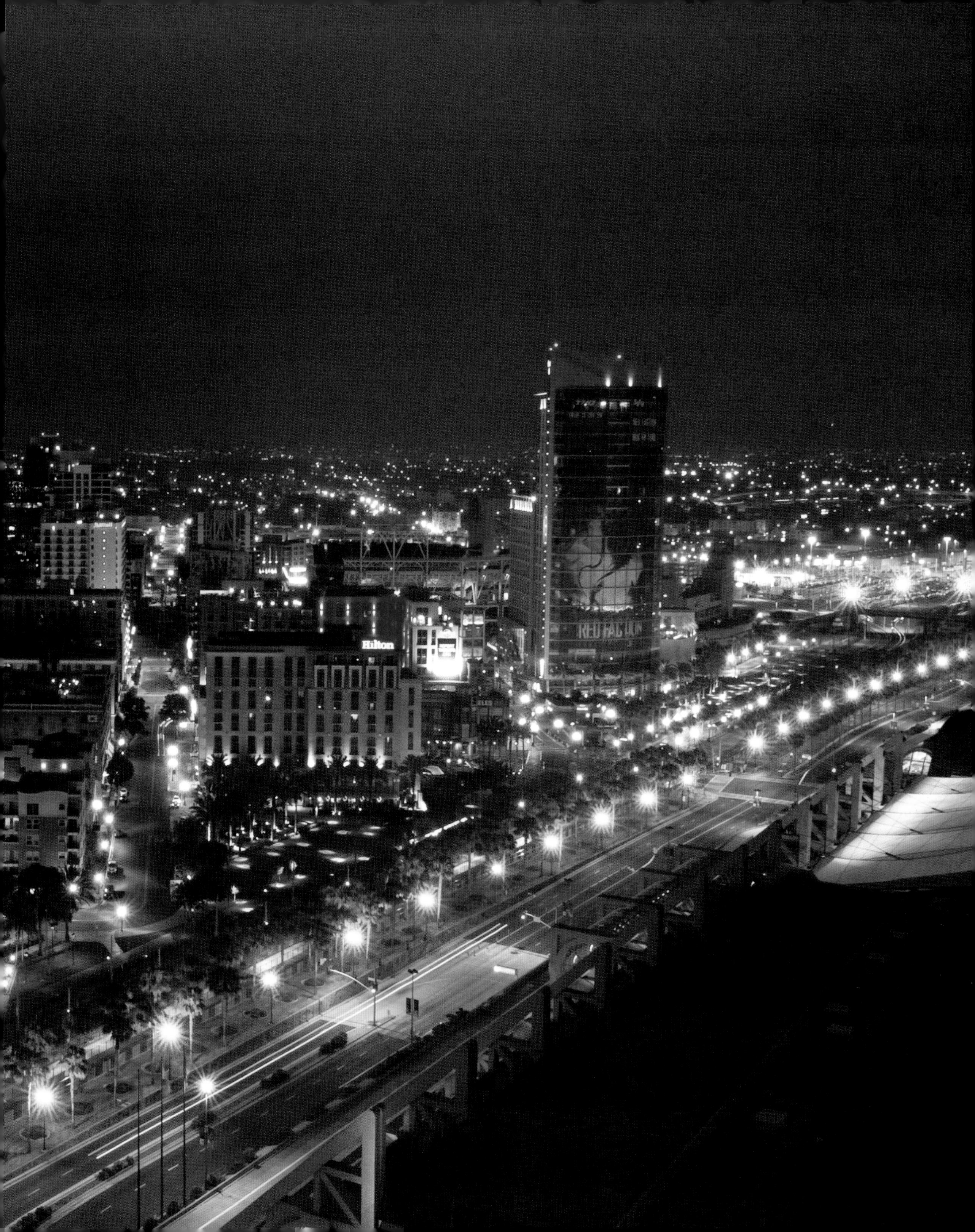
Hilton
RED FACTION

Adriana Basurto and
Thomas Alexander

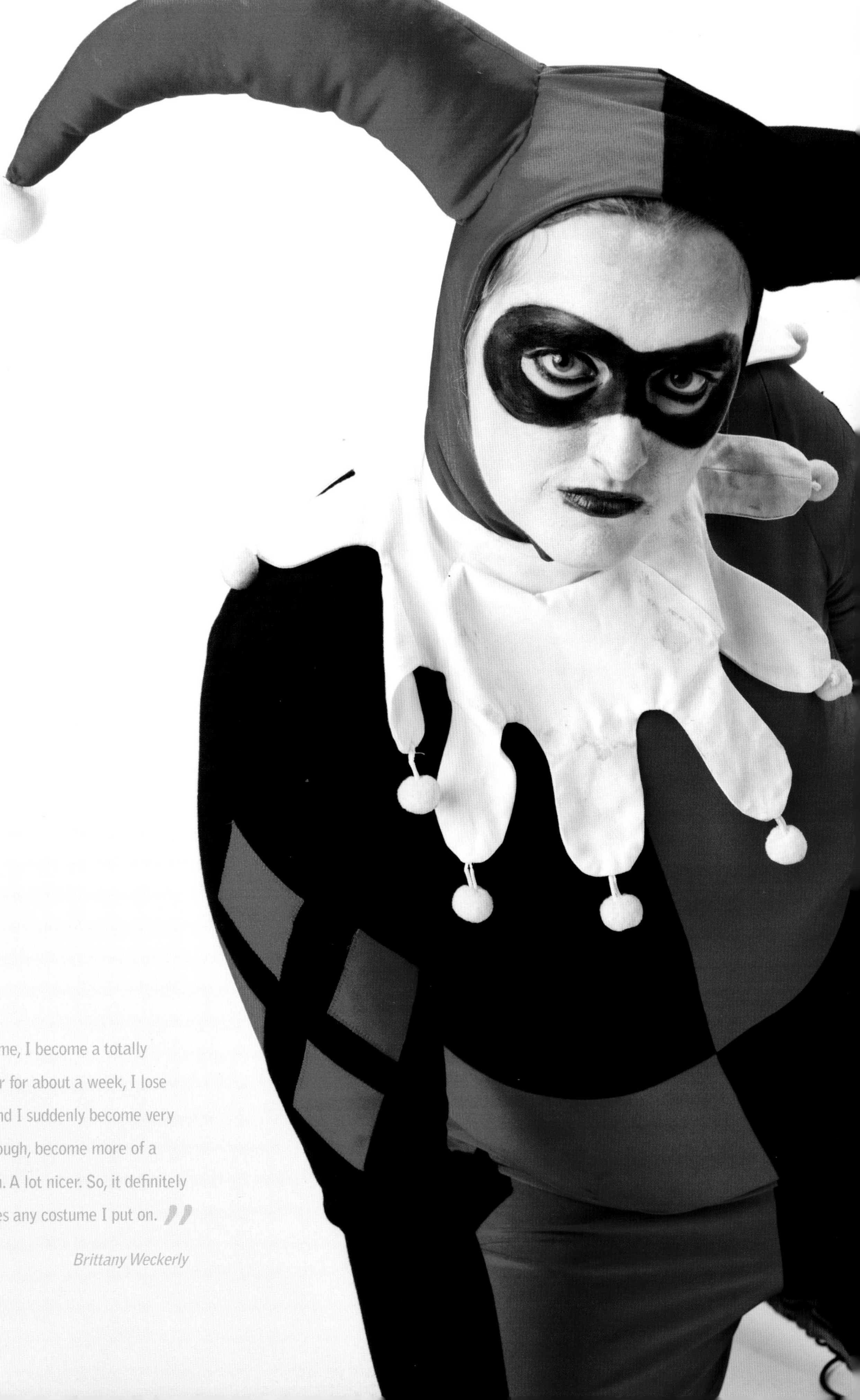

"When I get in this costume, I become a totally different person. I swear for about a week, I lose my IQ. It drops down, and I suddenly become very blondish. I definitely, though, become more of a confident, bubbly person. A lot nicer. So, it definitely changes me. As, too, does any costume I put on."

Brittany Weckerly

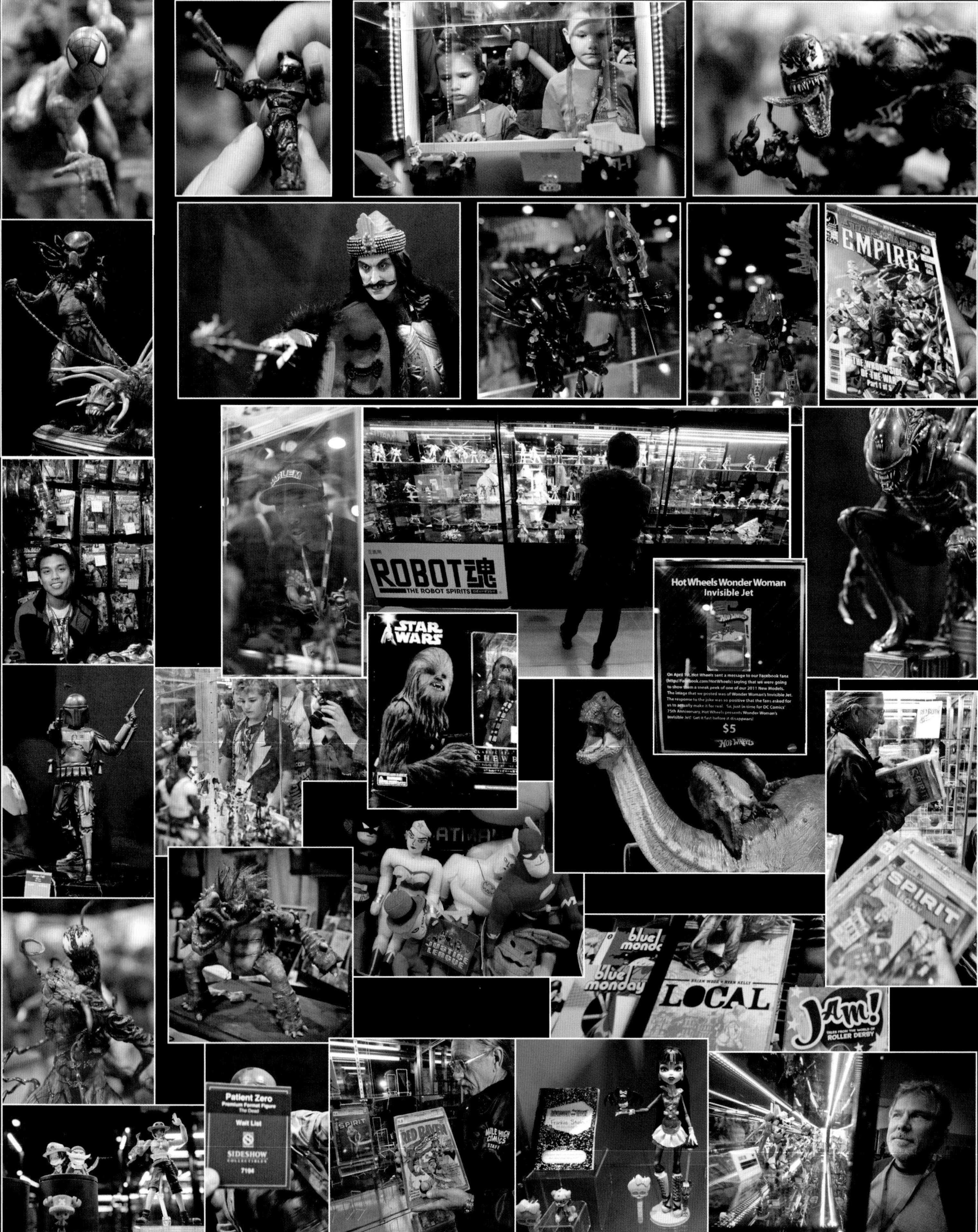
EMPIRE
ROBOT魂
THE ROBOT SPIRITS
STAR WARS
Hot Wheels Wonder Woman
Invisible Jet
$5
JUSTICE LEAGUE
blue monday
LOCAL
JAM!
ROLLER DERBY
SPIRIT
Patient Zero
Wait List
SIDESHOW
7194
RED RAVEN
MILE HIGH COMICS
STAFF

“I collect a lot of vinyl toys. I started with Bearbricks and Kubricks, which are made by MediCom…then I got into Kozik, who's an artist I met here. KAWS is a guy who makes toys that I collect a lot…that's one of the reasons it's cool to come here. You get to meet the guys who actually make these things.”

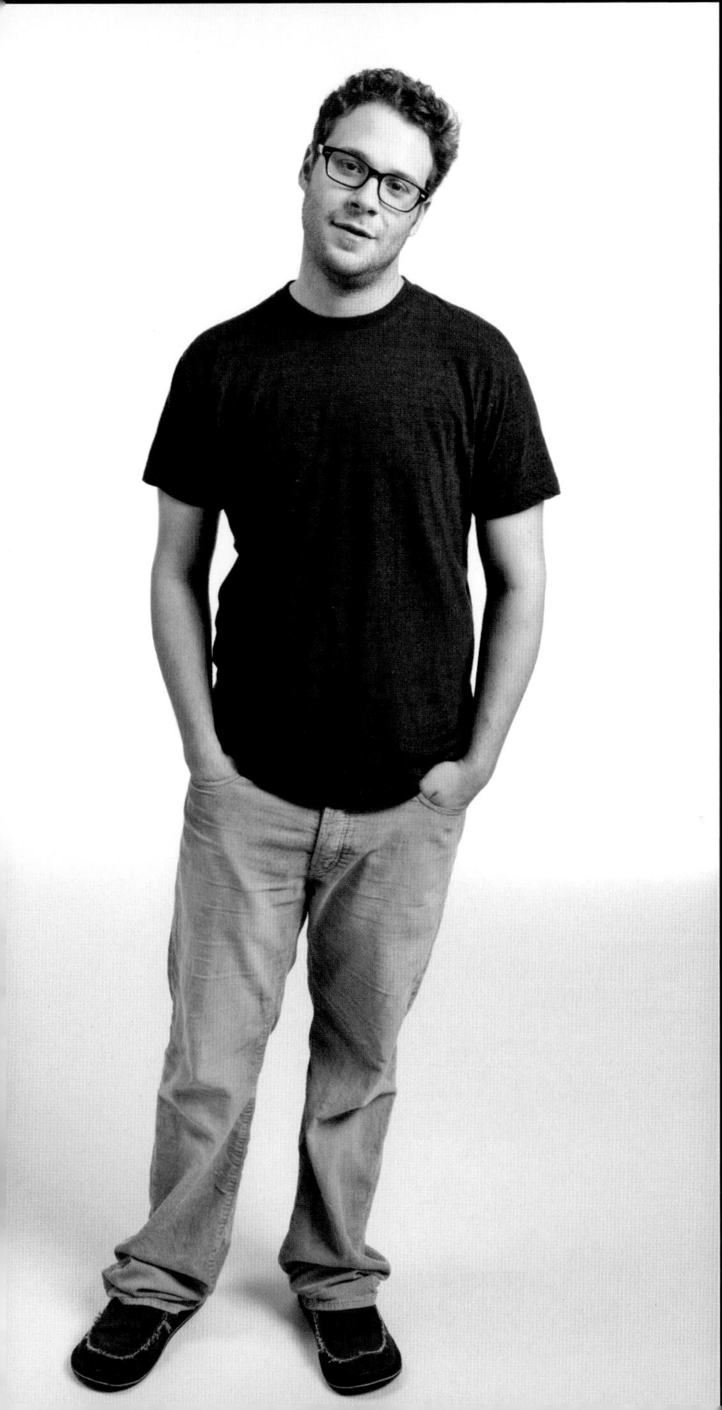

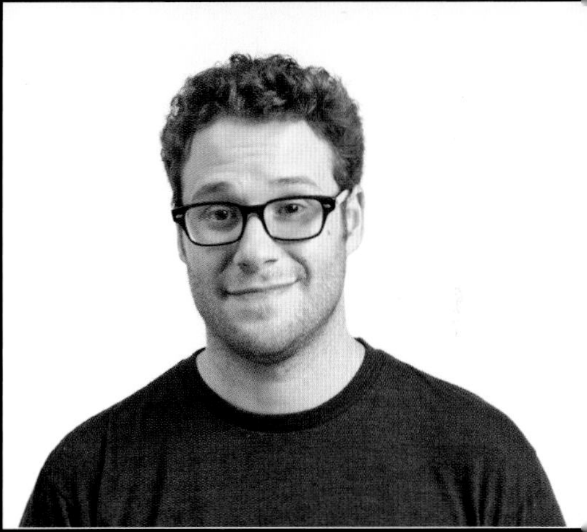

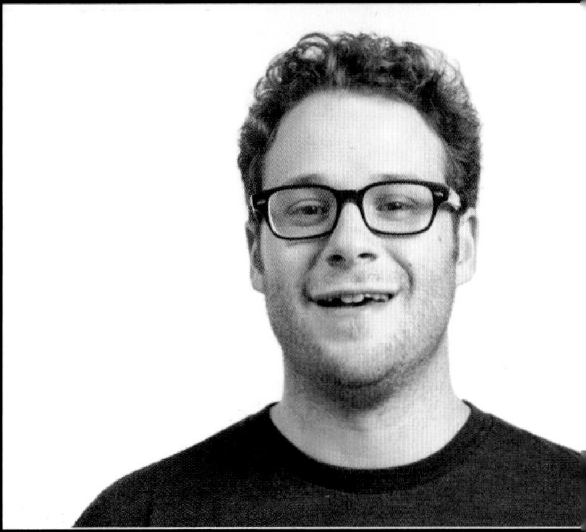

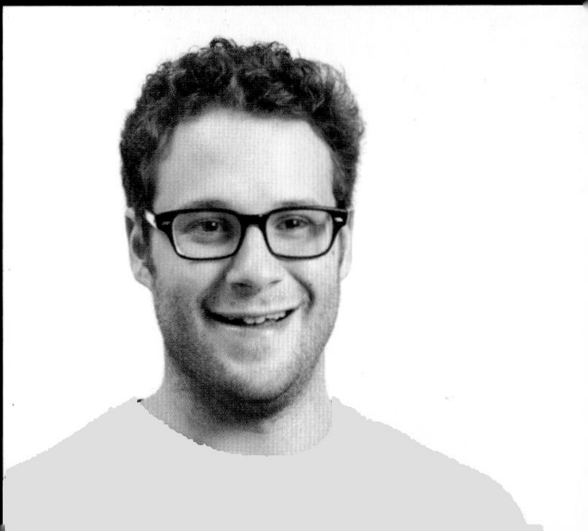

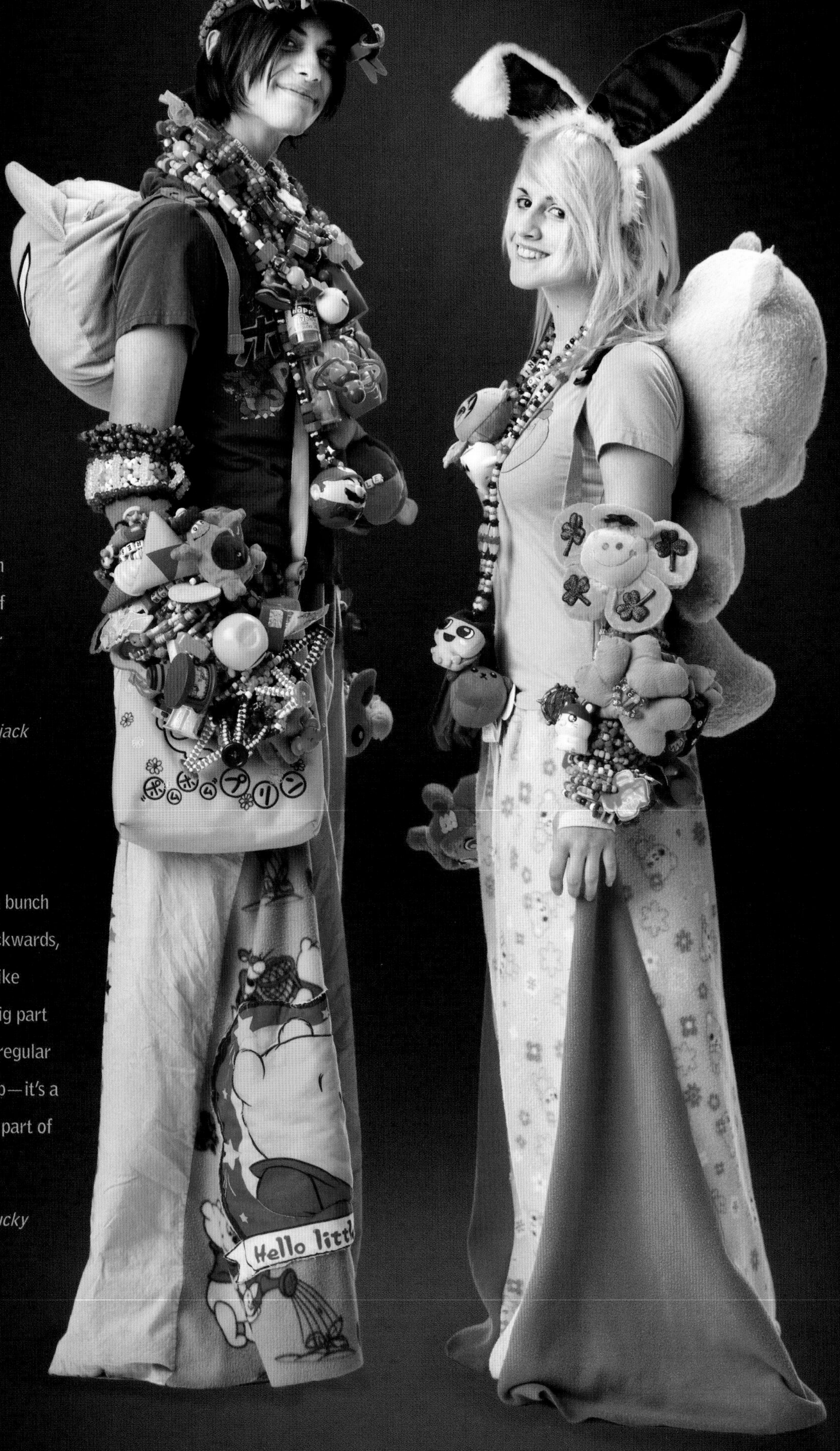
Hello litt

"Everyone's like all misshapen puzzle pieces that just kind of mesh and fit together in their own way. I like it."

Nathan Norton, a.k.a. Flapjack

"Our community is basically a bunch of older kids trying to go backwards, and not get older. We don't like growing up. Our music is a big part of our life. Happy hardcore, regular hardcore, hard style, dub step—it's a big part of our life and a big part of our community."

Sabrina Gruner, a.k.a. Lucky

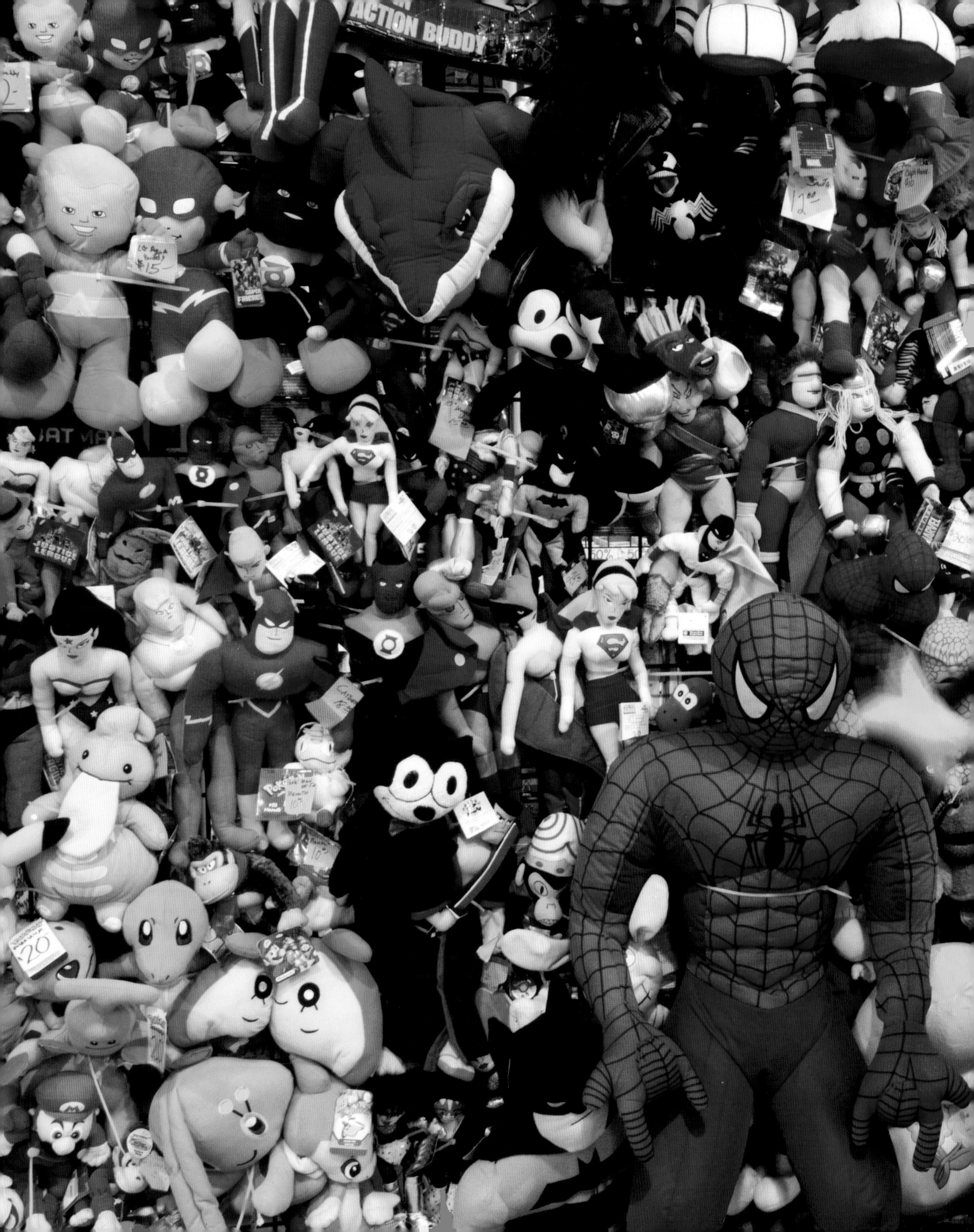
ACTION BUDDY
JUSTICE LEAGUE
JUSTICE LEAGUE
$15
20

tim bradstreet

artist | Vampire: The Masquerade, The Punisher, Hellblazer

“When people approach me to show me their work, trying to break into the industry, I can smell the guys who are really passionate about it. And for me, that conversation isn’t a critique of their work—it’s talking about why they do it, and what they love about it.”

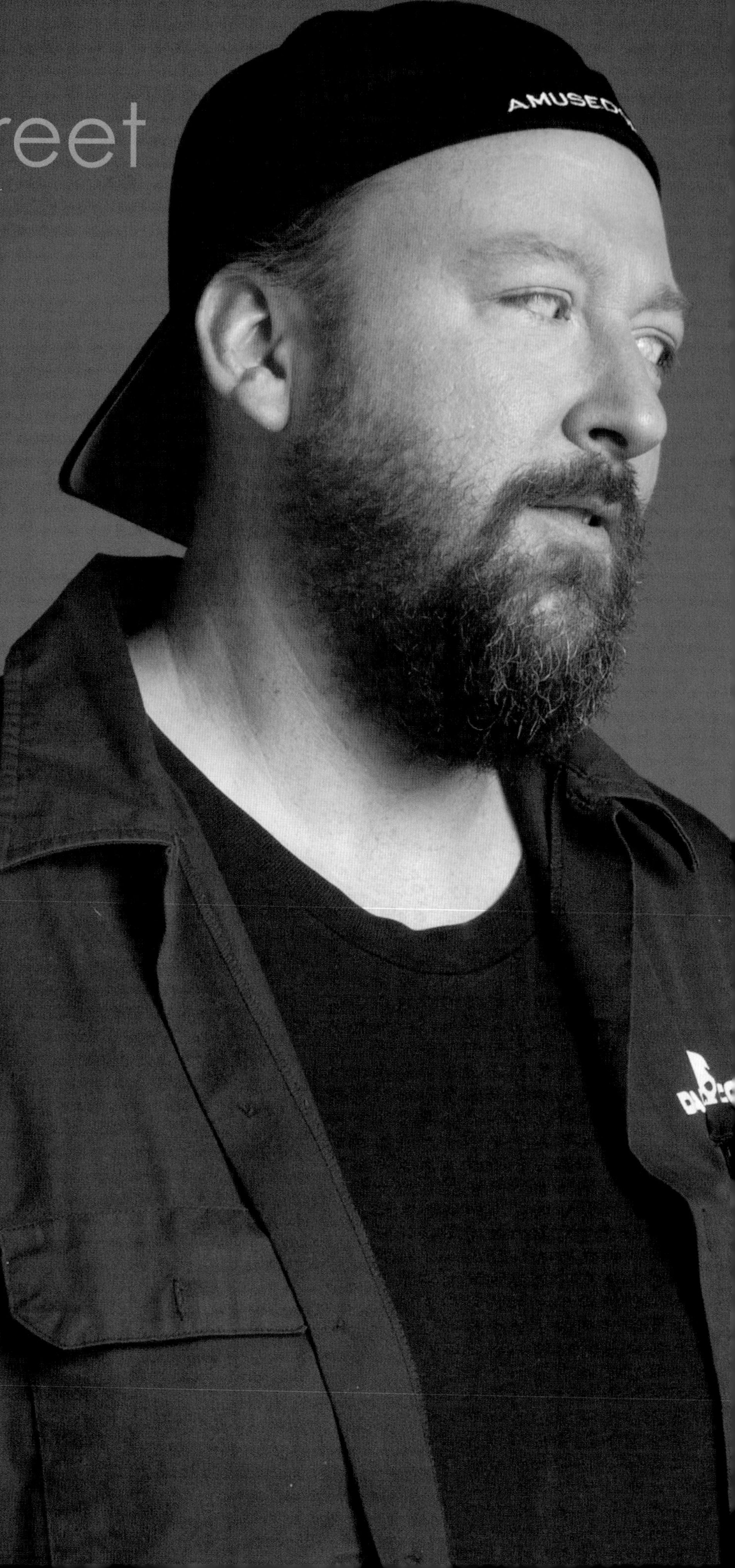

thomas jane

actor | The Punisher

"If you've been tuned in and turned onto art, real art and real writing, then it kind of becomes this organism that you try to find in regular life."

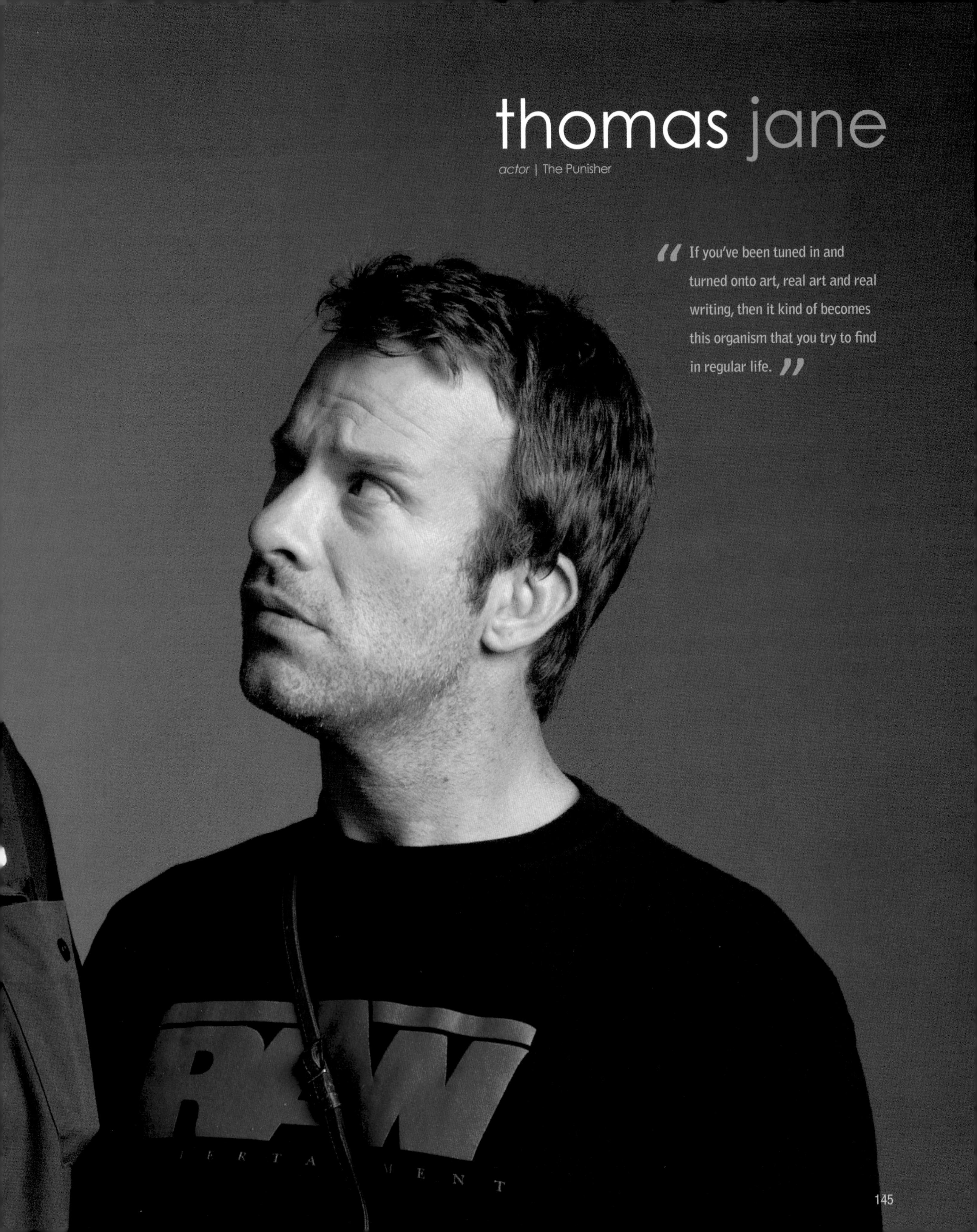
RAW

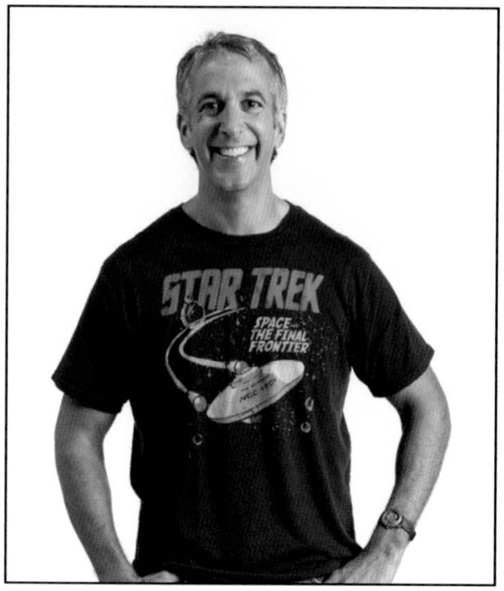
STAR TREK
SPACE THE FINAL FRONTIER

scott mantz

TV personality, film critic

“If you know which issue Gwen Stacy died in, then yes, you belong at Comic-Con. But if you go crazy for Robert Pattinson or you just love watching *Glee*, then now you belong at Comic-Con, too.”

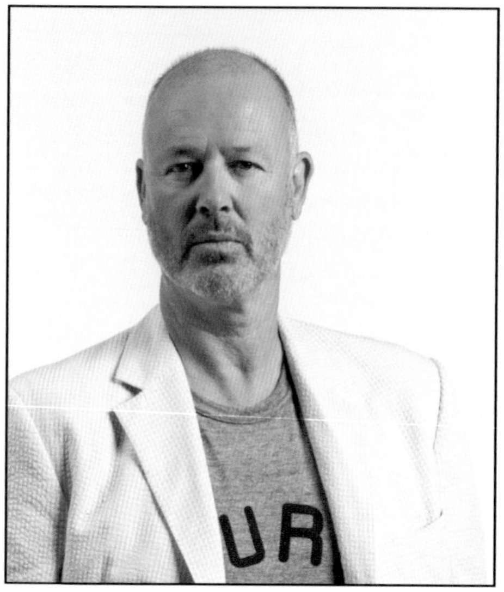

simon oakes

CEO | Hammer Films

“I think it plugs into lots of very deep-lasting and positive emotions that people have.”

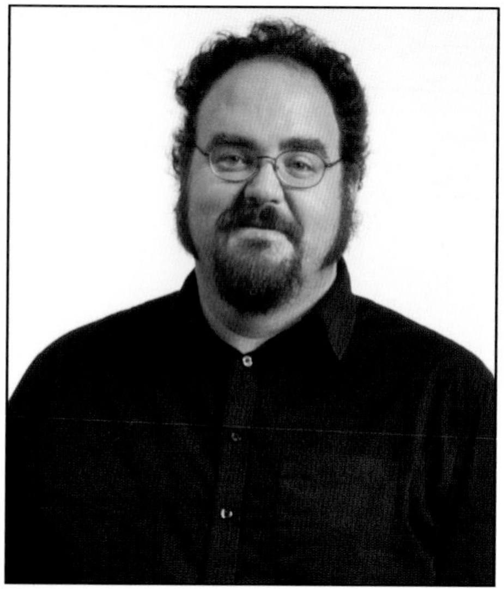

jon schnepp

creator, producer, director | Metalocalypse

“A die-hard conventioner is a person who's got the card games, they've dressed up, they go to Masquerade, they've got the backpack filled with strange dice that they roll with a strange book that's got their character chart in there. They also have their video game module controller that they can plug in and switch information with someone else. And they have a list: 'Daredevil number 51—check. Number 52—very fine, near mint, almost...must continue perusing.'”

alexandre aja

director | The Hills Have Eyes, Piranha 3D

" The audience here is much sharper. They don't see the genre as just a genre; they see the subtle subtext, the political comment, the satirical aspect of the genre. You think about those things when you're making a movie, and to find people who understand right away, who share with you the same kind of language—it's just amazing. I would like the audience everywhere to be like this. "

" I love science fiction. I always say that *Back to the Future* is maybe my favorite movie, and the sequels are great. "

michel gondry

director | The Green Hornet

betsy russell

actor | Saw

" Interacting with my fans on a one-on-one level is really awesome. The Saw fans are die-hards...they're so excited about all of the movies, and they're just really fun. "

tobin bell

actor | the Saw series

" The first time I came, I didn't know what to expect. And I was mightily impressed with the dedication and the passion and the sense of fun that Comic-Con visitors have. "

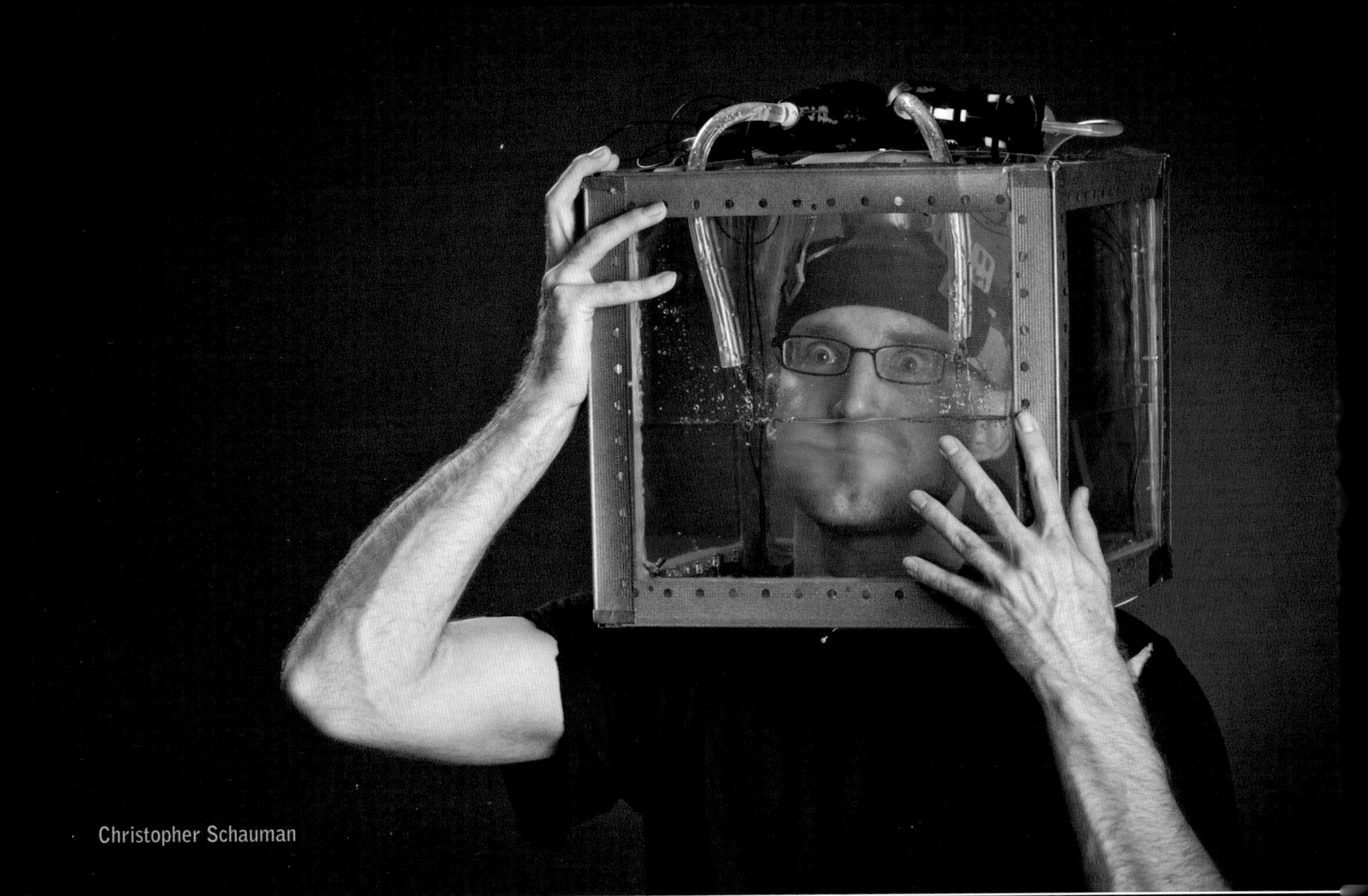

Christopher Schauman

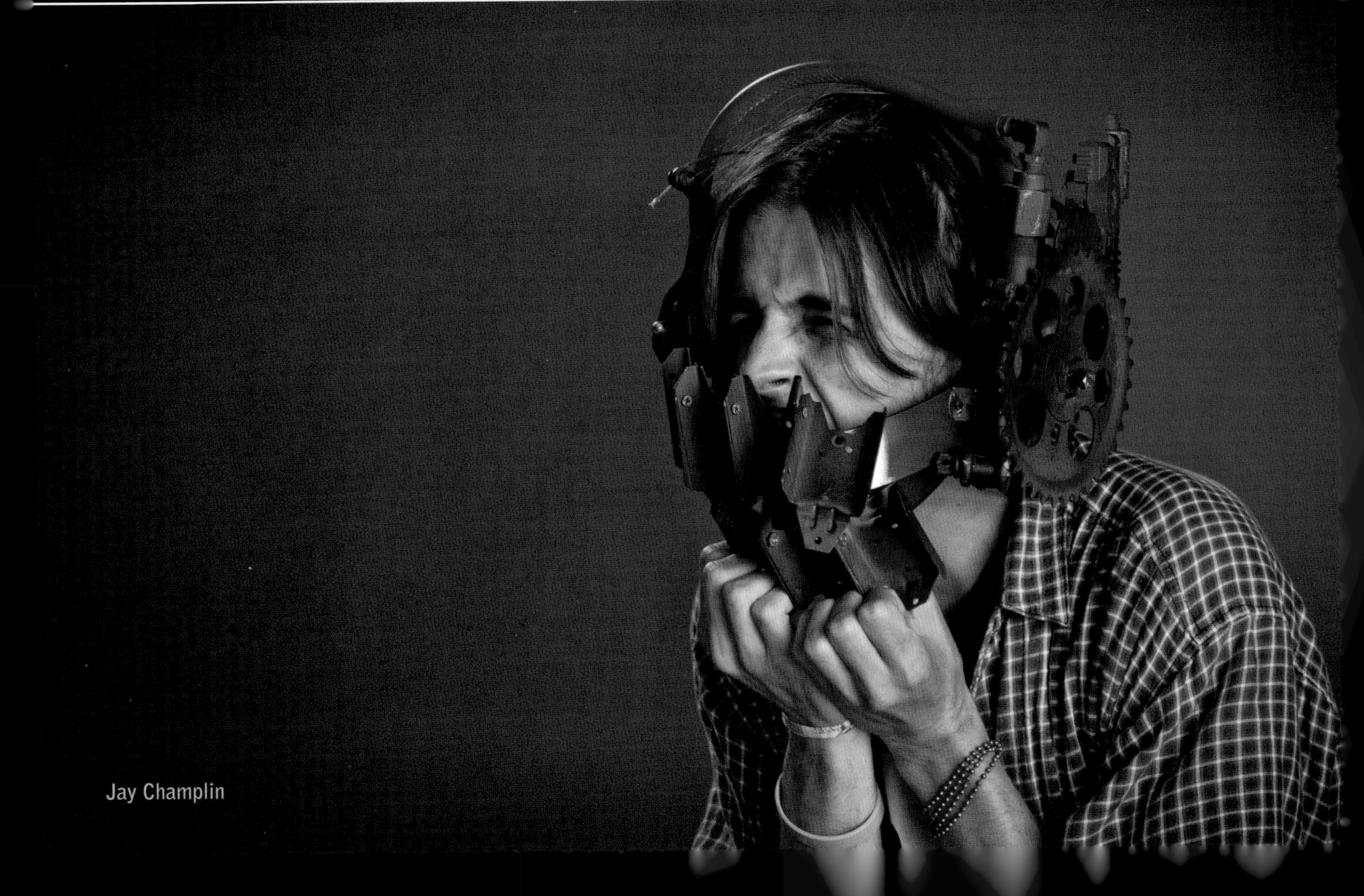

Jay Champlin

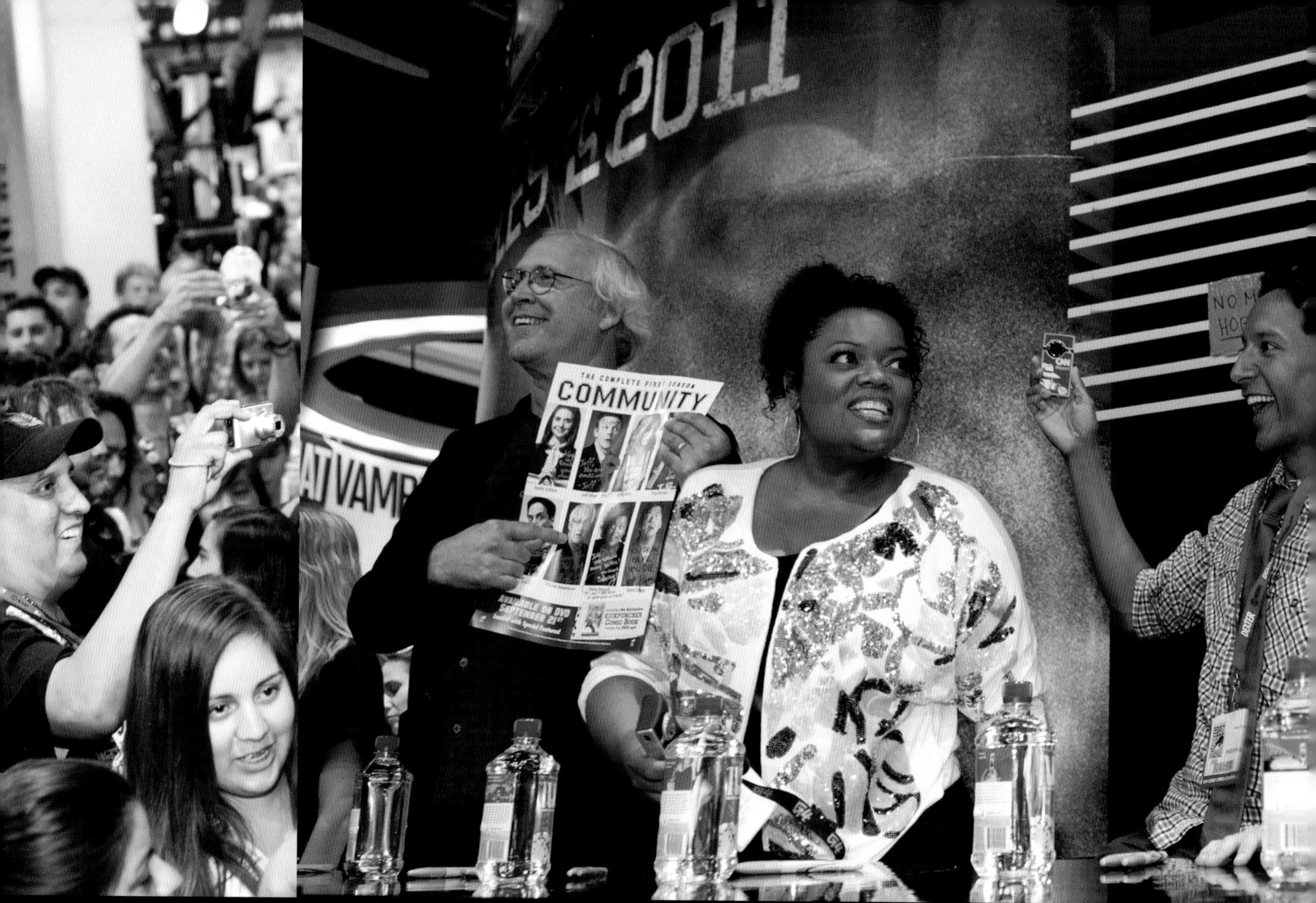
2011
THE COMPLETE FIRST SEASON
COMMUNITY

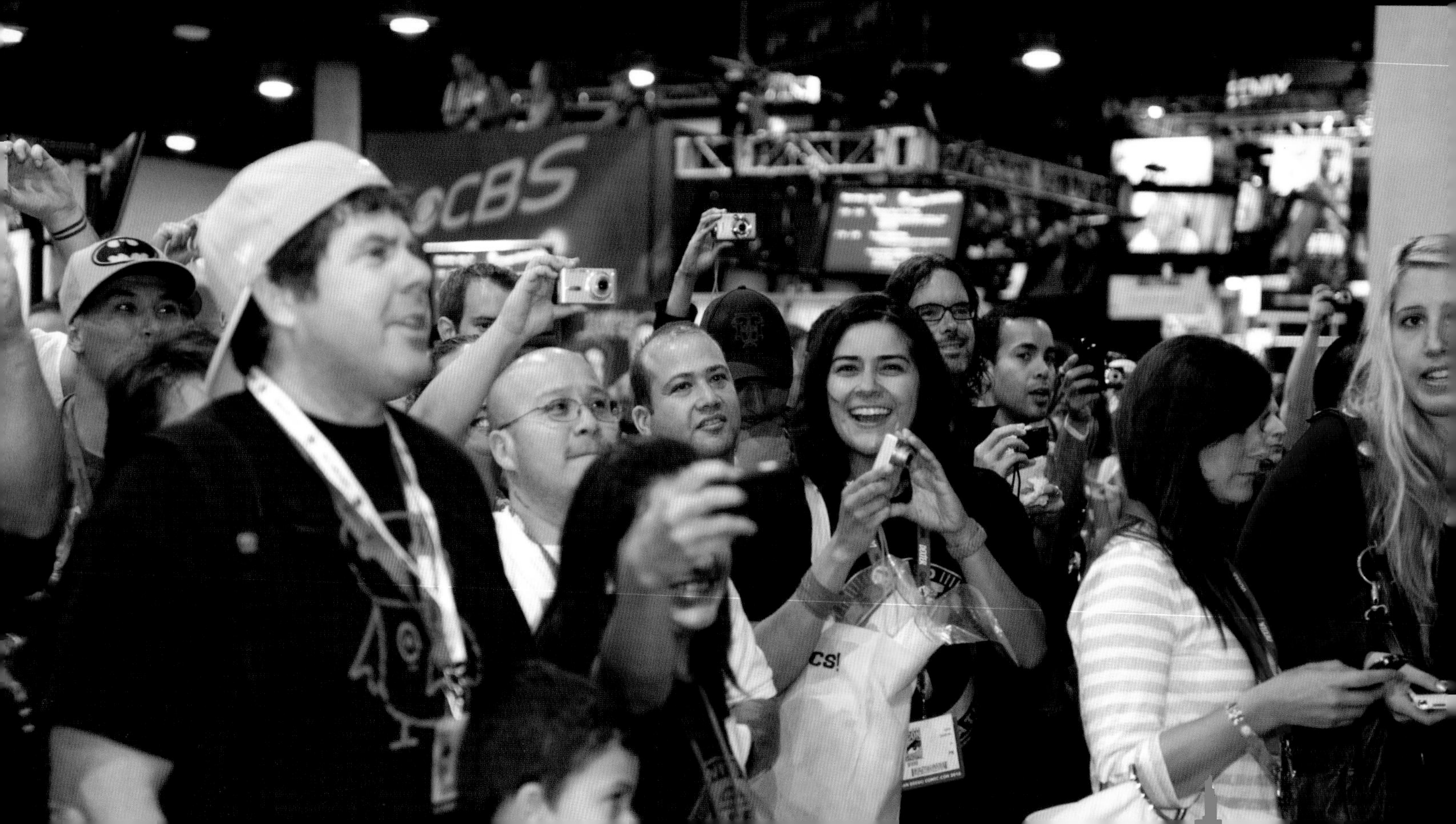
CBS

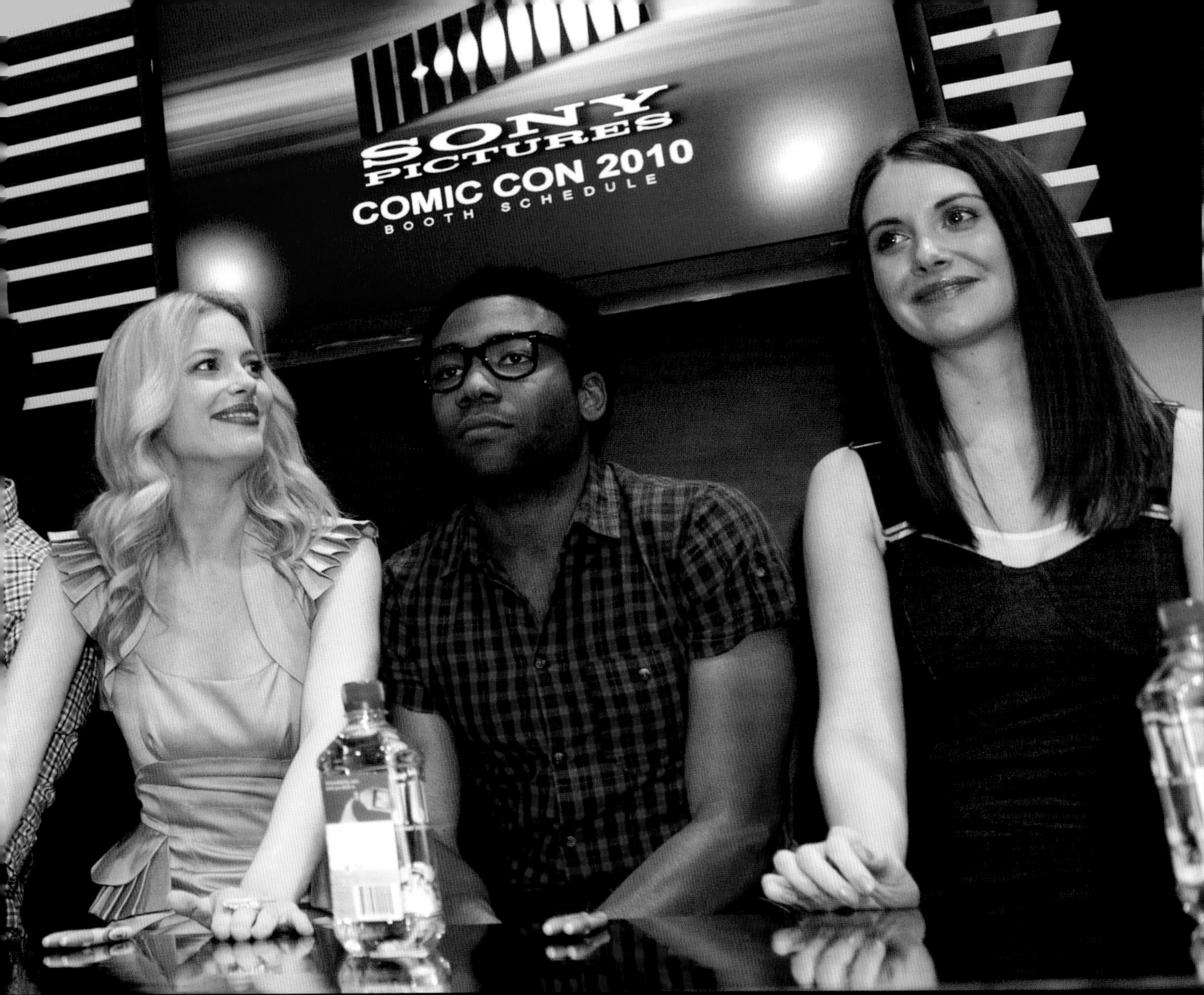
SONY
PICTURES
COMIC CON 2010
BOOTH SCHEDULE
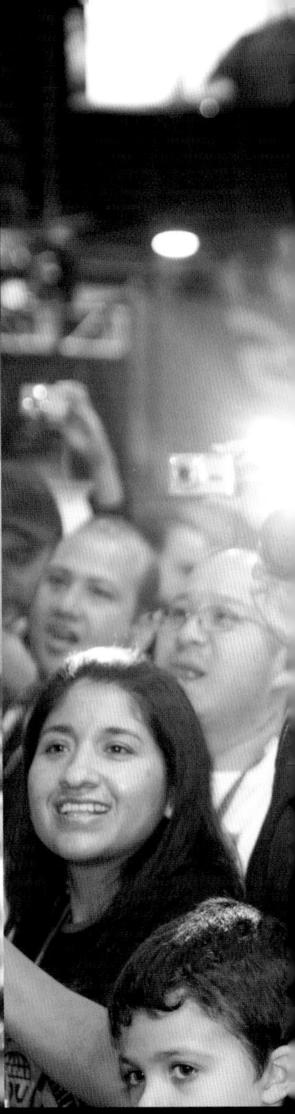
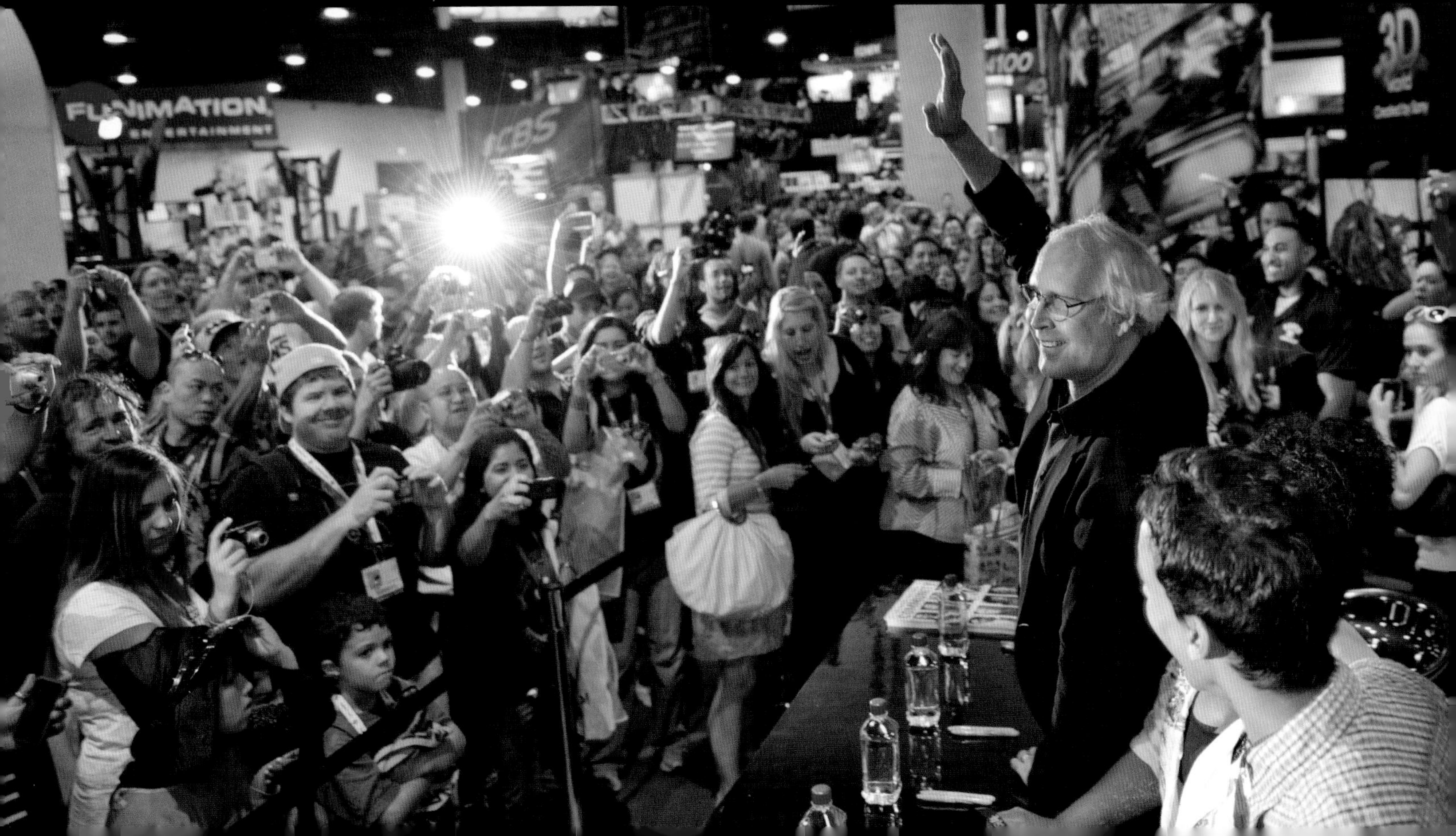
FUNIMATION
ENTERTAINMENT
CBS
3D

matt fraction

writer | The Invincible Iron Man, Uncanny X-Men

"We understand the world through the stories that we tell each other. And comics, be they sublime or ridiculous, are sort of the modern myth that is our *Iliad*, our *Odyssey*. It's these kinds of hero stories, this very Joseph Campbell kind of way that shows us, at its most simple, what we're capable of in our hearts and in our souls."

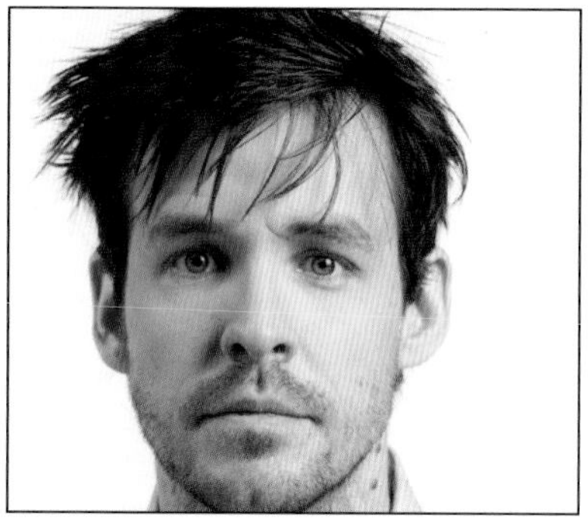
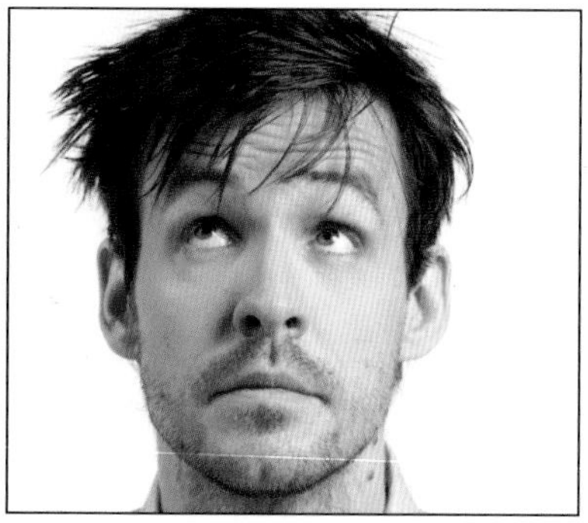
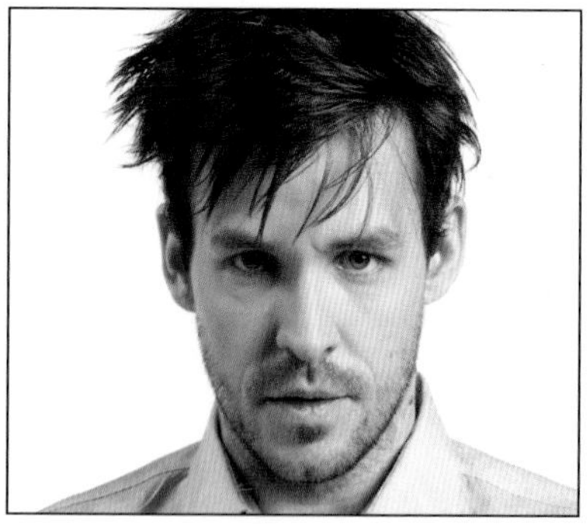
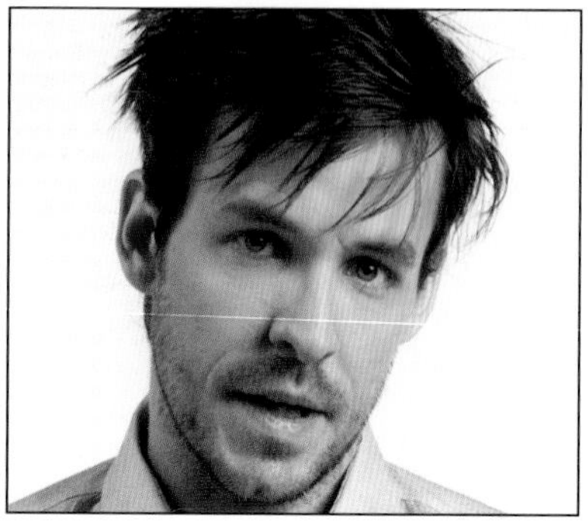
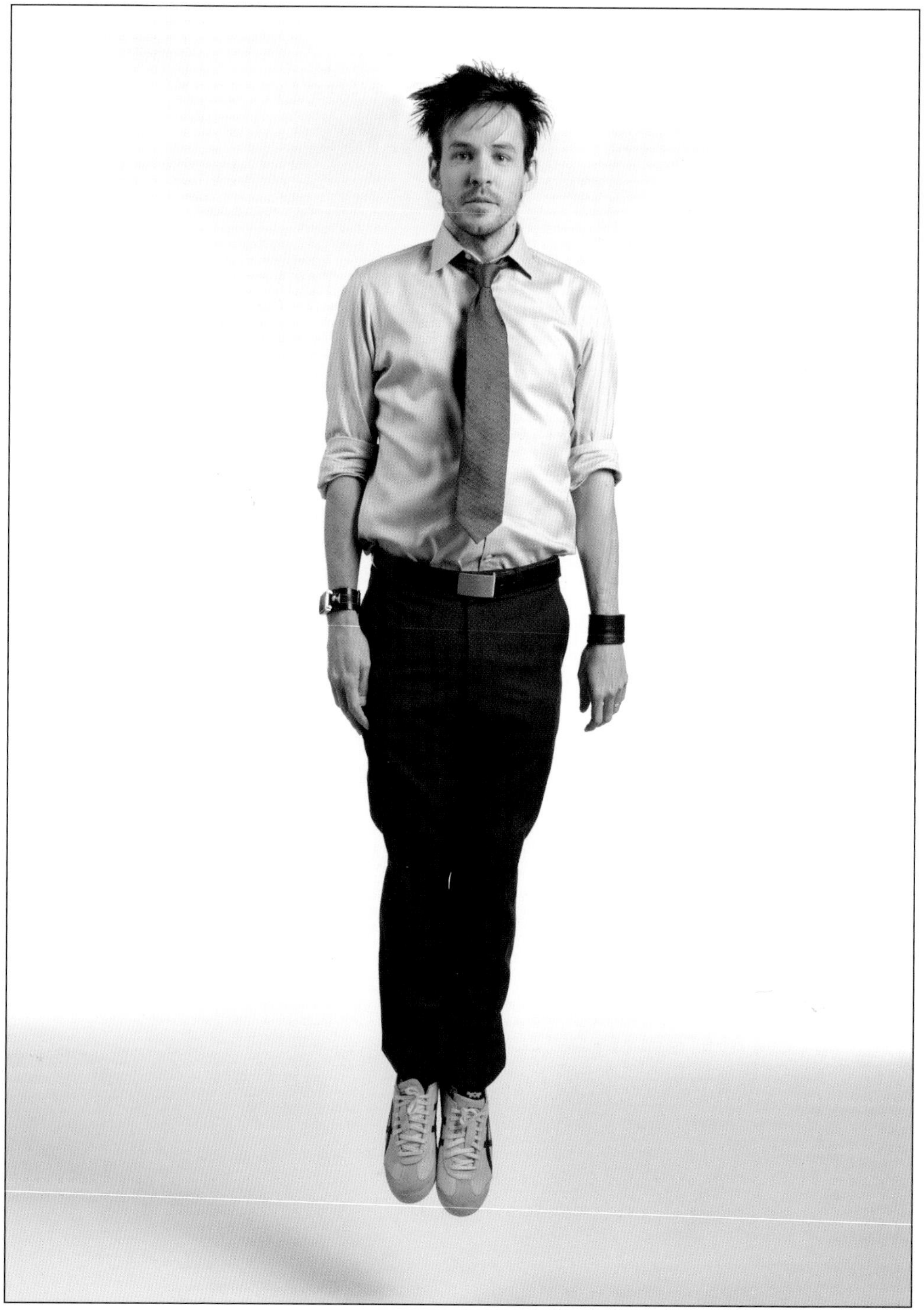

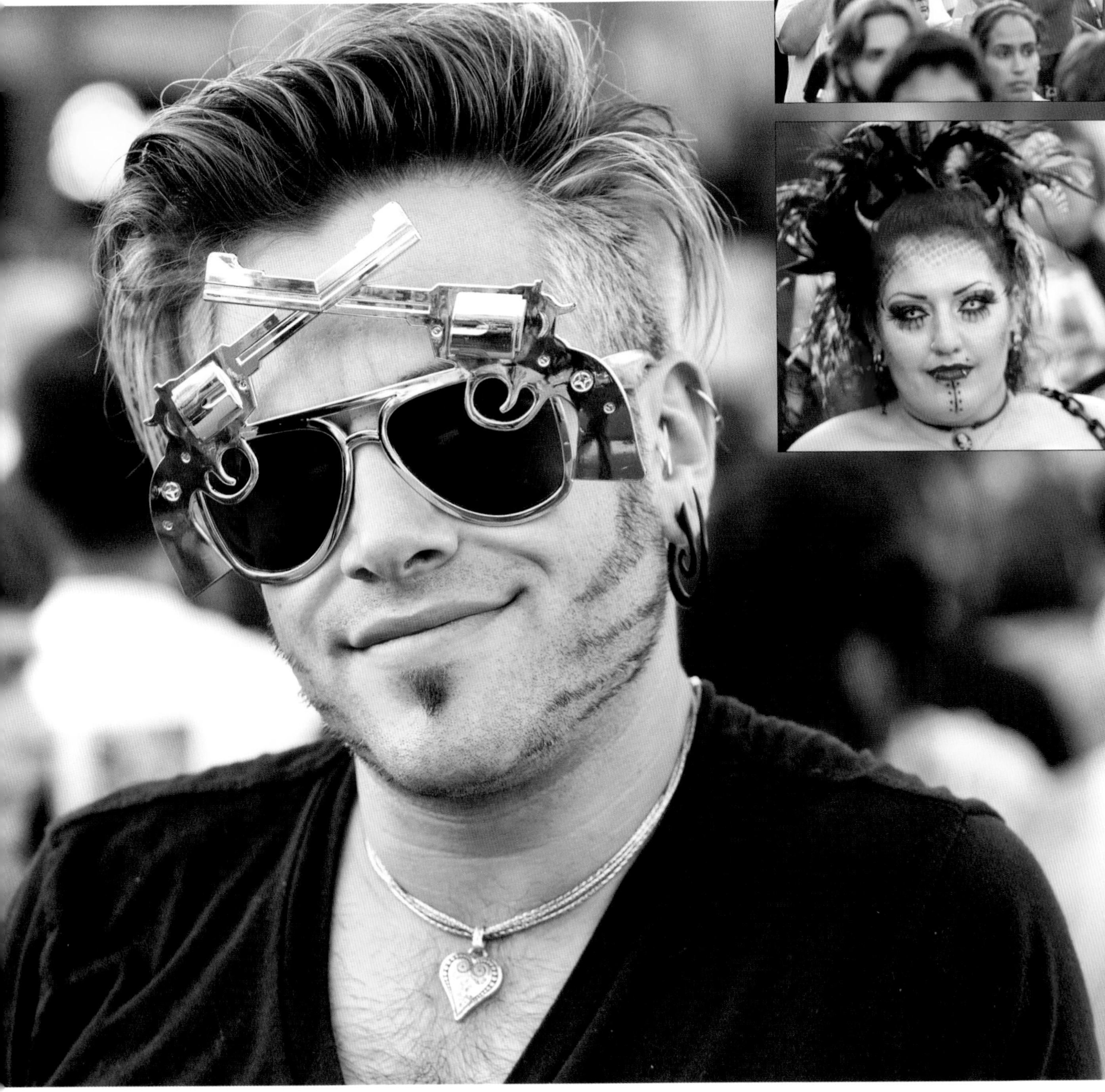

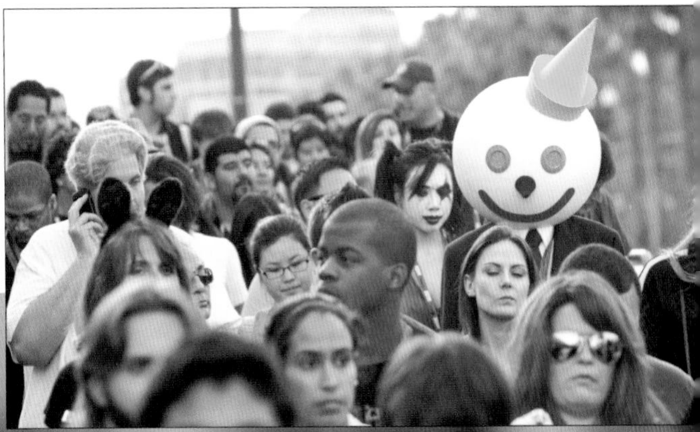

frank miller

comic book artist, writer | Batman: The Dark Knight Returns, Sin City, 300

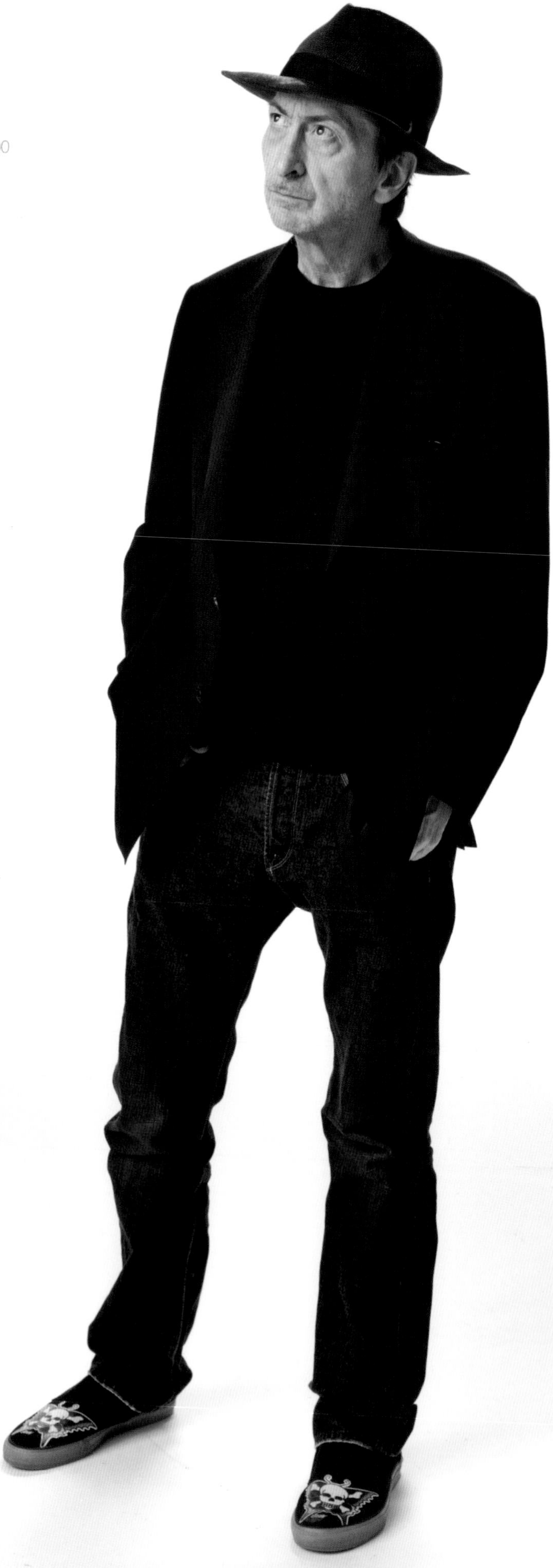

"It's very important in a field as intimate, as fantasy based, as comic books to stay in touch, to give back and to answer questions. It's become harder at Comic-Con to do so, because the mobs have gotten so intense. But I still love to do it, and the fans of fantasy, whether it's in comics or in movies, are among the sweetest people I've ever met in my life."

> "We need heroes for the same reason that we need stories. We need things that shine an arc of light on reality and make things a lot clearer."

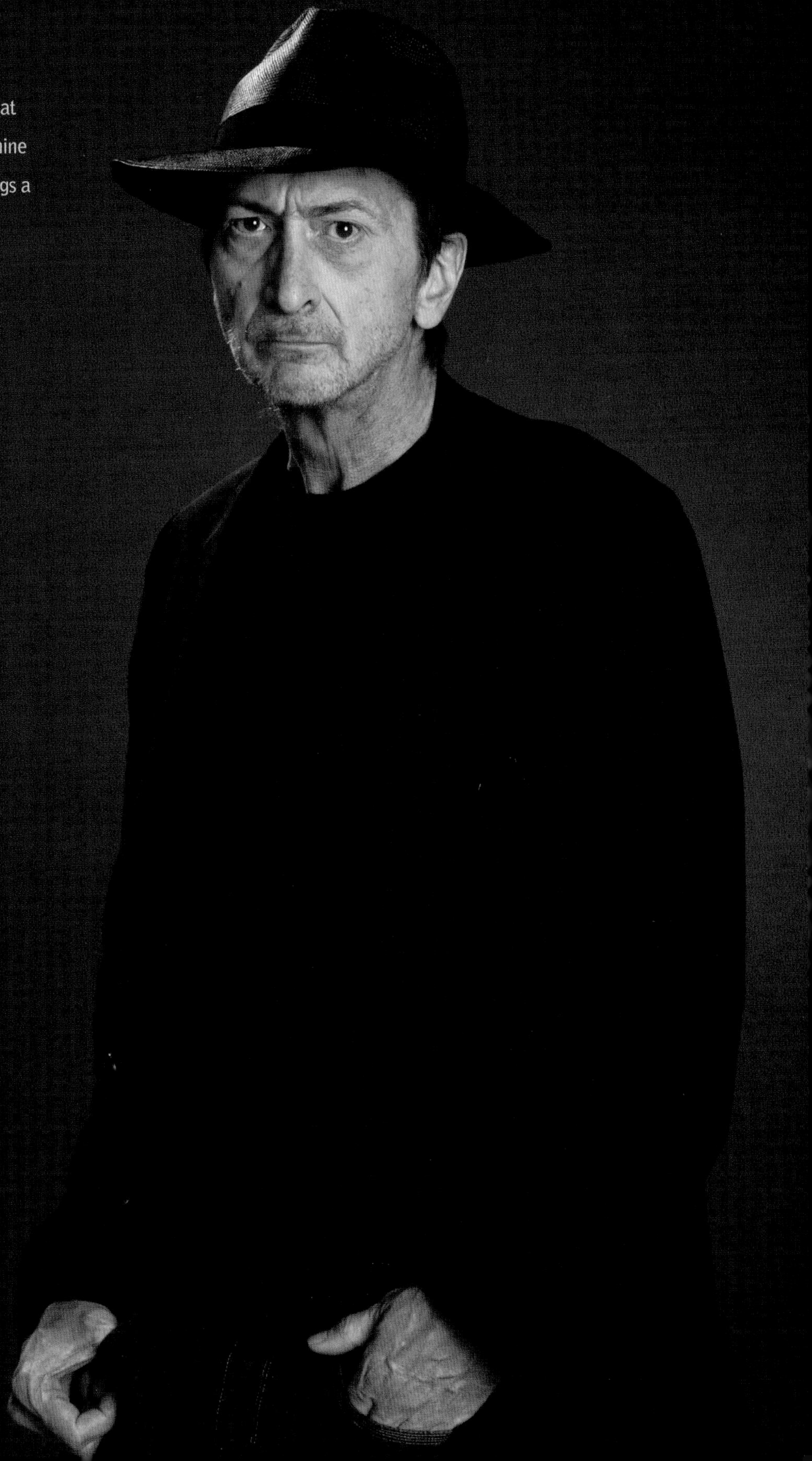

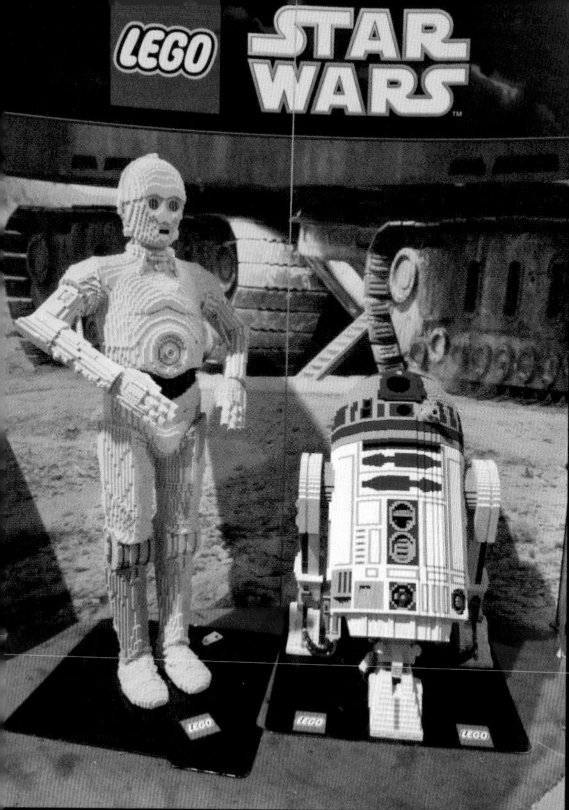
LEGO
STAR WARS
LEGO
LEGO
LEGO

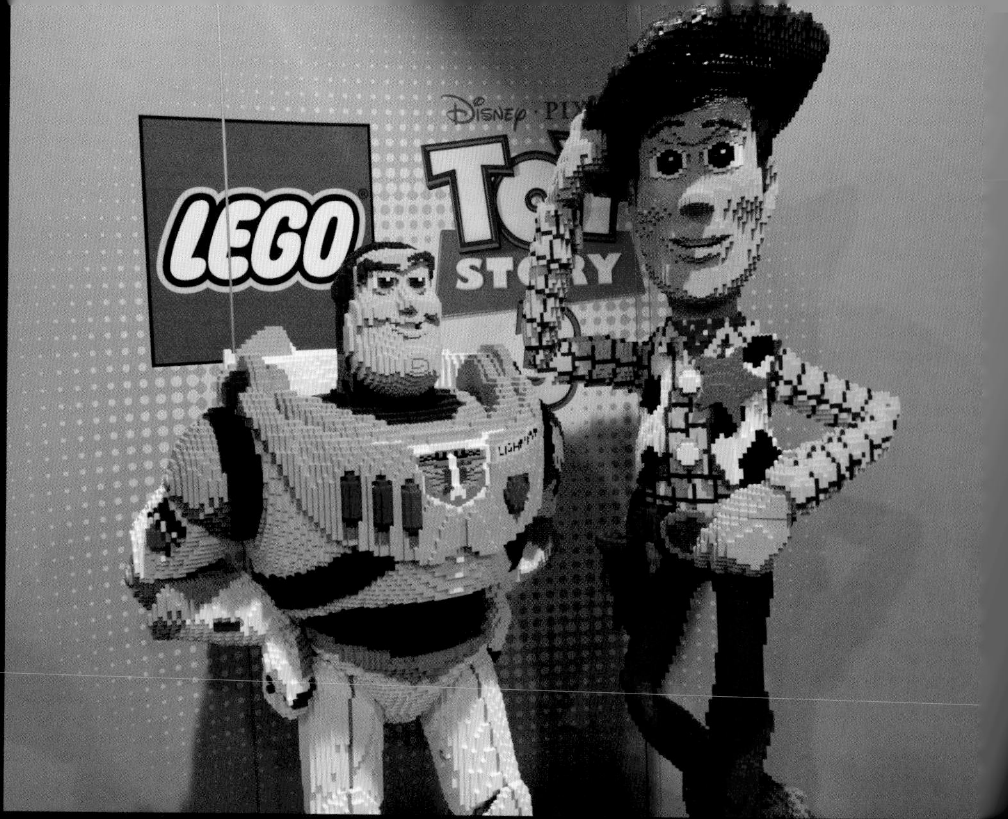
LEGO
STORY

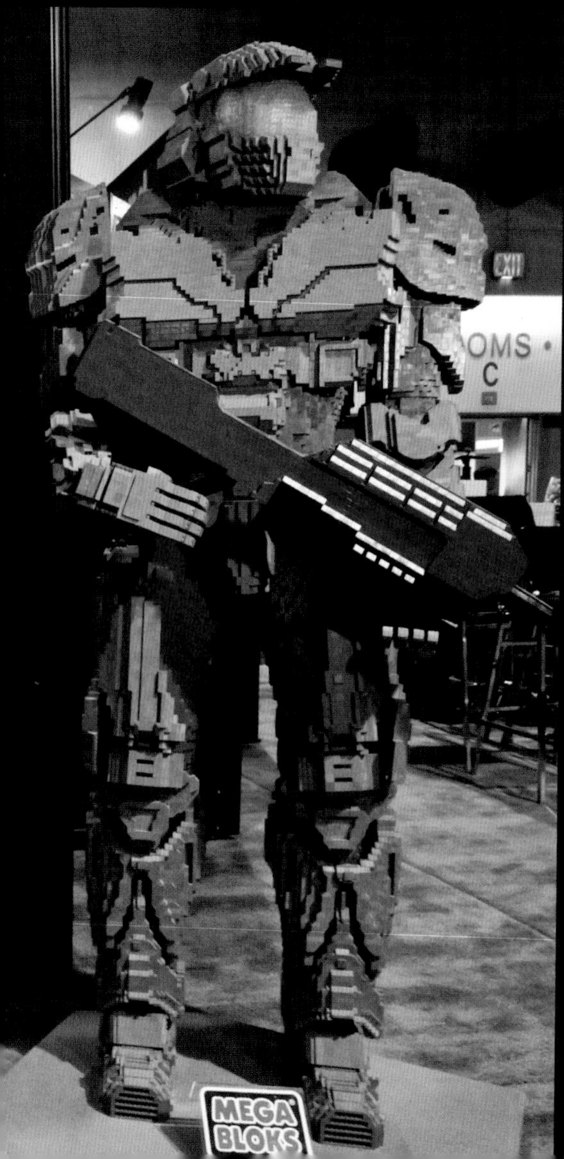
EXIT
OMS
C
MEGA BLOKS

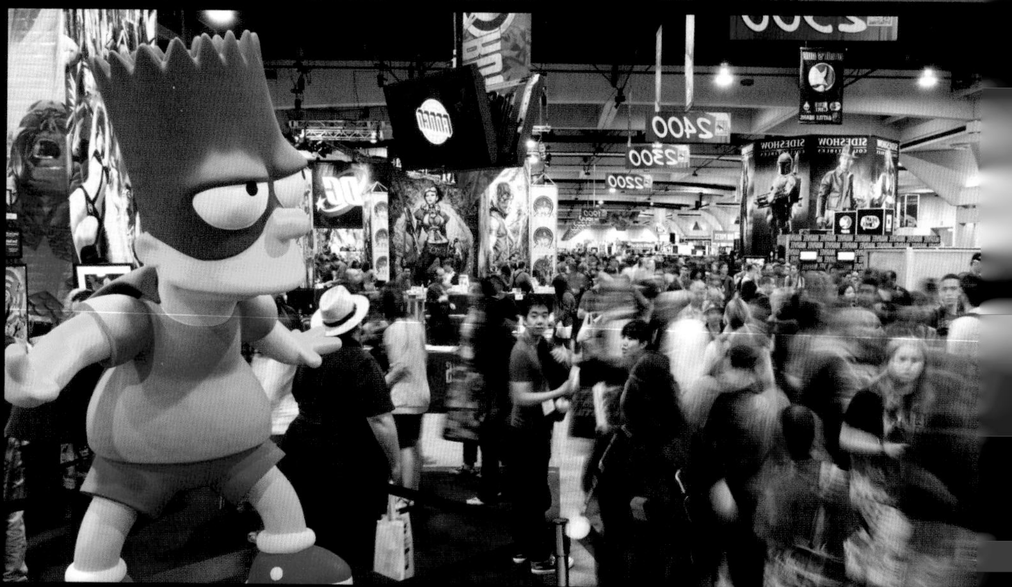
2400
2300
2200
SIDESHOW
SIDESHOW

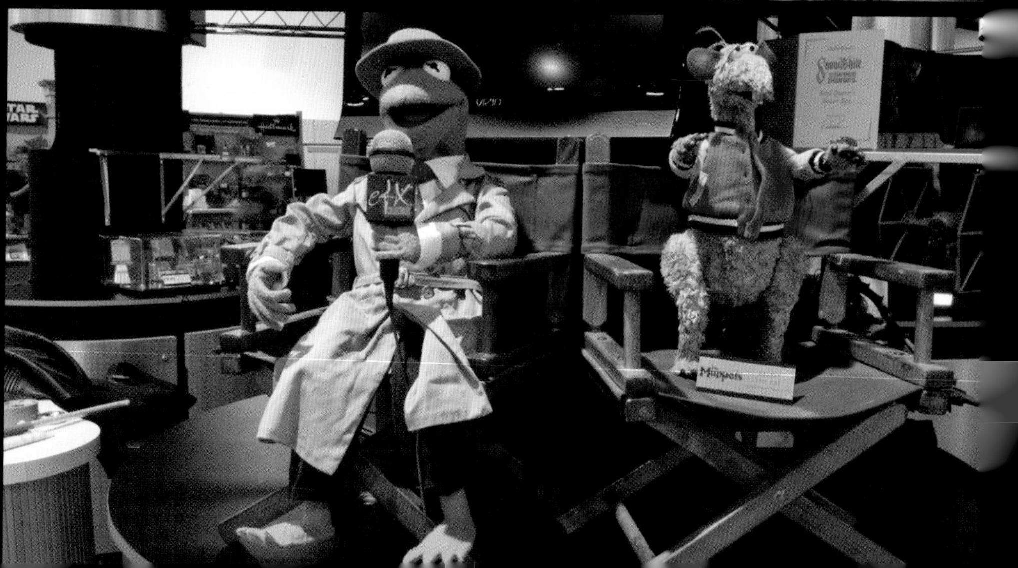
Muppets

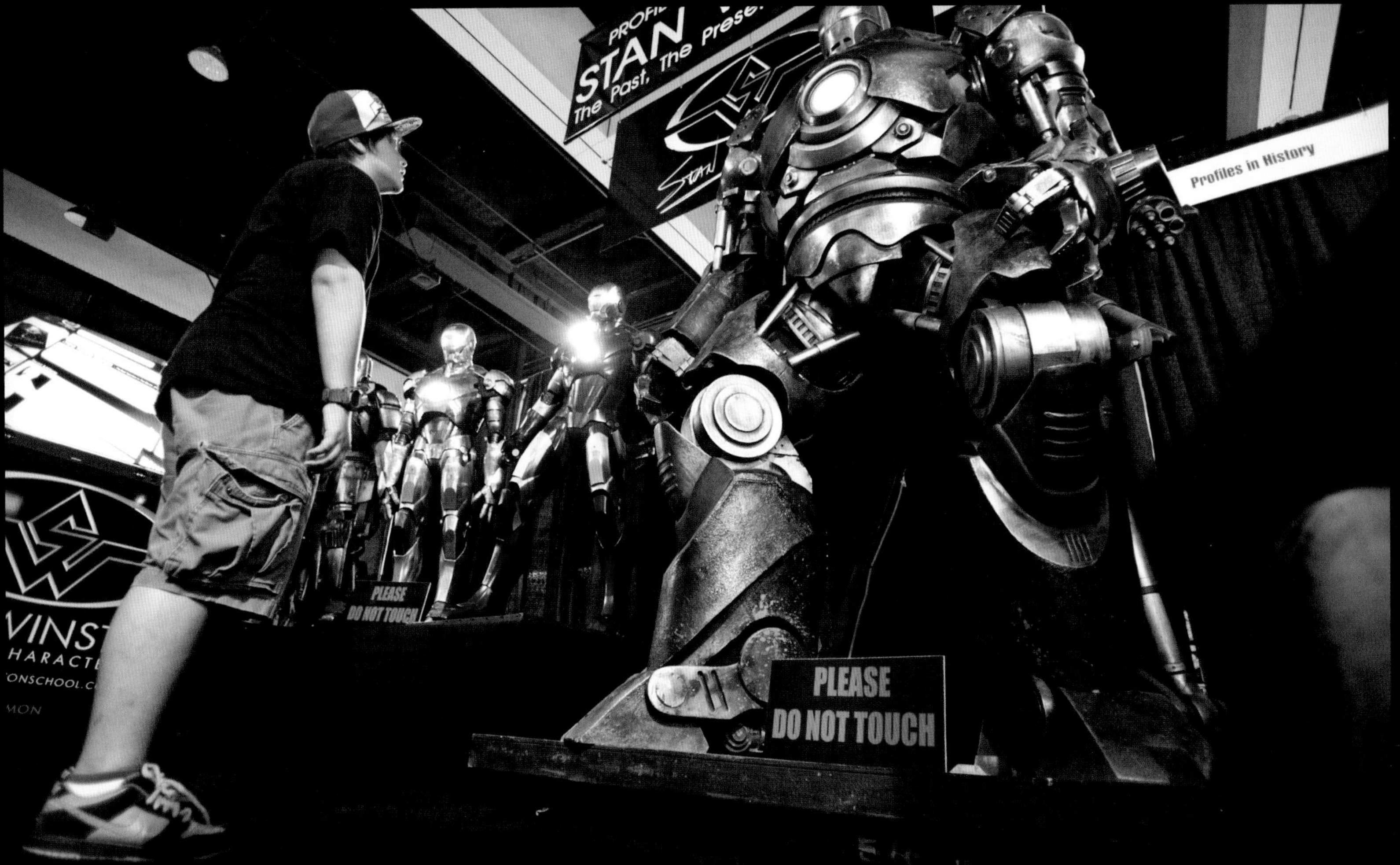
Profiles in History
PLEASE
DO NOT TOUCH
PLEASE
DO NOT TOUCH

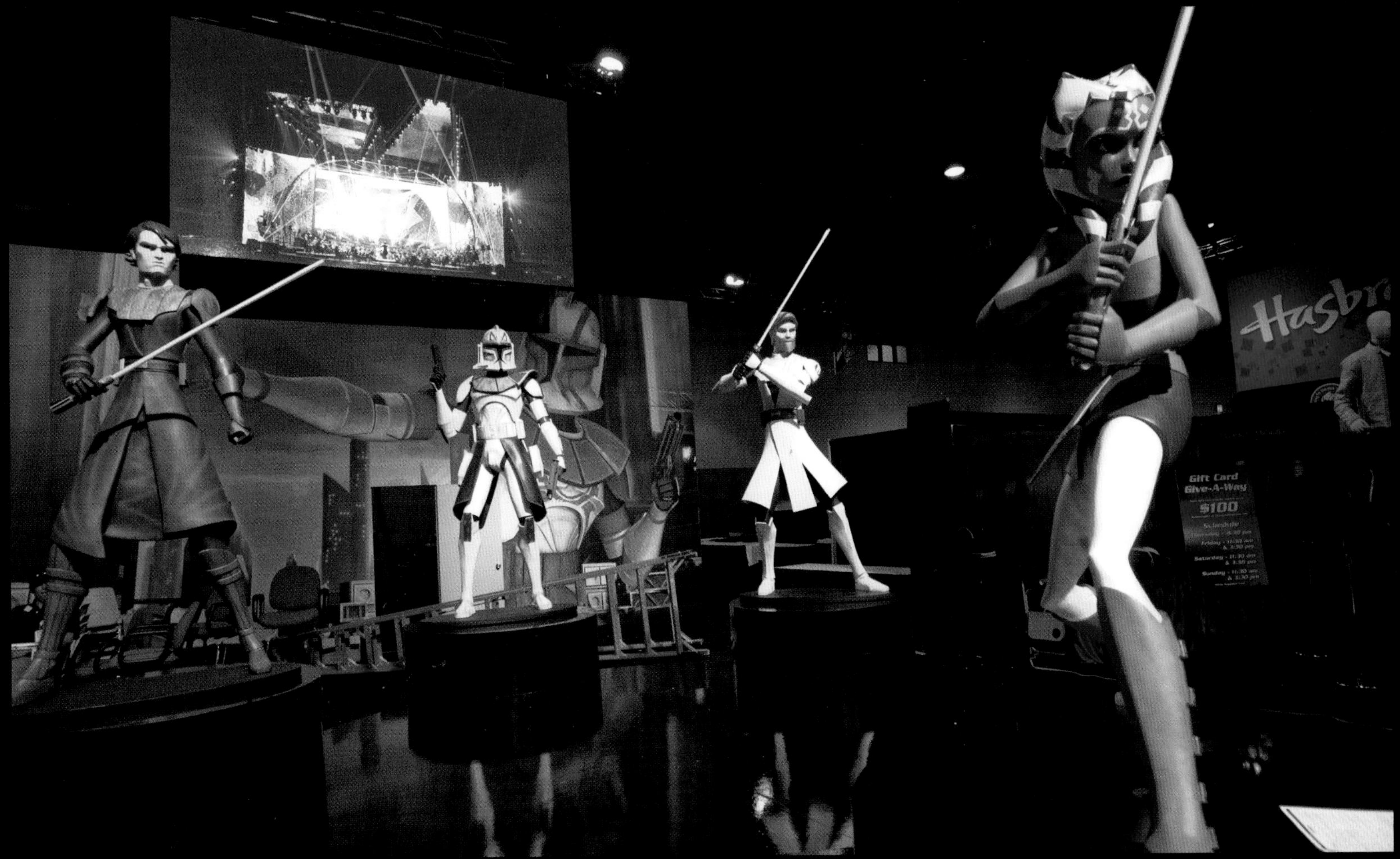
Gift Card
Give-A-Way
$100
Schedule

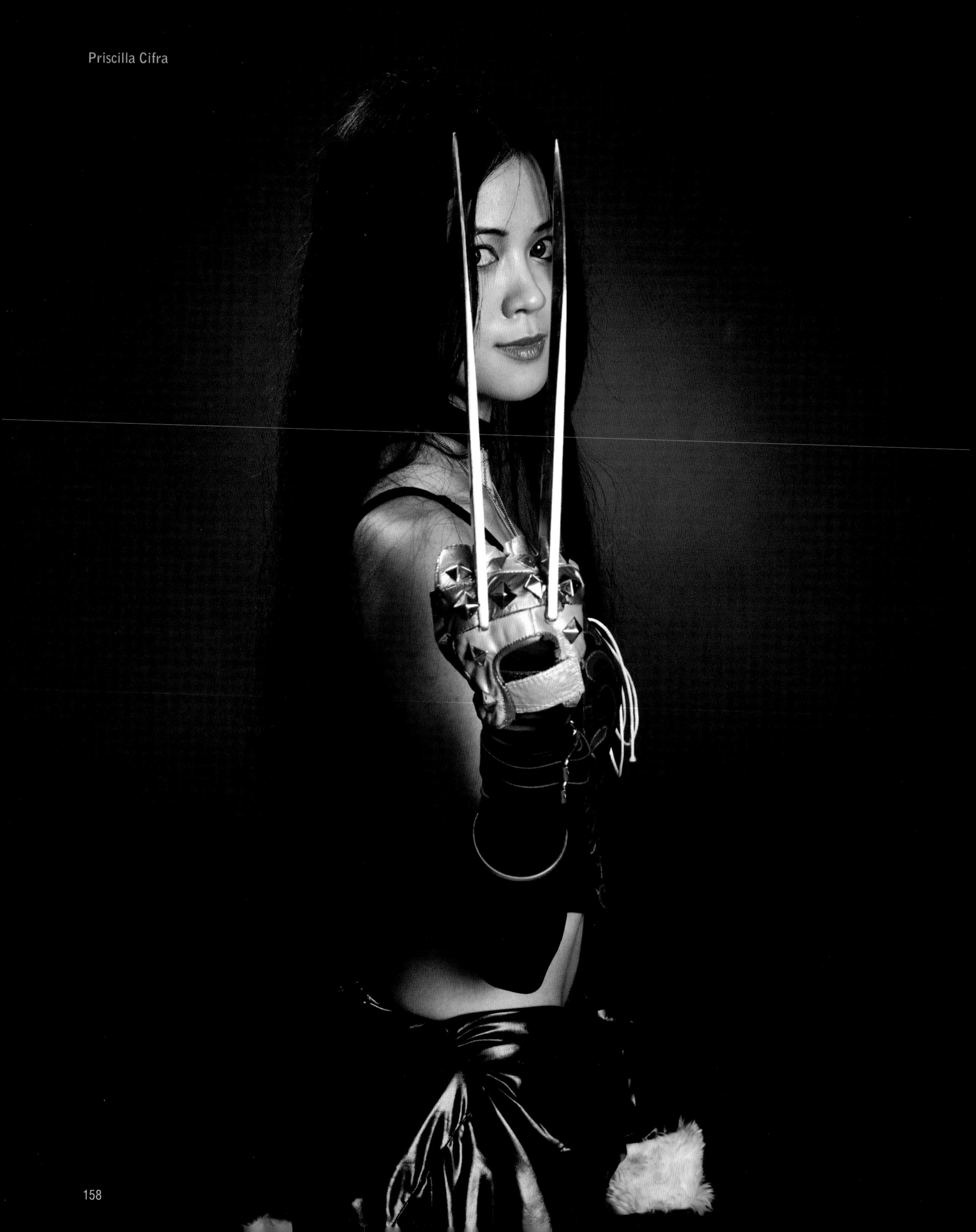

joe quesada

writer, creator | Event Comics

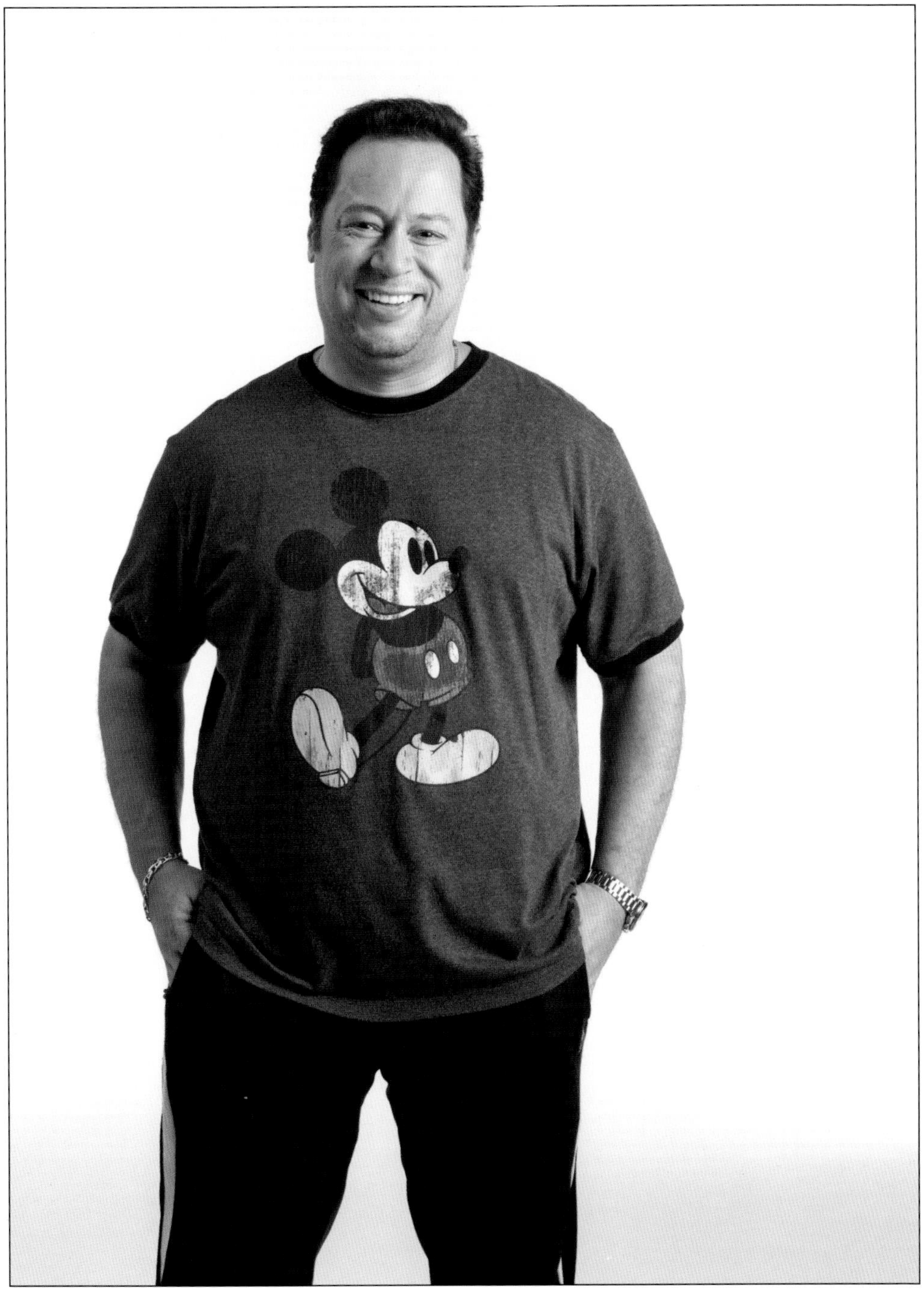

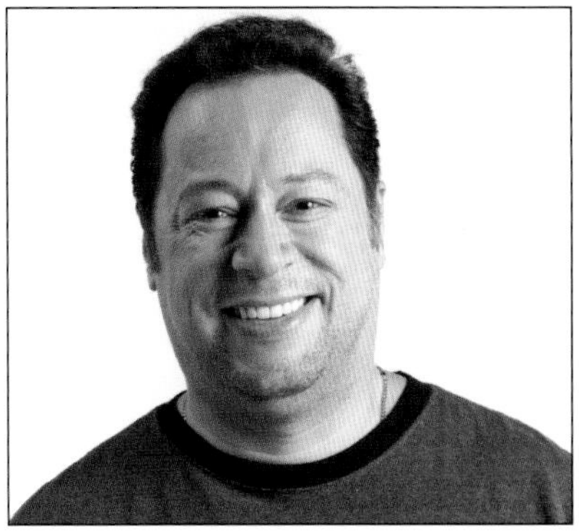

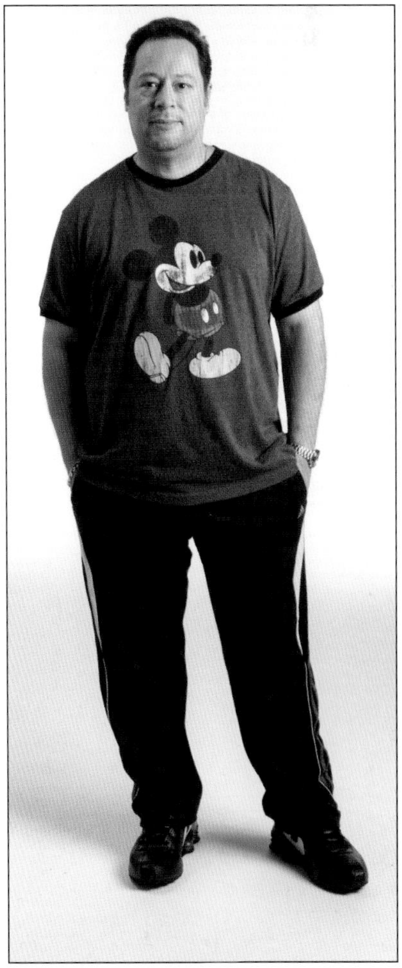

“You'll get a different vibe on the Internet than you would if you took a hundred people who are really angry about something and brought them down to Comic-Con. They'd all be happy. You'd never hear a single one of those complaints, because we're all in our element.”

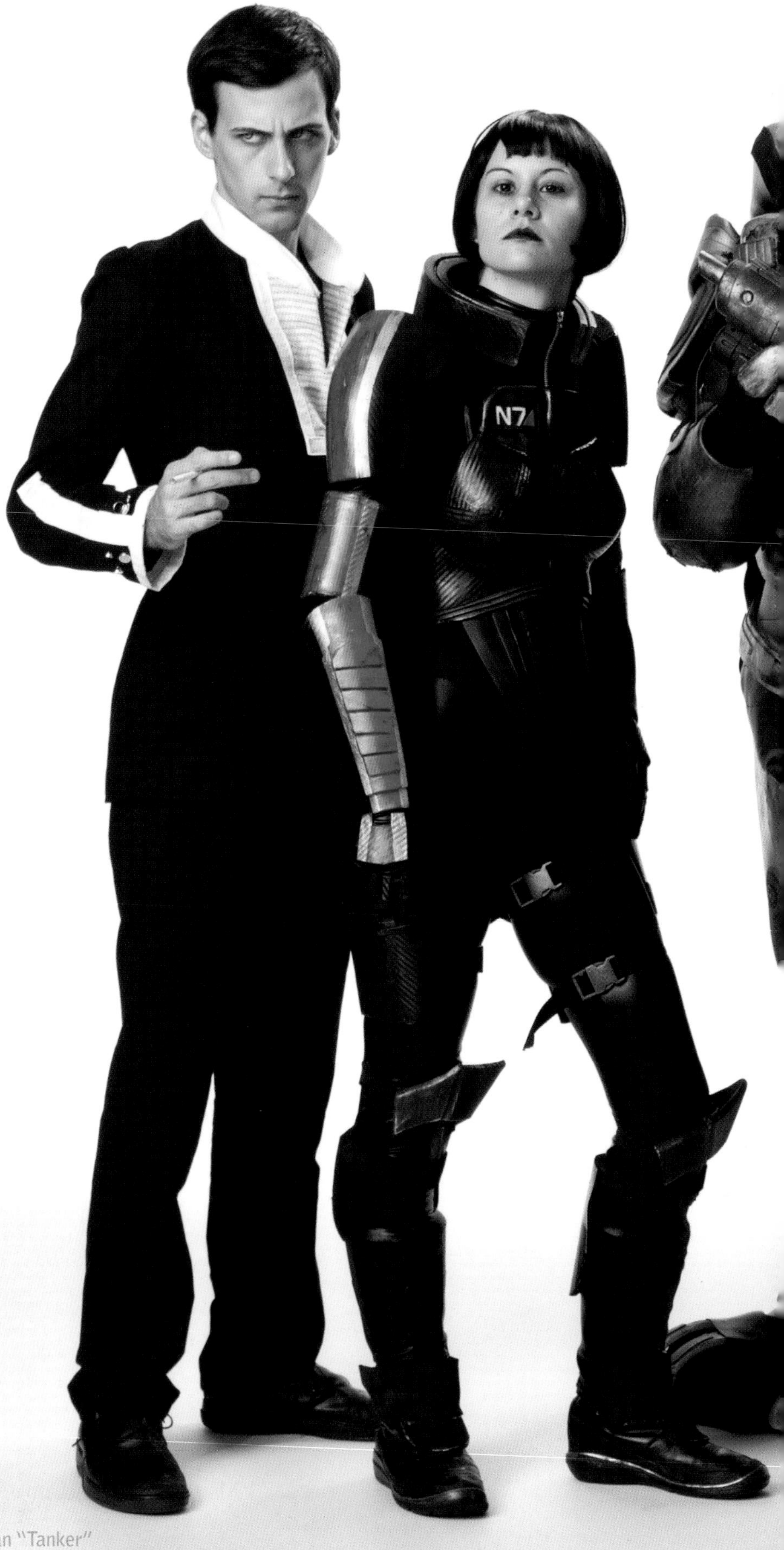
N7

(from left to right) Alex Gross, Holly Conrad, Sean "Tanker" Walsh, Tayler Hudson, Stephanie Werner, Jessica Merizan

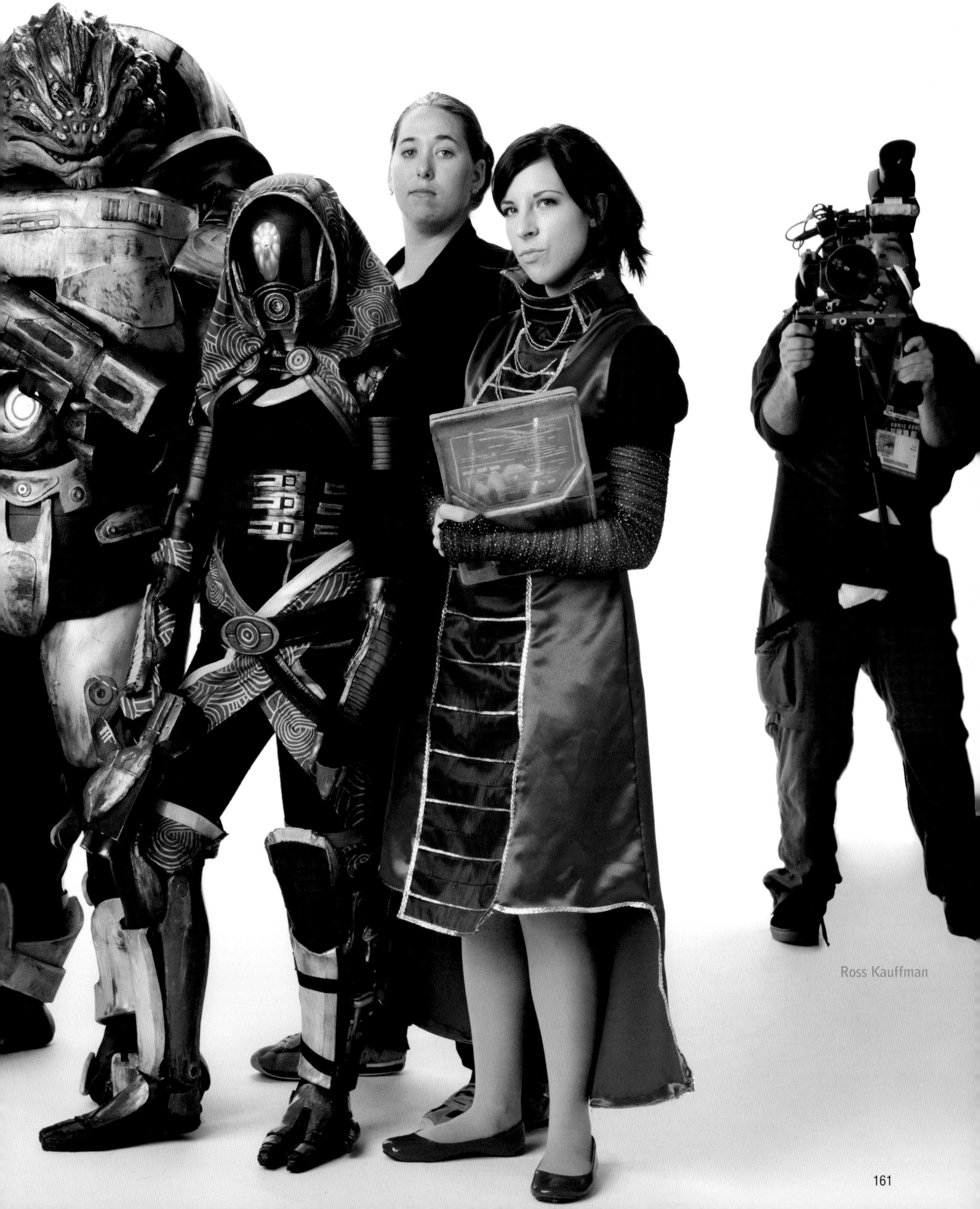

Ross Kauffman

nathan fillion

actor | Firefly

"I can tell you for me what drives fandom. I'm a fan. I used to collect comic books. I loved Spider-Man; I loved the escape that is fantasy. It's the unrealistic made real. And then on top of that, you can collect. And I think that's a neat thing, that you can come to Comic-Con and get pieces of the things that drive you wild."

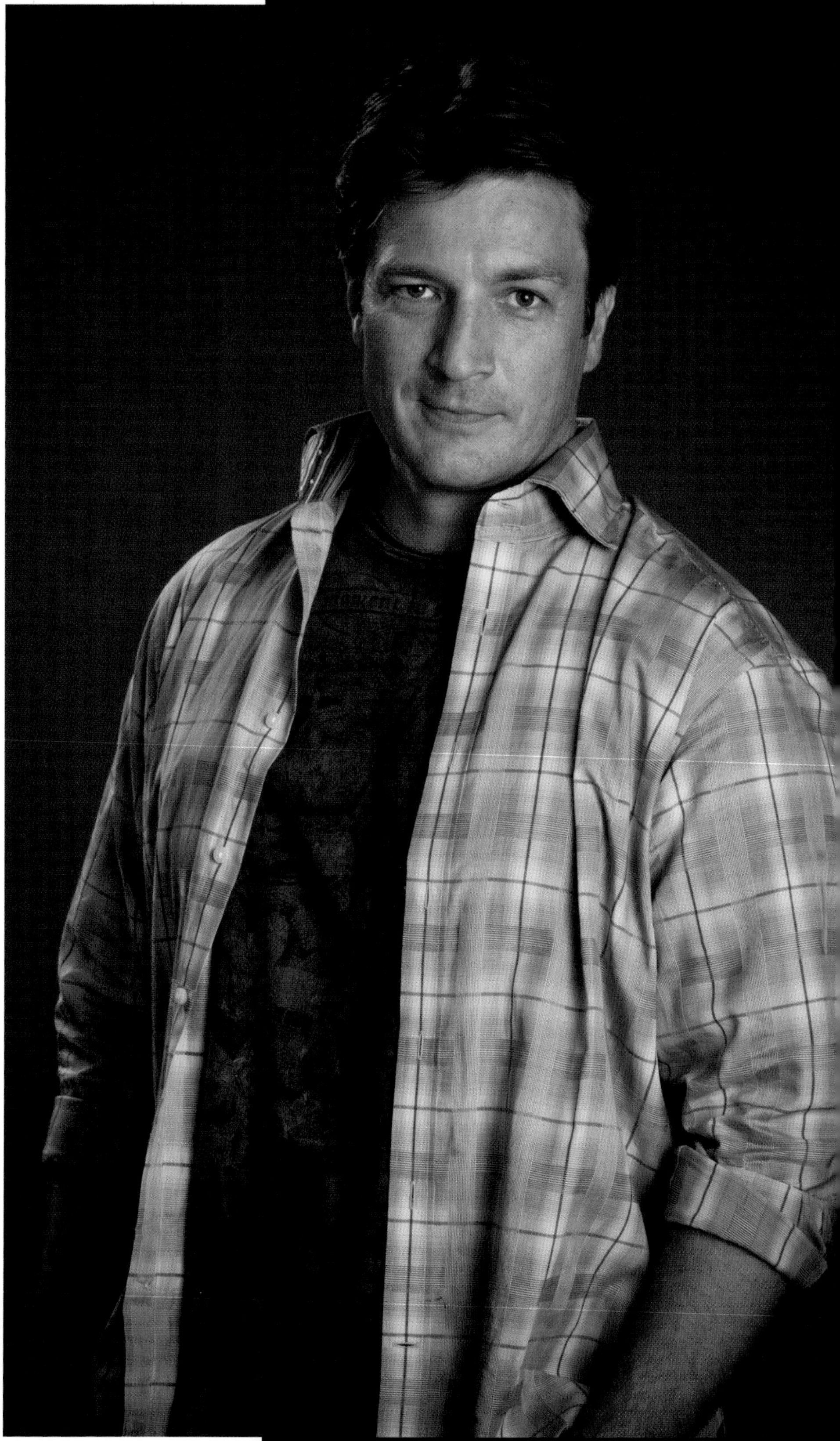

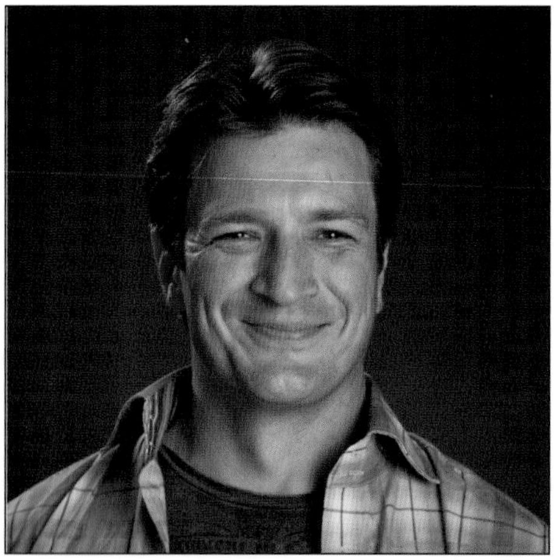

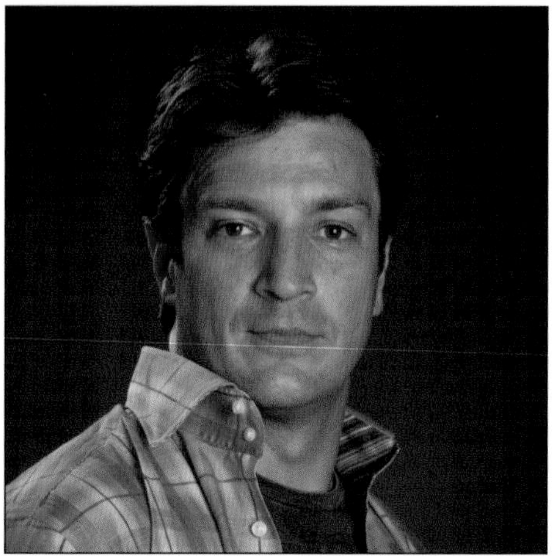

M. Rachel Butler

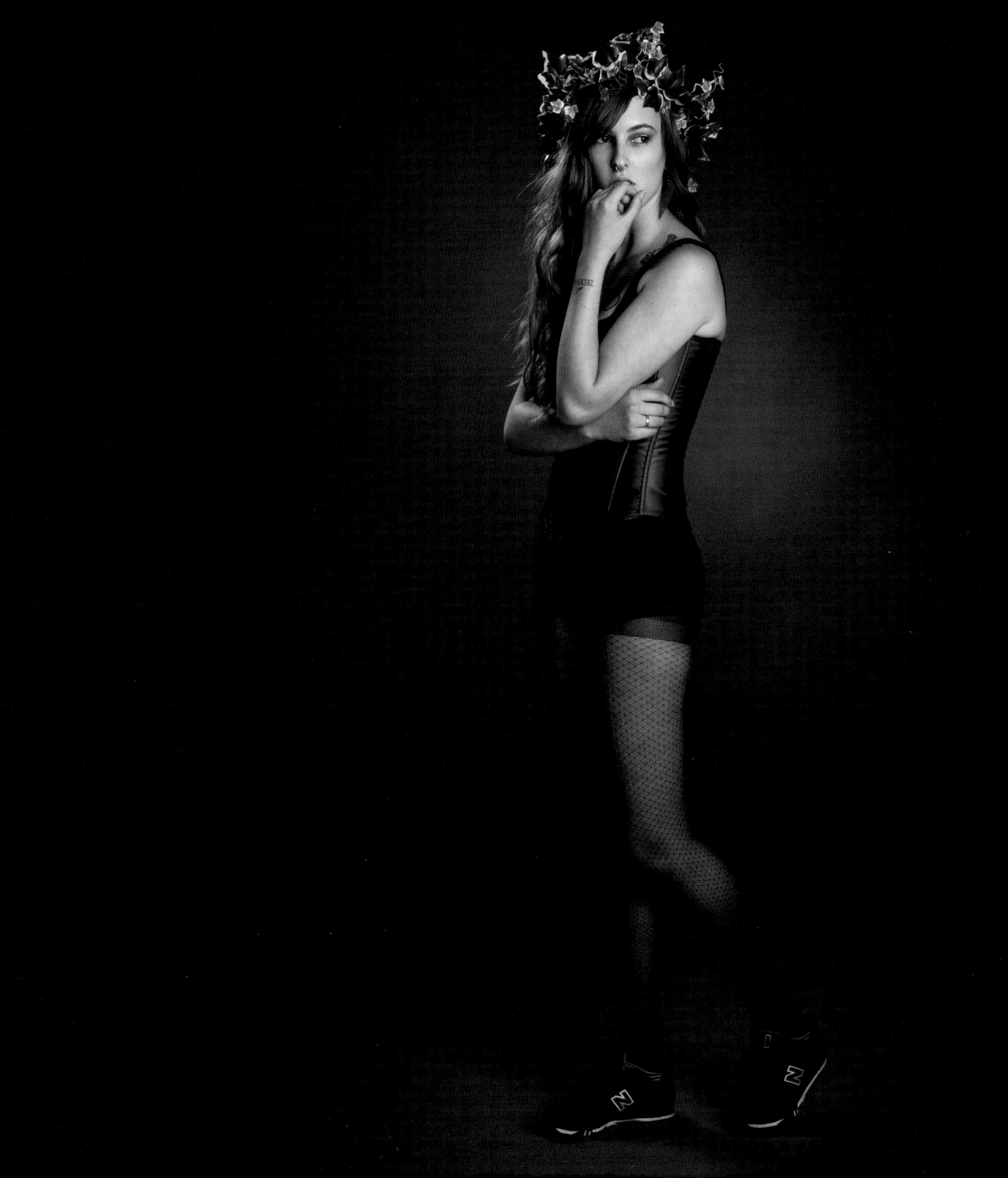

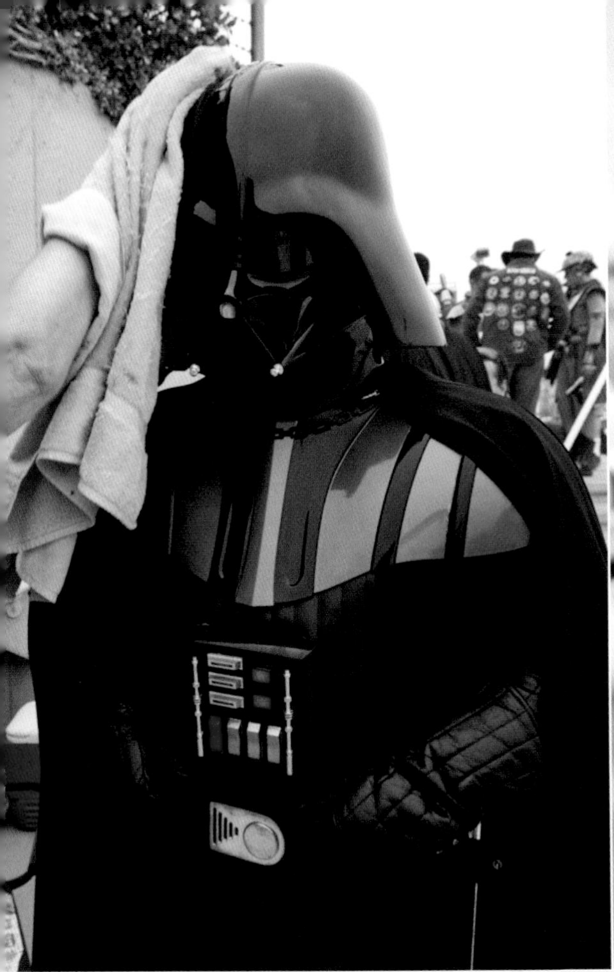
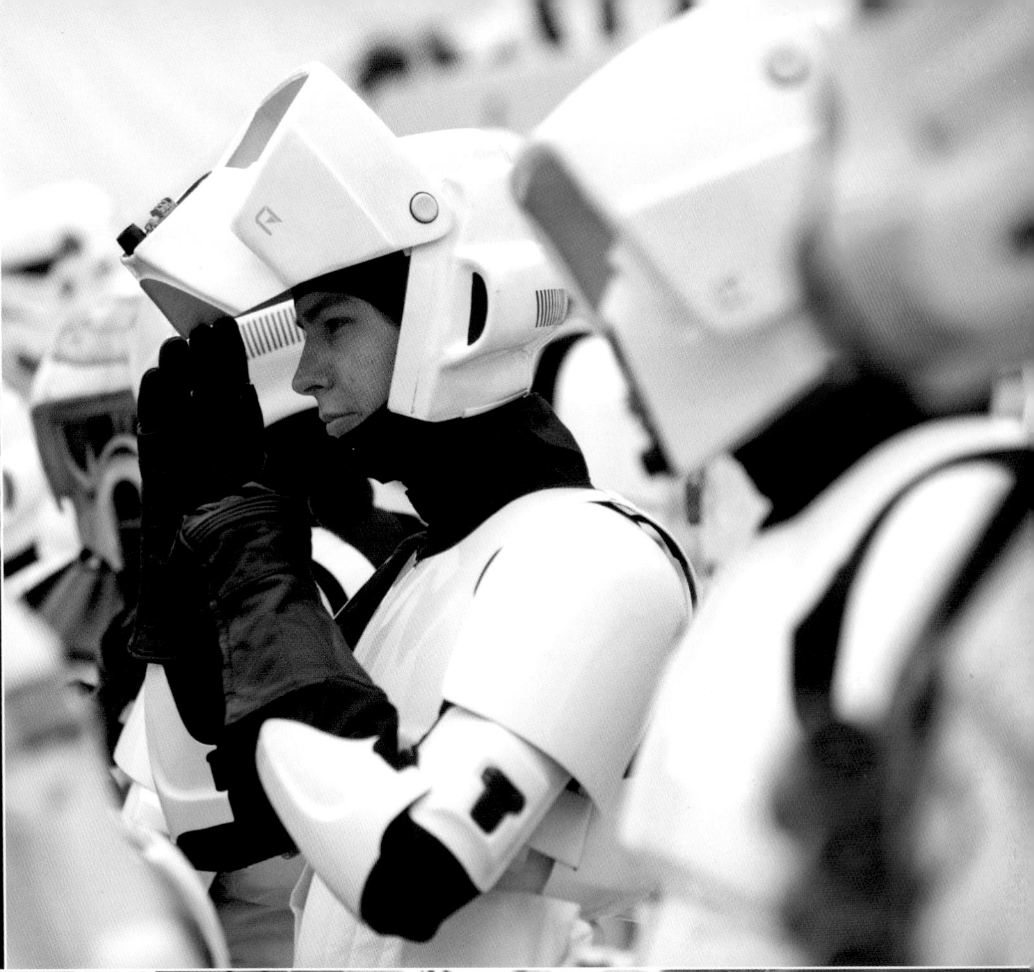
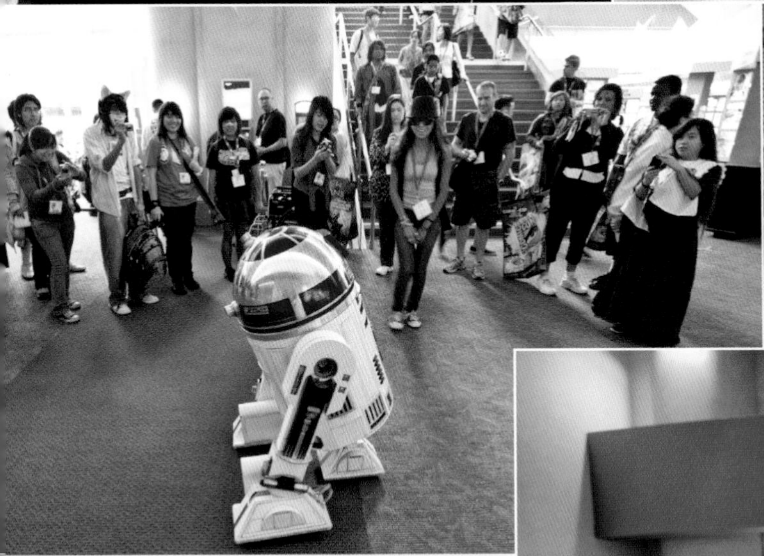
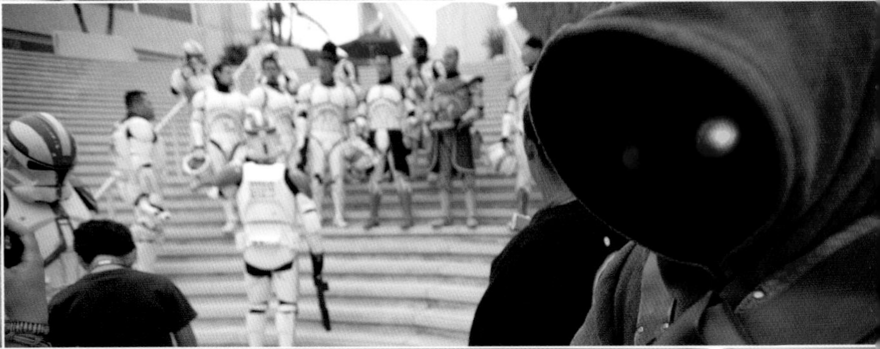
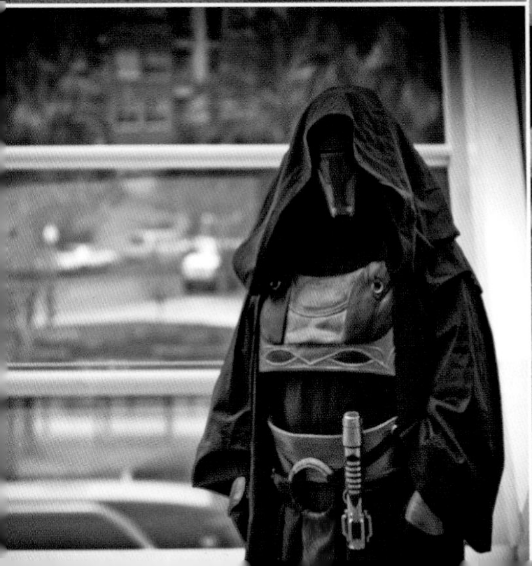
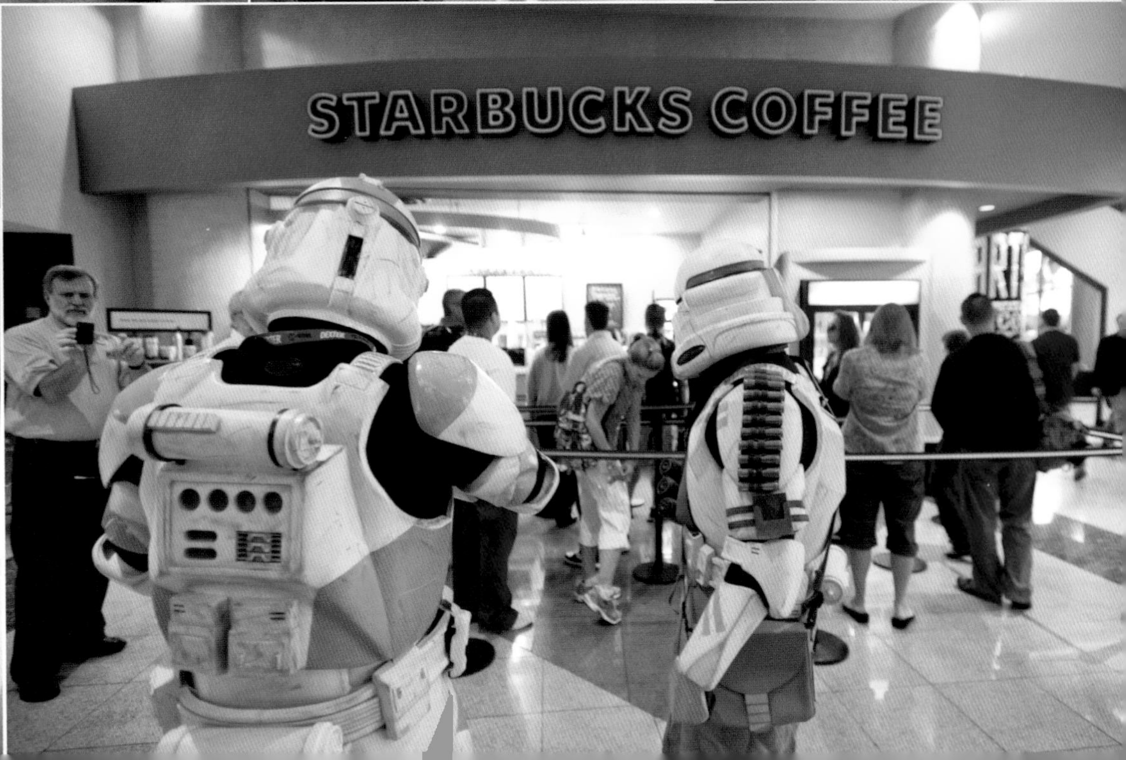
STARBUCKS COFFEE

grant morrison

writer | All Star Superman, New X-Men, Batman

> “We’re living in a world where every news broadcast we look at is telling us that we’re all doomed—we’re either going to be drowned by oil, or we’re going to die when the planet heats up, or asteroids will hit us. The future’s been cancelled for a long time for a lot of people, and I think the world of superheroes and extravagant characters is attractive because it offers a positive escape from that.”

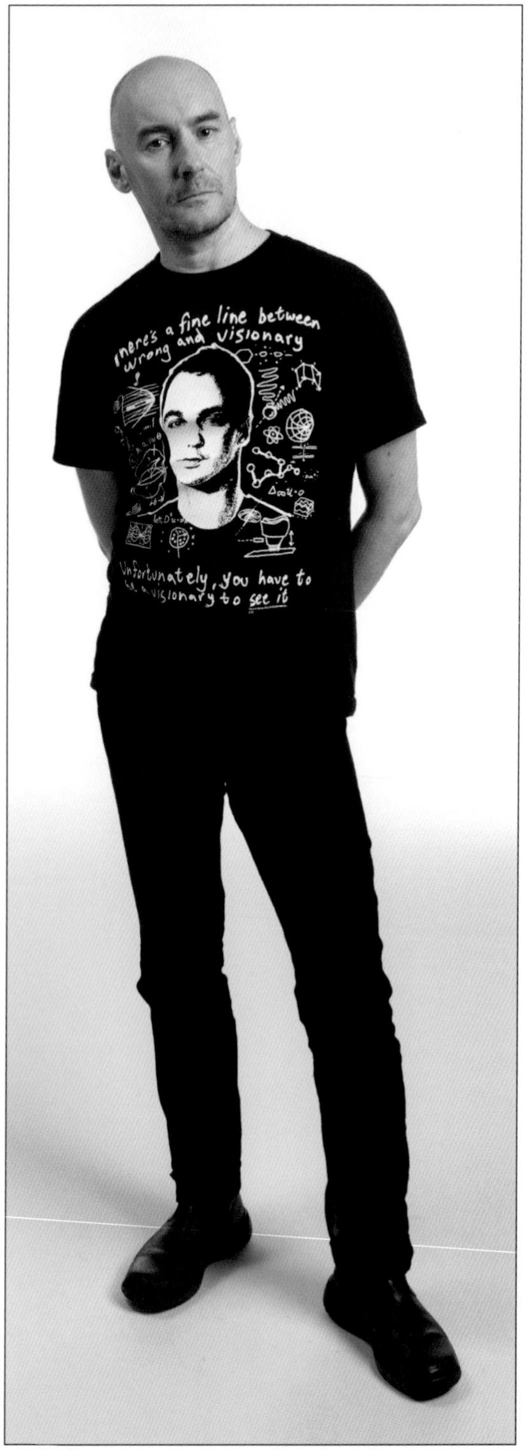
fine line between
wrong and visionary
Unfortunately, you have to
visionary to see it

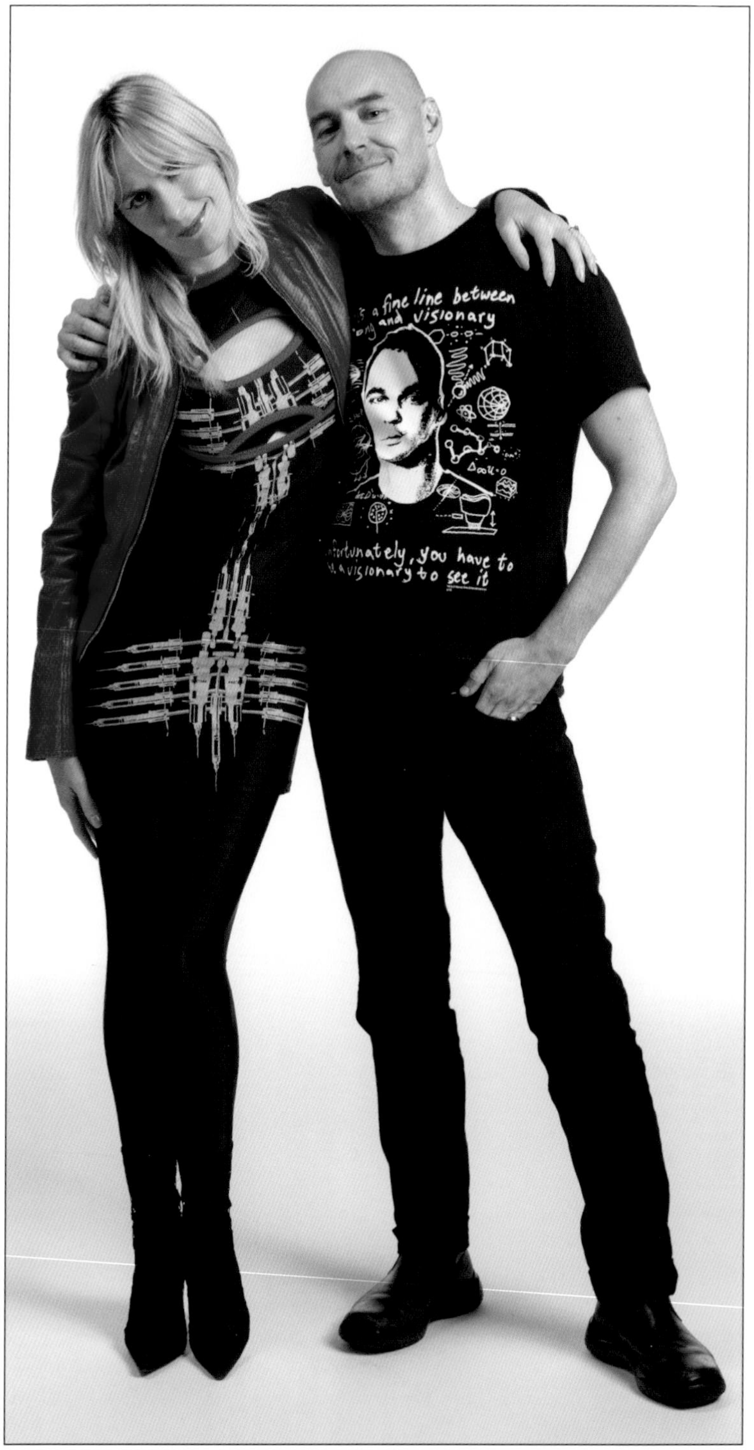

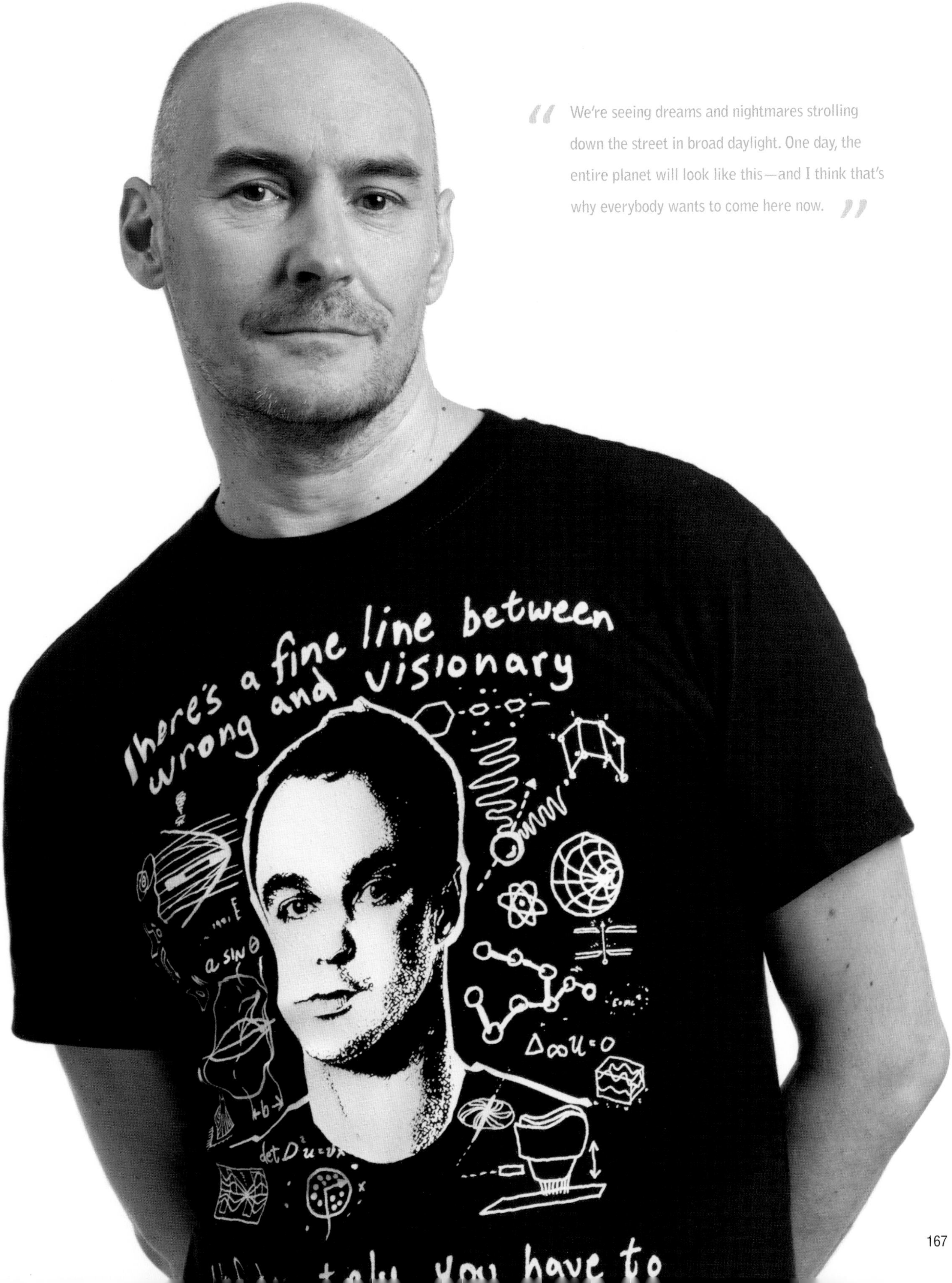
There's a fine line between
wrong and visionary
you have to

“We’re seeing dreams and nightmares strolling down the street in broad daylight. One day, the entire planet will look like this—and I think that’s why everybody wants to come here now.”

Sheyne Fleischer and Glenn Freund

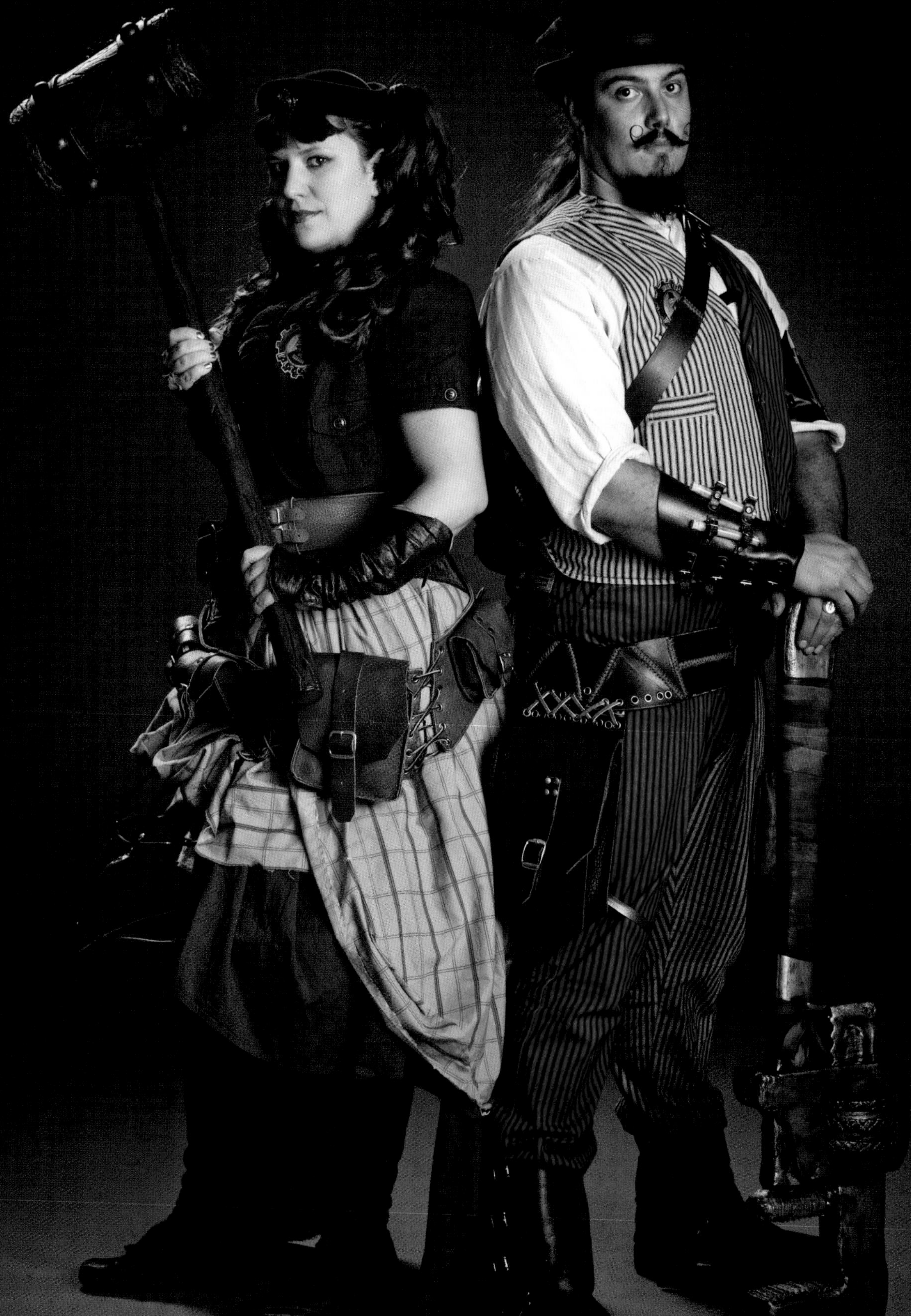

Mitchell Loren Brose

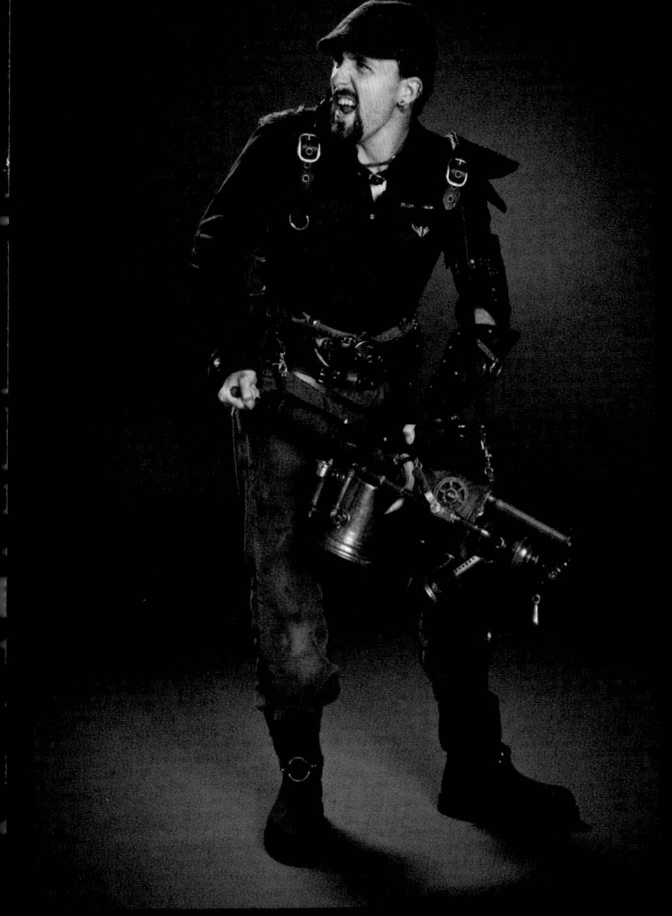

Benjamin Michael Brose

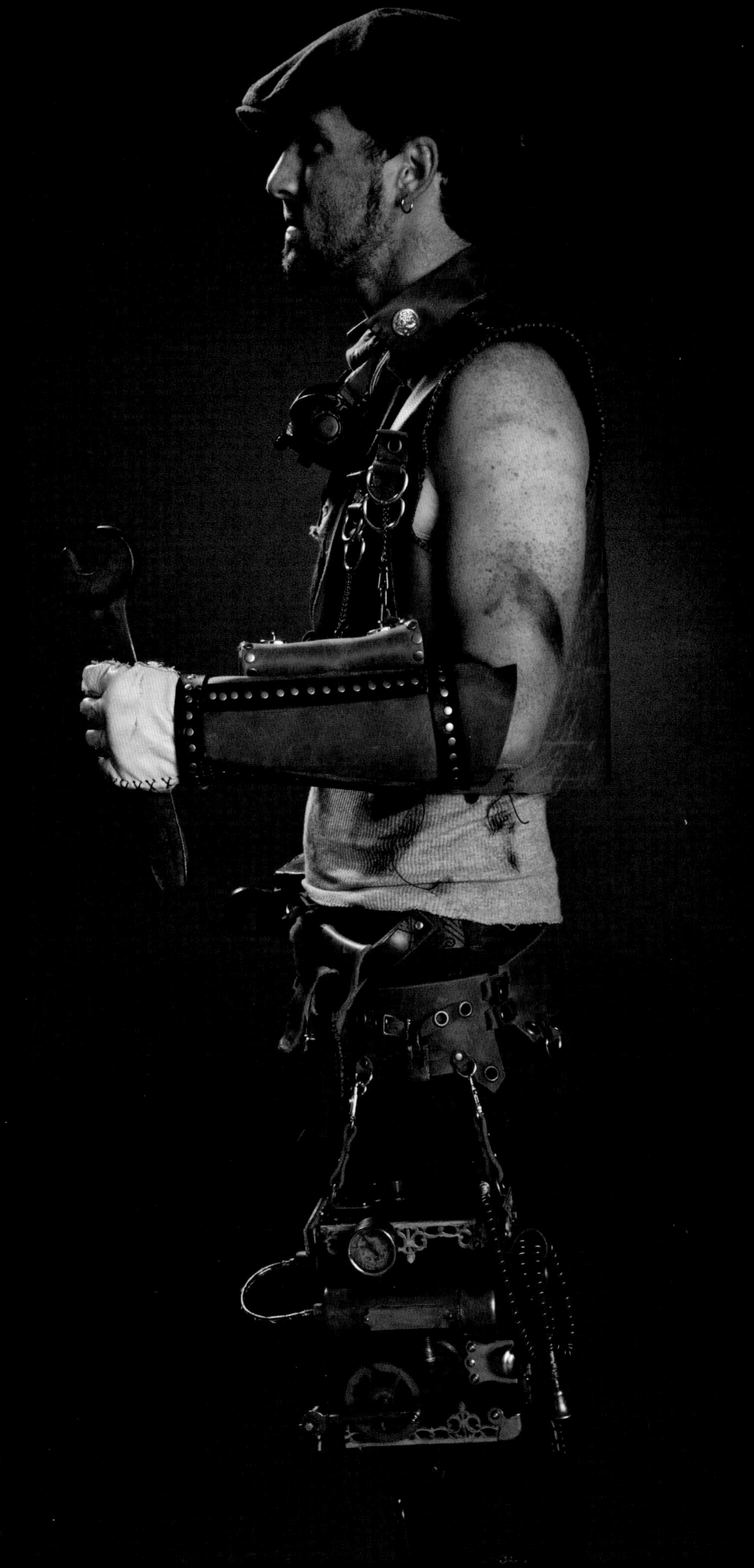

Casey Daniel Brose

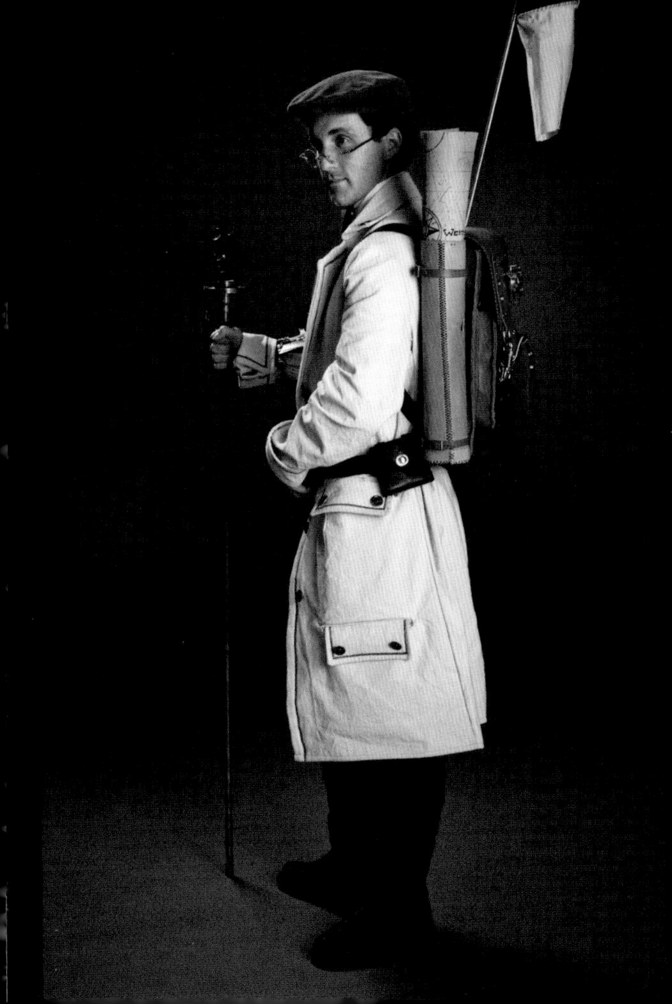

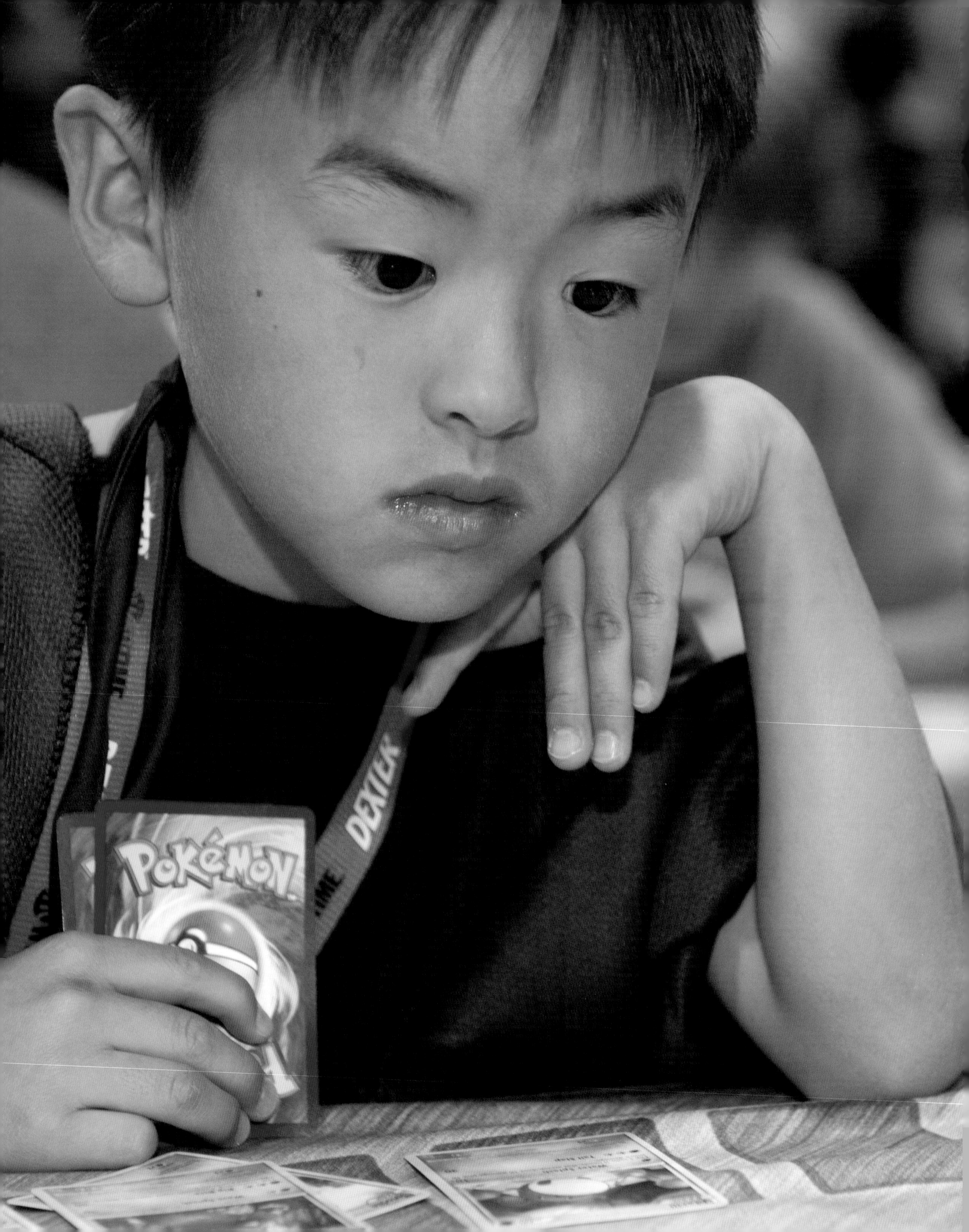
POKéMON
DEXTER

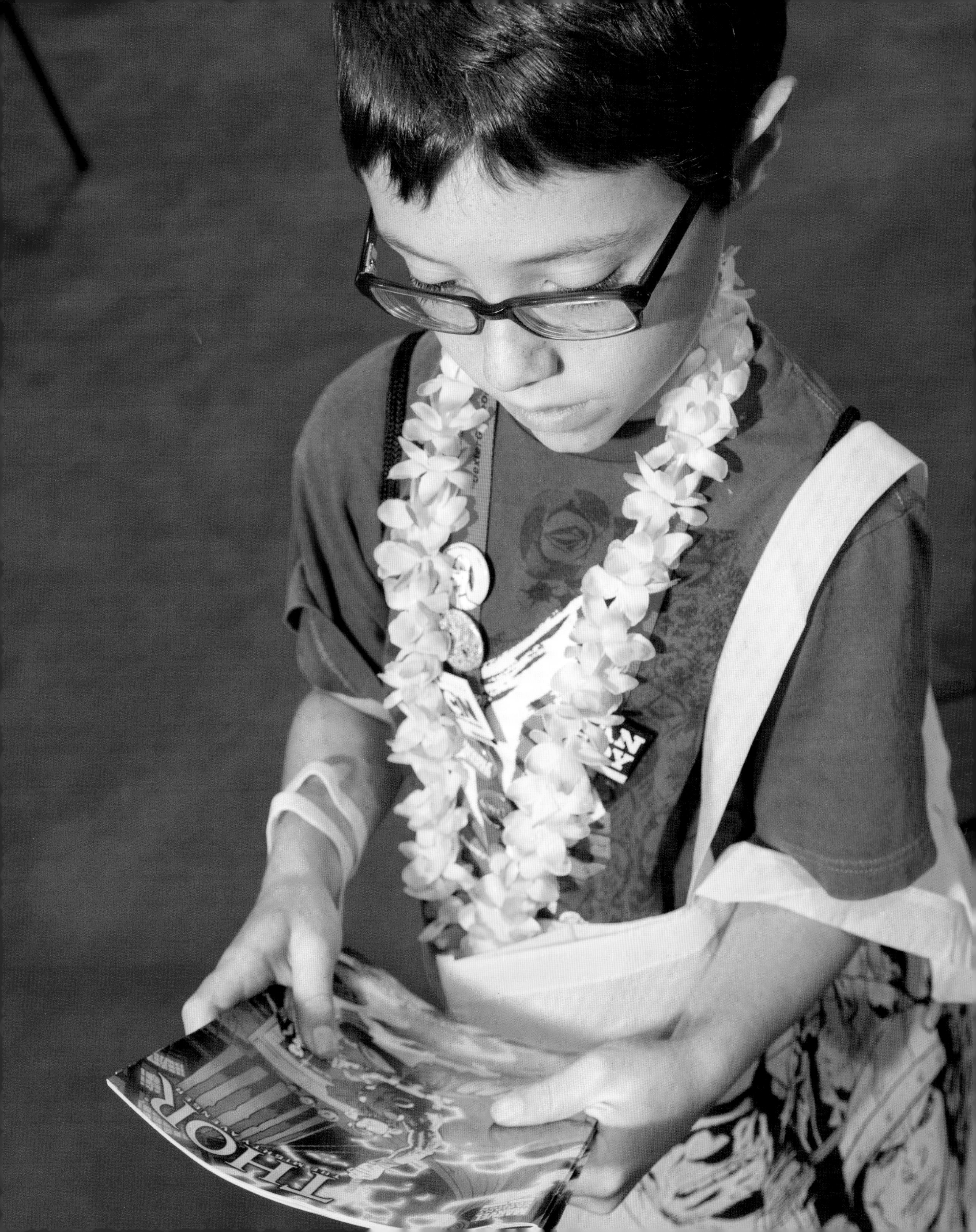
THOR

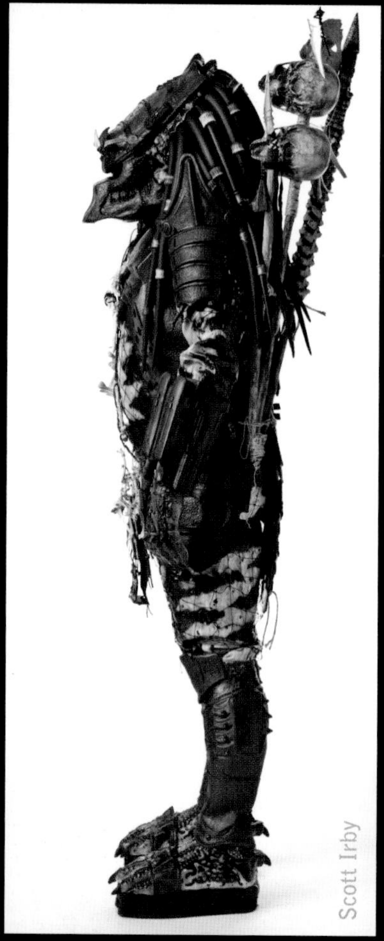
Scott Irby

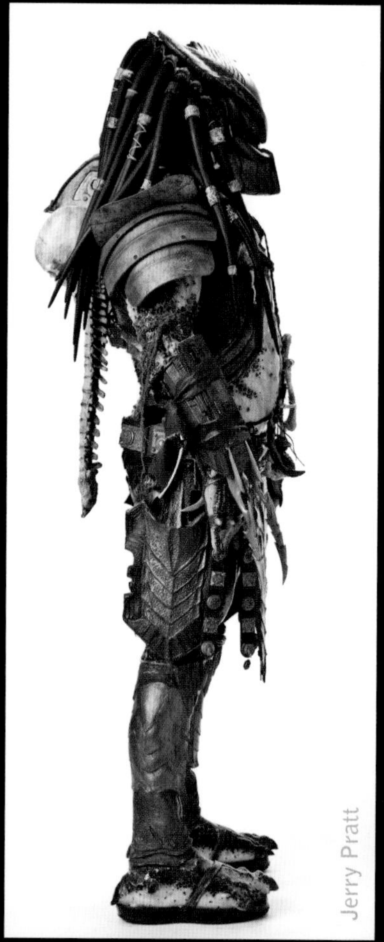
Jerry Pratt

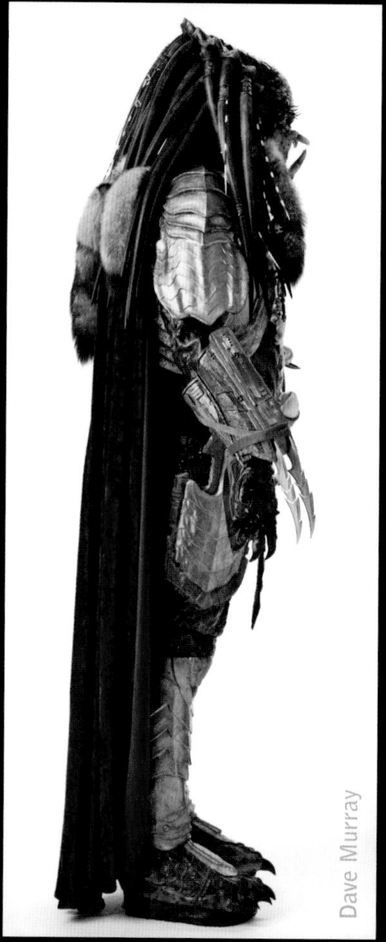
Dave Murray

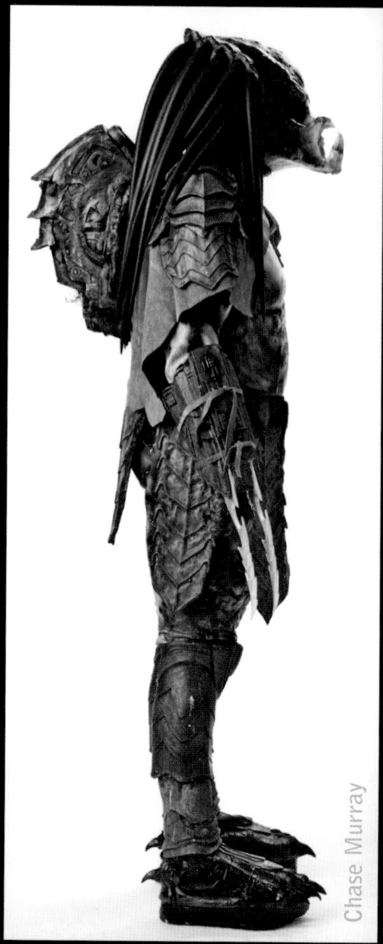
Chase Murray

Dean Vargo

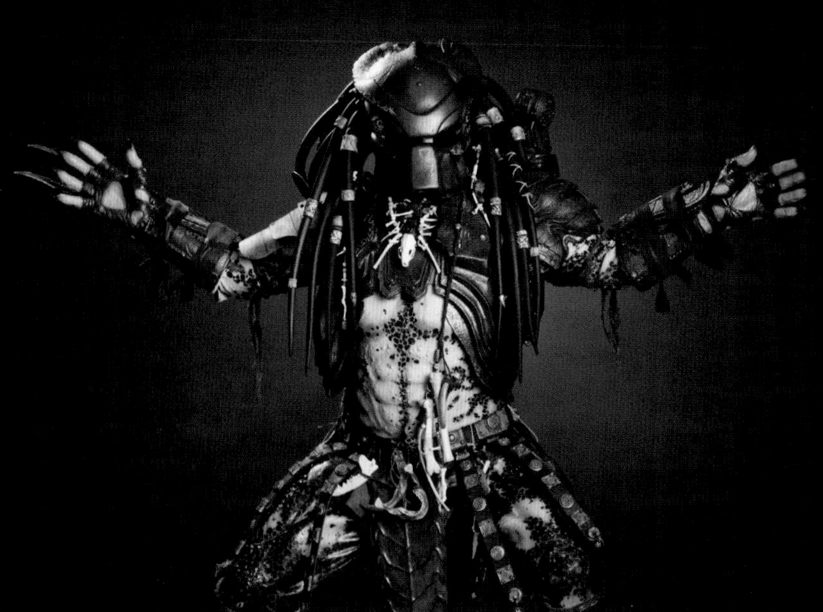

Jerry Pratt

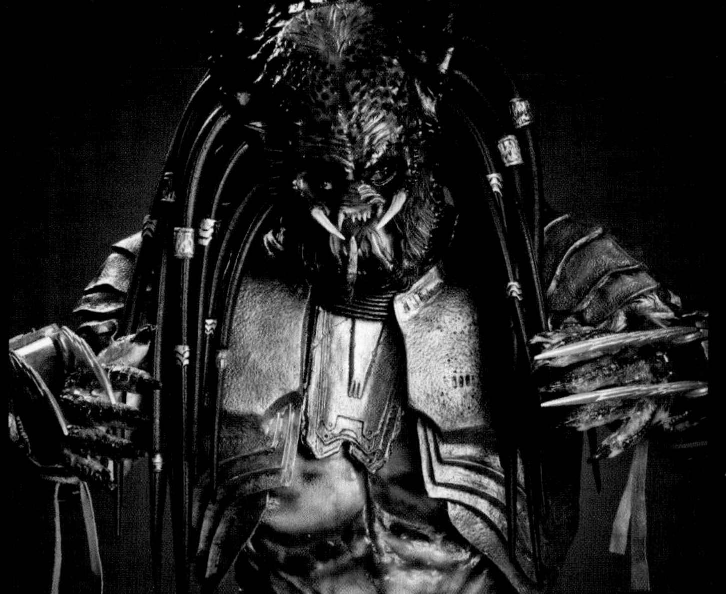

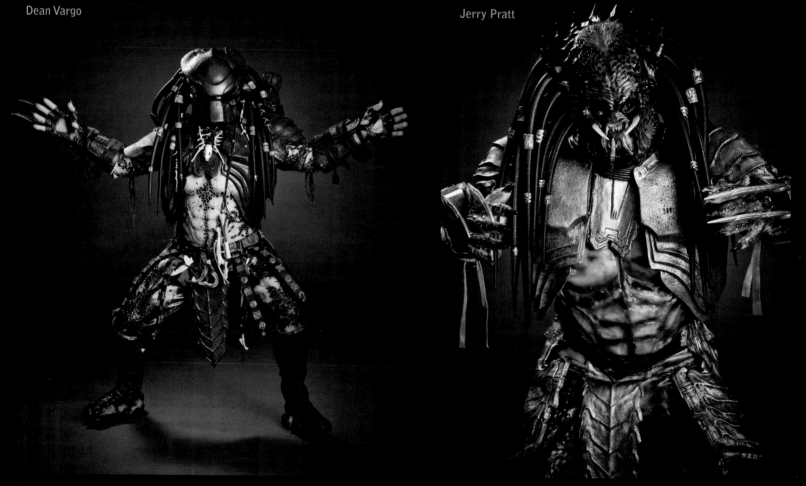

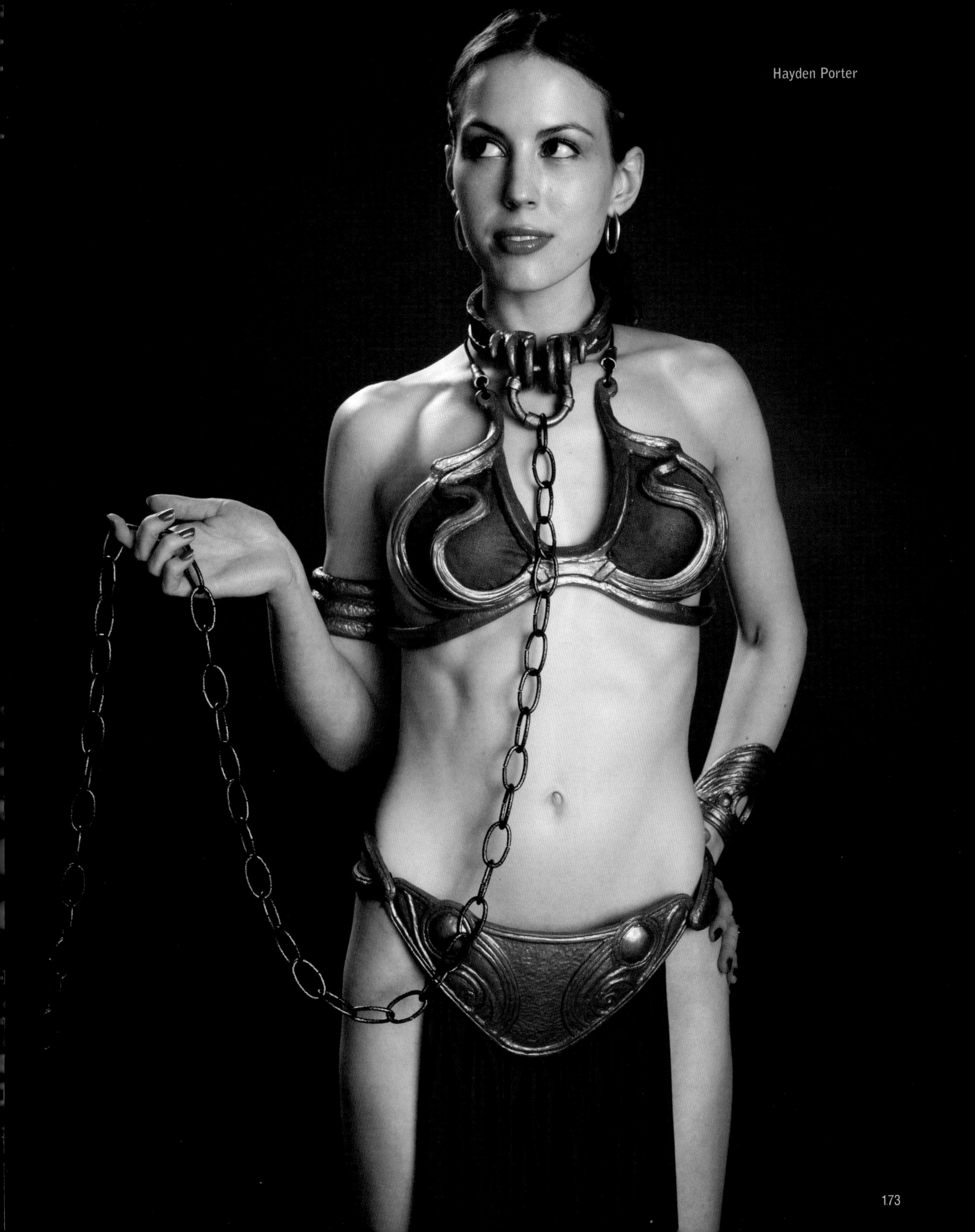

Hayden Porter

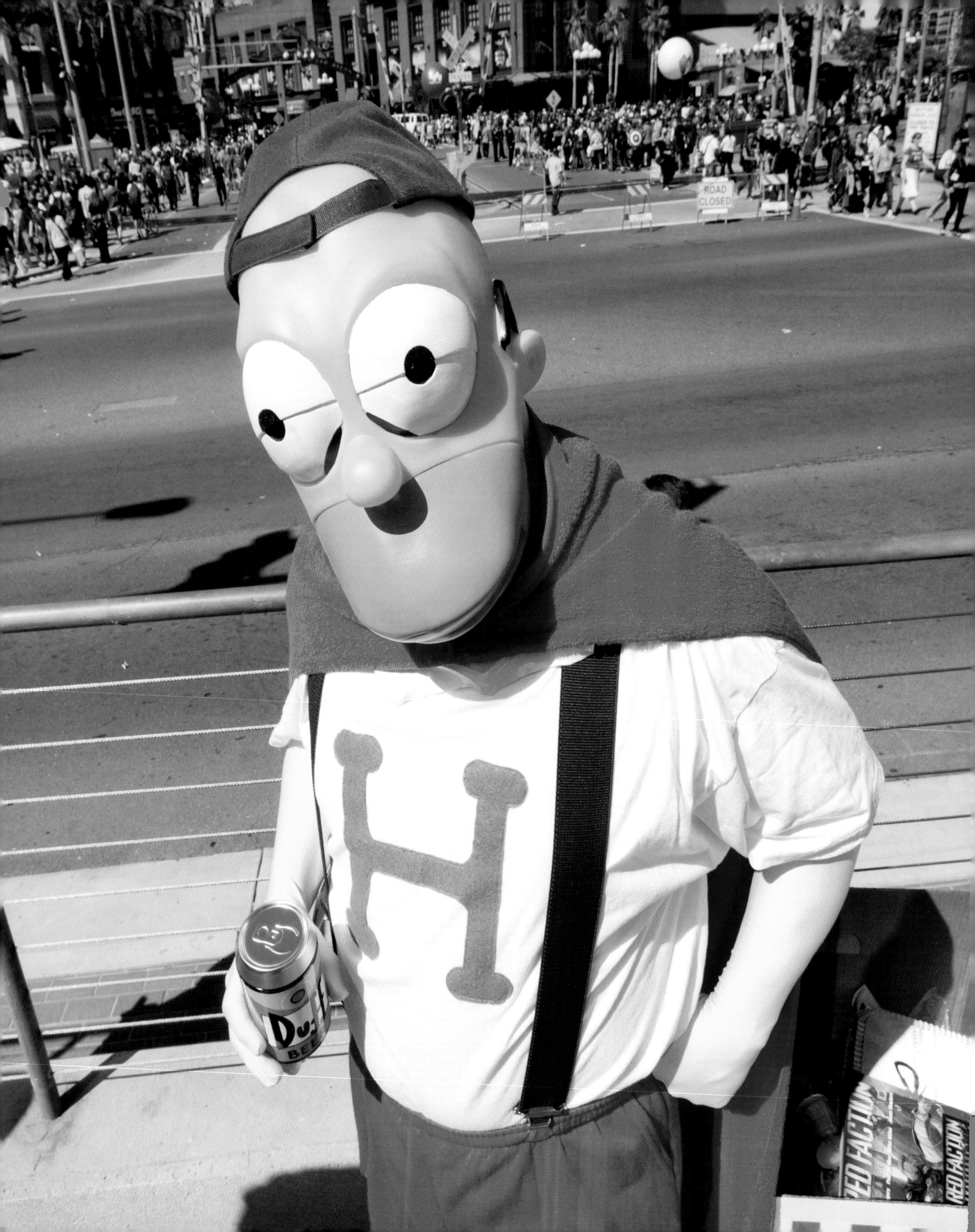
ROAD
CLOSED
RED FACTION
RED FACTION

matt groening

creator | The Simpsons, Futurama

" I think there is a love of the hand-drawn gesture in comics. Kids and nerds and adults and appreciators of fine art love it. People aren't buying CGI comics, right? Who wants that? You want to see a really good artist. "

" I was walking down one of the aisles and there was a dealer who had Simpsons merchandise— stuff I'd never seen before. I was looking at an item and he said, 'Oh, this is from Australia. It's a little diorama of the Simpsons at the beach, and it's a very rare item.' Then he went, 'Wait! Oh my god, are you the creator of *The Simpsons*?' And I said, 'Yes I am.' He said, 'It would be an honor to sell this to you.' "

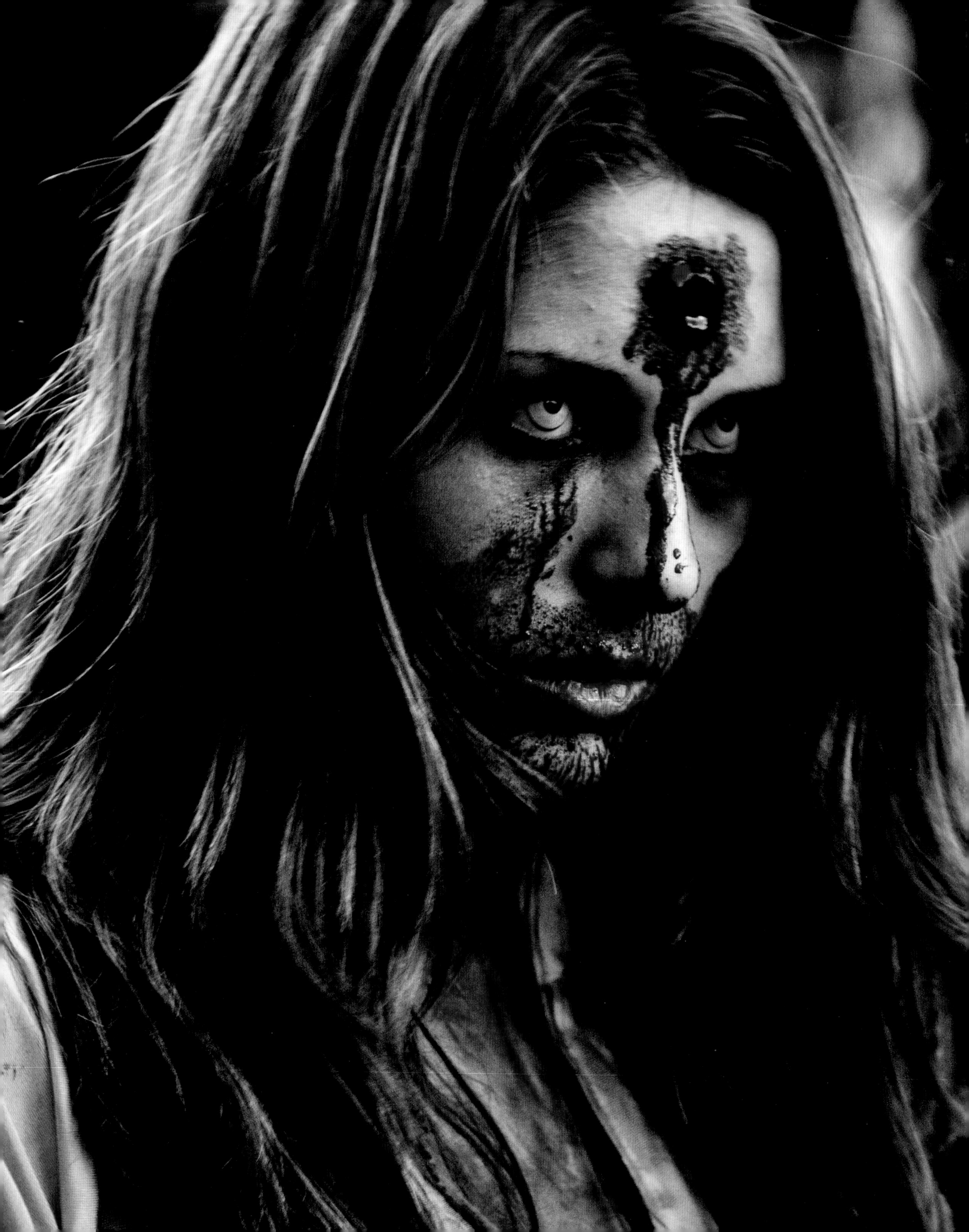

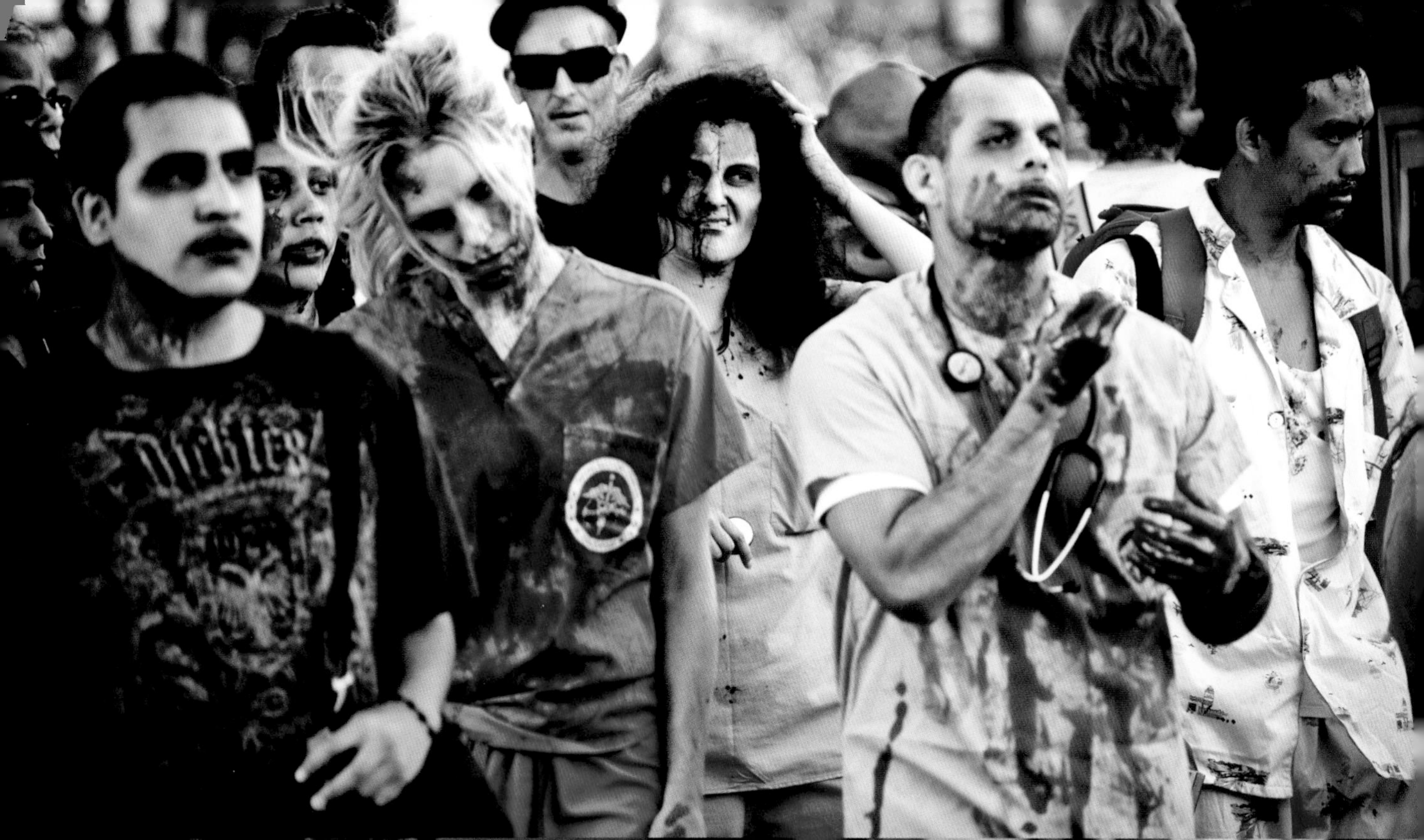

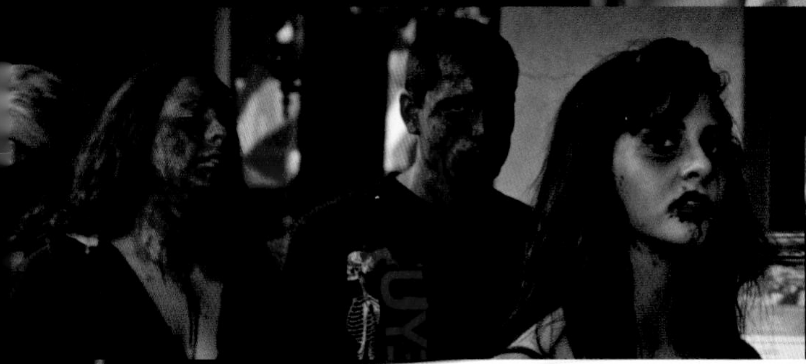

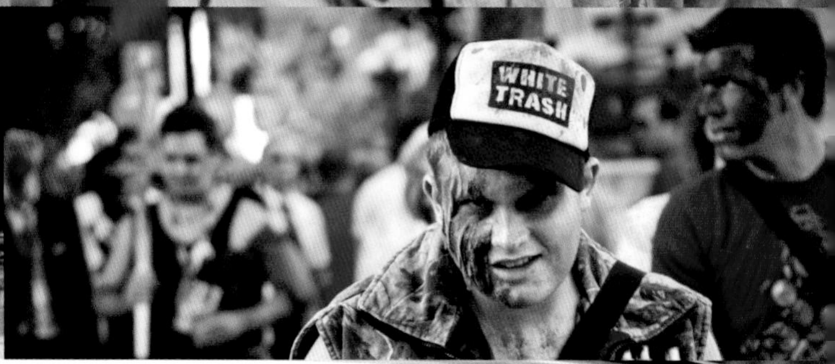
WHITE
TRASH

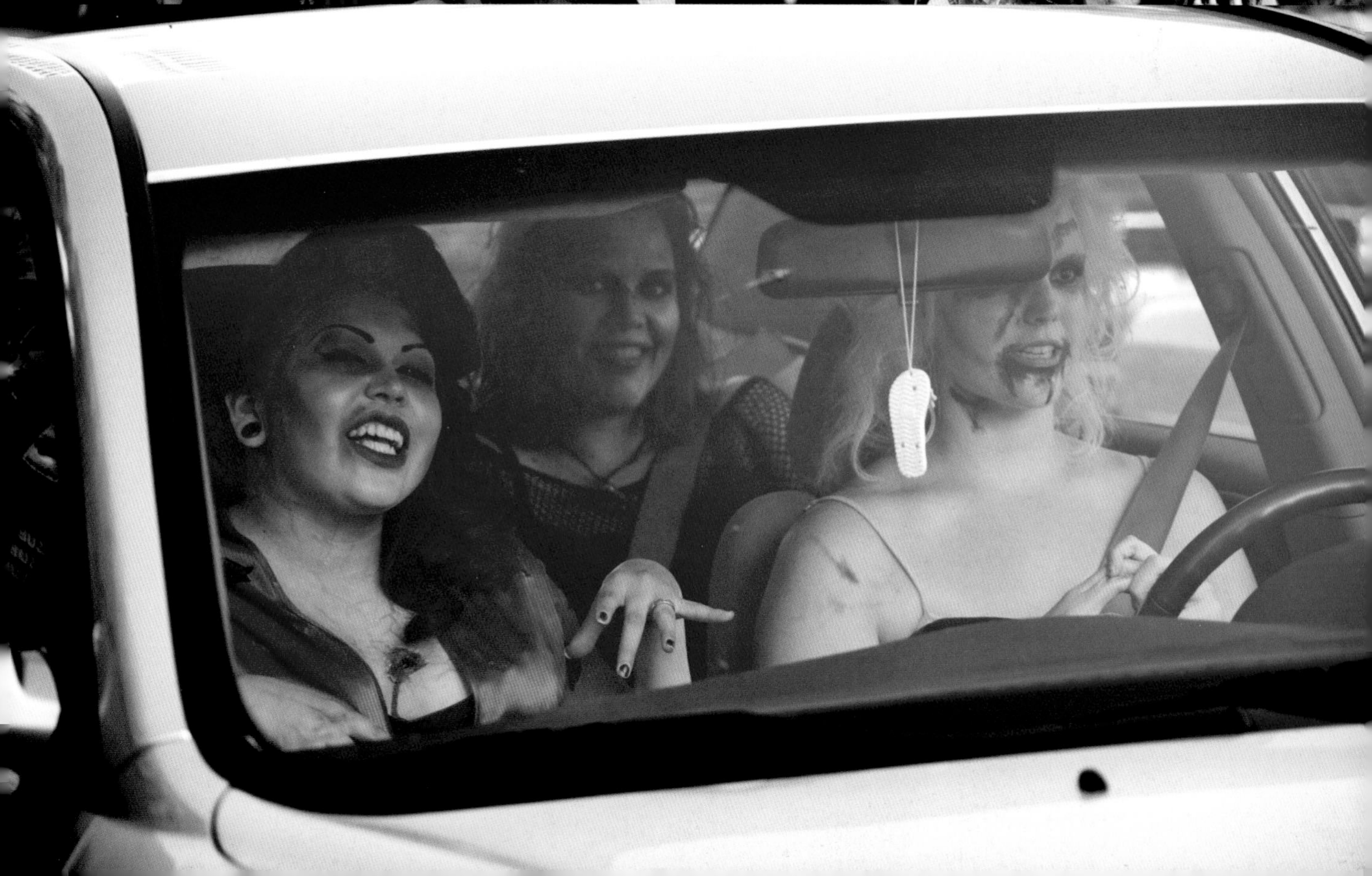

mike richardson

president | Dark Horse

" Comics are one of the few true original American art forms, much like jazz. And it's only now that comics are
really getting their due, as far as their effect on the culture. "

" I spent a couple hours yesterday just
talking with new talent. This is a
great place to find people who are
trying to break in. "

paul dini

writer, producer | Batman: The Animated Series, Superman: The Animated Series, Batman Beyond, Ultimate Spider-Man

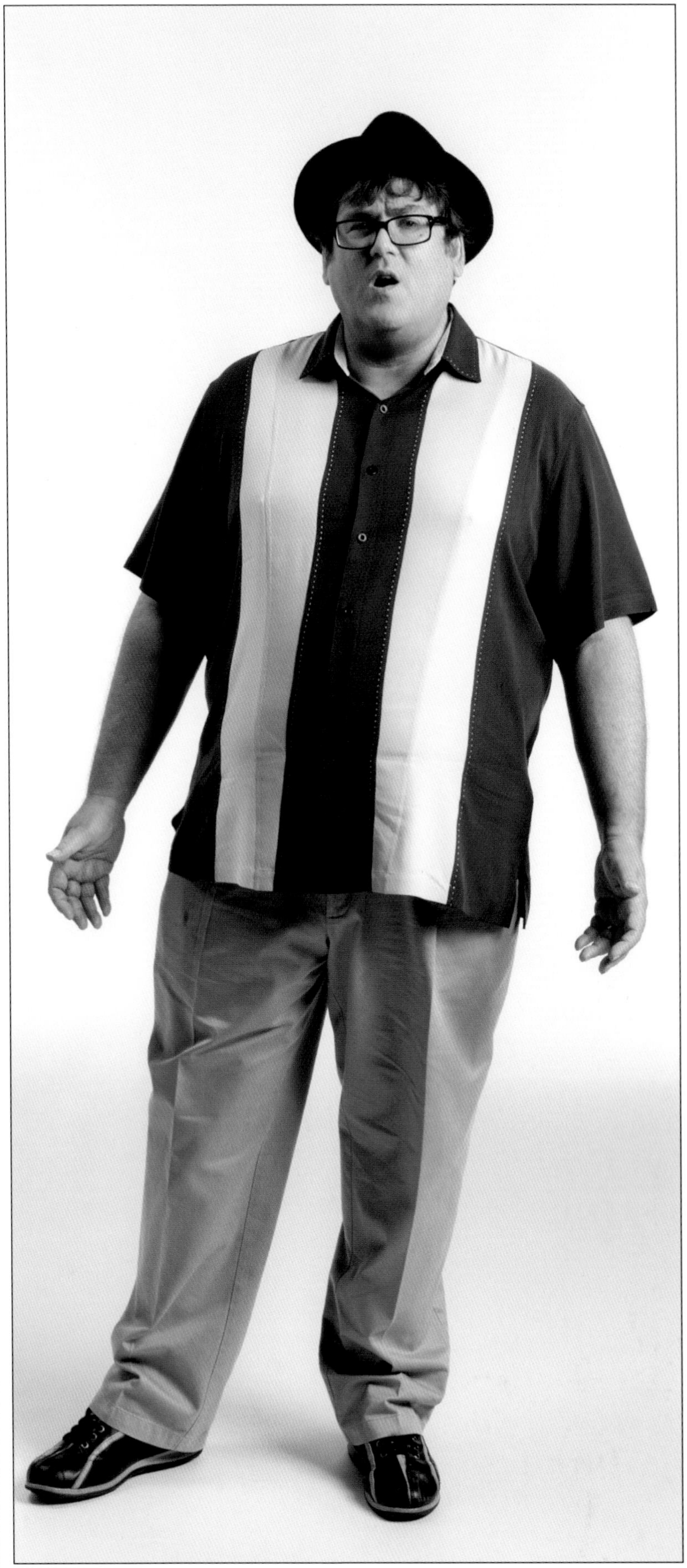

“There is a feeling of imagination and continuity and family, in a strange way, that draws people here, year after year.”

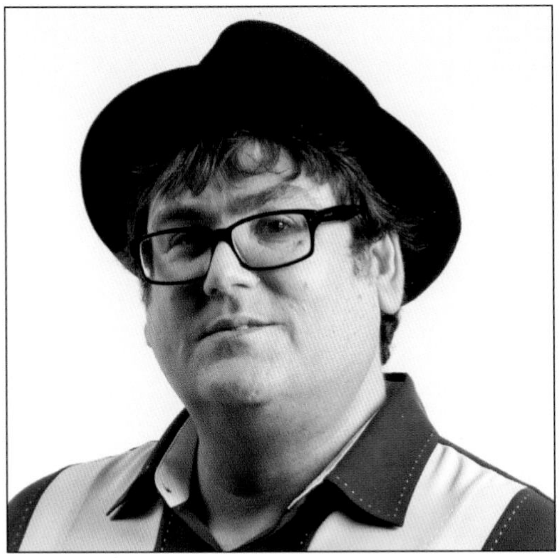

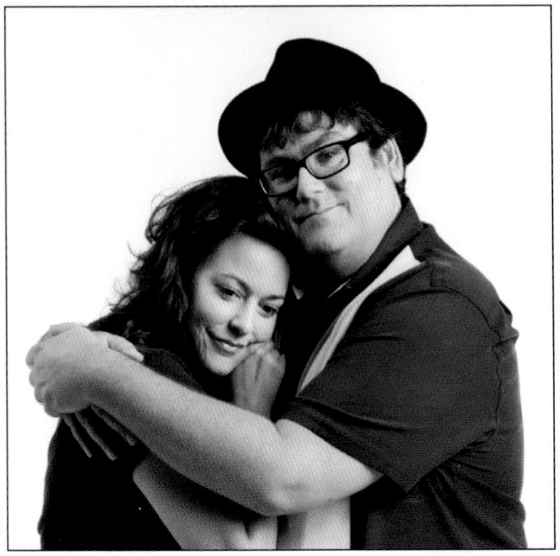

" I'm Hit Girl. From…I can't say. Because it's a bad word.

But yeah, I like this costume. "

Mina Knapp-Castillo

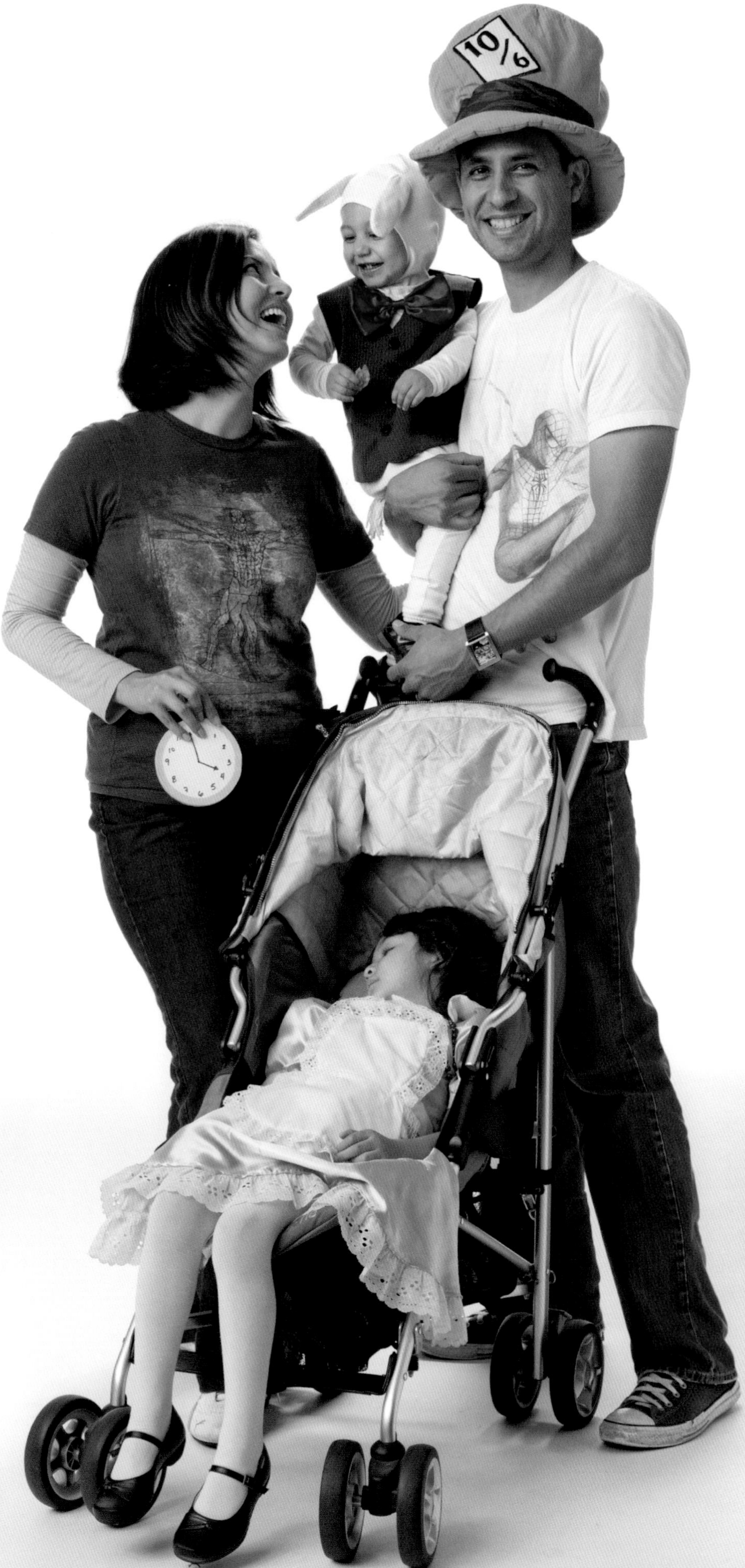
10/6

Sergio Esquivel,
Liliana Navaro,
Michelle and Ande
Esquivel

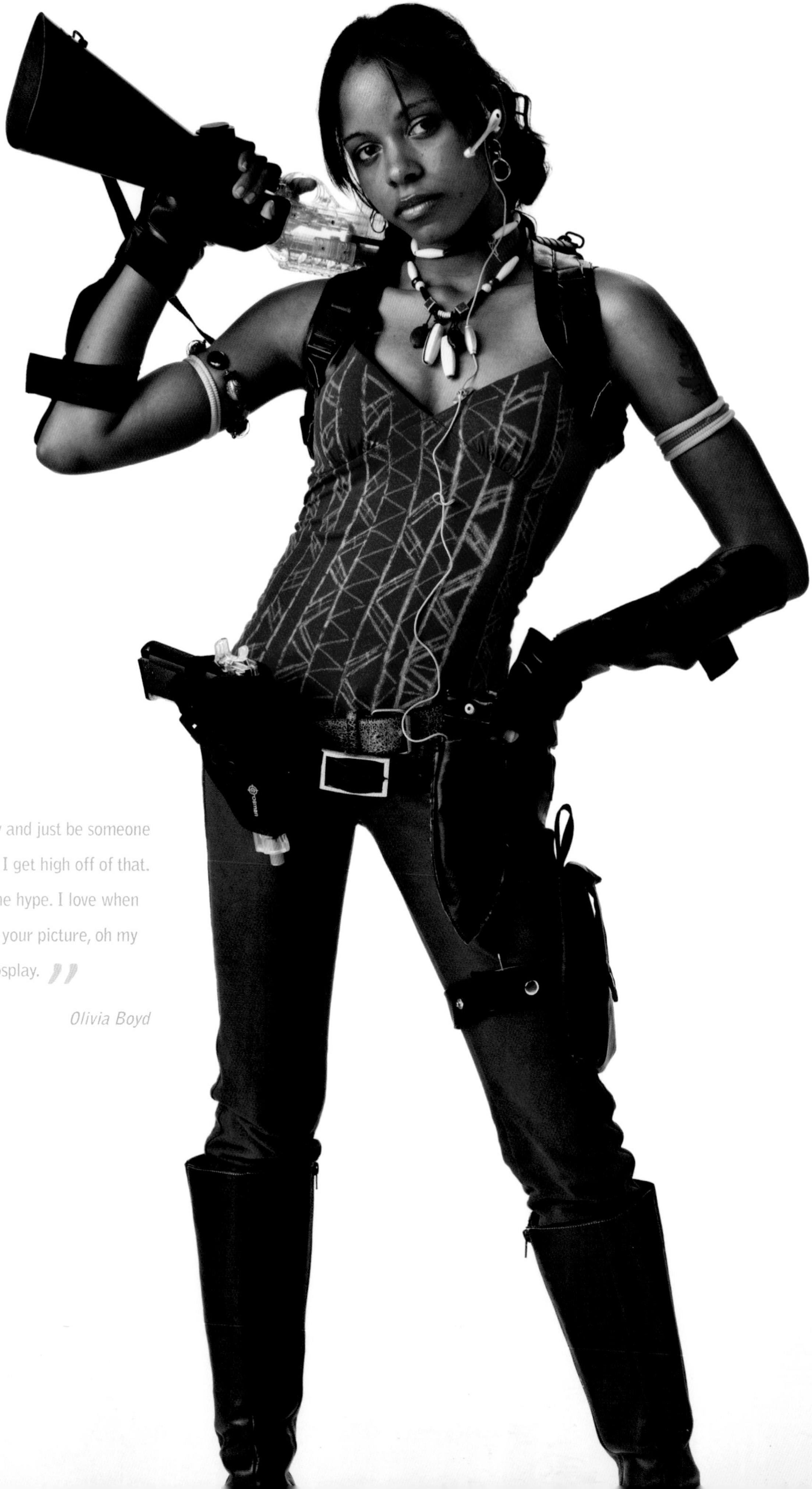

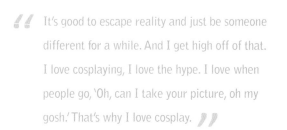

"It's good to escape reality and just be someone different for a while. And I get high off of that. I love cosplaying, I love the hype. I love when people go, 'Oh, can I take your picture, oh my gosh.' That's why I love cosplay."

Olivia Boyd

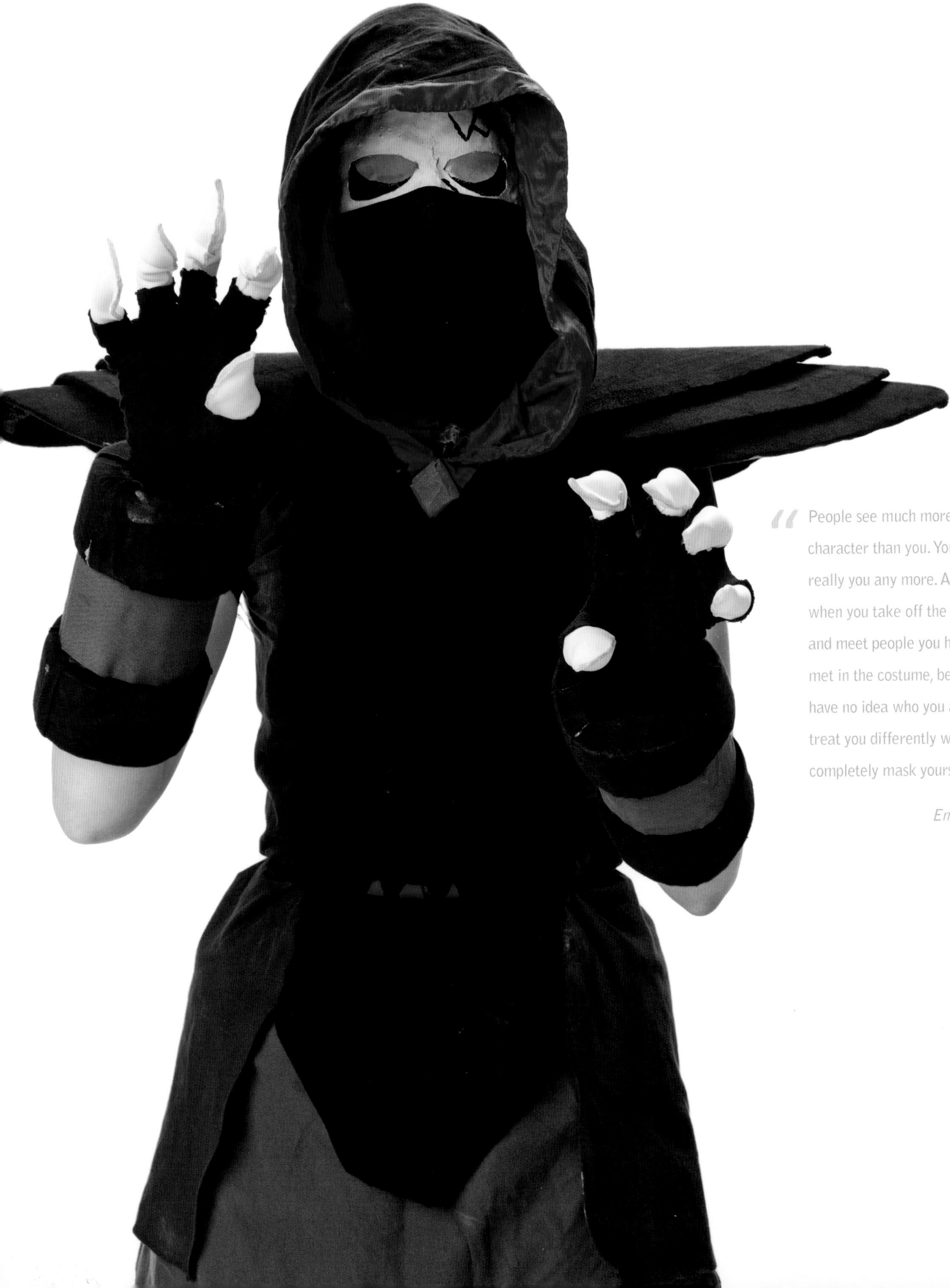

“People see much more of the character than you. You’re not really you any more. And it’s fun when you take off the costume and meet people you have only met in the costume, because they have no idea who you are. People treat you differently when you completely mask yourself.”

Emily Backlin

epilogue

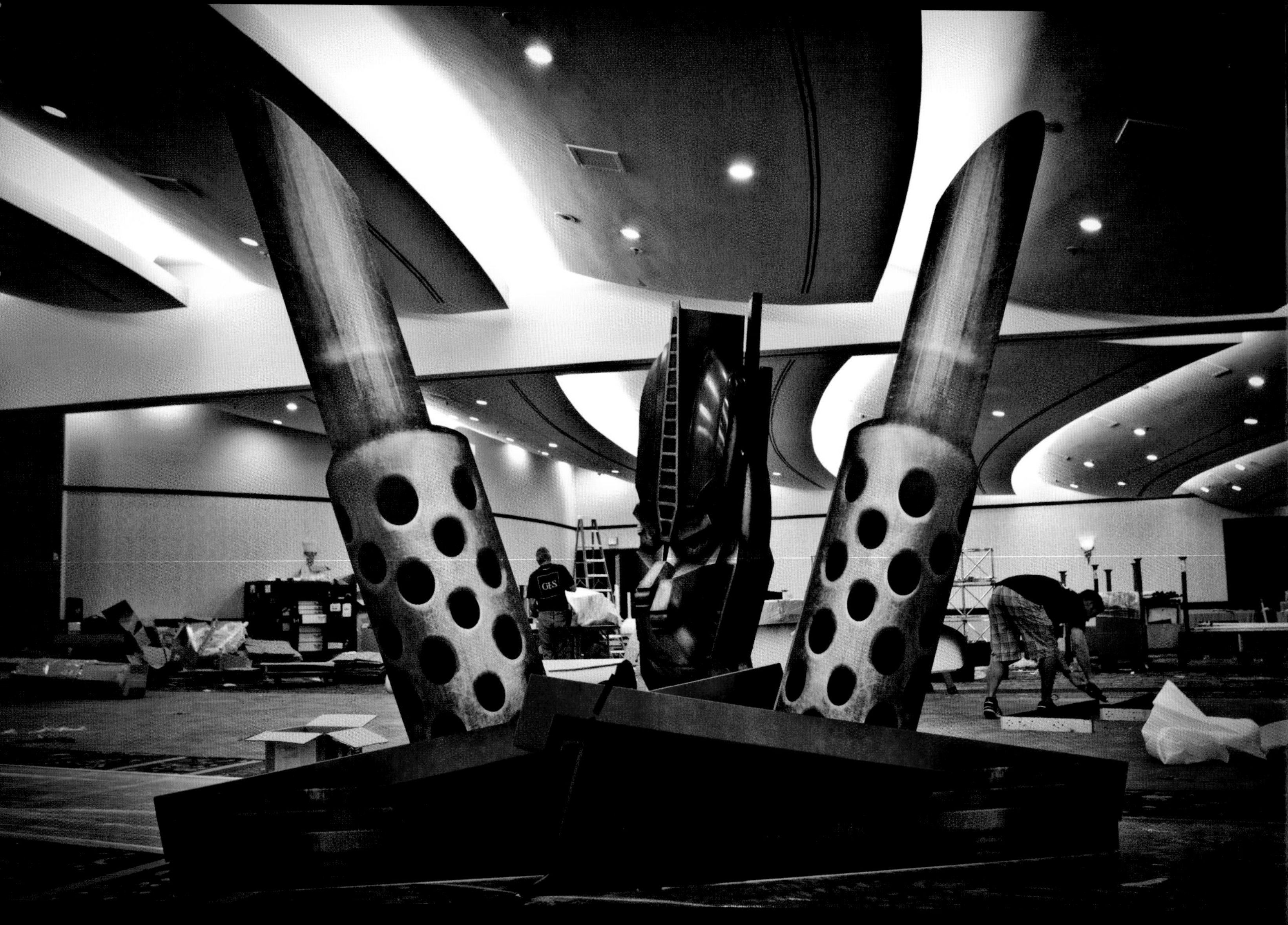
GLS

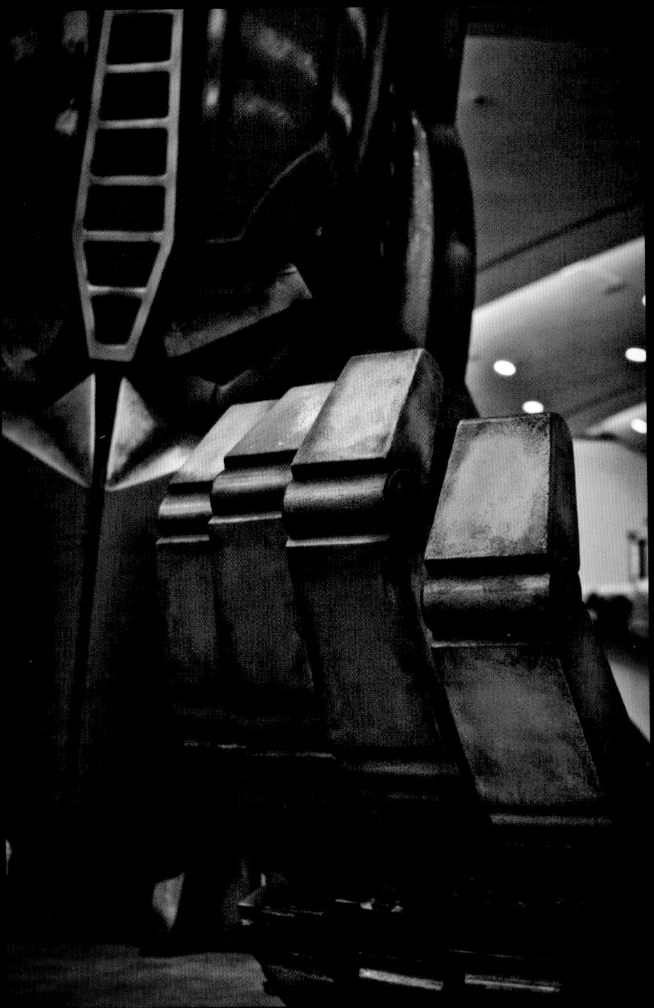

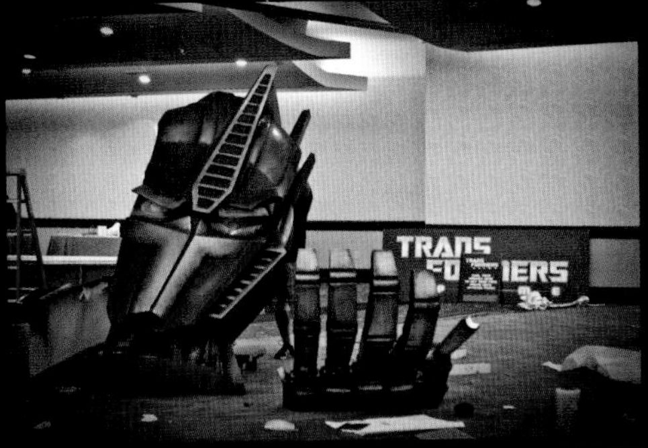
TRANS

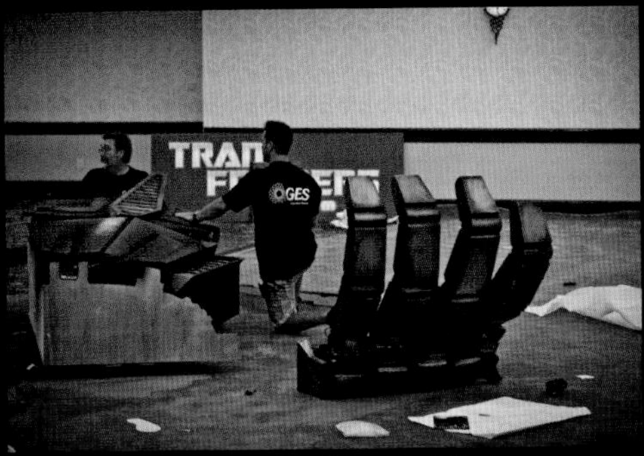
TRANS
GES

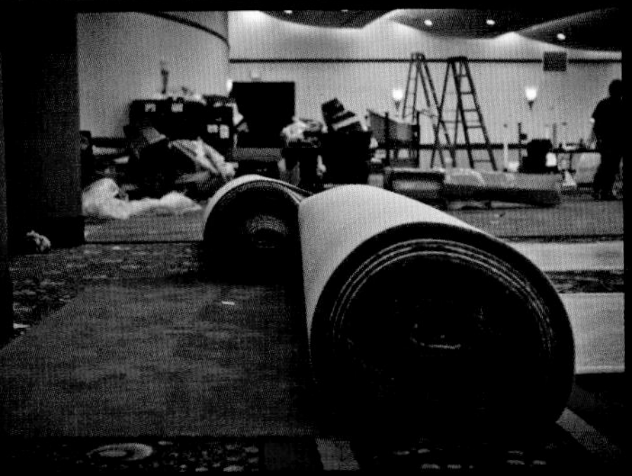

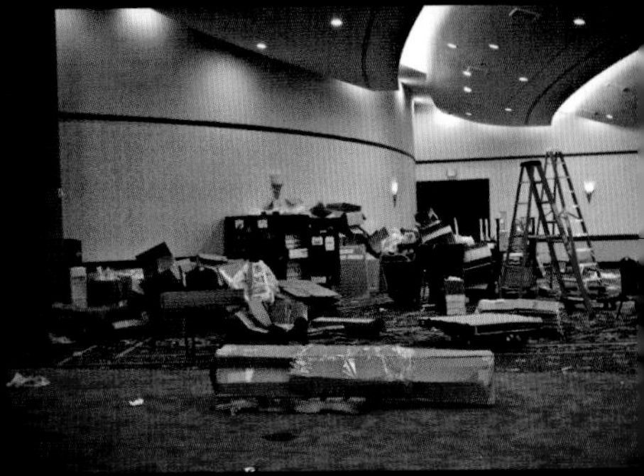

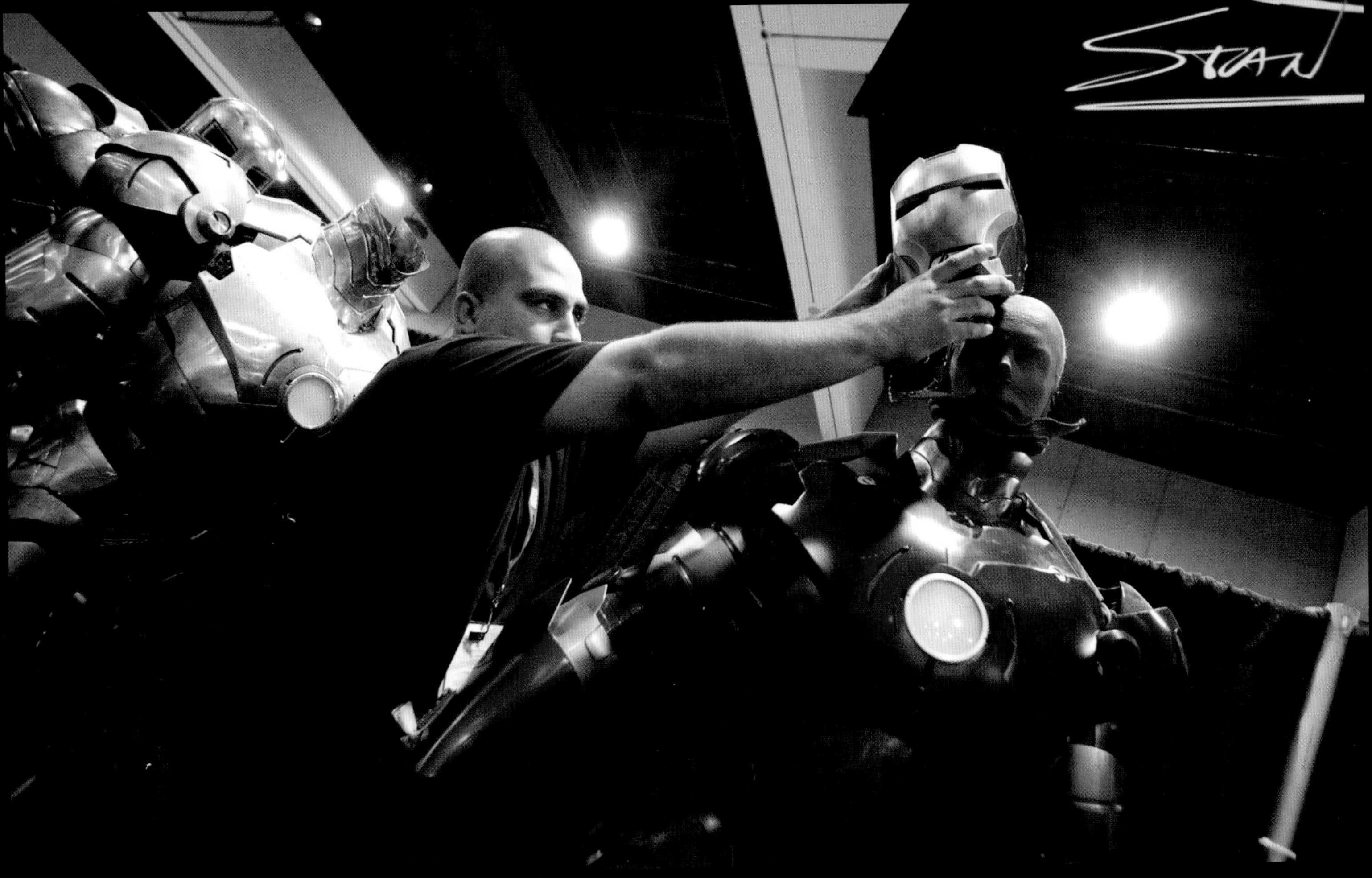

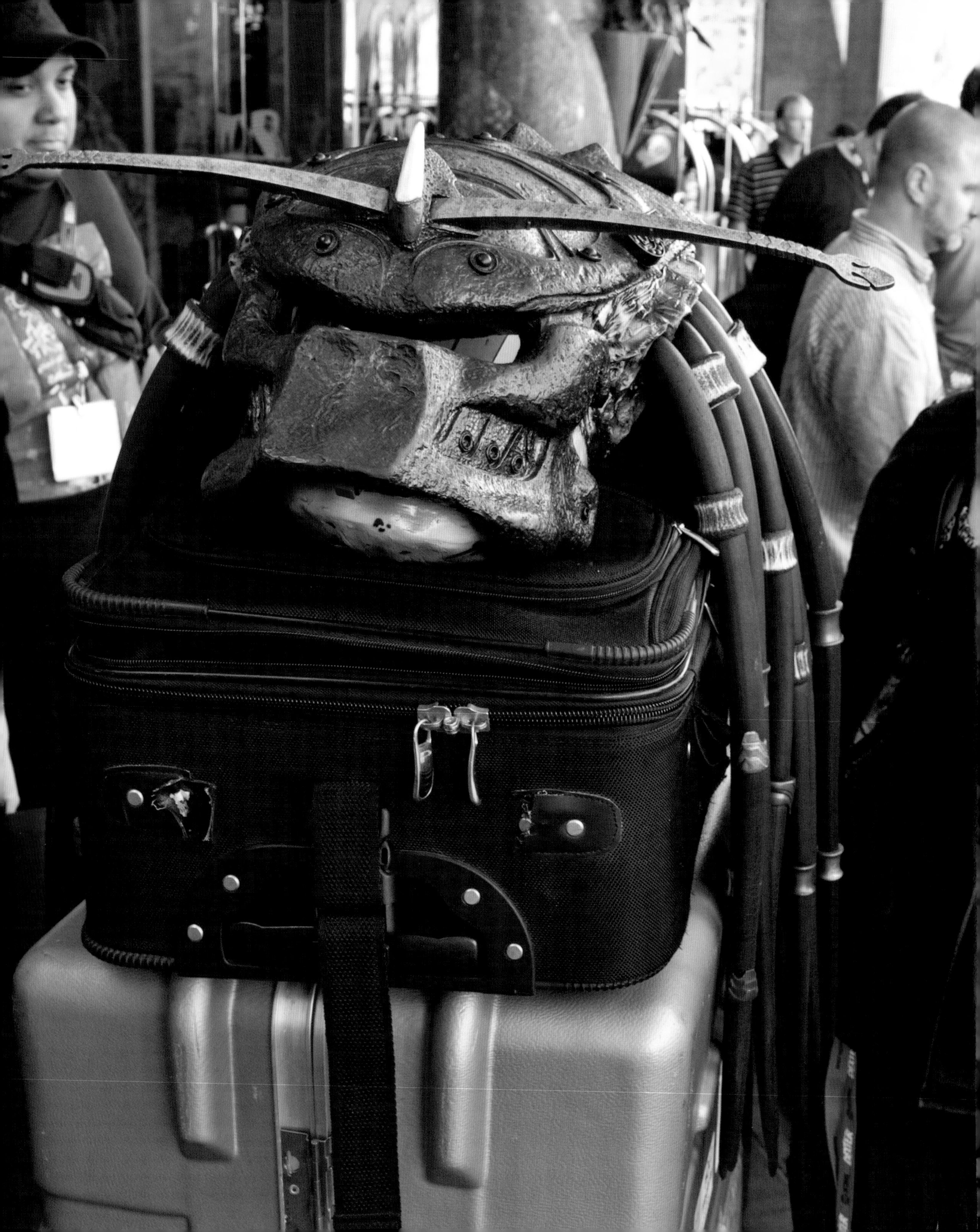

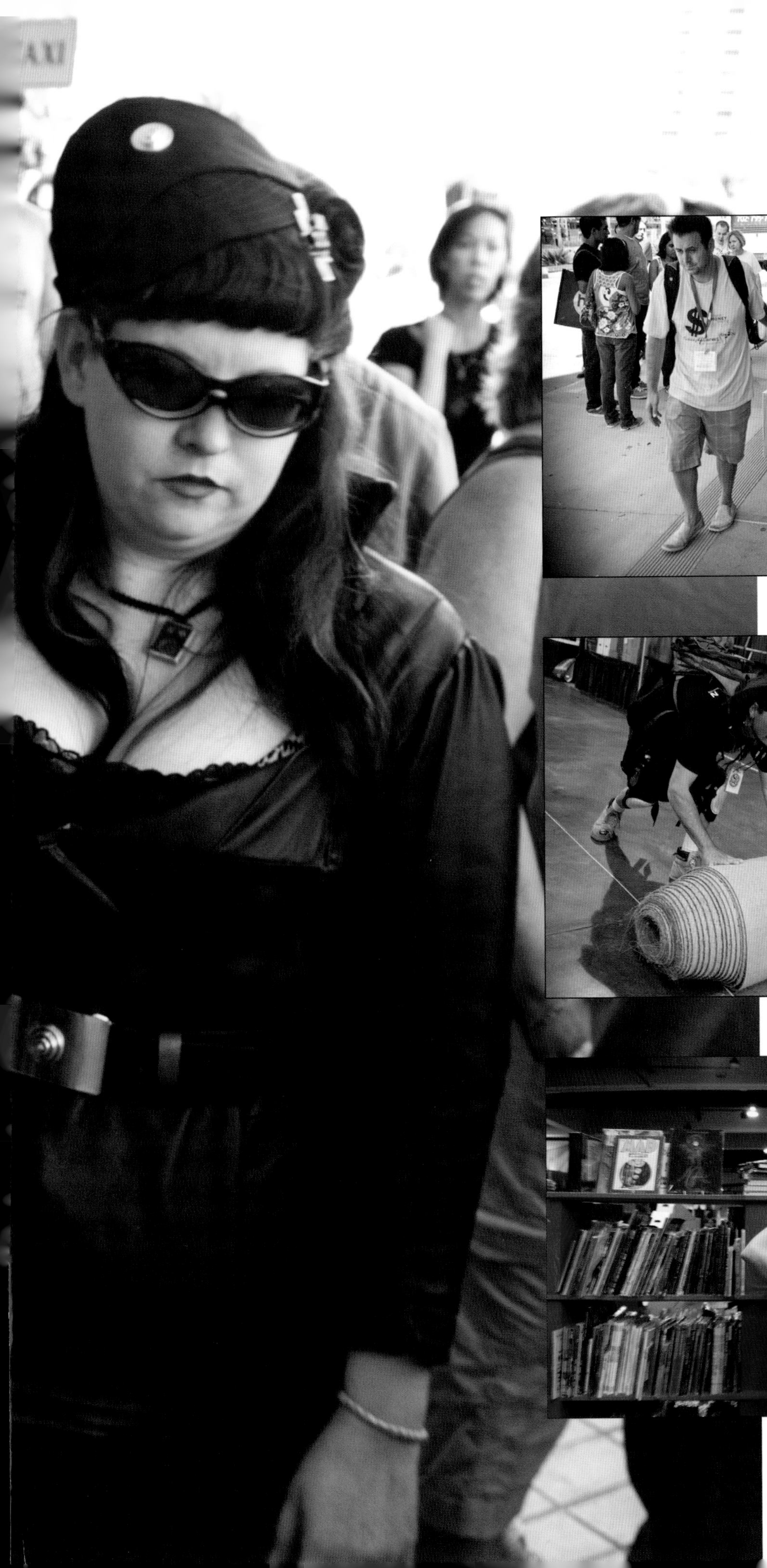

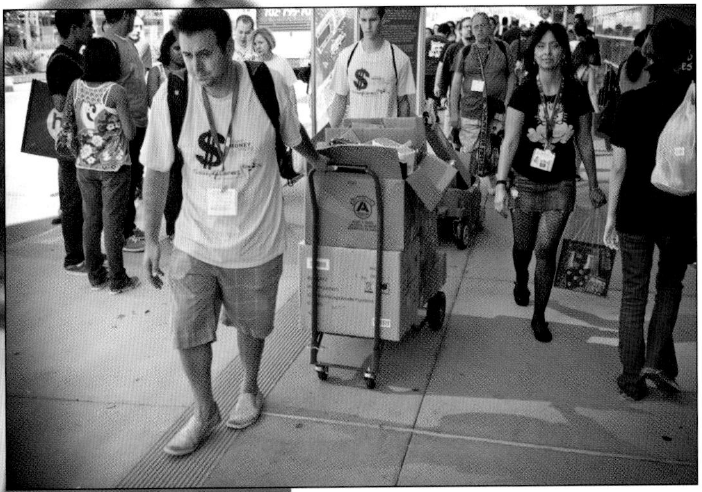

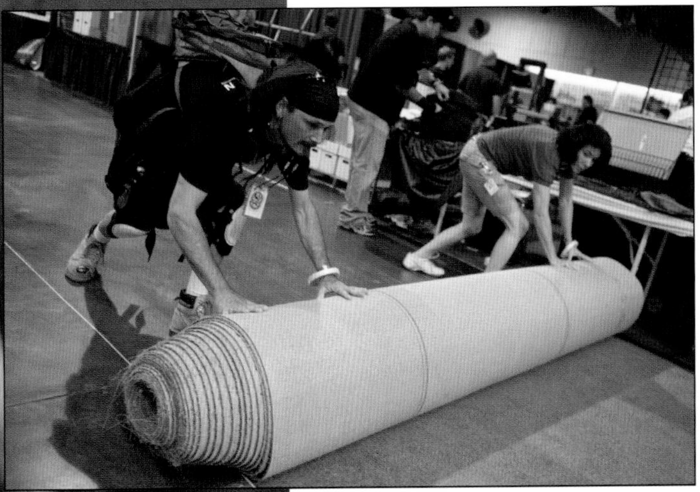

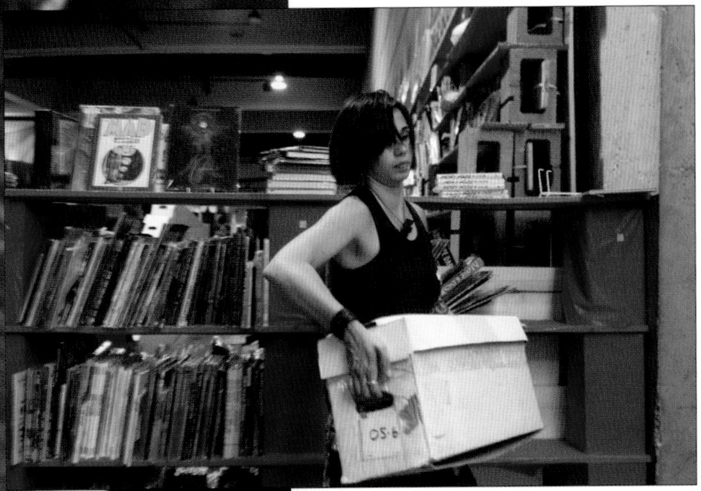

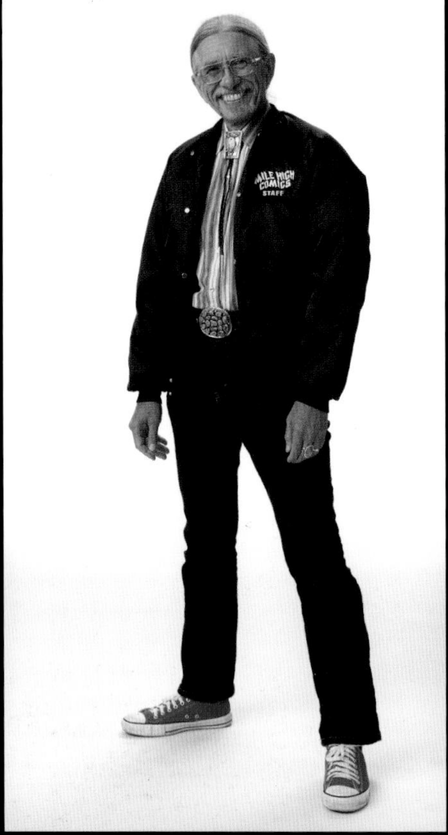
MILE HIGH
COMICS
STAFF
Chuck Rodanzki

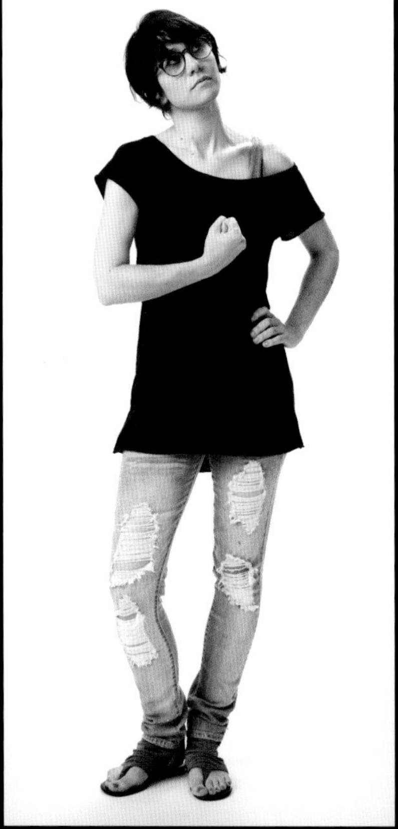
Holly Conrad

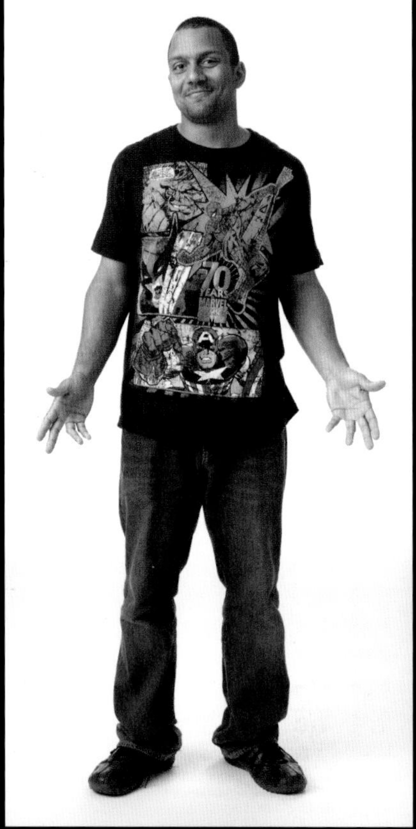
Eric Hensen

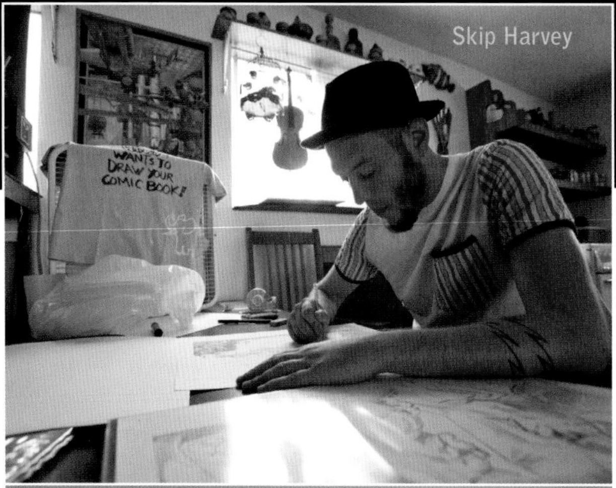
WANTS TO
DRAW YOUR
COMIC BOOK!
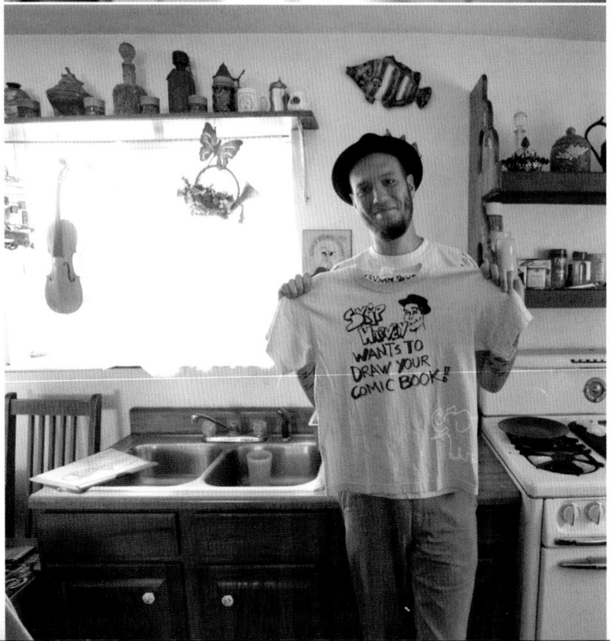
SKIP
HARVEY
WANTS TO
DRAW YOUR
COMIC BOOK!!
Skip Harvey

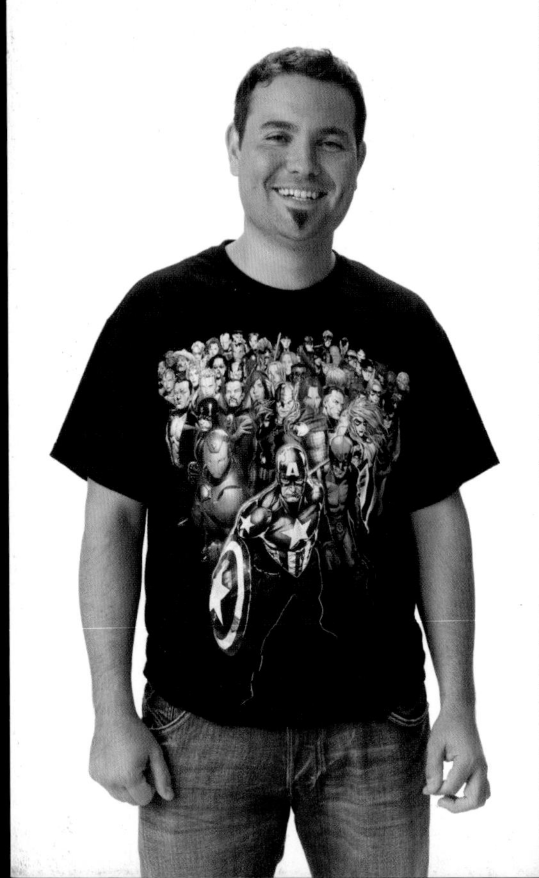
Anthony Calderon

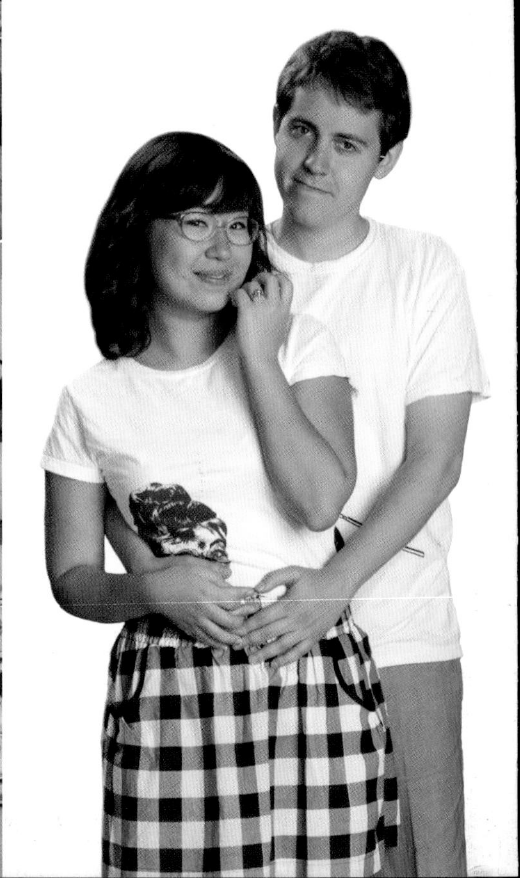
Se Young Kang and James Darling

a word from the publisher

Over the course of four days in July 2010, more than 130,000 fans made their yearly trek to sunny San Diego to indulge their obsession with video games, collectibles, anime, graphic novels, manga, cosplay, blockbuster films—and, of course, comic books. Since its inception in 1970, Comic-Con has always attracted a diverse group of fans—but in recent years it has expanded to become the place to bear witness to The Next Big Thing across all genres in popular culture.

DK started exhibiting at Comic-Con a decade ago, long before other book publishers recognized it as an invaluable event at which to interact with readers and fans. From our *Star Wars* and *Lost Encyclopedia* panels to opportunities to meet our authors and illustrators to giveaways and scavenger hunts, DK has always embraced Comic-Con as a place where we could hear, first-hand, what our readers like about our books and what they want to see more of. And, yeah—we've had some fun, too.

The natural pairing of DK with Morgan and Alba for the book that captures the spirit of Comic-Con is one that makes us nostalgic for Comic-Cons past, and excited for all the Comic-Cons yet to come.

See you in San Diego!

Rachel Kempster, Director of Marketing and Publicity
Michele Wells, Senior Editor

Check out more amazing work from our photographers!
Alba Tull: stillwaterimagery.com
Peter McCabe: petermccabephotography.com
8eyespictures.com

acknowledgments

Morgan Spurlock

This book and film would not have been possible without the guidance of Fae Desmond, David Glanzer, Mark Ytullarde, and all of the incredible staff at San Diego Comic-Con International.

I would also like to thank Stan Lee, Joss Whedon, Harry Knowles, Thomas Tull, Alba Tull, and the entire crew who made all the magic happen:

Matthew Galkin	Lisa Hepner	Damien Smith	Anthony Pang
Jeremy Chilnick	Michael Legum	Sharmila Ariathurai	Valeria Kohakura
Michelle Blumenschine	Scott Hedblom	Joyce Thorne	Marjon Javadi
Shannon Gibson	Brian Fish	Greg Ives	Mike Uslan
Sara Elyse	Paul Graff	Amelia Guimarin	Jonathan Knapp
Senain Kheshgi	Jeremy Habig	Max Wheeler	Jeremy Williams
Emmanuel Moran	Chip Plested	Alex Comery	Jeff Beachnau
Jennifer Jones	Joe Galath	Jerad Cullen	JT Bruce
Kaitlin Cunniff	Giles Khan	Sam Laughlin	Jeanne Bialik
Daniel Marracino	Eugene Thompson	Chris Kelishes	Lorena del Rio
Ross Kauffman	Alejo Ramos	Frank Wells	Danielle Arpon
Cameron Hickey	Paul Mendez	Shawn Elizabeth Curtis	Wendy Zhang
Rob Mursaskin	Matthew Sutton	Erik Altstadt	Jeremy Gabriel
Dave Ellis	Theresa Radka	Spencer Scranton	Eric Babajanian
Fortunato Procopio	Caleb Mose	Melissa Anderson	Priya Kanayson
Jermain Love	Abe Dolinger	Bekah Macias	Brian Wong
Jason Miller	Richard Walters	Ben Ganz	Jasmin Tabatabaee
Erik Messerschmidt	Joe Decarvalho	Damien Alexis Esparza	Amy Chiu
Matt Goodman	Kenny Rogers	Kimberly Bautista	Christine Kang
Paul Dokuchitz	Nick Berry	Bennett Bottero	Jason Torres
Guy Mossman	Layne McIsaac	Rebecca Waer	Melissa Valenzuela
Dane Lawing	Travis Williams	James Winston	Ed Silla
Tony Molina	Chris Andrus	Tim Zook	Ed Alva
Nick Higgins	James Allen	Adam Dyess	Rossy Mendez
Sandra Chandler	Eric Kieweg	Justin Oberman	Karen Mendez
Bryan Donnell	Dave Lichtenburg	Abbie Nissenson	Shawn Scarbarough
Tiffany Armour	Stephen Brou	Jed Goldberg	Peter Wisan
Mike Norman	Salvador Mariscal	Whitney Hodack	Nate Wisan
Beau Lambert	Patrick Divine	Heather Shreckengost	Brian Wong
Anthony Barrese	Jeycob Carlson	Carlos Paredes	Kestrel Thomas
Richard Hama	David Pleiss	Casey Kirkpatrick	Robert Tunstall
Zach Levy	Safi Kheshgi	Brett Hubbs	Oriana Yarid
Mark Landsman	Lenka Solmolova	Nick DeLuca	Nicole Tirosh
Gina Levy	Michael Sutton	Emily Gorski	Frank Hobbs
Kief Davidson	Mary Lively	Jason K Low	Brian Sanchez
Dara Horenblas	Kristin Meyer	Reese Avanessian	Jacqueline Monet
Minsa Cho	Sara Scott Farber	Ryan Broomberg	Brigit Bowers
Lucy Lesser	Nicole Anderson	Jacob Kang	Stella Kim
Joshua Weinstein	Brian Runnels	Pat Clark	Henry Lu
Chelsea Barnard	Elissa Cohn	Chris Guera	Jimmy Nguyen

Amanda Simons
Quynh Quach
Luis Meraz
David O'dere
Aaron Robinson
Andrew Baron-Varitan
Josh Krohn
Jeff Luong
Eric Polyn
Janell McCrensky
Michael C Poole
Michael Estrada
Alma Sanchez
Doris Lew-Jensen

Meagan Brown
Alba Tull
Peter McCabe
Richard Coleman
Roger Kruger
Sean Cassidy
Jesse Dhein
Stephanie Dana
Josh Reiss
Doug Wylie
Paul Taggart
David Newsom
Alex Finkel
Daniel Bergeron

Justin Sullivan
Rich Young
Chris Monberg
James Chapman
Jonathan Courtout
Nate Morse
Anne Northgraves
AJ Pinkerton
Matt Rigby
Gordon Stewart
Martin Torner
Kevin Warnecke
Michele Wells
Tim Murray

Abe Chang
David Magdael
Steven Wallace
Winston Emano

With a very special thanks to Micah Green, Richard Arlook, Paul Brennan, TED, Mom & Dad, and *Mad* magazine.

And my son Laken, who reminds me every day how important heroes are.

Alba Tull

I would like to thank my wonderful husband, Thomas, whose support has made my participation possible.

Special thanks to Morgan Spurlock for collaborating on this amazing project.

I also would like to thank Peter McCabe, who worked so hard producing this project, and David Newsom, who kept everything flowing with all the other contributing photographers...great job!

I also would like to thank DK Publishing, especially Michele Wells, for her dedication to the project.

Photo Page credits

Alba Tull — pages (6, 7, 9, 10, 11, 30, 31, 34, 35, 36, 41, 45, 46, 48, 52, 53, 55, 60, 61, 66, 67, 70, 71, 78, 79, 81, 86, 88, 91, 96, 98, 99, 103, 107, 116, 122, 126, 127, 132, 134, 135, 141, 145, 146, 147, 148, 152, 154, 155, 159, 162, 166, 167, 175, 178, 179, 190, 192)

Peter McCabe — pages (1, 4, 12, 13, 18, 19, 22, 28, 29, 37, 38, 39, 40, 44, 49, 50, 51, 54, 62, 63, 64, 65, 68, 72, 73, 74, 76, 80, 84, 85, 87, 90, 92, 93, 94, 95, 97, 102, 106, 108, 109, 110, 111, 112, 113, 117, 120, 121, 124, 125, 129, 130, 131, 133, 138, 139, 142, 149, 158, 161, 163, 164, 168, 169, 172, 173, 180, 181, 182, 183, 184, 185, 188, 190, 192)

Reportage

Paul Taggart — pages (4, 14, 15, 16, 17, 21, 25, 42,43, 56, 58, 75, 82,89, 100, 105, 114, 115, 118, 123, 140, 156, 157, 164, 165, 174, 188)

Josh Reiss — pages (17, 26, 47, 56, 57, 82, 89, 111, 114, 153, 185,186, 187)

David Newsom — pages (20, 136, 137)

Richard Coleman — pages (27, 42, 56, 75, 114, 176, 177)

Jesse Dhein — pages (20, 21, 105, 140, 143, 156, 171)

Doug Wylie — pages (20, 21, 33, 42, 69, 104, 140, 150, 151, 170)

Stephanie Dana — pages (20, 21)

Sean Cassidy — page (165)

Photographers' Assistants

Chris Monberg — (1st Assistant)
Daniel Bergeron — (1st Assistant)
Justin Sullivan — (2nd Assistant)
Richard David Young — (2nd Assistant)

Digital Archive Tech

Alexander Fink

Interviewer – Civilian/Costumed Cycloramas

Martin K. Torner

Production Assistants

Matt Rigby
AJ Pinkerton
Gordon Stewart III
James Heller Chapman
Jonathon Courtot
Nathan J. Morse
Anne Gould Northgraves

Special Thanks to

Leica Camera
Marty Glickman, for Mamiya Camera and Profoto Lighting
Mike D. at Samy's Rentals

about the contributors

Thomas Tull is Founder, Chairman, and CEO of Legendary Pictures, the production company behind blockbuster films such as *Inception*, *The Dark Knight*, *The Hangover*, and others. Tull is a board member of the American Film Institute (AFI); Hamilton College, his alma mater; the Fulfillment Fund; and the San Diego Zoo. He is also a minority partner in the Pittsburgh Steelers.

Stan Lee is the comic book legend revered by fans for creating Spider-Man, Iron Man, Thor, and other timeless superheroes of the 1960s. The former president and chairman of Marvel Comics, he took the company from a small imprint to a multimedia corporation. Today, he is a writer, editor, actor, producer, publisher, and television personality.

Joss Whedon is a producer, director, screenwriter, and founder of Mutant Enemy Productions. He is best known as the creator and showrunner of the television series *Buffy the Vampire Slayer*, *Angel*, *Firefly*, and *Dollhouse*. He has also done extensive work in film, comic books, and online media.

Morgan Spurlock is a documentary filmmaker, television producer, screenwriter, and journalist, best known for the Oscar-nominated film *Super Size Me*. The executive producer and star of the reality series *30 Days* and director of *The Simpsons 20th Anniversary Special—in 3-D! On Ice!*, his most recent projects include the feature-length films *Freakonomics* and *The Greatest Movie Ever Sold*.

Harry Knowles is an online film critic and the founder of the Ain't It Cool News website. A member of the Austin Film Critics Association, he holds a yearly event called Butt-numb-a-thon (BNAT), also called "Geek Christmas," a 24-hour celebration of film that features unofficial premiers and vintage films screenings.

Alba Tull is an accomplished photographer with a portfolio that includes well-known actors, musicians, and directors, including The Edge (of U2), Guillermo del Toro, Willie Nelson, Ellen Page, Jimmy Page, Bryan Singer, Jack White, Olivia Wilde, and Owen and Luke Wilson, among others. Her photographs have been exhibited at the Toronto Film Festival and published in *Rolling Stone* through Sony Classics. She was the photographer and an associate producer for Davis Guggenheim's *It Might Get Loud*, and she is currently working on a special book project for the American Film Institute (AFI) Historical Director Exhibit.